Occupational Health Psychology
Health Psychology

EUROPEAN PERSPECTIVES ON RESEARCH, EDUCATION AND PRACTICE

Manor Farm, Main Street, Thrumpton
Nottingham, NG11 0AX, United Kingdom

NOTTINGHAM

First published 2008
© Individual contributors

All rights reserved. No part of this publication
may be reproduced in any material form
(including photocopying or storing in any
medium by electronic means and whether or not
transiently or incidentally to some other use of
this publication) without the written permission
of the copyright holder except in accordance with
the provisions of the Copyright, Designs and
Patents Act 1988. Applications for the copyright
holder's written permission to reproduce any part
of this publication should be addressed to the publishers.

British Library Cataloguing in Publication Data
Occupational Health Psychology
Volume 3 - 2008

Editors: I. Houdmont, J. II. Leka, S.

ISBN 978-1-904761-82-2

Disclaimer

Every reasonable effort has been made to ensure that the material in this book is true, correct, complete and appropriate at the time of writing. Nevertheless the publishers, the editors and the authors do not accept responsibility for any omission or error, or for any injury, damage, loss or financial consequences arising from the use of the book. The views expressed by chapter contributors do not necessarily reflect those of the European Academy of Occupational Health Psychology.

Typeset by Nottingham University Press, Nottingham
Printed and bound by Hobbs the Printers Ltd, Totton, Hampshire, SO40 3WX

Occupational
Health Psychology
EUROPEAN PERSPECTIVES ON RESEARCH, EDUCATION AND PRACTICE

Volume 3: 2008

Editors:
Jonathan Houdmont
Stravoula Leka

Nottingham University Press

ea-ohp

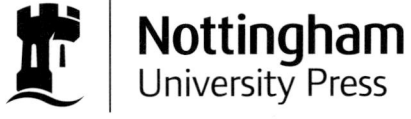

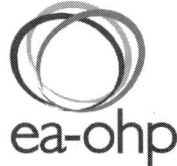

CONTENTS

Contributors   vii

Preface   xv

SECTION 1: RESEARCH

1. Need for recovery after work: An overview of construct, measurement and research   1

    Marc van Veldhoven

2. Knowledge development and content in occupational health psychology: A systematic analysis of the *Journal of Occupational Health Psychology*, and *Work & Stress*, 1996-2006   27

    Samantha Y. Kang, Alice K. Staniford, Maureen F. Dollard and Michiel Kompier

3. Self-determination theory: A theoretical and empirical overview in occupational health psychology   63

    Anja Van den Broeck, Maarten Vansteenkiste and Hans De Witte

4. Subjective occupational success: A resource in the stress process   89

    Simone Grebner, Achim Elfering and Norbert K. Semmer

5. Stress models: A review and suggested new direction   111

    George M. Mark and Andrew P. Smith

SECTION 2: EDUCATION

6. The definition of curriculum areas in occupational health psychology   145

    Jonathan Houdmont, Stavroula Leka and Carrie A. Bulger

SECTION 3: PRACTICE

7. **A participatory approach to promoting psychosocial health at work: Developing the Informing, Counselling and Advising (ICA) practices of occupational health psychologists**   171

    Päivi Jalonen, Sirkku Kivistö and Helena Palmgren

8. **Understanding the perception of occupational psychosocial risk factors in developing countries: Setting priorities for action**   191

    Evelyn Kortum, Stavroula Leka and Tom Cox

9. **Management competencies for preventing and reducing stress at work**   229

    Emma Donaldson-Feilder, Joanna Yarker and Rachel Lewis

10. **A case of teacher burnout**   257

    Pedro R. Gil-Monte

11. **The relationship between organisational justice and job stress: Insights, issues and implications**   281

    Andrew J. Noblet and John J. Rodwell

CONTRIBUTORS

Carrie A. Bulger is Associate Professor of Psychology at Quinnipiac University in Hamden, Connecticut, USA. She is the coordinator of the concentration in industrial-organisational psychology and is currently the chair of the Education and Training Committee for the Society for Occupational Health Psychology. In addition to her commitment to furthering the quality of education in occupational health psychology and industrial-organisational psychology, her current research interests focus on the interface between work and non-work. Specifically, she studies the positive and negative impact of technology on the boundaries around work and non-work, work/non-work interface issues for older workers, as well as other more general areas of occupational health and stress.
Contact: carrie.bulger@quinnipiac.edu

Tom Cox is Professor of Organisational Psychology and Director of the Institute of Work, Health & Organisations (I-WHO), University of Nottingham. He is the current President of the European Academy of Occupational Health Psychology. Tom's research and consultancy concerns the contribution of applied psychology to occupational health and safety with a special interest in the nature, management and prevention of work-related stress and associated legal and policy issues. Tom is Managing Editor of the international quarterly Work & Stress (Taylor & Francis), and a Book Series Editor for Issues in Occupational Health (also Taylor & Francis). He is a member of the Editorial Boards of the Journal of Occupational Health Psychology and Revista de Psicologia Aplicada Social.
Contact: tom.cox@nottingham.ac.uk

Maureen Dollard is Professor in Work and Organisational Psychology and Director for the Centre for Applied Psychological Research and Work & Stress Research Group at the University of South Australia. She is interested in the topics of rural work psychology, knowledge production in work stress, the ecology of work stress, psychosocial safety climate, and work stress prevention and intervention research. She is a consulting editor for Work & Stress (Taylor & Francis) and Co-Chair of the International Commission on Occupational Health-Scientific Committee Work Organisation and Psychosocial Factors.
Contact: maureen.dollard@unisa.edu.au

Emma Donaldson-Feilder is Director of Affinity Health at Work and combines research and practitioner roles with writing and presenting on

workplace well-being. Together with Joanna Yarker and Rachel Lewis, she has received funding from the Health and Safety Executive, the Chartered Institute of Personnel Development (CIPD) and Investors in People (UK) to identify the behaviours required by managers to manage subordinate stress effectively. Emma has worked with a wide range of clients in the public and private sectors, providing consultancy and learning & development interventions to help employers, leaders and managers improve staff well-being, productivity and engagement. She is also Consultant Editor for a CIPD subscription publication on well-being and performance.
Contact: emma@affinityhealthatwork.com

Achim Elfering is an Associate Professor in the department of Work and Organizational Psychology, University of Bern, Switzerland. In 1993 he graduated with a Masters degree in Clinical Psychology from the University of Wuerzburg, Germany. In 1997, he received his Ph.D. in General Psychology at the University of Frankfurt, Germany. His research interests include working conditions and occupational low back pain. This research has been internationally recognised by the SPINE Journal Young Investigator Research Award in 2001. His current research interests address positive work experiences, job satisfaction research, and work socialisation.
Contact: achim.elfering@psy.unibe.ch

Pedro R. Gil-Monte is Associate Professor of Work and Organizational Psychology at the University of Valencia, Spain. He is the Director of the "Unidad de Investigación Psicosocial de la Conducta Organizacional" (UNIPSICO), a scientific group oriented to the research of the quality of working life. He is author of more than 100 scientific publications in peer reviewed journals, books and chapters. His current research interests focus on: (i) stress and burnout, (ii) mobbing, (iii) work-family conflict, and (iv) occupational health psychology with particular emphasis on education and training.
Contact: pedro.gil-monte@uv.es

Simone Grebner is Assistant Professor for Occupational Health Psychology within the Psychology Department at Central Michigan University, USA. She received her Ph.D. in Work and Organisational Psychology from the University of Bern (Switzerland). She previously held an appointment at the University of Munich (Germany), the Federal Institute of Technology (Zurich, Switzerland), the University of Fribourg (Switzerland) and the University of Bern (Switzerland). Her current research interests focus on chronic and situation-related job stressors and resources, coping with job stress, evaluation of stress- and self-management trainings, and

physiological stress responses. One of her specific current interests is the nature and effects of subjective success experiences for the employee.
Contact: grebn1s@cmich.edu and simone.grebner@gmx.de

Jonathan Houdmont is a Lecturer in Workplace Health within the Institute of Work, Health and Organisations (I-WHO) at the University of Nottingham, UK. He is Programme Manager for the Institute's MSc in Workplace Health. He is also Executive Officer of the European Academy of Occupational Health Psychology. His current research interests focus on i) legal and policy issues in organisational health and safety and specifically in respect of work-related stress and ii) the discipline of occupational health psychology with particular emphasis on education and training.
Contact: jonathan.houdmont@nottingham.ac.uk

Päivi Jalonen is Head of Development at the Finnish Institute of Occupational Health, Helsinki. The topic of her doctoral thesis was on early retirement as a function of work stress. Her later research interests have included organisational commitment and work-related stress in hospital workers. Recently, Päivi has studied occupational health service activities; especially health education and communication, and community work in occupational safety and health. She is a specialist in occupational health psychology and is responsible for the education of occupational health psychologists in Finland.
Contact: paivi.jalonen@ttl.fi

Samantha Kang is a PhD candidate with the Work & Stress Research Group, Centre for Applied Psychological Research at the University of South Australia. She is completing a Master of Work and Organisational Psychology at University of South Australia. Her research interests are in work psychology in Eastern cultures, examining best practice models in enterprise bargaining, and the ecology of work stress.
Contact: samantha_kang@hotmail.com

Sirkku Kivistö works as team leader and senior psychologist in a Work and Mental Health team and as a board member in the Centre for Expertise for Work Organizations at the Finnish Institute of Occupational Health. She is involved in the statutory training of occupational health psychologists in Finland and in developmental projects for Occupational Health Services. She has been actively involved in the Healthy Mind at work project that focused on the management of sickness absence in cooperation with the employer, occupational health and rehabilitation services.
Contact: sirkku.kivisto@ttl.fi

Contributors

Michiel Kompier has a full Chair in Work and Organisational Psychology at the Radboud University of Nijmegen, The Netherlands. He has published many national and international articles, books and book chapters on topics such as work stress, job design, prevention and intervention research, working time arrangements, work-home interaction, and working conditions policies. He is associate-editor of the Scandinavian Journal of Work, Environment and Health, and member of the editorial boards of Work and Stress, Journal of Occupational Health Psychology, and the International Journal of Stress and Health.
Contact: m.kompier@psych.ru.nl

Evelyn Kortum holds a BSc in Psychology and an MSc in Occupational Psychology from Birkbeck College, London University. Her research interests include differences between high- and low-income countries in the perception and understanding of psychosocial risks and work-related stress, awareness about the hazards to health, interventions, and more. Her long-term goal is to promote an integrated preventive approach encompassing traditional and emerging occupational hazards, in particular work-related stress and its consequences on psychological and physical health.
Contact: lwxek1@nottingham.ac.uk

Stavroula Leka is Associate Professor in Occupational Health Psychology at the Institute of Work, Health & Organisations, University of Nottingham, and Director of its World Health Organization programme. She is a member of the Planning Committee of the WHO Network of Collaborating Centres in Occupational Health and manages its programme of work on Practical Approaches to Identify and Reduce Occupational Risks. She is a Chartered Psychologist and member of the British Psychological Society, a Fellow of the Royal Society for Public Health, an Executive member of the European Academy of Occupational Health Psychology and Secretary of the International Commission on Occupational Health Scientific Committee Work Organization & Psychosocial Factors. Stavroula is also a member of an expert consortium supporting the European Parliament in occupational health and safety. Her research is focused on the translation of occupational health and safety knowledge and policy into practice. Currently, this research is expressed through studies on psychosocial risk management, corporate social responsibility and occupational health and safety and health and safety practices in small and medium-sized enterprises.
Contact: stavroula.leka@nottingham.ac.uk

Rachel Lewis is a Research Associate at Goldsmiths, University of London. She specialises in organisational research and consultancy, particularly

in the areas of leadership and employee well-being. For the last 3 years, Rachel has worked, with Emma-Donaldson-Feilder and Joanna Yarker, on a project to identify the behaviours required by managers to manage subordinate stress effectively. In this time she has also been completing a PhD part-time. Rachel combines her academic career with a range of consultancy work primarily in the areas of selection and assessment and employee well-being. She works within both academic and practitioner fields to enable her to apply current research and innovative approaches in her work.
Contact: r.lewis@gold.ac.uk

George Mark is an Occupational Psychologist working in the welfare-to-work sector. He currently works for a "Pathways to Work" provider, helping those on incapacity benefit get back into work. A former PhD student at Cardiff University (UK), his interests include (i) the effects of individual differences in the stress process, (ii) job characteristics and interactions with individual differences, (iii) self efficacy and job seeking, (iv) mental health and job retention, (v) mental health and return to work, and (vi) CBT and Motivational Interviewing in return to work.
Contact: gmark@a4e.co.uk

Andrew Noblet is a Senior Lecturer in Organisational Behaviour at Deakin Business School, Deakin University (Australia). Andrew's research interests are in the areas of occupational stress, job redesign, organisational justice, leader-member relationships and employee performance. He is currently a Chief Investigator on two, three-year research projects funded by the Australian Research Council and undertaken in conjunction with a state-based police service and a group of health and aged-care facilities. Within these projects, Andrew and his colleagues are particularly interested in the individual and organisational characteristics that contribute to a range of health- (e.g., job stress) and performance-related (e.g., extra-role behaviours) outcomes.
Contact: andrew.noblet@deakin.edu.au

Helena Palmgren works as a researcher in the Finnish Institute of Occupational Health, Helsinki. Since 2003, she has been the researcher in charge of an extensive research project on health education and communication in Occupational Health Services. Her other research interests include health, well-being and leadership; especially in the context of small firms and entrepreneurship. She is a specialist in qualitative research methods. Helena also acts as an instructor in the professional training for occupational health personnel in Finland.
Contact: helena.palmgren2@ttl.fi

Contributors

John Rodwell is Professor of Management at the Deakin Business School, Deakin University (Australia). His current research interests focus on employee-level issues such as work stress in large organisations (especially in healthcare management), with an aim toward making healthier, more productive workplaces and preventing employee turnover. John has published in journals that include: Human Resource Management, Work & Stress, Human Relations, Group & Organization Management, and the International Journal of Human Resource Management.
Contact: john.rodwell@deakin.edu.au

Norbert K. Semmer is Professor for the Psychology of Work and Organizations at the University of Bern, Switzerland. He studied psychology in Regensburg (Germany), Groningen (The Netherlands), and Berlin (Germany), and received his PhD from the Technical University of Berlin in 1983. His major interests refer to (1) stress at work and its implications for health and productivity, (2) efficiency in work behavior: its characteristics, and its training, and (3) human error and its implications for quality and safety. His current work focuses on the concept of "Stress as Offense to Self", largely within the context of the Swiss Centre for "Affective Sciences (cf. the chapter by Semmer et al. in Vol 2 of this series). He is member of the editorial boards of a number of journals in the field of Work Psychology (e.g., European Journal of Work and Organizational Psychology) and Occupational Health (e.g., Journal of Occupational Health Psychology; Scandinavian Journal of Work, Environment and Health). Norbert is involved in teaching at the university, research, and teaching/consulting outside of the University.
Contact: norbert.semmer@psy.unibe.ch

Andy Smith is Professor of Psychology and Director of the Centre for Occupational and Health Psychology at Cardiff University (UK). He has published over 250 papers and given over 200 invited talks and conference papers. His current research interests in the area of Occupational Health Psychology are: (i) combined effects of occupational health hazards, (ii) fatigue offshore and psychological markers for adjustment to shift work offshore, (iii) the scale and impact of prescribed medication and illegal drug use by workers, (iv) ethnicity, work characteristics, stress and health, (v) emotional stress in nurses and care workers, (vi) mental health and job retention, (vii) stress in those starting work, and (viii) positive work characteristics and well-being at work.
Contact: smithap@cardiff.ac.uk

Alice Staniford is a Research Associate with the Work and Stress Research Group and the Human Factors and Safety Systems Group at the University of South Australia. She is currently completing a Master of Work and

Organisational Psychology at University of South Australia. Her research interests lie in the areas of rural psychology, work-related stress, health psychology, occupational safety behaviour, positive work psychology, and organisational change and development.
Contact: alice_staniford@pkf.com.au

Marc van Veldhoven is an Associate Professor in the Department of Human Resource Studies, Faculty of Social and Behavioural Sciences, Tilburg University, the Netherlands. His current research is focussed on the connections between HRM, well-being (including health) and performance and tries to build bridges between the academic fields of HR studies and occupational health psychology.
Contact: m.j.p.m.vanveldhoven@uvt.nl

Anja Van den Broeck is working at the Motivation Psychology Center at the University of Leuven, Belgium. She is preparing a PhD dissertation on Self-Determination Theory within the context of Occupational Health Psychology. The key emphasis of her work is on the basic psychological needs and how their satisfaction can explain and stimulate optimal functioning at work in terms. She is furthermore interested in the goal pursuit, the Job Demands Resources model, burnout, engagement as well as work and well-being in general.
Contact: anja.vandenbroeck@psy.kuleuven.be

Maarten Vansteenkiste works as a Professor at Ghent University, Belgium. Through his research, he tries to expand Self-Determination Theory in various ways. He is especially interested in theoretically and empirically linking Self-determination Theory with other well-established motivation theories and in studying the effect of pursuing intrinsic relative to extrinsic goals on well-being, performance, and social functioning.
Contact: maarten.vansteenkiste@ugent.be

Hans De Witte is full Professor at the Department of Psychology of the Katholieke Universiteit Leuven, Belgium. He teaches Work (and Organisational) Psychology and is member of the Research Centre for Work-Organizational and Personnel Psychology (WOPP) of his Department. His research includes the study of the psychological consequences of job insecurity, unemployment, temporary employment and downsizing, as well as mobbing and stress versus engagement at work.
Contact: hans.dewitte@psy.kuleuven.be

Joanna Yarker is a lecturer at Goldsmiths, University of London. Her research is focused on health at work, particularly the role of managers and leaders in supporting health at work interventions. Together with

CONTRIBUTORS

Emma-Donaldson-Feilder and Rachel Lewis, Joanna has received funding from the Health and Safety Executive, the Chartered Institute of Personnel Development and Investors in People (UK) to identify the behaviours required by managers to manage subordinate stress effectively. In recent years she has also conducted research in the area of cancer and chronic ill-health at work to better understand the adjustments required by employees returning to work following long-term sick leave, and the managers' role in the return process.
Contact: j.yarker@gold.ac.uk

PREFACE

Welcome to the third volume in the annual book series from the European Academy of Occupational Health Psychology. The publication of this volume has been scheduled to coincide with the Academy's eighth conference which takes place this year in Valencia, Spain. Whether you are reading this upon having received a copy of the book in your conference delegate pack, or have purchased a copy from the online bookstore of the Academy's publisher and distributor (www.nup.com), thank you for taking the time to open the volume. We hope you will find that its contents make a useful contribution to your professional or study-related activities.

For readers who are unfamiliar with the series a brief overview may be warranted here. Initiated in 2006, the regular volumes offer a set of chapters each of which has its focus on a discreet topic of current pertinence within the occupational health psychology (OHP) umbrella. All contributions are authored by individuals who are recognised by the international community as experts in the particular area of activity on which they are writing. The chapters within each volume are divided across three sections: research, education and professional practice, a structure that reflects the three pillars of activity on which the Academy operates. Chapters are designed to be of interest to a broad range of researchers, practitioners, educators and students of the discipline. Consistent with the Academy's constitutional objective to enhance awareness, knowledge and understanding of OHP, the series is affordably priced to ensure broad access. Back copies may be purchased at Academy conferences and online at www.nup.com.

The current volume contains eleven chapters produced by OHP researchers, educators and practitioners working throughout Europe and beyond. The research section opens with a chapter that demonstrates a particular facet of the book series: the opportunity that it provides for the presentation of material from research traditions that have primarily been published in languages other than English and thus which a large portion of the OHP community has not had the privilege of accessing. Marc van Veldhoven (Tilburg University, the Netherlands), reviews research on the 'need for recovery after work' construct and its measurement. To date, many of the studies in this area have been published only in Dutch; this review offers the first English-language overview of an important strand of research.

In Chapter 2, Samantha Kang, Alice Staniford and Maureen Dollard (University of South Australia), along with Michiel Kompier (Radboud University of Nijmegen, The Netherlands), review themes evident in the OHP research that has appeared over an eleven year period in the discipline's two flagship journals: the Journal of Occupational Health Psychology and Work & Stress. The analysis demonstrates that OHP research published in these two journals has primarily focused on work factors and individual influences, an emphasis that may have been at the expense of a consideration of external and organisational factors. It is further noted that most of the studies were conducted in industrialised countries among urban populations using particular research methodologies. Suggestions are advanced for the development of a more truly inclusive OHP research agenda.

Next, Anja Van den Broeck (Katholieke Universiteit Leuven, Belgium), Maarten Vansteenkiste (Ghent University, Belgium) and Hans De Witte (Katholieke Universiteit Leuven, Belgium), consider the role of Self Determination Theory (SDT) in OHP. This theory of human motivation and optimal functioning has been applied with success in numerous scientific areas; the authors take it upon themselves to examine the scope for extending its application into the OHP domain. In line with SDT, conclusions are drawn in relation to those aspects of work design, management and organisation that may foster and impede workers' intrinsic motivation.

In recent times, a number of OHP researchers (Macik-Frey, Quick & Nelson, 2007; Schaufeli, 2004) have noted the need for a move away from a preoccupation with what Inness & Barling (2003) have described as the "grimmer facets of human life" towards a focus on "positive, valued subjective human experiences and strengths that have the potential to buffer individuals from illness and enhance their well-being and personal fulfilment" (p. 8). In line with this trend towards positive psychology initiated, in large part, by Martin Seligman (Seligman & Csikszentmihalyi, 2000), Chapter 4 has its focus on the notion of occupational success. Simone Grebner (Central Michigan University, USA) along with Achim Elfering and Norbert Semmer (University of Bern, Switzerland), introduce the concept of subjective occupational success, defined as positive and meaningful experiences at work that are goal-related and salient for an individual or a group, in terms of subjective goal attainment or reasonable movement toward a goal. The authors offer a description of its antecedents, consequences and measurement, and argue that the study of subjective occupational success is important on the basis that it may act as a causal agent for human strengths and optimum functioning. It will be interesting to observe the degree to which this novel construct will be integrated into OHP studies as the positive psychology agenda unfolds within the discipline of OHP.

In Chapter 5, George Mark and Andy Smith (University of Cardiff, UK) consider the evolution of theoretical models of the work-related stress concept. They question whether there is scope for the development of new models that sit comfortably between interactional models that have their focus on exposure to potentially hazardous job characteristics and transactional models that centre on the dynamic process that represents the ongoing and ever changing relationship between an individual and the work environment. The merits of various ways forward are considered and a framework for further research presented.

OHP education is in a process of gradual evolution. That youthfulness is reflected in the brevity of the education section of this volume. Jonathan Houdmont, Stavroula Leka (University of Nottingham, UK) and Carrie Bulger (Quinnipiac University, USA) report on a collaborative study supported by the European Academy of Occupational Health Psychology and the Society for Occupational Health Psychology. The chapter has its focus on the imperative for and development of consensus surrounding OHP curriculum areas. Results are presented from an international survey of OHP academics which revealed that consensus can be achieved on the importance of sixteen topics to an educational curriculum. Among these, six topics were identified as core. The study constitutes an important step in the road towards the development of agreed curriculum frameworks and possible professional governance structures.

The professional practice section of this volume opens with a chapter authored by Päivi Jalonen, Sirkku Kivistö and Helena Palmgren (Finnish Institute of Occupational Health) who explore the unique contribution that occupational health psychologists may offer to the operation of occupational health service teams. Using their experience of an action-research project conducted in a Finnish hospital as a case study, the authors chart the opportunities and challenges faced in establishing an Information, Counselling and Advising (ICA) occupational health service. The chapter concludes by highlighting the important role of the occupational health psychologist in awareness-raising in relation to psychosocial issues as well as designing and implementing psychosocial interventions.

In light of the conclusion from the study reported in Chapter 2 concerning the paucity of OHP research activity in developing countries, it is perhaps timely and appropriate that this volume contains a chapter that addresses the perception of occupational psychosocial risk factors in such countries. In Chapter 8, Evelyn Kortum, Stavroula Leka and Tom Cox (University of Nottingham, UK), describe a study that aimed to explore similarities and differences in the conceptualisation and nature of work-related stress and psychosocial risks in industrialised and developing countries. A series of recommendations are made towards developing priorities for action in developing counties.

Chapter 9 provides an example of OHP research commissioned by government (in this case the British government through the agency of the Health and Safety Executive) that has important and useful implications for practitioners. Emma Donaldson-Feilder (Affinity Health at Work, UK), Joanna Yarker and Rachel Lewis (Goldsmiths, University of London, UK), describe a series of applied studies that set out to identify management behaviours associated with the effective prevention of stress at work. The development of a framework identifying the behavioural competencies required by managers to prevent stress in employees, together with a questionnaire measure of the relevant behaviours generated a number of implications for practitioners that are explored alongside implications for employers, line managers and national policy.

Chapter 10 offers a first for the book series: a consideration of the role of the OHP practitioner in the provision of diagnoses and evidence in legal claims. By reference to theory and the empirical literature, Pedro Gil-Monte (University of Valencia, Spain) describes the development of a case of burnout in a school teacher. Under Spanish law burnout is not considered a compensable work-related illness; rather, claims for compensation may be pursued through the courts where it is recognised as an occupational accident. Interaction with legal systems and procedures is not a novel area of activity for OHP practitioners – in the UK, for example, OHP academics have been called upon many times to describe to the court the ways in which the psychosocial work environment may have contributed to the development of a psychological disorder. It is, however, an area of expertise that is ill-defined in the context of a professional competency framework for OHP practitioners and one that existing OHP educational provision may not adequately equip graduates for. Thus, the chapter serves the important function of highlighting the scope for OHP practitioners to identify and exploit opportunities to interface with legal systems while flagging up the need for developments in OHP education towards this end.

In the spirit of inclusiveness this book series contains contributions from authors operating outside of Europe who, through their research and practice, seek to advance the application of psychology for the enhancement of occupational health and safety. In this vein we are delighted to present a chapter on the topic of organisational justice, or fairness, by Andrew Noblet and John Rodwell (Deakin University, Australia). The chapter outlines the concept of organisational justice as it relates to worker health and broader measures of organisational functioning such as commitment, absenteeism and performance. It then considers the implications of existing knowledge on the sources and effects of organisational justice for occupational health practice in the context of stress-prevention programmes.

Finally, it goes to say that this is *your* book series; it is designed to add value to the activities of all those with a vested interest in OHP. As such, the editors would be pleased to enter into discussion with potential contributors about ideas for future volumes.

Best wishes,

Jonathan Houdmont
jonathan.houdmont@nottingham.ac.uk

Stavroula Leka
stavroula.leka@nottingham.ac.uk

REFERENCES

INNES, M. & BARLING, J. (2003). Putting health back into occupational health psychology. In *British Psychological Society Occupational Psychology Conference Book of Proceedings, 8-10 January 2003*, (pp. 8-14). Leicester, UK: British Psychological Society.

MACIK-FREY, M., QUICK, J.C. & NELSON, D.L. (2007). Advances in occupational health: From a stressful beginning to a positive future, *Journal of Management, 33*, 809-840.

SELIGMAN, M. & CSIKSZENTMIHALYI, M. (2000). Positive psychology: An introduction, *American Psychologist, 55*, 5-14.

SCHAUFELI, W. (2004). The future of occupational health psychology, *Applied Psychology: An International Review, 53*, 502-517.

RESEARCH

NEED FOR RECOVERY AFTER WORK
AN OVERVIEW OF
CONSTRUCT, MEASUREMENT AND RESEARCH

Marc van Veldhoven

CHAPTER OVERVIEW

Work-related fatigue is a classic research topic in occupational health psychology. The roots of this type of research go back to the late 19th century. Since then, knowledge on fatigue has increased substantially. This knowledge relates to the biological processes involved and their motivational, cognitive and emotional concomitants. A specific subfield of study concerns the fatigue experience. Meijman (1991) provides an overview of this part of the fatigue literature. He classifies previous research on the fatigue experience into four main categories: psychological pressure, reduction in the willingness to perform, reduction in the capacity to perform, and the state of fatigue. He then goes on to develop a scale for measuring the fatigue experience during work. Such a measure is of great importance for research on fatigue in relation to work performance in terms of quality of output, quantity of output, safety, pro-activity on-the-job et cetera. Another possible angle recognised by Meijman (1989; 1991) is to measure the fatigue experience not during work itself, but towards the end of work and/or (just) after work. This approach focuses on the carry-over of the cumulative effects of work effort to the situation outside work. This carry-over approach is directly relevant to the quality of private life, but depending on the amount of recovery it is indirectly also relevant to future work performance.

Meijman's work on carry-over has stimulated a line of research that later received considerable attention from researchers under the term of "need for recovery after work". To date, however, no overview on need for recovery (NFR) after work is available in the literature. As the NFR construct originally evolved during the period 1985-1995 in a series of studies that are only available in the Dutch language, such an overview is especially relevant in order to introduce the roots of the construct to a wider international audience. It is the purpose of this chapter to provide such an overview. After introducing the construct of need for recovery and the effort-recovery model from which it was framed, a psychometric scale is presented and its measurement quality discussed. Consequently, existing research on need for recovery is overviewed in several categories. The chapter concludes with some recent developments and future prospects.

CONSTRUCT

Need for recovery after work needs to be understood within the framework of the Effort-Recovery Model (Meijman 1989; Meijman and Mulder 1998; Meijman and Schaufeli, 1996). An adaptation is represented in figure 1.

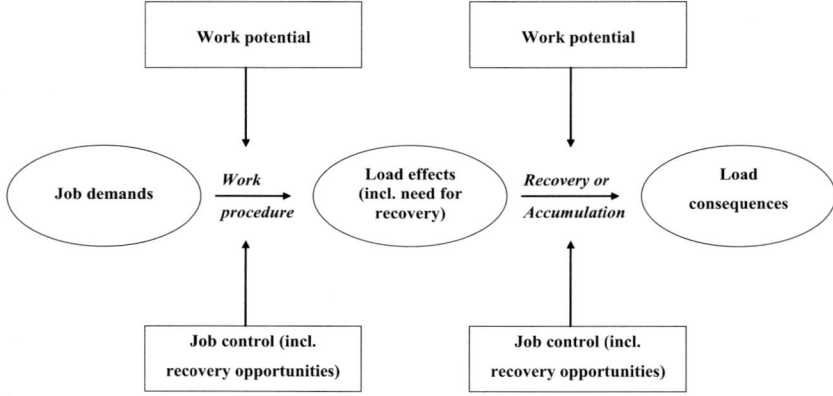

Figure 1: The effort-recovery model (based on Meijman, 1989; Van Veldhoven, 1996; Meijman & Mulder, 1998).

In the Effort-Recovery Model "job demands" produce costs in terms of "load effects". Load effects concern an array of emotional, cognitive, and behavioural symptoms that are reversed when work stops. This is what constitutes short-term fatigue at work (Meijman and Schaufeli, 1996). How job demands translate into load effects depends to a large extent on other job characteristics, especially "job control". It also depends on characteristics of the worker involved. These last characteristics are collectively referred to in the model as "work potential". Meijman (1989) draws specific attention to the job control characteristics that are concerned with opportunities for recovery, such as work breaks, holidays, beginning and ending times of the work day. By using the term "work strategy" it is emphasised in the model that the way work is performed is not static, but that it depends on the present, dynamic combination of situational and personal characteristics.

Short-term fatigue symptom reversal takes a certain time span, but ideally within the same working day and/or the following night reversal takes place. With enough time and possibilities to recuperate (during working time and after work) a worker will arrive at the next working day with no residual symptoms of previous effort. Within this normal recuperation cycle the concept of need for recovery after work refers to the extent that the work task induces a collection of symptoms, characterised by temporary feelings of overload, irritability, social withdrawal, lack of energy for new effort, and reduced performance. This need for recovery can be observed especially during the last hours of work and immediately after work.

As Jansen, Kant and Van Den Brandt (2002) discuss, the concept is related to Glass and Singer's concept of "post-work irritability" (Glass and Singer, 1972). Mohr (1986) formulated a similar construct under the name of "irritation". Need for recovery, being a variant of the fatigue experience, includes all the major categories that Meijman (1991) described for the fatigue experience in general: psychological pressure, reduction in the willingness to perform, reduction in the capacity to perform, state of fatigue. It concerns the manifestation of these symptoms just before finishing work and/or (just) after work.

When normal possibilities for recuperation are not sufficient, the worker starts the next working day with a residual level of need for recovery. Starting from here, a "cumulative process" is postulated (Kompier, 1988) that can produce more serious, adverse "load consequences", like health symptoms and work incapacity in the long run (Van Dijk, Van Dormolen, Kompier and Meijman, 1990). As part of this cumulative process the need for recovery increases, the worker reports more serious psychological feelings of pressure, further reduced willingness to perform, further reduced capacity to perform and worsened state of fatigue. When activation is sustained for a long time more serious long-term fatigue-related syndromes develop, like burnout and vital exhaustion. In this ultimate stage, recovery opportunities do not automatically reduce feelings of pressure, nor bring back the willingness or capacity to perform, nor lift the state of fatigue. Indeed, the mechanism of recuperation itself now seems to fail, and the employee primarily experiences this failure rather than only a high "need for recovery".

If high need for recovery is present for a prolonged period of time, this can be considered an indicator of failing recovery that might have substantial individual health consequences, apart from the fact that such a condition is indicative of severely lowered quality of private life during an extended period of time. The latter may also be considered a problematic condition in itself. Work performance and safety behaviour at work may also be compromised.

Finally, the model in Figure 1 also makes explicit how the process of strain accumulation is influenced, again, by the two factors of work potential and job control (the latter again including opportunities for recovery).

Meijman (2000) connects fatigue and the experience of fatigue to biological survival and sustained optimal functioning of the organism. He draws parallels with other basic human needs and the emotions associated with them. Rest, sleep and recuperation are considered a basic human need and the fatigue experience (especially that after work or during strain accumulation, e.g. NFR) shows similar characteristics as other human emotions: it "seizes" us when our resources are at stake, and it motivates behaviour directed at protecting our resources. For these reasons he calls fatigue the "STOP"-emotion. In line with the above, Sonnentag and Zijlstra (2006) have described need for recovery as the "sense of urgency to take a break from the demands (p. 331)". NFR is conceived by these authors as a "conscious emotional state characterised by a temporal reluctance to continue with the present demands or to accept new demands. It is associated with a wish for low baseline activity ... and with the expectation that such a break is necessary in order to be able and willing to confront future demands (p. 331)".

Need for recovery contrasts from the regular fatigue experience in two ways: First, fatigue in a more narrow sense only refers to a general feeling of lack of energy. NFR broadens this scope to the functional aspect of fatigue: reduced willingness to perform and reduced capacity to perform. Second, it contrasts with experiences of fatigue during work. Need for recovery after work relates to the broader issue of recovery from work effort (Sonnentag, 2005). Workers can reflect on much more than just their need for recovery: their recovery experience also concerns the activities they perform to recover, the strategies they pursue to achieve recovery, as well as how they rate their control over leisure time (Sonnentag and Fritz, 2007). In this broader context of work-related recovery, need for recovery might be considered an indicator of the effectiveness of recovery.

EARLY STUDIES

The first study using items to measure "need for recovery" was that by Meijman, Cavalini, Van Dormolen, Gloerich, Hellinga and Van Noord (1985). At this stage, these items were simply referred to as the "recovery scale". Since then, the items and the idea behind them developed over a period of time in the context of research at the universities of Groningen and Amsterdam. Early on, the items were especially used in studies on carry-over and sustained activation in extended/intensified work days (Meijman, 1989). These items would complement physiological measures of carry-over and sustained activation processes. Later, the items would also be used in more paper-and-pencil type of studies on psychosocial job conditions, work-related fatigue and occupational health. Most of this research was published only as departmental reports to funding bodies. All of this work is in Dutch.

A study by Furda (1995) used similar items, but under the term "recovery complaints". He reports a study in an insurance firm. Job demands (high) are related to "recovery complaints" (high) in a cross-sectional study, but changes in job demands (higher) are also related to changes in "recovery complaints" (higher) in a longitudinal study with a 1.5 year time interval.

During 1992-1994 the author conducted a project to develop a series of scales for use by Dutch occupational health services. He conducted a scale construction study that, amongst others, comprised the items from the "recovery list". The list was extended to a 21-item scale called "negative carry-over from work to private life". The scale construction study showed that the "rumination" items in the 21-item scale were a related, but also substantially different latent factor. Experiencing pain just before finishing work/just after work similarly was not systematically related to the NFR-items. Neither were several items about mood just after work. These results led to the proposition of a downsized scale labelled "need for recovery" by Van Veldhoven and Meijman (1994).

PSYCHOMETRIC SCALE

The need for recovery-scale is an 11-item, dichotomous (yes/no) scale. The items of the need for recovery scale inquire about the severity and duration of symptoms that indicate that the respondent is not fully recovered from work effort. English translations of this scale have been published by Sluiter, Van Der Beek and Frings-Dresen (1999) and by Van Veldhoven and Broersen (2003), the latter being presented in table 1.

The simplicity of dichotomous answering categories (yes or no) was preferred to a polychotomous scale, because of the intended application at the individual level in occupational health practice: the scale had to be as easy to fill in and score as possible. Scale length was determined by minimum requirements formulated for reliability and unidimensionality (.40 for unidimensionality (Loevinger´s H) and .80 for reliability (Cronbach´s alpha)), thus not compromising measurement quality by choosing for dichotomous answering possibilities.

Because the NFR scale was intended for use alongside separate scales for measuring workload, no item content was used in the scale to indicate psychological pressure. These might cause artificial stressor-strain correlations with scales measuring workload, especially quantitative

Table 1. Items of the "need for recovery scale"

1. I find it difficult to relax at the end of a working day.
2. By the end of the working day, I feel really worn out.
3. Because of my job, at the end of the working day I feel rather exhausted.
4. After the evening meal, I generally feel in good shape.
5. In general, I only start to feel relaxed on the second non-working day.
6. I find it difficult to concentrate in my free time after work.
7. I cannot really show any interest in other people when I have just come home myself.
8. Generally, I need more than an hour before I feel completely recuperated after work.
9. When I get home from work, I need to be left in peace for a while
10. Often, after a day's work I feel so tired that I cannot get involved in other activities.
11. A feeling of tiredness prevents me from doing my work as well as I normally would during the last part of the working day.

The answer "yes" signals unfavorable situations, except for item 4, where "no" signals an unfavorable situation.

workload (time pressure, deadline pressure). Therefore, from the viewpoint of the four categories of fatigue experience, item content was focused on the remaining three: feelings of fatigue/energy, reduced capacity to perform, and reduced willingness to perform.

MEASUREMENT QUALITY

Available research so far suggests that the psychometric qualities of the 'need for recovery scale' are good: reliability, expressed in Rho (comparable with Cronbach's Alpha), was found to be .87 at the construction stage (Van Veldhoven, 1996) and .86 in an independent replication study (Weel and Broersen, 1995). Unidimensionality of the scale, expressed in Loevinger's H, was also good in both studies: .48 and .46 respectively. In Mokken analysis, scales with a Loevinger's H above .40 are considered unidimensional (Mokken and Lewis, 1982). Additionally, recent results suggest that the need for recovery scale is an adequate measurement scale for different types of employees. Van Veldhoven and Broersen (2003) reported Cronbach's alpha for subgroups in the Dutch working population, split by age class, gender and education level. Alpha ranged between .81 and .92, with a value of .88 reported for the total sample (N = 68,775).

Not many results are available on the temporal stability of need for recovery. Van Veldhoven (unpublished) found a stability coefficient of .53 between two measurement moments of need for recovery with a one-year interval in 101 health care workers. This value suggests less stability than would be expected of a trait-type of measure (like neuroticism or negative affectivity), but more stability than expected for a typical state-type of measure (work effort).

De Croon, Sluiter and Frings-Dresen (2006) examined test-retest reliability for 526 truck drivers and 144 nurses. Furthermore, they calculated test-retest reliability taking into account ratings by the employees of the stability in their work environment. For truck drivers, ICC values for a two-year interval are moderate to good (.55 - .69). Generally, this is also the case for nurses, whether a two-year, one-year or two-week interval is concerned (48-.80). However, the ICC is rather low for nurses that rate their environment as unstable over a two-year period. Here ICC drops to .30, which is poor. As expected, for nurses the ICC-values decrease with the length of the time interval between test and retest. Overall, the authors rate the test-retest characteristics of the NFR scale as favourable.

CONTENT VALIDITY

Comparisons of the scores on the 'need for recovery scale' with scores of the same respondents on other measurement scales about fatigue (at work) can support our claim that the 'need for recovery scale' can be used to measure (early indications of) cumulating fatigue at work. Based on these comparisons we can draw conclusions on whether the 'need for recovery scale' has sufficient content validity.

The Utrecht Burnout Scale (UBOS) by Schaufeli and Van Dierendonck (2000), especially the sub-scale 'emotional exhaustion', is a first possibility for content validation of the need for recovery scale. This is the same scale as the General Version of the Maslach Burnout Inventory (MBI-GS). The 'emotional exhaustion'-scale correlated .84 with need for recovery in a study among 742 occupational physicians (Schaufeli and Van Dierendonck, 2000). In a study among 559 policemen, the correlation between the 'need for recovery scale' and the 'emotional exhaustion scale' was .75 (Schaufeli and Van Dierendonck, 2000).

The Checklist Individual Resilience, 20-item version (CIS-20; Bültmann, 2002) is a questionnaire originally developed to measure fatigue in groups of patients in a clinical setting, independent of the working situation. The CIS-20 consists of four sub-scales, of which the scale 'subjective fatigue' is the closest to need for recovery in terms of item content. In 1998, the need for recovery scale and the subjective fatigue-scale were measured together in two large-scale research projects (Schellekens, Brouwer and Meijman, 1999; De Croon, Blonk, Frings-Dresen and Van Der Beek, 2000). The correlation coefficients between the two scales were .66 (N = 1,637 in the building and construction sector) and .71 (N = 3,458 in the transport sector) respectively. In view of the difference between the two scales in their relation to work, we consider this correlation to be high. This concurs with a study by Beurskens, Bultmann, Kant, Vercoulen, Bleijenberg and Swaen (2000). These authors found comparable discriminative characteristics (between two regular employee groups (healthy blue/white collar employees), two medical patient groups (after hernia operation, pregnant) and a mental fatigue group for the CIS-20, the MBI-GS (exhaustion scale), and the NFR-scale.

De Vries, Michielsen and Van Heck (2003) compared six work-related fatigue scales in a random sample of 351 Dutch employees, including the NFR-scale. The highest correlations found for the NFR scale in this study were those with the emotional exhaustion- subscale from the MBI-GS/UBOS (.80) and the Fatigue Assessment Scale or FAS (.79), developed by these authors. Somewhat lower correlations were reported with the CIS-20 (.66), the WHO Quality of Life-scale on Energy and fatigue (.57) and .68 with the fatigue scale by Chalder, Berelowitz, Pawlikowska, Watts, Wessely, Wright and Wallace (1993).

Sonnentag and Fritz (2007) also provide relevant information as to the content validity of the NFR scale. Their study focuses on the recovery experience rather than the fatigue experience. It is the validation study of their "recovery experience questionnaire". A sample of 270 employees filled in Sonnentag and Fritz's scales on Recovery experiences (2007) as well as several scales on psychological well-being at work. Again, NFR showed the highest correlation with the emotional exhaustion subscale from the MBI-GS/UBOS (.82). NFR also demonstrated a substantial (-.52) negative correlation with the "psychological detachment" scale constructed by these authors.

A final issue concerns the question of whether need for recovery is different from fatigue during work. Meijman (1991) developed a scale for measuring fatigue during work. Of the nearly 70,000 workers reported on in Van Veldhoven and Broersen (2003) just about 13,425 also filled in the fatigue during work scale. The correlation between the scales is .42, illustrating both relatedness and difference between these constructs. Workers' fatigue/energy levels during work are thus related, but not very strongly related, to carry-over effects like NFR.

All in all, the NFR scale can justifiably be called a fatigue experience scale. It is most strongly related to the emotional exhaustion subscale from the UBOS/MBI-GS. This is somewhat remarkable because the 'emotional exhaustion'-scale (as part of a burnout-scale) is expected to measure more serious, late symptoms of work-related fatigue, whereas the 'need for recovery scale' is expected to measure less serious, early symptoms. The conceptual transition from less serious and short-term to more serious and long-term symptoms of work-related fatigue apparently is somewhat diffuse.

Now that we have presented the construct of need for recovery and its measurement, we can turn to the research evidence that has accumulated about need for recovery. Below, an overview is presented without trying to be exhaustive. It is divided into four parts: antecedents, biological process correlates, consequences and intervention-related research.

ANTECEDENTS

Research on the antecedents of need for recovery can be categorised into several subcategories. We start out with demographic and personality variables. The next category of antecedents is psychosocial factors at work. We conclude with time-related aspects of work and work-life balance.

Demographic and personality variables

In 1999 Van Veldhoven and Broersen reported results on a cumulative database consisting of nearly 70,000 Dutch employees. In univariate analyses there were hardly any differences between men and women for need for recovery. Need for recovery increased slightly with age. Effects were also found for education level, with need for recovery rising with the level of education. Health care and education, as well as other non-profit services, were the branches of industry reporting the highest levels of need for recovery. Multivariate analyses, combining age, gender and education level showed women above 45 with higher levels of education (vocational, university) to have specifically high scores on need for recovery. Recently Kiss, De Meester and Braeckman (2008) studied differences between younger and older workers in need for recovery among over a thousand public sector workers. After controlling for a multitude of other demographic variables, psychosocial work conditions and life conditions, high need for recovery was still significantly more prevalent in older workers than in younger workers.

Furda (1995) reports correlations between need for recovery and two personality characteristics: locus of control and coping style. High need for recovery correlates with an external locus of control (.33). High need for recovery also correlates with an avoidance (.32) rather than an approach (-.14) type of coping style.

Results from a study in 101 workers from a health care institution showed that negative affectivity (trait anxiety) was positively associated with sustained need for recovery over a period of one year. Four different coping styles were also investigated. Three out of four coping styles did not show any significant effects. However, employees with a preference for palliative coping showed lower levels of sustained need for recovery, contrary to expectations based on the existing literature (Van Veldhoven, unpublished).

Psychosocial factors at work

Van Veldhoven and Broersen (2003), working with a heterogeneous sample of nearly 70,000 workers, found quantitative workload (e.g. work speed and quantity) to have the highest correlation with need for recovery (.36). When both workload and need for recovery were aggregated to department means, this correlation increased. In all departments with at least 5 respondents (nearly 4,000 departments) the correlation was .49. In all departments (nearly 700) with at least 25 respondents the correlation increased further to .54. For qualitative aspects of workload, such as emotional workload and physical workload, the results were less strong.

Sonnentag and Zijlstra (2006) conducted a diary study for a period of five days in 96 health service employees. They found that, based on measures averaged over the five days, the strongest situational antecedents of need for recovery were situational constraints (.36). Other relevant antecedents were time pressure (.24), job control (-.24), and low-effort activities during leisure time (-.22). In the same paper, they also report cross-sectional survey results for a heterogeneous sample of 700 full-time Dutch employees. This time the most important situational antecedents were daily hazards and/or lack of support (.35), quantity of work (.34) and task control (-.28).

De Raeve, Vasse, Jansen, Van Den Brandt and Kant (2007) contributed to the literature on the situational antecedents of need for recovery by reporting a longitudinal analysis on the Maastricht Cohort Study data (N > 2,000). Changes in job demands and job control were significantly related to changes in need for recovery, and directions of these associations were consistent with theoretical assumptions, higher demands and lower control being associated with higher NFR.

The study by Sluiter, De Croon, Meijman and Frings-Dresen (2003) researched stressor-strain relationships in six specific occupational groups:

coach drivers, public bus drivers, construction workers, ambulance workers, hospital nurses, and truck drivers. Need for recovery showed different correlations for the psychosocial job characteristics investigated, depending on the occupation. Work demands/workload were found to be a consistent strong predictor in all occupations, however. Depending on the group an amount of variance between 14% and 48% could be explained in need for recovery, based on a combination of work demands, age and baseline need for recovery.

Sluiter, Van Der Beek and Frings-Dresen (1999) did a study among over 360 coach drivers. The strongest situational predictors of need for recovery in this case were need for break control and the number of work hours per week. De Croon, Sluiter, Blonk, Broersen and Frings-Dresen (2004) did a study in almost 700 truck drivers. The best situational predictors for need for recovery in this study were psychological job demands (.56), physical job demands (.41), supervisor job demands (.40) and job control (-.32). Finally, Eriksen, Ihlebaek, Jansen and Burdorf (2006) conducted a study in over 750 workers in home care. Here, psychological job demands were the most important antecedent of high need for recovery.

Time-related aspects of work and work-life balance

A specific category of antecedents of need for recovery are time-related aspects of work such as overtime, extended working hours, shift schedules, and work-life balance.

Jansen, Van Amelsvoort, Kristensen, Van den Brandt and Kant (2003) as well as Jansen, Kant, Van Amelsvoort, Nijhuis and Van den Brandt (2003) have shown that increased need for recovery can be found in workers in shift work and/or overtime work conditions. In a related study by Jansen, Kant, Kristensen and Nijhuis (2003) an increased need for recovery was also demonstrated in relation to work-family conflict.

Van Amelsvoort, Jansen, Swaen, Van Den Brandt and Kant (2004) reported a study on another work schedule variable: forward and backward rotation. Only workers in three-shift schedules were studied. Compared to forward rotation, backward rotation was associated with an increased need for recovery. Using longitudinal data De Raeve, Jansen and Kant (2007) researched whether changes in working time arrangements are accompanied by changes in need for recovery. In men, changes in work schedule and working hours were accompanied with concomitant changes in need for recovery. Also, transitions in working overtime were related to changes in need for recovery for both men and women. All of these studies are based on the Maastricht Cohort Study data, a large prospective cohort study on work-related fatigue.

Josten, Ng-A-Tham and Thierry (2003) found relevant associations between an extended working day and need for recovery in health care workers. The extended working day studied here in particular was a 9-hour shift schedule.

Finally, Van Der Hulst, Van Veldhoven and Beckers (2006) reported a study in a national sample of nearly 1,500 full-time employees in municipalities. In the full sample there was no significant association between overtime and need for recovery. Such association appeared to depend on the psychosocial job conditions. Only in "high strain" jobs as characterised by Karasek (1979) did the expected association between overtime and need for recovery appear to be significant.

Overall, when we look at research on the antecedents of NFR we can say that:

- the research evidence on need for recovery in relation to demographic and personality variables is still quite scarce;
- need for recovery is a strongly workload-related construct; and
- need for recovery appears to be clearly associated with important time-related aspects of work.

BIOLOGICAL PROCESS CORRELATES

The construct of need for recovery was originally conceived in the context of work psychology research that combined field and laboratory methods (Meijman, 1989). In this context some first attempts were made to connect need for recovery-type of measures to psychobiological measures related to activation and fatigue. Nothing explicit was reported about this connection, however, until one decade later.

Neuro-endocrine measures and work characteristics were significant predictors for the amount of need for recovery after work and for health status in a study by Sluiter, Frings-Dresen, Van Der Beek and Meijman (2001). Although this empirical result is promising, the results on the relationships between neuro-endocrine measures (adrenaline, cortisol) and need for recovery were inconclusive from a more theoretical point of view. Significant correlations between physiological indices and need for recovery were found, but they did not correspond exactly with theoretical frameworks on the regulation of activity and recovery.

Veldhuizen, Gaillard and De Vries (2003) investigated relationships between facial EMG and fatigue- and effort-related measures, including need for recovery, in the laboratory using 46 students as subjects. Need for recovery appeared to be associated with lowered facial EMG, where the latter is interpreted by the authors as an indicator of increased psychophysiological system demands for compensatory effort to maintain task performance.

Need for recovery might be an important correlate of psychobiological processes involved in work, activation and recovery. Currently the information in this area is still very limited, however.

CONSEQUENCES

Much of the research interest in need for recovery has been fuelled by the expectation (on the grounds of the Effort-Recovery Model) that it is an early indicator for more serious consequences of accumulating job strain like health problems, absenteeism/work incapacity, voluntary turnover, accidents at work and deterioration of job performance. In this section an overview is presented on the research so far on these possible consequences of need for recovery. We start with absenteeism/work incapacity and (mental) health consequences, followed by turnover, safety, and job performance.

Absenteeism/work incapacity and (mental) health

Van Veldhoven (1996) demonstrated the predictive validity of the 'need for recovery scale' for sickness absence as registered among 411 workers in a health care organisation during an interval of 6 months after completion of the questionnaire. The need for recovery scale was predictive of both frequency and duration of absenteeism. Sluiter, De Croon, Meijman and Frings-Dresen (2003) reported, similarly, that need for recovery was a predictor of prospective absenteeism in hospital nurses (one year follow-up) and truck drivers (two-year follow-up). Analyses on the prospective cohort study in truck drivers were reported separately in more detail by De Croon, Sluiter and Frings-Dresen (2003). In this study, high baseline need for recovery after work was associated with an increased risk for subsequent sickness absence (self-report data), after adjusting for the effects of age, previous sickness absence, marital status, educational level, and company size. The odds-ratio was 2.19 (confidence interval between 1.13 and 4.24). However, need for recovery was not found to mediate the relationship between stressful working conditions and sickness absence.

Sluiter, Van Der Beek and Frings-Dresen (1999) conducted a study on health in coach drivers. Need for recovery was found to be a major predictor of psychosomatic complaints and sleep complaints. In 2003 the same research group reported a study in multiple occupational groups (Sluiter, De Croon, Meijman and Frings-Dresen, 2003). Cross-sectional data showed need for recovery to be an important predictor of subjective health complaints in coach drivers, public bus drivers, construction workers, ambulance workers and hospital nurses. For hospital nurses, prospective analyses were also reported. Need for recovery appeared to strongly predict subjective health complaints after one year in this particular occupational group.

Van Amelsvoort, Kant, Bültmann and Swaen (2003) reported a study on the risk of cardiovascular disease in relation to need for recovery. They used data from the Maastricht Cohort Study on over 12,000 employees. During a period of 32 months follow-up after a baseline survey, 42 incidents were reported of cardiovascular disease. The highest tertile of scorers on need for recovery at baseline had a relative risk of 3.16 (confidence interval between 1.34 and 7.48) of experiencing such a CVD incident, in comparison to the lowest tertile.

In a study in the financial sector, the 'need for recovery scale' and a measure of psychosomatic health complaints correlated .63 (N = 3,011) (Van Veldhoven, unpublished). Of the nearly 70,000 workers reported on in Van Veldhoven and Broersen (2003) exactly 12,420 also filled in the sleep quality scale (measuring the number of sleep complaints in a series of 14 yes/no questions. The correlation between the two scales is .52. High need for recovery is therefore related to high sleep complaints.

In another study, principal component analysis revealed obvious separation between need for recovery items on the one hand, and psychological distress items on the other hand. This supports the notion that need for recovery and psychological distress represent different underlying psychometric constructs. Although need for recovery and psychological distress were frequently co-morbid, they also clearly occurred as separate entities in this research sample (Jansen, Kant and Van Den Brandt, 2002). Finally, Sonnentag and Fritz (2007) reported a .52 correlation with subjective health complaints, and a .55 correlation with depressive symptoms in a sample of 270 workers.

Turnover

The occupational group of truck drivers in the Netherlands provided an opportunity to study the longitudinal impact of need for recovery on turnover (De Croon, Sluiter, Blonk, Broersen and Frings-Dresen, 2004). Data on turnover were gathered using self-reports with a two-year time interval. Similar data were available for job demands and need for recovery.

The study group comprised 820 truck drivers. The impact of job demands on turnover was mediated by need for recovery. High need for recovery furthermore seemed to stimulate inter-occupational turnover more than intra-occupational turnover. Furthermore, the former type of turnover was associated with the highest decrease in need for recovery. These findings suggest that high need for recovery is a factor pushing truck drivers into other jobs, in search for a less stressful job and/or workplace.

Accidents

In the Maastricht Cohort Study, need for recovery was studied prospectively as a risk factor for being injured in an occupational accident (Swaen, Van Amelsvoort, Bultmann and Kant, 2003). The sample contained over 7,000 workers in the Southern part of the Netherlands. Accident injury was monitored for one year after the survey. After adjustment for age, gender, education, smoking, shift work, and work environment rather strong effects on the risk of being injured in an occupational accident were found. Compared to the lowest tertile on need for recovery, the highest tertile had a relative risk of 2.28 (confidence interval between 1.41 and 3.66).

Job performance

Considering the conceptual linkage between need for recovery and the reduced capacity to perform, one would expect the need for recovery construct and/or scale to have been used in studies on task performance in laboratory studies. This, however, is not the case. So far, need for recovery has only been connected to (decreased) job performance in the long run, much in a similar manner as health and safety risks are expected to increase in the long run due to the gradual accumulation of fatigue over time.

Demerouti, Taris and Bakker (2007) investigated the link between need for recovery and in-role performance in 123 employees from 8 different companies. The employees responded to two surveys with a time-lag of one month. Moreover, the authors investigated whether lack of concentration might mediate the link between need for recovery and in-role performance. As expected, need for recovery had negative, lagged effects on concentration, whereas concentration had a positive lagged effect on in-role performance. To complete the picture, the results from this study also suggest that the effect of need for recovery is reciprocally, negatively related to home-work interference.

Van Veldhoven (2005) studied the relationship between need for recovery (amongst other survey measures) and the financial performance of branches of a large financial services organisation. Over 18,000 employees participated in this survey study. Financial performance information was collected at the branch level using objective data of business transactions for over 200 branches in the year before and in the year after the survey. Need for recovery was not among the important predictors of prospective financial performance. However, good financial performance in the year before the survey was a modest predictor of low need for recovery.

In summary, we can say about research on the consequences of NFR that:

- the link between need for recovery and health, absenteeism and work incapacity has been substantiated to a certain extent;
- turnover and safety consequences have received attention in isolated studies only; these links deserve more future research; and,
- the need for recovery-job performance link also deserves further study, especially in relation to short-term, in-role job performance and in relation to tasks that require concentration.

INTERVENTION-RESEARCH AND MONITORING/SCREENING OF RISK GROUPS

Previous research has shown that high need for recovery is associated with relevant health, safety and performance problems. Monitoring need for recovery in working populations therefore makes sense: it can help in the (early) detection of possible cases of cumulating fatigue in workers. Along with this purpose of screening/monitoring comes the question of whether the need for recovery scale might also be used to detect changes, especially changes as instigated by efforts to improve working conditions/stress symptoms.

Bekker, Nijssen and Hens (2001) reported a study evaluating the effect of stress prevention training. Participants were surveyed before the training, immediately after and three months after. Participants reported a significant decrease in need for recovery after the training, whereas a control group did not. This positive effect was maintained at follow-up three months later.

Kuijer, Van Der Beek, Van Dieën, Visser and Frings-Dresen (2005) did an intervention study in refuse collectors. In this occupational group job rotation (between collecting refuse and driving a refuse truck) was investigated as a possible means of prevention for developing effort-related health problems. Participants were surveyed at baseline and one year after the introduction of the job rotation scheme. Compared to a control group without rotation, job rotation seemed to coincide with a reduced need for recovery.

De Croon, Kuijer, Broersen and Frings-Dresen (2004) investigated the possible negative effects on need for recovery of introducing on-board computer systems for lorry drivers, but no such negative effects were substantiated.

Finally, De Croon, Sluiter and Frings-Dresen (2006) reported on the sensitivity of the need for recovery scale to detect fatigue-relevant changes in working conditions, in this particular case an increase in working hours. Two-year longitudinal data of truck drivers and nurses were used for this purpose. Their study found a significant and substantial increase in need for recovery scale scores in employees who reported increased working hours. No such change was found in employees reporting stable working hours during the same period.

For workers with a long-term disease and/or handicap, fatigue often is a concomitant factor that is important in the context of recovering from/managing the disease/handicap. It can also be an issue in their work reintegration. Need for recovery has therefore been suggested as a specific measure for monitoring/screening purposes in specific patient groups. In this area of application, the construct's relevance is diverse, depending on the target group involved.

Weijman, Kant, Swaen, Ros, Rutten, Schaufeli, Schabracq and Winnubst (2004) studied need for recovery in diabetes patients in comparison to healthy workers. Diabetics without other concomitant health problems were not different from healthy workers. Diabetics with co-morbidity, however, showed significant increased levels of need for recovery.

Need for recovery has also been investigated in the context of low back pain (Eriksen, Ihlebaek, Jansen and Burdorf, 2006; Alexopoulos, Burdorf and Kalokerinou, 2006; Alexopoulos, Burdorf and Kalokerinou, 2003; Elders and Burdorf, 2001), because a similar process of strain accumulation is expected to exist in the development of musculoskeletal disease as the one that is involved in the development of long-term fatigue/burnout. Results from this series of studies imply that need for recovery indeed seems to play an important role in the accumulation process involved in low back pain.

Summarising, the need for recovery scale is sensitive to relevant work-related changes and in this context it can be put to purpose as a measure for screening (identifying high-risk individuals for treatment) as well as monitoring (evaluating changes at the individual and/or workplace level in relation to interventions) in occupational health psychology.

SOME RECENT DEVELOPMENTS AND FUTURE PROSPECTS

Now that we have presented an overview of the existing work on need for recovery, we can ask the question: what's next? Several things are worth mentioning here.

The original need for recovery scale (Van Veldhoven and Meijman, 1994) was targeted for use in Dutch occupational health services. For this reason it employed a yes/no dichotomous answering scale, in order to make the scale compatible with health symptom checklists used in this context by occupational health physicians. Psychological practitioners and researchers have ever since pointed out the problematic nature of a dichotomous answering scale for questions on need for recovery. Some have resorted to using the same items, but with a four-point answering scale (always, often, sometimes, never). Based on these projects we can report that the scale characteristics improve only slightly because of this intervention, but more importantly the scale average (when put on a similar scale as the dichotomous version) goes down. For future research purposes/translations of the scale it might be wise to adopt a four-point scale from the beginning.

The need for recovery scale has been translated into English, French, German and Malaysian. There are more translations under way, but until now only very few research reports on need for recovery come from outside the Netherlands, as this chapter shows. Also, only very limited information is currently available on the existing translations. One exception is the translation into French, which was done as part of a national effort in Belgium to build a reference database on psychosocial job conditions and stress at work (Notelaers and Van Veldhoven, 2002). More importantly, cross-cultural or cross-language area comparisons of need for recovery are completely un-investigated up to this point. This is an important prospect for future research. In this context it is important to note that the scale was constructed from the point of view of the typical Northern European/Dutch work setting and worker. For instance: item number four in the scale refers to the period "after the evening meal", because for many workers in the Northern part of Europe/the Netherlands, there is a significant amount of time available after evening meal (which usually takes place around six to seven o'clock in the evening). In Southern parts of Europe and many other parts of the world this makes little sense, however: the evening meal is usually consumed only briefly before sleep (usually around nine to ten o'clock in the evening). For international research on need for recovery a scale would be necessary that doesn't have the limitation of cultural bias.

In the Netherlands, the scale has meanwhile been used in over 5,000 practical and scientific research projects. This has resulted in its inclusion in national survey systems for monitoring trends in working conditions (2003 and 2005). The same is true for the Flemish part of Belgium (2004 and 2007). In occupational health care practice it has by now become a standard procedure to compare need for recovery scores in a specific group (department, occupational group) to norm scores of general and specific reference groups. Especially specific reference groups are much in demand, and some sectors have therefore instigated their own reference database projects. This has generated several new research issues.

For example, it has been investigated what minimum sampling requirements a specific reference group should meet, before it can be accepted as a reference value for a specific branch of industry or occupational group (Van Veldhoven and Broersen, 1999). These requirements concern things like: N of cases, number of different constituting samples, and maximum size of the largest constituting samples.

Also, there is a demand for a cut-off value based on the simple 11-item yes/no-scale. Broersen, Fortuin, Dijkstra, Van Veldhoven and Prins (2004) report an analysis that suggests that a score of 6 or higher (out of 11 items) identifies the high-risk group for need for recovery in the best possible way. The criterion used to determine this cut-off is the amount of contrast between a group of healthy workers and a group of workers referred to an occupational health psychologist for stress management counselling. In the Netherlands this identifies 21% of the work force as "at risk". Another way to determine a cut-off point is to ask several groups of stakeholders what would be an unacceptable level of need for recovery to them, based on the same 11 questions. The author did just this, with separate focus groups of employee representatives, employer representatives, occupational physicians, and researchers in the area of work-related fatigue. This exercise suggests that a cut-off point of 4 or higher is closer to the "shared opinion" on what is considered unacceptable in the cultural and economic context of the Netherlands. This means that no less than 33% of the Dutch workforce scores above this cut-off. Indeed, having a higher need for recovery than would be considered "acceptable" appears to be quite common. The adequate use of reference databases and norms, including the establishment of cut-off values, is a further area of possible development in NFR research.

CONCLUSION

Several concluding remarks can be made based on the overview presented in this chapter.

From a conceptual point of view, the added value of the need for recovery construct over and above existing constructs like work-related fatigue and burn-out is an issue open to debate. Particularly striking is the height of the correlation with the emotional exhaustion-subscale that is an established part of burnout measures (UBOS/MBI-GS). Apparently, emotional exhaustion is also common in the short term fatigue cycle, rather than only in the long-term fatigue accumulation stage. One might therefore consider the need for recovery construct and measure superfluous. However: can energy resources be considered "exhausted" if recuperation from this level of exhaustion is possible overnight? One might want to reserve a strong term like "exhaustion" for the clinical stage where energy resources of a worker are (nearly) depleted and recovery from this condition is very hard, taking considerable time and treatment. A term like need for recovery might capture better the early stages of strain accumulation, which can ultimately lead to exhaustion.

In terms of measurement, the 11-item scale seems adequate for most purposes in its current cultural context. If individual psychometrics is the main purpose, it might be wise to adopt four-point rather than two-point answering categories. Also, a culturally unbiased version of the scale would be necessary for comparisons between countries/cultures.

In research on need for recovery, data on validity have by now accumulated to a considerable extent. However, validity issues remain in relation to important topics like sleep quality and mood in working populations. A considerable number of studies are now available on the predictors of need for recovery. Most of these studies are cross-sectional, however. Longitudinal data on the development of need for recovery are still relatively scarce. In general, the time course of (accumulating) need for recovery deserves further research, preferably also involving psychobiological process correlates.

Finally, in serious clinical cases of burnout and exhaustion it is found that symptom reversal does not take place in response to time off the job and rest. Indeed, the recovery mechanism itself appears to fail (Meijman and Schaufeli, 1996). An important issue for the future might be to determine at which point strain accumulation and a lack of recovery (as witnessed by high need for recovery after work, but responsiveness to rest) changes into exhaustion and failing recovery (high need for recovery after work, but no responsiveness to rest).

ACKNOWLEDGMENTS

The author would like to acknowledge Yvonne Prince for her assistance in preparing this chapter.

REFERENCES

ALEXOPOULOS, E.C., BURDORF, A., & KALOKERINOU, A. (2003). Risk factors for musculo-skeletal disorders among nursing personnel in Greek hospitals. *International Archives of Occupational and Environmental Health, 76,* 289-294.

ALEXOPOULOS, E.C., BURDORF, A., & KALOKERINOU, A. (2006). A comparative analysis on musculoskeletal disorders between Greek and Dutch nursing personnel. *International Archives of Occupational and Environmental Health, 79,* 82-88.

BEKKER, M.H.J., NIJSSEN, A., & HENS, G. (2001). Stress prevention training: Sex differences in types of stressors, coping, and training effects. *Stress and Health, 17,* 207-218.

BEURSKENS, A., BULTMANN, U., KANT, I., VERCOULEN, J., BLEIJENBERG, G., & SWAEN, G.M.H. (2000). Fatigue among working people: Validity of a questionnaire measure. *Occupational and Environmental Medicine, 57,* 353-357.

BROERSEN, J.P.J., FORTUIN, R.J., DIJKSTRA, L, VAN VELDHOVEN, M., PRINS, J. (2004). Monitor Arboconvenanten: kengetallen en grenswaarden [Monitor Working Conditions Agreements: indicators and cut-offs]. *Tijdschrift voor Bedrijfs- en Verzekerings-geneeskunde [Journal of Occupational and Insurance Medicine], 12,* 100-104.

BÜLTMANN, U. (2002). *Fatigue and psychological distress in the working population: the role of work and lifestyle.* Maastricht: University Press Maastricht. Ph.D. thesis.

CHALDER, T., BERELOWITZ, G., PAWLIKOWSKA, T., WATTS, L., WESSELY, S., WRIGHT, D., WALLACE, E.P. (1993). Development of a fatigue scale. *Journal of Psychosomatic Research, 37,* 147-153.

DE CROON, E.M., BLONK, R.W.B., FRINGS-DRESEN, M.H.W., & VAN DER BEEK, A.J. (2000). *Stress in het beroepgoederenvervoer: eindrapport [Stress in transport: final report].* Amsterdam: Coronel Institute.

DE CROON, E.M., KUIJER, P., BROERSEN, J.P.J., & FRINGS-DRESEN, M.H.W. (2004). Information technology and road transport industry: How does it affect the lorry driver? *Applied Ergonomics, 35,* 313-320.

DE CROON, E.M., SLUITER, J.K., BLONK, R.W.B., BROERSEN, J.P.J., & FRINGS-DRESEN, M.H.W. (2004). Stressful work, psychological job strain, and turnover: A 2-year prospective cohort study of truck drivers. *Journal of Applied Psychology, 89,* 442-454.

DE CROON, E.M., SLUITER, J.K., & FRINGS-DRESEN, M.H.W. (2003). Need for recovery after work predicts sickness absence: a 2-year prospective cohort study in truck drivers. *Journal of Psychosomatic Research, 55,* 331-339.

DE CROON, E.M., SLUITER, J.K., & FRINGS-DRESEN, M.H.W. (2006). Psychometric properties of the need for recovery after work scale: Test-retest reliability and sensitivity to detect change. *Occupational and Environmental Medicine, 63,* 202-206.

DE RAEVE, L., JANSEN, N.W.H., & KANT, I. (2007). Health effects of transitions in work schedule, work hours and overtime in a prospective cohort study. *Scandinavian Journal of Work Environment & Health, 33,* 105-113.

DE RAEVE, L., VASSE, R.M., JANSEN, N.W.H., VAN DEN BRANDT, P.A., & KANT, I. (2007). Mental health effects of changes in psychosocial work characteristics: A prospective cohort study. *Journal of Occupational and Environmental Medicine, 49,* 890-899.

DE VRIES, J., MICHIELSEN, H.J., & VAN HECK, G.L. (2003). Assessment of fatigue among working people: a comparison of six questionnaires. *Occupational and Environmental Medicine, 60,* i10-i15.

DEMEROUTI, E., TARIS, T.W., & BAKKER, A.B. (2007). Need for recovery, homework interference and performance: Is lack of concentration the link? *Journal of Vocational Behavior, 71,* 204-220.

ELDERS, L.A.M., & BURDORF, A. (2001). Interrelations of risk factors and low back pain in scaffolders. *Occupational and Environmental Medicine, 58,* 597-603.

ERIKSEN, H.R., IHLEBAEK, C., JANSEN, J.P., & BURDORF, A. (2006). The relations between psychosocial factors at work and health status among workers in home care organizations. *International Journal of Behavioral Medicine, 13,* 183-192.

FURDA, J. (1995). *Werk, persoon en welzijn. Een toetsing van het job demand-control model [Work, person and well-being. A test of the job demand-control model].* Enschede: Copyprint 2000. Ph.D. Thesis.

GLASS, D.C., & SINGER, J.E. (1972). *Urban stress: experiments on noise and social stressors.* New York: Academic Press.

JANSEN, A.W.H., KANT, I., KRISTENSEN, T.S., & NIJHUIS, F.J.N. (2003). Antecedents and consequences of work-family conflict: A prospective cohort study. *Journal of Occupational and Environmental Medicine, 45,* 479-491.

JANSEN, N.W.H., KANT, I., VAN AMELSVOORT, L., NIJHUIS, F.J.N., & VAN DEN BRANDT, P. (2003). Need for recovery from work: Evaluating short-term effects of working hours, patterns and schedules. *Ergonomics, 46,* 664-680.

JANSEN, N.W.H., KANT, I., & VAN DEN BRANDT, P.A. (2002). Need for recovery in the working population: Description and associations with fatigue and psychological distress. *International Journal of Behavioral Medicine, 9,* 322-340.

JANSEN, N.W.H., VAN AMELSVOORT, L.G.P.M., KRISTENSEN, T., VAN DEN BRANDT, P.A., & KANT, IJ. (2003). Work schedules and fatigue: a prospective cohort study. *Occupational and Environmental Medicine, 60,* 47-53.

JOSTEN, E.J.C., NG-A-THAM, J.E.E., & THIERRY, H. (2003). Nursing and health care management issues. The effects of extended workdays on fatigue, health, performance and satisfaction in nursing. *Journal of Advanced Nursing, 44,* 643-652.

KARASEK, R.A. (1979). Job demands, job decision latitude, and mental strain: implications for job design. *Administrative Science Quarterly, 24,* 285-308.

KISS, P., DE MEESTER, M., & BRAECKMAN, L. (2008). Differences between younger and older workers in the need for recovery after work. *International Archives of Occupational and Environmental Health, 81,* 311-320.

KOMPIER, M.A.J. (1988). Arbeid en gezondheid van stadsbuschauffeurs [Work and health of city bus drivers]. Delft: Eburon. Ph.D. thesis.

KUIJER, P., VAN DER BEEK, A.J., VAN DIEEN, J.H., VISSER, B., & FRINGS-DRESEN, M.H.W. (2005). Effect of job rotation on need for recovery, musculoskeletal complaints, and sick leave due to musculoskeletal complaints: A prospective study among refuse collectors. *American Journal of Industrial Medicine, 47,* 394-402.

MEIJMAN, T.F. (1989). Belasting en herstel: een begrippenkader voor arbeids-psychologisch onderzoek van werkbelasting [Effort and recuperation: a conceptual framework for psychological research of workload]. In T.F. Meijman (Ed.), *Mentale Belasting en Werkstress: een Arbeidspsychologische Benadering [Mental Workload and Job Stress: a Work Psychological Approach]* (pp. 5-20). Assen/Maastricht: Van Gorcum.

MEIJMAN, T.F. (1991). *Over vermoeidheid [about fatigue].* Amsterdam: Studie-centrum Arbeid en Gezondheid. Ph.D. thesis.

MEIJMAN, T.F., CAVALINI, P., CREEMER, R., VAN DORMOLEN, M., GLOERICH, F., HELLINGA, P., & VAN NOORD, F. (1985). *Onderzoek taakbelasting rijexaminatoren [Research workload driving examiners].* Groningen: Department of Work Psychology, University of Groningen.

MEIJMAN, T.F., & MULDER, G. (1998). Psychological Aspects of Workload. In: P.J.D. Drenth & H. Thierry (Eds.), Handbook of Work and Organizational Psychology (Vol. 2, pp. 5-33). Hove: Psychology Press.

MEIJMAN, T.F., & SCHAUFELI, W.B. (1996). Psychische vermoeidheid en arbeid [psychological fatique and work]. *De Psycholoog [The Psychologist], 6,* 236-242.

MOHR, G. (1986). *Die Erfassung psychischer Befindensbeeinträchtigungen bei Industriearbeitern [Measuring the Psychological State of Industrial Workers].* Frankfurt: Lang.

MOKKEN, R.J., & LEWIS, C. (1982). A nonparametric approach to the analysis of dichotomous item responses. *Applied Psychological Measurement, 6,* 417-430.

NOTELAERS, G., VAN VELDHOVEN, M. (2002). Interroger le "vécu du travail": présentation d'un outil spécifique d'analyse de la charge psychosociale de travail [The QEEW: introducing a specific analytical tool for measuring psychosocial workload]. Bruxelles: Institut National de Recherche sur les Conditions de Travail.

Schaufeli, W.B., & Van Dierendonck, D. (2000). UBOS - de Utrechtse Burnout Schaal. Handleiding. [UBOS - the Utrecht Burnout Scale. Manual]. Lisse: Swets & Zeitlinger.

Schellekens, J.M.H., Brouwer, J., & Meijman, T.F. (1999). Determinanten en effecten van werkdruk in de bouw- en houtnijverheid en de woningbouwcorporaties. [Determinants and effects of work pressure in building and construction, wood industry and house rental institutions]. Groningen: Department of Work Psychology, University of Groningen.

Sluiter, J.K., De Croon, E.M., Meijman, T.F., & Frings-Dresen, M.H.W. (2003). Need for recovery from work related fatigue and its role in the development and prediction of subjective health complaints. *Occupational and Environmental Medicine, 60*, 62-70.

Sluiter, J.K., Frings-Dresen, M.H.W., Van Der Beek, A.J., & Meijman, T.F. (2001). The relation between work-induced neuroendocrine reactivity and recovery, subjective need for recovery, and health status. *Journal of Psychosomatic Research, 50*, 29-37.

Sluiter, J.K., Van Der Beek, A.J., & Frings-Dresen, M.H.W. (1999). The influence of work characteristics on the need for recovery and experienced health: A study on coach drivers. *Ergonomics, 42*, 573-583.

Sonnentag, S. (2005). Burnout research: Adding an off-work and day-level perspective. *Work and Stress, 19*, 271-275.

Sonnentag, S., & Fritz, C. (2007). The recovery experience questionnaire: development and validation of a measure for assessing recuperation and unwinding form work. *Journal of Occupational Health Psychology, 12*, 204-221.

Sonnentag, S., & Zijlstra, F.R.H. (2006). Job characteristics and off-job activities as predictors of need for recovery, well-being, and fatigue. *Journal of Applied Psychology, 91*, 330-350.

Swaen, G.M.H., Van Amelsvoort, L., Bultmann, U., & Kant, IJ. (2003). Fatigue as a risk factor for being injured in an occupational accident: Results from the Maastricht cohort study. *Occupational and Environmental Medicine, 60*, 88-92.

Van Amelsvoort, L., Jansen, N.W.H., Swaen, G.M.H., Van den Brandt, P.A., & Kant, IJ. (2004). Direction of shift rotation among three-shift workers in relation to psychological health and work-family conflict. *Scandinavian Journal of Work Environment & Health, 30*, 149-156.

Van Amelsvoort, L., Kant, IJ., Bultmann, U., & Swaen, G.M.H. (2003). Need for recovery after work and the subsequent risk of cardiovascular disease in a working population. *Occupational and Environmental*

Medicine, 60, 83-87.
VAN DER HULST, M., VAN VELDHOVEN, M., & BECKERS, D. (2006). Overtime and need for recovery in relation to job demands and job control. *Journal of Occupational Health, 48,* 11-19.
VAN DIJK, F.J.H., VAN DORMOLEN, M., KOMPIER, M.A.J., & MEIJMAN, T.F. (1990). Herwaardering model belasting-belastbaarheid [Revaluation of the model work load-work capacity]. *Tijdschrift Sociale Gezondheidszorg [Journal Social Health Care], 68,* 3-10.
VAN VELDHOVEN, M. (1996). *Psychosociale arbeidsbelasting en werkstress. [Psychosocial job demands and job stress].* Lisse: Swets & Zeitlinger. Ph.D. thesis.
VAN VELDHOVEN, M. (2005). Financial performance and the long-term link with HR practices, work climate and job stress. *Human Resource Management Journal, 15,* 30-53.
VAN VELDHOVEN, M., & BROERSEN, J.P.J. (1999). *Psychosociale arbeidsbelasting en werkstress in Nederland. [Psychosocial job demands and job stress in the Netherlands].* Amsterdam: Foundation for Quality Improvement in Occupational Health Care.
VAN VELDHOVEN, M., & BROERSEN, S. (2003). Measurement quality and validity of the "need for recovery scale". *Occupational and Environmental Medicine, 60,* 3-9.
VAN VELDHOVEN, M., & MEIJMAN, T.F. (1994). *Het meten van psychosociale arbeidsbelasting met een vragenlijst: de vragenlijst beleving en beoordeling van de arbeid (VBBA). [The measurement of psychosocial job demands with a questionnaire: the questionnaire on the experience and evaluation of work (QEEW)].* Amsterdam: Dutch Institute for Working Conditions.
VELDHUIZEN, I.J.T., GAILLARD, A.W.K., & DE VRIES, J. (2003). The influence of mental fatigue on facial EMG activity during a simulated workday. *Biological Psychology, 63,* 59-78.
WEEL, A.N.H., & BROERSEN, J.P.J. (1995). *Verslag van het project PAGO-module werkstress [Report on the project POHE-module work stress].* Amsterdam: Dutch Foundation for Quality Improvement in Occupational Health Care.
WEIJMAN, I., KANT, IJ., SWAEN, G.M., ROS, W.J.G., RUTTEN, G., SCHAUFELI, W.B., SCHABRACQ, M.J., WINNUBST, J.A.M. (2004). Diabetes, employment and fatigue-related complaints: A comparison between diabetic employees, "healthy" employees, and employees with other chronic diseases. *Journal of Occupational and Environmental Medicine, 46,* 828-836.

KNOWLEDGE DEVELOPMENT AND CONTENT IN OCCUPATIONAL HEALTH PSYCHOLOGY
A SYSTEMATIC ANALYSIS OF THE *JOURNAL OF OCCUPATIONAL HEALTH PSYCHOLOGY*, AND *WORK & STRESS*, 1996-2006

Samantha Y. Kang, Alice K. Staniford, Maureen F. Dollard[1]
and Michiel Kompier

CHAPTER OVERVIEW

The nature of work has changed rapidly in the past decade principally due to economic and social developments such as globalisation of economic and business practices, workforce diversity, and advancements in technology. Does our current knowledge reflect these ecological influences and inform us adequately about the implications of such changes for workers' health? As an indication of what papers have been published in Occupational Health Psychology (OHP) in international journals we systematically analysed the 631 papers published over 11 years (1996 – 2006) by two journals that explicitly publish OHP research: *Journal of Occupational Health Psychology* (JOHP) (N = 334 articles), and *Work & Stress* (W&S) (N = 297 articles). We found that OHP research published in those journals primarily focused on work factors (e.g. workload) (11.2%, JOHP; 11.6%, W&S), individual influences (e.g. motivation) (16.8%, JOHP; 18.4%, W&S), and a combination of work and individual contextual factors (40.8%, JOHP; 41.9%, W&S) as opposed to external or organisational factors. Most studies were located in industrialised nations (e.g. North Americas 56.4%, JOHP; 15.9%, W&S; Europe 33.9%, JOHP, 66.5%, W&S), among urban participants (82.9%, JOHP; 81.2%, W&S). Studies of rural samples represented at best 20% of research analysed, a significant under-representation of research into rural based occupations globally given that rural workers comprise over 50% of the total world population. Cross-sectional designs were most frequently used (59.9%, JOHP; 62.6%, W&S). Longitudinal studies were fewer in number, but are tending to increase (22.7%, JOHP; 16.2%, W&S). Finally, intervention studies only accounted for 7.2% of studies in JOHP and 6.4% in W&S.

---

[1] Author for correspondence

This suggests either limited translation of research to practice, a limited evaluation of it or a lack of research that reaches journal benchmarks for high quality publications. The majority of papers were from Europe or the US, which suggests a need for more research in other regions, or for better distribution of resources to enable researchers from other areas to reach publishable standards in the international literature. We also identified a propensity to look at the individual and work contexts rather than upstream factors (such as government policy, industrial legislation, and the effects of globalisation). We intend that this up-to-date account of knowledge development in the area will stimulate useful new insights for OHP researchers and policy makers, which may improve the scope of research in the area leading to improvements in the quality of workers' lives worldwide by setting OHP firmly within an international context.

INTRODUCTION

Occupational Health Psychology (OHP) has as its major goal "the application of psychology to improve the quality of work life, and to protect and promote the safety, health and well-being of workers" (US National Institute of Occupational Safety and Health, 2007). Despite its brief history, this area of psychology first identified by Jonathan Raymond (Raymond, Wood, & Patrick, 1990) has become an important focus of research, development and practice within psychology (Quick, 1999). It seeks to integrate research findings and practical experience from different disciplines within and beyond psychology in order to apply them to matters of employee safety, health, and well-being (Schaufeli, 2004). Meanwhile, the nature of work and employment is undergoing rapid change as a result of economic and social developments, globalisation of economic and business practices, workforce diversity, and advances in technology (Kompier, 2006; Sauter & Hurrell, 1999). These changes are fundamentally re-shaping people's experience of their working lives in countries all over the world and thus forcing a re-appraisal of our understanding of the dynamic relationship between the worker, their environment and their health (Cox, et al., 2004; Tokyo Declaration, 1999). Researchers and experts in the field have pointed out that the rapidly changing world of work is challenging the current OHP knowledge base (Cox, et al., 2004). Some have even questioned whether these changes have out-paced our knowledge development (Schaufeli, 2004). A major motivation for conducting the current study was to assess whether these global changes are reflected in the development and content of OHP knowledge. Thus, the aim of this study is to assess the scope of published OHP research in terms of: level of ecological focus, geographical location and methodology, and map these against putative needs in order to identify gaps in current occupational health psychology knowledge. To achieve this we review 11 years worth of publications from two of the most influential journals in the field that focus on OHP, the *Journal of Occupational Health Psychology* (JOHP), and *Work & Stress* (W&S).

THE ORGANISATION OF WORK

The world and its societies are evolving at a rapid rate. Organisations and job requirements are constantly influenced by economic change, government policy, technology, and social developments at both national and international levels (Kompier, 2006). Schabracq and Cooper (2000) describe the need for organisations to adapt to these environmental demands as 'the survival of the fittest' (p. 227). With these pressures come consequences for the working lives of employees. Emerging social and human work-related risks and trends reported by European experts identifies changing labour markets (i.e. unstable labour markets, job insecurity, precarious contracts, the increased use of new forms of employment contracting practices), and globalization (which can lead to changing labour markets as above but also to lean production, outsourcing, work intensification, high work load and work pressure) as the most important upstream factors likely responsible for a range of psychosocial risks we see in the workplace today (i.e. long working hours, work intensification, poor work-life balance) (Van den Bossche, Smulders & Houtman, 2006). Major transformations in work in recent times have stimulated comprehensive multilevel modeling of environmental factors impinging on worker health and well-being. A recent framework proposed by Steven Sauter and colleagues (NIOSH, 2002) in the US National Occupational Research Agenda (NORA) (shown in Figure 1), has highlighted a three - level hierarchical relationship between the economic and social context, organisational context, and job context. The framework emphasises the continuity and distinction between a number of elements:

(1) The external context, which includes economic, political, technological and social factors at a national and international level;

(2) The organisational context, which includes organisational structure, supervisory practices, production methods and human resource policies; and

(3) The work context, which includes job-related and workplace characteristics (NIOSH, 2002).

This multi-level ecological model implies that upstream external and organisational contexts influence directly or indirectly the individual's occupational health, safety and well-being (see Schaufeli, 2004). This

Organization of Work

External Context

Economic, legal, political, technological, and demographic forces at the national/international level

- Economic developments (e.g., globalization of economy)
- Regulatory, trade, and economic policies (e.g., deregulation)
- Technological innovations (e.g., information/computer technology)
- Changing worker demographics and labor supply (e.g. aging populations)

Organizational Context

Management structures, supervisory practices, production methods, and human resource policies

- Organizational restructuring (e.g., downsizing)
- New quality and process management initiatives (e.g., high performance work systems)
- Alternative employment arrangements (e.g., contingent labor)
- Work/life/family programs and flexible work arrangements (e.g., telecommuting)
- Changes in benefits and compensation systems (e.g., gainsharing)

Work Context

Job Characteristics

- Climate and culture
- Task attributes: temporal aspects, complexity, autonomy, physical and psychological demands, etc.
- Social-relational aspects of work
- Worker roles
- Career development

Figure 1. Model of the organisation of work (NIOSH, 2002).

framework is useful for understanding how different ecological contextual levels influence worker occupational health and safety. Thus each level may be considered in terms of its etiological influence on worker health (see Johnson & Hall, 1996).

Evidence in support of an ecological framework for theorizing on work-related stress for example can be found in several recent studies. For example, a study examining the Australian dairy industry showed that dairy farmers experienced higher levels of distress compared to other occupations in Australia (Wallis & Dollard, 2008). This was despite their responses which indicated they had 'active jobs' (i.e. high task demands, and relatively high job control) (Karasek & Theorell, 2000), which is usually indicative of lower than average levels of distress. Instead, the authors found that external demands arising from government deregulation and free market forces, and environmental demands, were significant factors accounting for much of the acute and chronic effects upon farmers' psychological health beyond that of task demands and control (Wallis & Dollard, 2008).

Another illustrative study used Participative Action Research to investigate the psychological well-being of a group of frontline service staff in a South Australian government owned metropolitan rail organisation (Kang, Pannell, & Dollard, 2008). The employees identified a mismatch between the State Government's enthusiasm to promote the city's public transport system and its commitment to improve the current outdated rail system. This impacted significantly on both the organisation's operation and the employees' daily work. The increasing demand for public transport and a lack of resources to provide it caused a great deal of dissatisfaction among the commuters. As a result, managing dissatisfied commuters had become a major cause of interpersonal conflicts at work, posing significant emotional demands on the employees. Under pressure from both government and public, the company focused on meeting demands, such as maintaining the services' time-keeping and increasing service frequency. Consequently some employees experienced reduced job satisfaction and work stress, which cost the company in terms of sick leave and workers' compensation for stress related injuries (Kang, Pannell, & Dollard, 2008). This study clearly demonstrated how the safety, health and well-being of workers were not only affected by job-related and personal influences, but by an ecology of forces (e.g. organisational and external).

The majority of the OHP literature, at least within the work-stress research domain, has been strongly influenced by work stress models such as the Demands-Control Model (Karasek, 1979; Karasek & Theorell, 1990), and the Effort-Reward Imbalance Model (Siegrist, 1998). These emphasise the contextual features of the work environment. In addition there is a strong contribution of psychological models which emphasise individual differences in perceptions, such as the cognitive-phenomenological model (Lazarus & Folkman, 1984) and the Person-Environment Fit theory (French, Caplan, & Harrison, 1984; Dollard, 2003; Schnall, Landsbergis, & Baker, 1994). These models and theoretical frameworks have provided valuable insight into the etiological links between the psychosocial aspects of work environment, as well as individual characteristics, and the health and well-being of workers. However, they have been criticised for promoting an over simplified two-dimensional view of the world of work (Johnson & Hall, 1996). According to Johnson and Hall, (1996) if more comprehensive models where worker-environment interactions are framed within a broader societal context are not taken into consideration, understanding of aspects of work and health outcomes may be incomplete, and causal factors overlooked. Moreover, without a more complete understanding of the workplace as a social context comprising political, economic and social elements, understanding and reform of the ecology in which workers operate cannot be made (Johnson & Hall, 1996). For example by nesting the sources of work stress within the organisational structure of the workplace, connections with broader concepts such as labour conflicts, worker's collectives, personal alienation, power, and management can be made (Kristensen, 1996) with the potential benefit of identifying the true sources of work stress.

Prima facie there is a clear need to build knowledge of the organisation of work and its influences on worker health from a multi-level perspective. Thus we assessed the scope of OHP studies in relation to the contextual level(s) of investigation (i.e., External, Organisational, Work or Individual Context factors).

GLOBAL AND REGIONAL INTERESTS

Over the past two decades, global economic activity has grown rapidly. Therefore understanding and improving work conditions across all nations and regional areas is increasingly important (Aycan, 2000). The insights of OHP have hitherto evolved within a North American and European cultural context (Kristensen, 1996) and tended to focus on "developed industrial countries" (Kompier, 2006, p. 2). Work-family conflict research in Eastern cultures for instance has received little attention to date (Hassan, Dollard, & Winefield, 2007). This raises concerns about the hegemony of OHP knowledge production, the social origins of OHP knowledge, and whether OHP is translatable to other socio-geographical locations. The sociology of knowledge contends that specialised bodies of thought and knowledge are influenced by the social and cultural contexts in which they are produced (Mulkay, 1979). It is reasonable to propose that knowledge is most useful in the contexts in which it is generated. This implies an imperative to conduct OHP research globally, not simply in developed industrialised countries. The WHO *Global plan of action on workers' health 2008-2017* notes that "large gaps exist between and within countries with regard to the health status of workers and their exposure to occupational risk" (p. 4).

Occupational health, especially work-related psychosocial issues such as work stress, has become a growing concern in developing countries due as well to the impact of globalisation (Houtman, Jettinghoff, & Cedillo, 2007). It is difficult to estimate the effects of globalisation on worker health and well-being given the limited amount of available OHP information. However some researchers are concerned that the impact of work changes may affect developing economies even more than industrialised nations (Dollard, 2007). The reality is that the impact of global changes in work has benefited industrialised or strong economies rather than those that are weak (Loewenson, 2001). Thus while the impact of work changes are of concern in industrialised nations their impact appears even worse in the developing economies (The International Labour Organisation, 2004).

Within developing economies, globalisation, commercial agreements with industrialised countries, and World Bank policies have led to a major decline in the agriculture sector, where a large proportion of workers were employed traditionally (Houtman, Jettinghoff, & Cedillo, 2007). At the same time, the differences between rural and urban areas in terms of development and availability of resources, income and jobs have increased. Overall population growth and the offer of industry and service work in urban areas has increased and has stimulated migration to the cities (Houtman, Jettinghoff, & Cedillo, 2007). In addition, deregulation associated with globalisation has resulted in decreased protection of workers' rights such as health and retirement benefits (Rama, 2003). Child labor (ILO, 2004) is a pertinent issue in many developing economies. And an increasing number of people are facing job insecurity, unemployment, under-employment and substandard jobs due to trade liberalisation in formerly protected sectors (Houtman, Jettinghoff, & Cedillo, 2007; Rama, 2003).

The pace of industrialised development itself poses a major issue in many developing countries (Dollard, 2007). While the level of industrial development in Western societies has been the result of a gradual process over the last two hundred years, the development in many emerging economies such as China and India has transpired in just over two decades. The migrant worker has evolved from a rapid transformation from traditional occupations (e.g., farming, fishing and traditional workshops) to manufacturing industries both on-shore and off-shore. These workers not only need to adjust to the new work environment, life style and social network in an unfamiliar place, they also carry a tremendous responsibility and pressure to provide better living conditions for their families back home (Tan, 2008).

A lack of awareness and understanding of worker psychosocial well-being has hindered policy development and occupational health services coverage in relation to work-related psychosocial health issues in non-industrialised countries (Houtman, Jettinghoff, & Cedillo, 2007). In sum there is a growing need for OHP research and consequential policies and practice in developing economies. A major challenge for OHP research is to develop knowledge within a complex counterpane of broad cultural dimensions such as individualism versus collectivism, spirituality and religion, and in different economic systems.

Rural work is also under-represented in the international OHP literature (Staniford, Dollard, & Guerin, 2007). Yet the rural population accounts for 51.3% of the world's population, and 73.3% of the population in least developed countries (e.g. Cambodia, Ethiopia, Somalia, Sudan, Tuvalu & Uganda) (PDDESAUNS). There is evidence which raises concern for the psychological well-being of the farming population. For instance, Kelly and Bunting (1998) found that farmers as an occupational group had one of the highest risks for suicide. In addition their proportional mortality ratio was twice that of the general population recorded between 1982-1987 in England and Wales. This trend continued throughout the 90s. More recent studies have also suggested that the mental and physical health of farmers is under threat in many countries. This is in the context of changing government policies, growing global competition, increasing consumer demands, as well as natural disasters such as flood, drought and diseases in crops and animals (e.g. Gorgievski-Duijvesteijin, 2005; Staniford, Dollard & Guerin, 2007). Furthermore, there is an increasing pressure on world governments to address the needs and well-being (including psychological health) of workers in primary industries suffering from the effects of climate change and increasing oil prices.

At a national and regional level governments need evidence based information to guide their decisions on public policies (Quick, 1996). Quick suggests that: "Scientists and researchers are responsible to provide the evidence that meets these criteria, and then public officials and policy makers are responsible to take action to protect, defend, and enhance the health of their constituencies" (Quick, 1996, p.348). We argue therefore that there is an imperative for OHP researchers to move beyond the occupation groups they usually study and include populations of need identified here within developing countries and rural regions. In the review therefore we assessed where OHP studies are predominantly grounded e.g., industrial vs developing economies; urban vs. rural locations.

RESEARCH METHODOLOGY

Increased interventional research and more thorough data collection targeting improved worker health and safety has also been identified as an important issue for guiding research in OHP (Landsbergis, 2003; NIOSH, 2002). However, there is a mismatch between the need for interventions and the number of published intervention studies (Schaufeli, 2004; Van der Klink et al., 2001). Particularly there is a lack of well-designed and well-implemented preventative interventions (Kompier et al., 1998). Traditionally intervention studies have been predominantly reactive and aimed at individuals (Kompier et al., 1998). This is disconcerting considering the strong etiological link between the psychosocial work environment and health. Furthermore, prevailing legislation for working conditions (at least in some industrialised economies) emphasises primary prevention for work stress i.e. interventions at the organisational or work level. More recently, there has been an increase in well-documented intervention studies into the psychosocial work environment targeting improved job design (Dollard, Zapf, Cox, & Petkov, forthcoming; Kompier & Taris, 2005; Semmer, 2003; 2006). In this study we intend to quantify the number of intervention studies published in the journals.

Researchers have previously commented on the under-utilisation of longitudinal OHP research. Cross-sectional designs are limited in their ability to demonstrate causal relationships and to explain effects of third variables (Zapf, Dormann, & Frese, 1996). By comparison, longitudinal research allows the examination of patterns of change over time, and may assist to establish causal direction and reciprocal relationships. Longitudinal designs also have the capacity to assess within-individual change (Farrington, 1991; Goodman & Blum, 1996). Alternatively cross-sectional designs are better adapted to monitoring/surveillance (see Kompier, Taris, & Schaufeli, 2004), fact counting, and trends research but are inadequate for the study of causality and time-dynamics. Thus, more systematic longitudinal designs of OHP studies are needed to complement cross-sectional studies (Taris & Kompier, 2003). Therefore we sought to assess the prevalence of longitudinal research in the field.

THE PRESENT STUDY

We wanted to determine existing patterns of research and knowledge development in the OHP field. In order to achieve this we assessed papers in terms of: 1. the main topic areas covered and changes in topic focus over time, 2. contextual levels of focus, 3. participant locations, and 4. the range of designs employed in studies. By identifying emphases or omissions in knowledge production mapped against potential need, we expected new opportunities could arise for future research and knowledge generation to assist policy makers to improve the quality of workers' lives worldwide.

Several international journals, such as *Work & Stress,* the *Scandinavian Journal of Work Environment and Health,* and the *Journal of Occupational Health Psychology* (JOHP), have as a core mission to serve the development of and dissemination of OHP research. OHP studies can be found elsewhere, such as in the *Journal of Applied Psychology* and in journals of other disciplines such as management, medicine and OH&S. However we decided to select data from OHP focused journals only. The main reason for this decision was to delimit the analysis.

We selected the JOHP as the journal publishes articles concerning psychological factors related to all aspects of occupational health and safety, specifically focusing on the work environment, the individual, and the work-family interface (American Psychological Association, 2007). We analysed all articles published since its inception in 1996.

We also selected the journal *Work & Stress* (W&S) which, although also international, is based in Europe. W&S is a well-established premier journal with a considerably longer history in the field (since 1987). Nevertheless we matched publications from the same 11 years in the analysis. We believed that eleven years of development and publication of OHP knowledge in the JOHP and W&S collectively would provide a rich database within which to examine the research questions.

Five research questions were posed:

Q1: What are the main topics covered in the JOHP and W&S and have these changed over time?

Q2. To what extent has the literature in the past decade endorsed a multi-level approach to OHP issues?

Q3: Does the development of the OHP literature reflect the increasing needs and interests for more culturally and globally representative research?

Q4: What is the proportion of intervention studies in comparison to non-intervention studies in the JOHP and W&S?

Q5: What are the proportions of cross-sectional vs longitudinal study designs used in OHP research?

METHOD

A systematic search of the published articles in the *Journal of Occupational Health Psychology* (JOHP) was conducted using a computerised search of the PsycARTICLE database, which resulted in 334 articles. Two raters (Authors 1 and 2) independently analysed every paper backward from volume 11, 2006 to volume 1, 1996. Details of the study title, author(s), year of publication, design methodology, participants, research setting (country and region), level of contextual influences according to the Model of the Organization of Work (NIOSH, 2002) (see Figure 1) outcome measures, and results were recorded (see Table 2 for a sample). In addition, we categorised the articles into OHP topic areas using thematic analysis (Boyatzis, 1998) and also assessed whether the intervention method(s) were the focus of the studies. Eleven years of the published articles (297 articles) in *Work & Stress* (W&S), from volume 20, 2006 to volume 10, 1996, were analysed. Because of time constraints, all other details of the articles were recorded in the same fashion as the first round of analysis with the exception of the results (see Table 3 for a sample)[1].

During the categorisation process, a new dimension emerged - Individual Context - which included personality, individual differences, coping strategies and motivation, and demographic factors such as age, gender, and race. The raters collaboratively added this dimension to the NIOSH taxonomy.

Raters divided this fourth dimension, the Individual Context into three distinct levels: Individual Factors, Family Factors (e.g. family-to-work conflict or enrichment) and Inter-Domain Factors (where work factors influence other areas of life such as family and relationships). By consensus between raters, this categorisation of articles was then used for all articles (see Table 1 adapted from NIOSH, 2002 used by the raters).

Table 1 shows the codes used to categorise each level, the names given to each contextual level of work, and basic inclusion criteria used for each level. An illustrative sample of the categorised articles is presented in Table 2 for JOHP and in Table 3 for W&S. Five types of design were used to categorise the methodology employed by the articles. These were: Cross-sectional, Longitudinal, Meta-analysis, Review, and Editorial.

Furthermore, four types of settings in which the samples of the studies were located were identified: Urban, Rural, National, and Military. National

---

[2] A full version of these tables is available upon request from the third author

Table 1. Level code, level name and inclusion criteria for each context used in rating articles in OHP

Level Code	Contextual Level of Work	Inclusion Criteria
4	External Context	Economic, legal, political, technological, and demographic forces at the national and international level
3	Organizational Context	Management structures, supervisory practices, production methods, and human resource policies
2	Work Context	Job characteristics such as climate and culture, task attributes, social-relational aspects of work, worker roles, and career development
1a	Individual Factors	Personality, motivation, coping strategies, and demographics (e.g. age, gender and race)
1b	Family Factors	Family demands, conflicts, enrichment
ID	Inter-domain Factors	Influences of work on other domains e.g. family, relationships

refers to a nation-wide sampling base. Military samples were separated from other types because these samples might include participants who were located in urban military bases or deployed to remote rural areas. We found that most studies identified the towns or cities where their participants were located, especially when the studies involved rural populations, but there were a few studies which did not specify the location. Those studies have been categorised as National since their sample might contain participants from rural areas.

In sum, we systematically analysed a total number of 334 articles in eleven volumes of the *Journal of Occupational Health Psychology* from the years 1996-2006 and 297 articles in *Work and Stress* from the same time period. To answer question 1 we assessed major topics researched in the journals across three different time periods; '1996 to 1998', '1999 to 2002' and '2003 to 2006'.

RESULTS

Figure 2 for JOHP and Figure 3 for W&S show the total frequency of each topic, and a breakdown of the frequency of each topic. The most frequently covered topic areas in JOHP were: work-family interface (n = 38), work and health (psychological/physiological outcomes) (n = 35), safety at work (n = 23), internal resources (n = 22), and interpersonal conflict/aggression/violence (n = 19). Some topic areas, particularly work-family interface, interpersonal conflict/aggression/violence, problematic

Table 2. Categorization of articles from the JOHP.

Study (Author, Year of Publication)	Design	Participants	Organisation of Work	Outcomes	Results	Intervention
1. 'The interactive effects of positive affect and conscientiousness on strain' (Zellars, Perrewé, Hochwater & Anderson, 2006)	Cross-sectional	188 nurses(USA/ Urban)	**Level 1a:** - Positive affect (PANAS) - Conscientiousness (NEO-FFI)	Strain variables: - Job burnout (emotional exhaustion & depersonalisation on Maslach Burnout Inventory) - Job tension	The combination of high positive affect and high levels of conscientiousness was associated with lower levels of all strain variables. Conscientiousness was found to strengthen the negative relationship between PA and job strain.	No
2. 'Development and validation of a multidimensional scale of perceived work–family positive spillover'(Hanson, Hammer & Colton, 2006)	Cross-sectional	*Study 1:* 136 employees from a distribution centre *Study 2:* 135 employees from a public utility company & electronics design company (USA / Urban)	**Level ID:** Multidimensional work-family positive spillover	*Study 1:* EFA on construct validation of WFPS *Study 2:* CFA on construct validation of the new multidimensional WFPS measure.- job satisfaction, family satisfaction & self-reported mental health (SF-12v2 Health Survey)	Work-family positive spillover (PS) can be broken into 6 subdimensions: (1) work-to-family affective PS; (2) work-to-family behaviour-based instrumental PS; (3) work-to-family value-based instrumental PS; (4) family-to- work affective PS; (5) family-to-work behaviour-based instrumental PS; (6) family-to-work value-based instrumental PS. All dimensions demonstrated adequate dimensionality and internal consistency.	No

Table 2. Contd.

Study (Author, Year of Publication)	Design	Participants	Organisation of Work	Outcomes	Results	Intervention
3. 'Psychosocial work stressors in the development and maintenance of insomnia: A prospective study'(Jansson & Linton, 2006)	Longitudinal	2,179 randomly selected Swedish residents (part of the Orebro Insomnia CohortStudy) (Sweden/Urban)	**Level 2:** Psychosocial work stressors - autonomy and control - influence over decisions - professional compromise - role conflict - work demands - peer support - leader support - role clarity - feedback	Sleep (Basic Nordic Sleep Questionnaire	Findings indicated that some stressors at work (work demands, leader support, and influence over decisions) are involved in developing and maintaining insomnia, whereas other work stressors are less substantial. Insomnia may be partly work related and, associated with perceived specific stressors at work.	No
4. 'Divergent effects of transformational and passive leadership onemployee safety' (Kelloway, Mullen, & Francis, 2006)	Cross-sectional	158 undergraduate students (Canada/Urban)	**Level 3:** - Leadership styles: Safety-specific transformational leadership and safety-specific passive leadership (MLQ-5(Bass & Avolio, 1990)).	- Injuries - safety climate - safety consciousness	Passive leadership contributes incrementally to the prediction of safety-related variables, beyond transformational leadership alone. Further analyses via structural equation modelling showed that both transformational and passive leadership have opposite effects on safety climate and safety consciousness, and these variables predict safety events and injuries.	No

Table 2. Contd.

Study (Author, Year of Publication)	Design	Participants	Organisation of Work	Outcomes	Results	Intervention
5. 'Organizational adoption of pre-employment drug testing' (Spell & Blum, 2001)	Cross-sectional	360 organizations. (data obtained from HR managers) (USA/Urban)	**Level 4:** - Area density (the proportion of worksites adopting drug testing in the geographic area) - Industry density (the nationwide proportion adopting within the industry). - Period effects (Reagan, Bush and Clinton administrations) **Level 3:** - Size (number of full time employees at the worksite) - Safety (extent that safety was an important concern for the worksite) - Internal labour market. - Union presence at worksite - Ave. annual voluntary turnover - Perceptions of drug problem. **Level 1a:** - Demographics (gender and racial distribution)	Adoption of drug testing by the organization	Both internal organizational and environmental variables predicted adoption of drug testing. Results indicate that the higher the proportion of drug testers in the worksite's industry, the more likely it would be to adopt drug testing. Also, the extent to which an organization uses an internal labor market, voluntary turnover rate, and the extent to which management perceives drugs to be a problem were related to likelihood of adoption of drug testing.	No

NOTE: A full table is available from the third author.

Table 3. Categorization of articles from the W&S

Study (Author, Year of Publication)	Design	Participants	Organisation of Work	Outcomes	Interventions
1. 'Evaluation of an intervention programme based on empowerment for eldercare nursing staff' Petterson, Donnersvärd, Lagerström & Toomingas (2006)	Longitudinal	200 eldercare nursing staff (Sweden/Urban setting)	**Level 1a** Competence programme **Level 2 & 3** Worksite competence circles Worksite improvement projects	Workload Staff resources Health & Well-being Health resources Quality of care	Yes
2. 'Organizational change in the public sector: Augmenting the demand control model to predict employee outcomes under New Public Management' Noblet, Rodwell, & McWilliams (2006)	Cross-sectional	1,155 staff from the Australian public sector (Australia/Urban setting)	**Level 1a** Coping: Problem vs. emotion focused **Level 2** Job demands Job control Social support: work & non-work **Level 3** Organisational-specific stressors (Unrewarding management; Tight organisational resourcing; Draining environment)	Psychological health Job satisfaction Organisational commitment	No
3. 'Is there a relationship between burnout and objective performance? A critical review of 16 studies' Taris (2006)	Meta-analysis	16 studies dealing with burnout-performance relationship (N/A)	**Level 1a:** Burnout	Performance	No

Table 3. Contd.

Study (Author, Year of Publication)	Design	Participants	Organisation of Work	Outcomes	Intervention
4. 'Beyond demand–control: Emotional labour and symptoms of burnout in teachers' Näring, Briët & Brouwers (2006)	Cross-sectional	365 mathematics teachers (Netherlands/Urban setting)	**Level 2** Social Support (SSL-D) Control Quantitative demands (VOS-D)	Emotional labour (surface acting; deep acting; suppression; emotional consonance) (D-QEL) Burnout (MBI-NL-Ed)	No
5. 'Measuring exposure to bullying at work: The validity and advantages of the latent class cluster approach' Notelaers, Einarsen, De Witte, & Vermunt (2006)	Cross-sectional	6,175 employees from 18 organisations (Belgium/Urban setting)	**Level 1a** Exposure to bullying at work (NAQ)	Symptoms of work stress	No
6. 'Success or failure? Interpreting and understanding the impact of interventions in four similar worksites' Nielsen, Fredslund, Christensen, & Albertsen (2006)	Longitudinal (2-wave)	118 employees from 4 industrial canteens (Denmark/Urban setting)	Interventions: **Level 1a** Individual health (weight loss course; exercise; smoking cessation course; massage; health profiles, etc.) Psychosocial activities (First-aid training; self-managing work teams; etc. **Level 2** Team building activities Physical environment (ergonomics; training on heavy lifting; noise regulation)	Social support (COP-SOQ) Job satisfaction (COP-SOQ) Opportunities for personal development (COPSOQ) Symptoms of stress BMI Vitality	Yes

Table 3. Contd.

Study (Author, Year of Publication)	Design	Participants	Organisation of Work	Outcomes	Intervention
7. 'Variables related to psychiatric sick leave taken by Spanish secondary school teachers' Antonio Moriana & Herruzo (2006)	Cross-sectional	200 secondary school teachers from 29 centres (12 urban and 17 rural) (Spain/ Urban & Rural)	**Level 1a** Age; Number of children; Years working; Substitute teacher; Civil servant; Gender; Marital status; Degree; Job status; Cigarette smoking; Alcohol; Anxiety; Somatic symptoms; Depression; Competitiveness; Impatience; Hostility; Emotional exhaustion; Depersonalisation; Personal accomplishment; Job satisfaction **Level 2** Work overload	Psychiatric sick leave	No
8. 'Combined workplace stressors and their relationship with mood, physiology, and performance' Wellens & Smith (2006)	Longitudinal	84 participants (UK/Urban)	**Level 1a** Gender **Level 2** Temporal stressors (Shift work; Night work; Long/unsociable hours of work; Unpredictable hours of work)Physical hazards (Inhale harmful substances; Handle/touch harmful substances; Left with ringing in the ears; Background noise disturbs work)	Mood (alertness; sociability; anxiety) Physiological (systolic BP; diastolic BP; heart rate; salivary cortisol) Performance (VF-P SRT task; focused attention task; categoric search task)	No

Table 3. Contd.

Study (Author, Year of Publication)	Design	Participants	Organisation of Work	Outcomes	Intervention
9. 'Work and mental disorders in a German national representative sample' Roesler, Jacobi, & Rau (2006)	Cross-sectional	2329 employees (Germany/National)	**Level 1a** Demographics (gender, age, social class, marital status, number of children, unemployment) **Level 2** Physical workload (unvaried posture; carrying heavy objects) Stress at workplace (pressure of time or to perform; high need on concentration, bad working climate) Overtime, long working hours	Anxiety disorders (specific phobia, social phobia, panic disorder, generalized anxiety disorder) Somatoform disorders (pain disorder) Affective disorders (major depression, dysthymic disorder, bipolar disorder) Substance abuse or dependence (nicotine dependence, alcohol abuse or dependence, drug abuse or dependence)	No
10. 'Exploring work- and organization-based resources as moderators between work–family conflict, well-being, and job attitudes' Mauno, Kinnunen, & Ruokolainen (2006)	Cross-sectional	1,252 employees from 3 organisations (Finland/Urban)	**Level 1D** Work-to-family conflict (time-based & strain-based) (SWING) **Level 2** Job control (time control, method control) Career development Working hours Organizational-based self-esteem **Level 3** Family supportiveness of management	Job satisfaction (PMI)	No

work behavior, and organisational change were published increasingly over time. Others, such as job loss/insecurity and unemployment and OHP research issues, were published more frequently during the earlier period of the review.

By comparison with the JOHP, we found that publication in W&S were more concentrated on the topic of work and health (psychological/physiological outcomes) (n = 86), although other topics such as OHP research issues (n = 28), internal resources (n = 27), and burnout (n = 26), were also frequently covered in the journal. Topics including organisational factors, burnout, and work-family interface were published increasingly over the period reviewed. Others such as internal resources and theory/model development were more frequent during the earlier period of review. Articles investigating issues that did not appear to fit under a broad recurring topic theme were classed as miscellaneous. This included 29 articles in JOHP and 21 in W&S.

In addressing question 2 we first excluded 30 articles (7 editorials, 20 review articles, 1 meta-analysis, and 2 empirical studies) from JOHP and 30 articles (13 editorials, 16 review articles and 1 empirical study) from W&S. This was because they did not study any contextual level of influence on individual occupational health and safety. Thus, the final number of articles included in the analysis was 304 in JOHP and 267 in W&S.

Many of these studies employed more than one level of influence. We identified 15 different combinations of measured contextual levels in each journal. Because of the large range of combinations, Figures 4 and 5 display the breakdown of levels of contextual influences measured by five or more articles only. The most frequently observed contextual levels of influences in the articles in order were: a combination of Work and Individual contextual factors (Level 2 and Level 1a) (n = 124, 40.8%, JOHP; n = 112, 41.9%, W&S); Individual Factors level (Level 1a) only (n = 51, 16.8%, JOHP; n = 49, 18.4%, W&S) and; the Job Context level (Level 2) (n = 34, 11.2%, JOHP; n = 31, 11.6%, W&S). Other levels of influence were given considerably less attention, especially the External Factors level (Level 4). We found 63 articles (20%) in JOHP and 48 articles (18%) in W&S included organisational context as the focus, either alone or in combination of the studies. Nonetheless, as shown in Figures 2 and 3, organisational context increasingly became more prevalent as a study focus. There were only 6 articles from each journal which included external influences only as the focus of their studies.

In addressing question 3, we first excluded all editorials, review articles and meta-analysis studies and papers where they did not identify the

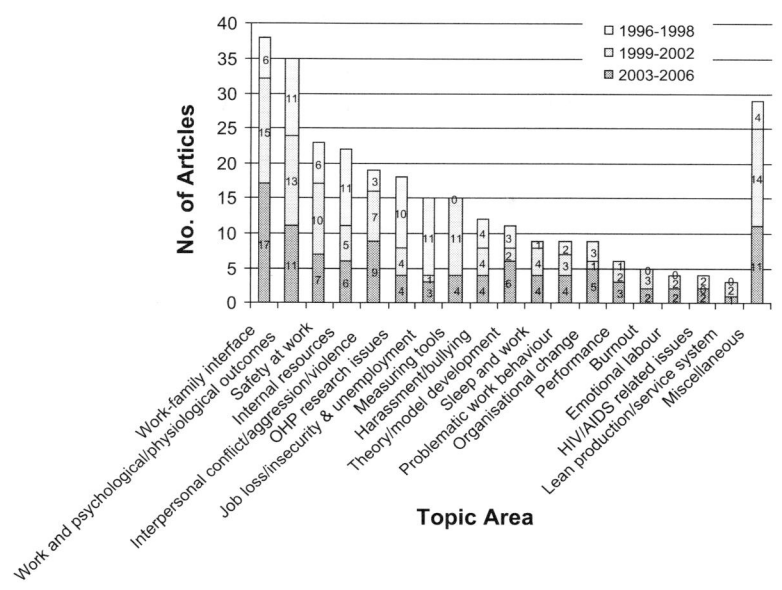

Figure 2. Graph showing the breakdown of frequency of topic areas covered in JOHP articles across three time periods: 1996-1998, 1999-2002, 2003-2006.

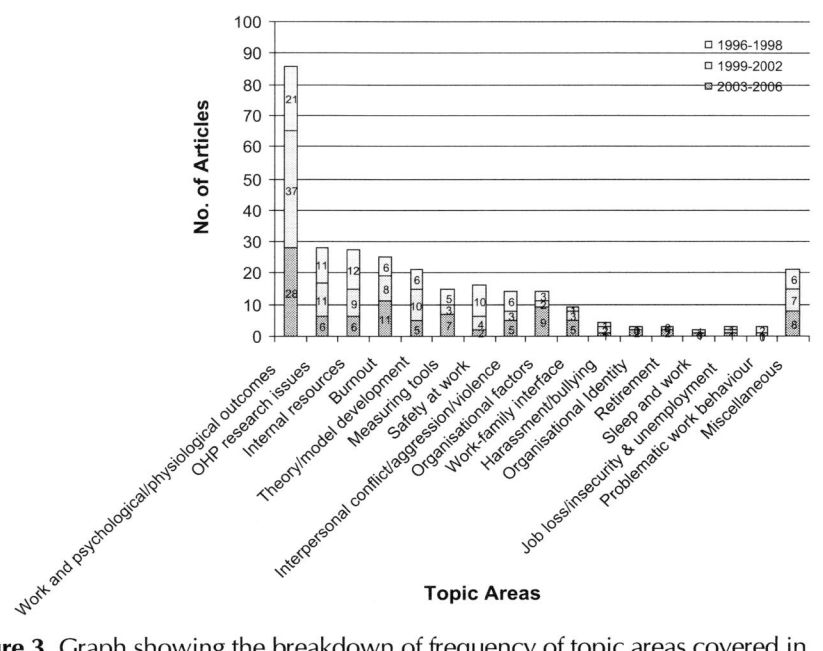

Figure 3. Graph showing the breakdown of frequency of topic areas covered in W&S articles across three time periods: 1996-1998, 1999-2002, 2003-2006.

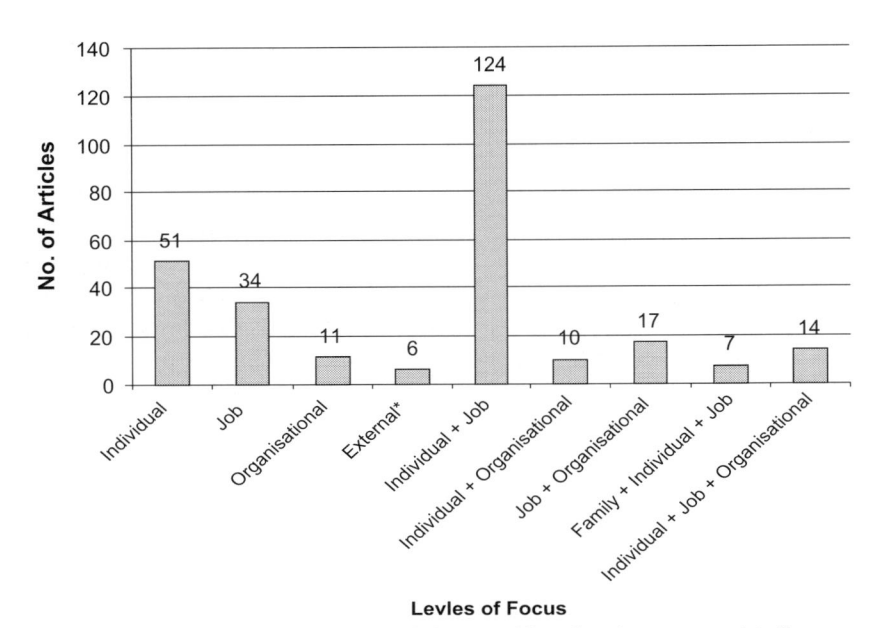

Figure 4. Graph showing the breakdown of levels of contextual influence on variables measured in JOHP studies.

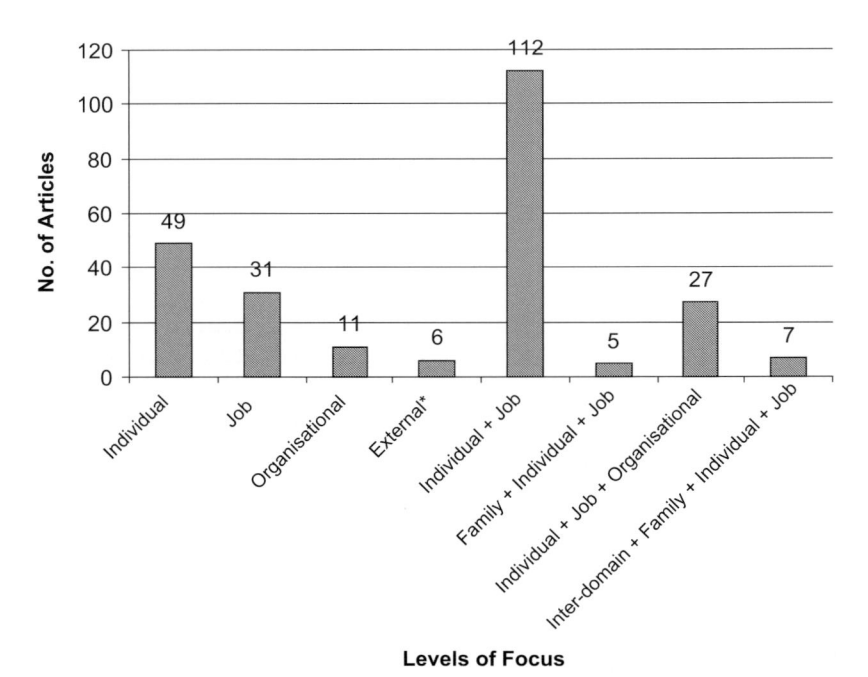

Levels of Focus (Individual: 51, Job: 34, Organisational: 11, External*: 6, Individual + Job: 124, Individual + Organisational: 10, Job + Organisational: 17, Family + Individual + Job: 7, Individual + Job + Organisational: 14)

Figure 5. Graph showing the breakdown of levels of contextual influence on variables measured in W&S studies.

Levels of Focus (Individual: 49, Job: 31, Organisational: 11, External*: 6, Individual + Job: 112, Family + Individual + Job: 5, Individual + Job + Organisational: 27, Inter-domain + Family + Individual + Job: 7) geographical-location of the research (excluded 54 articles, JOHP; 56 articles, W&S).

Of the remaining studies (289 JOHP; 239 W&S) most were located in North America (n = 158, 56.4%, JOHP; n = 38, 15.9%, W&S) and Europe (n = 95, 33.9%, JOHP; n = 159, 66.5%, W&S). The 'Europe' studies were predominantly conducted in Western Europe where many industrialised countries are located, except for one study in W&S which was conducted in Poland. In addition there were 13 studies (4.7%) in JOHP and 21 (8.8%) in W&S from Australia; 7 (2.5%) studies in JOHP and 4 (1.7%) in W&S from the Middle East (2.5%); 2 (.7%) in JOHP and 4 (1.7%) in W&S from Asia; 4 studies (2.5%) in W&S were from New Zealand, and 1 study in JOHP was from South America (.4%).

In addition, there were 2 (.7%) articles in JOHP and 5 (2.1%) in W&S that were collaborative studies between the industrial nations; and 2 (.7%) studies in JOHP and 1 (.4%) in W&S were collaborative efforts from industrial nations and developing countries. No study was located in an African nation, including the collaborative studies.

Figure 6 shows the distribution of studies across nations represented on a world map in order to visually illustrate differences in study geo-location.

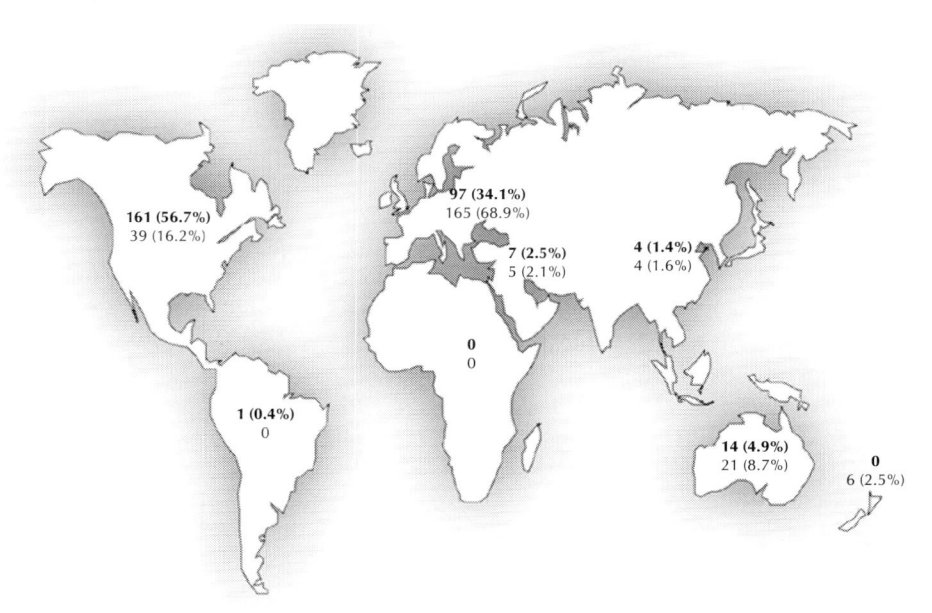

Figure 6. Distribution of studies in OHP over the globe (1996-2006)
(Figures in bold = JOHP; figures not in bold = WS)

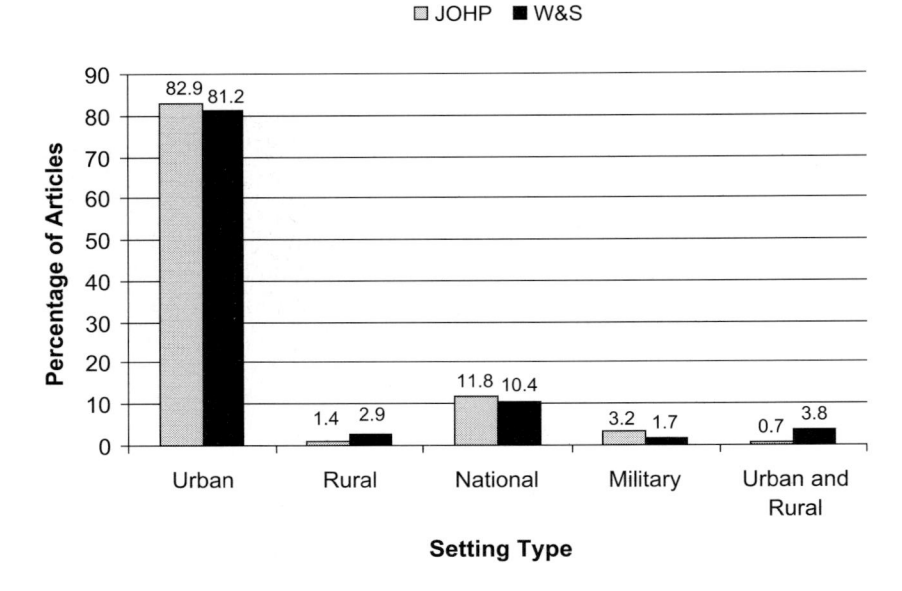

Figure 7. Graph showing the breakdown of setting of OHP studies

The figures shown vary from those mentioned above as they are inclusive of each country's collaborative studies (e.g. for a collaborative study between the US and China one study was counted towards North America's total and one towards Asia's total). Furthermore, as shown in Figure 7, the participant samples employed by the majority of studies were located in urban settings (n = 232, 82.9%, JOHP; n = 194, 81.2%, W&S).

Finally in relation to study design (Question 5), among the 334 articles in JOHP and 297 articles in W&S, only 7.2% (n = 24) in JOHP and 6.4% in W&S (n = 19) were intervention studies (see Figure 8). We found that 200 studies in JOHP employed cross-sectional methodology (59.9%), 76 studies employed longitudinal methodology (22.7%), 7 were meta-analyses (2.1%), and 4 articles included both cross-sectional and longitudinal data (1.2%). There were 7 editorials (2.1%) and 40 review articles (12.0%). Similar results were observed in W&S: we found 186 studies used cross-sectional design (62.6%), 48 studies were longitudinal (16.2%), 2 were meta-analyses (.7%), and 5 studies included both cross-sectional and longitudinal data (1.7%). There were also 13 editorials (4.4%) and 43 review articles (14.5%) (see Figure 9).

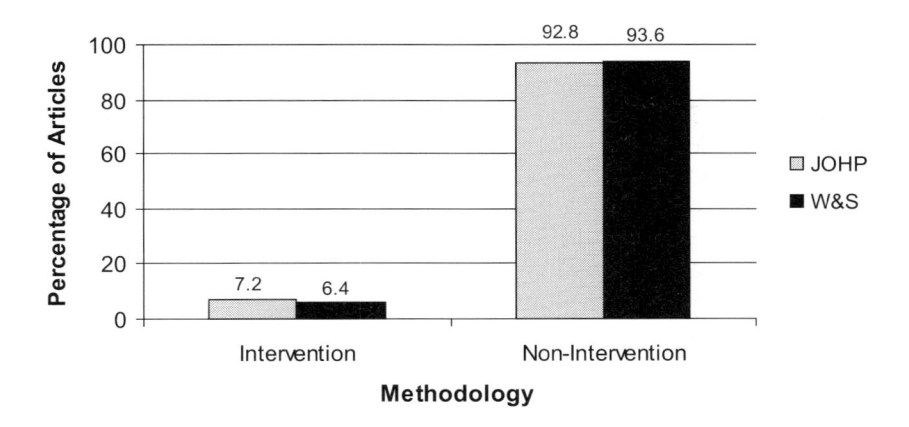

Figure 8. Graph showing the frequency of non-intervention vs. intervention designs used in OHP studies.

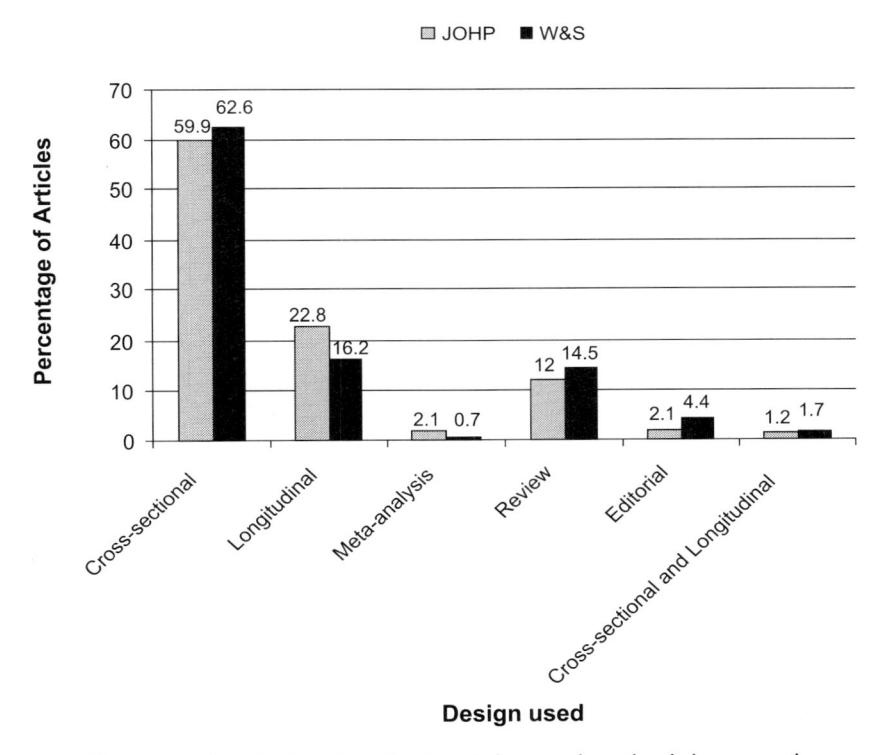

Figure 9. Graph showing the breakdown of methodology used in OHP studies.

DISCUSSION

Significant efforts have been given to the study of OHP, as evidenced by 631 papers published in just two leading OHP journals in the past 11 years. Many OHP topics and issues have been researched and discussed over the past decade. We discerned changes in topic pattern over time. Most research published in the JOHP and W&S focused on Individual Factors and/or Job Contextual issues. Most studies were conducted in industrialised nations including the US, UK and other European countries, and a notably higher proportion of studies were located in urban settings compared to rural settings. Very few intervention studies were reported, and cross-sectional study designs predominated over longitudinal or other designs. The results from this study highlight important patterns in OHP research as published in two international journals over the last eleven years.

The OHP research areas published in the JOHP are extensive, and cover a wide range of issues. We found an increase in reported research on organisational factors, work family conflict and burnout over time. This compared with a reduction of papers on job loss insecurity, and unemployment over time. Some topics remained consistent in presentation over the period e.g., work and health - psychological/physiological outcomes. W&S concentrated more on the topic of work and health. Topics including organisational factors, burnout, and work-family interface were published increasingly over the period reviewed. These trends hopefully reflect societal needs rather than researcher preference or convenience research. OHP research topics might be expected to vary in company with change in societal concerns.

The need for a more comprehensive, multi-layered research approach to OHP issues has been articulated (e.g., Aycan, 2000; NIOSH, 2002) to reflect an "ecology of exposure" (e.g., Johnson & Hall, 1996, pg. 362). However the patterns in the published OHP research we examined did not reflect this ideal. We found evidence of an increasing trend of studies into the effects of organisational behaviors. These included organisational restructuring, new HR and operational practices, and leadership styles. However the majority of OHP research appeared to focus on the individual context, including values, beliefs, cognitions and overt behaviour. Further, there was a preponderance of studies that focused etiological inference on the job context (e.g. job demands, control and social support), rather than on an ecology of forces, including factors at the external level such as economic and social developments and government policies, and the organisational level such as organisational structures and management practices. We were especially surprised about the small number of studies looking at the effects of external influences on people's working lives, considering influences like globalisation have received significant attention in many fields of study.

As we move closer towards a 'borderless' global community, it is perhaps more evident that worker health clearly exists within a complex ecological context of *interacting* forces, resulting from 'metaexposure' to political, economic and social forces in addition to the person-work organisation interaction (Johnson & Hall, 1996). As highlighted in Aycan's review (2000) of industrial and organizational psychology literature higher-level factors (e.g. external, social) are increasingly more prominent influences in all areas of our lives. Yet there is little empirical evidence in OHP literature regarding the influence of these factors on people's working life. Our review enables us to argue that OHP researchers study too easily the work context (the job characteristics in Figure 1) as independent factors, i.e. factors that influence our health and well-being, but are conceptualized as 'just being there'. We argue that there is also a need to study where these 'independent factors' (job characteristics) come from.

There is a need for OHP to conceptualise job characteristics, not only as factors that influence other factors (motivation, health and well-being), but also as factors that are influenced by other factors (organisational context → job design → health). Evidence in support of this pathway is provided by Dollard and Bakker (2008) where Psychosocial Safety Climate (PSC), which refers to "employee perceptions regarding the extent of psychosocial care, reflected through policies procedure and practice relating primarily to psychosocial safety" was shown to predict changes in job demands and control over time, and in turn worker health and showed direct effects on work outcomes (job engagement). The study provides some insights into the origins of job design elements and points to a different source for primary intervention other than job redesign (i.e. the improvement of PSC). Indeed, evidence in support of the organisational context → work context → employee outcomes pathway can be found in research on job redesign (e.g. Sprigg & Jackson, 2006) and the impact of lean production systems (Parker, 2003). Thus, we suggest more empirical studies also conceive of job characteristics as mediators or as dependent variables.

Extending from this we argue that all contextual levels of influence on employees' safety, health and well-being are important for investigation to provide organisations with guidance as they attempt to create healthy work environments for their employees (Bliese & Jex, 1999). We additionally argue for multi-level theoretical conceptualisation and models, as well as new measuring tools (see Schaufeli, 2004), to assist in the development of new OHP knowledge for global and local application.

Despite the increasing need and interest for a more culturally and globally representative OHP research, the findings from the present study did not show a trend in this regard in either JOHP or W&S in the past decade. Rather, the findings concur with the observation that published OHP (e.g. work stress) research is almost entirely derived and developed within North American or European cultures and settings (Kristensen, 1996). This is problematic as OHP issues emerge globally. Further, the dramatic under representation of rural samples, at most around 20% of papers, is really striking given a conservative estimate of the rural population worldwide at over 50% in the global population. Sociologists suggest that organisational knowledge should be thought of as 'distributed social expertise: that is, knowledge-in-practice situated in the historical, socio-material, and cultural context in which it occurs' (Gherardi & Nicolini, 2000, p. 330). Similarly, OHP knowledge that was developed and based in Western, industrialised cultures may not be as applicable to other workers in diverse parts of the world. Alternatively, issues that are significant to particular 'other' groups may not have been encountered by Western industrialised cultures. Furthermore, it has been demonstrated that workers' occupational health benefits more from job control where national research and development activity is greater (Daniels, Tregaskis, & Seaton, 2007). Thus, it is logical to suggest that local and (inter)national research and development in the field of occupational health potential could play a crucial role in improving a country's work conditions and workers' health.

Although we found a clear preponderance of Western European and North American papers in these journals, this may not be unexpected since this reflects their geo-location. It could also be that papers submitted from less developed countries do not meet the aims and standards of the journals. To address this we suggest that more researchers build cooperative research[2] with academics and workers from other parts of the world, in rural and developing countries/regions to ensure more wide ranging improvements in world health and work conditions for the global population. Researchers can also work with industry partners who have business experiences in developing countries. There is also a need for OHP researchers from less developed countries/regions such as China, India, Africa and South America, and researchers specialising in rural and remote populations to receive financial resources and expertise to meet the joint objectives of conducting vital research for their own economies and to meet journal standards. Main-stream OHP journals may consider setting up special scientific committees to provide guidance and assistance to less

---

2 Truly cooperative research builds a cooperative knowledge including using emic approaches focused on the construction of local meaning and theory rather than (re) through applying western OHP theory and methods using universal etic approaches (i.e. grand theory).

experienced researchers to meet the quality standards of international peer-reviewed journals.

We found that intervention studies occupied a very small proportion of the literature, despite the strong need for more intervention studies identified in OHP research. Knowing *what works* to improve occupational health rather than focusing only on identifying problems is useful for OHP practitioners. Evidence shows that interventions can benefit both the workers and their employers, if they are well-designed and well-implemented with a combination of thorough risk assessments, and stress management methods (Kompier & Taris, 2005). Finally, we acknowledge that a great deal of effort has been put into conducting longitudinal studies, considering the difficulties and costs associated with conducting such studies, but there is room for more of these studies. Therefore, OHP researchers in the future should be encouraged to increase the use of longitudinal and interventional studies.

GENERAL LIMITATIONS

The results of the present study must be considered in light of its limitations. We understand that systematic analysis of two journals may not accurately generalise to OHP research in its entirety. Although we chose two journals to offset selection bias we can not be confident that all conclusions would be the same for all other journals that canvas OHP issues. However, from this study we see a general lack of published OHP research from developing countries and on rural samples, and a need for more such research. The World Health Organization (WHO) for example notes that: "The majority of the developing countries have very poor investment in research and still have many unsolved problems; these are maybe the main cause that explains the paucity in generating proper data and evaluating the impact of the change at work (p.11)"(Houtman, Jettinghoff & Cedillo, 2007). Flagship journals and their attendant researchers in the OHP field might consider a joint role to play to remedy this situation.

Another limitation is that in the categorisations we used race, gender, and education as individual level phenomenon as this is how they were mainly operationalised. We acknowledge that these phenomena may also be indicative of social level factors that influence the experience of work and the labor market (Johnson & Hall, 1996).

Regarding interventions, again it may be that reports of intervention research do not meet the standards required of a high impact journal. This could be partly because of the difficulty of conducting such research.

Finally we used an adapted NIOSH framework against which to map OHP research, and our conclusions are framed by this. It may be argued that this approach "neglects more fundamental research questions that may generate in-depth knowledge about the psychological processes and mechanisms that might explain how the organisation of work affects individual workers" (Schaufeli, 2004). A balance of research in areas of psychological processes and mechanisms and the full ecology of factors impinging on the psychological worker could be a fruitful way forward.

Additionally there may be other relevant frameworks against which to map OHP knowledge development. An important contribution would be to focus on vulnerable groups (e.g. part-time, contingent, temporary, women and lower socio-economic status workers) as outlined in the NIOSH research agenda. Analysis of specific types of OHP research undertaken (e.g. explanatory research, descriptive research, tool development, intervention research, organisational change) would also be of interest (Schaufeli, 2004).

FUTURE DIRECTIONS

The apparent gaps in research and knowledge published in these two international journals represent areas that need more support and resourcing in terms of finance and expertise, and also toward which OHP researchers and practitioners, may fruitfully turn their attention. Lack of publication in crucial areas means that knowledge is not developed and integrated into the OHP curriculum. Of immediate concern is the possibility that OHP literature is outpaced by the rapid changes in the nature of work to the detriment of worker health. It is recommended that future research in OHP aims to:

1. Build a research agenda consistent with the WHO, Workers' Health; Global Plan of Action 2008-2017.
2. Develop multi-layered approaches to OHP issues, through developments in theory and measurement tools that capture the full ecology of influences of health work, increasing our knowledge of these issues (Dollard, 2007).
3. Broaden the range of locations and settings in which studies are conducted to build a more representative body of international research. Specifically, conduct studies using cooperative techniques and appropriate techniques with rural/indigenous populations and those living in emerging developing economies, for example, African, Asian, Middle Eastern and South American nations.

4. Cross-national risk factors surveillance systems, may also be a very important component to the process of building a more thorough and practically useful research base (e.g., Dollard, Skinner, Tuckey, & Bailey, 2007).
5. Use thorough data collection methods including longitudinal designs and intervention research where relevant and possible.

CONCLUSION

This study provides a stock-take of the parameters of research and knowledge development in OHP analyzing 631 articles from 2 journals. It may therefore be used to establish an agenda for future knowledge building in OHP research in areas that need help and attention. In the two journals specifically reviewed there is evidence of change in topics overtime presumably (although not conclusively) in response to societal needs (e.g. work-family conflict in JOHP). Looking at the research patterns more specifically, we found that there are some limitations and omissions in the current OHP research, either due to a lack of attention by researchers, or research not reaching the standard required for publication in those journals. We also identified a lack of a comprehensive, multi-level approach to issues relating to workers' health, safety and wellbeing, a tendency to measure low levels of contextual influence (i.e., individual and work context) rather than upstream level influences (i.e., external and organisational context), a focus on industrialised nations over developing countries, a paucity of research in rural contexts, and minimal use of intervention studies.

In light of these, we have highlighted a number of important research directions to consider in order to build a truly international OHP project and bridge gaps between information built and that required. Firstly, there is a need for more studies focused on upstream/external and organisational factors, and studies aimed towards multi-layered approaches to problems in order to capture both upstream influences and downstream costs. There is also a need to extend the focus of attention to rural people and to emerging or developing economies in African, Asian, Middle Eastern and South American nations, and to utilise more comprehensive data collection methods, including longitudinal designs and intervention research.

The patterns of research in OHP revealed by the current study must be considered in light of the complexities of today's organisations and the emergence of a global business community in which 'upstream' or external pressures are becoming more and more influential in worker's lives. In accord with the WHO *Workers' health; global plan of action* 2008-2017, the need to know about organisations and workers in a range of different nations all over the world and the need to conduct more thorough, empirical research is required to inform organisational, national and international policy and practice is required. It is important that research and development in OHP 'keep up' with the pace of these changes and stay abreast of what is important to guide effective and efficient OHP practice, even if it is not simple or convenient to conduct the type of research that can help fulfill this aim.

REFERENCES

American Psychological Association (2007). *Journal of Occupational Health Psychology Journal Description*. Retrieved January 23, 2007, from APA Web site: http://www.apa.org/journals/ocp/description.html

Aycan, Z. (2000). Cross-cultural industrial and organizational psychology: Contributions, past developments and future directions. *Journal of Cross-Cultural Psychology, 31*, 110-128.

Bliese, P.D., & Jex, S.M. (1999). Incorporating multiple levels of analysis into occupational stress research. *Work and Stress, 13*(1), 1-6.

Bliese, P.D., & Jex, S.M. (2002). Incorporating a multilevel perspective into occupational stress research: Theoretical, methodological, and practical implications. *Journal of Occupational Health Psychology, 7*(3), 265-276.

Boyatzis, R.E. (1998). *Transforming qualitative data: Thematic analysis and code development*. California, USA: Sage Publications.

Cox, T., Leka, S., Ivanov, I., & Kortum, E. (2004). Work, employment and mental health in Europe. *Work & Stress, 18*(2), 179-185.

Daniels, K., Tregaskis, O., & Seaton, J.S. (2007). Job control and occupational health: The moderating role of national R & D activity. *Journal of Organizational Behavior, 28*, 1-19.

Dollard, M.F. (2007). Necrocapitalism: Throwing away workers in the race for global capital. In J. Houdmont & S. McIntyre & (Eds), *Occupational Health Psychology: European Perspectives on Research, Education and Practice (Vol. 2)*, Maia, Portugal: ISMAI Publishers. pp. 169-193

Dollard, M. F. (2003). Introduction: Costs, theoretical approaches, research designs. In M.F. Dollard, A.H. Winefield, & H. R. Winefield, *Occupational Stress in the Service Professions*, London: Taylor & Francis, pp1-43.

Dollard, M.F., & Bakker, A.B. (2008). *Psychosocial safety climate: Longitudinal impacts on health, engagement and sickness absence. Manuscript under review*.

Dollard, M.F., le Blanc, P., & Cotton, S. (2007). Participatory action research as work stress intervention, In Ed Katharina Näswall, Johnny Hellgren, & Magnus Sverke *Balancing work and well-being: The individual in the changing working life* (pp. 351-353). Cambridge University Press.

DOLLARD, M. F. SKINNER, N., TUCKEY, M. R., & BAILEY, T. (2007). National surveillance of psychosocial risk factors in the workplace: An international overview. *Work & Stress, 21, 1-29*.

DOLLARD, M.F., ZAPF, D., COX, T. & PETKOV, J. (submitted). An Exposure Evaluation of a Longitudinal PAR Risk Management Stress Prevention Study in an Australian Public Sector Sample

FARRINGTON, D.P. (1991). Longitudinal research strategies: Advantages, problems, and prospects. *Journal of American Academy of Child and Adolescent Psychiatry, 30*(3), 369-374.

FRENCH, J.R.P., JR., CAPLAN, R.D., & VAN HARRISON, R. (1984). *The mechanisms of job stress and strain.* New York: Wiley.

GHERARDI, S. & NICOLINI, D. (2000). To transfer is to transform: The circulation of safety knowledge. *Organization Articles, 7*, 329-348.

GOODMAN, J.S, & BLUM, T.C. (1996). Assessing the non-random sampling effects of subject attrition in longitudinal research. *Journal of Management, 22*, 627-652.

GORGIEVSKI-DUIJVESTEIJIN, M.J., BAKKER, A.B., SCHAUFELI, W.B., & VAN DER HEIJDEN, P.G.M. (2005). Finances and well-being: A Dynamic Equilibrium Model of Resources. *Journal of Occupational Health Psychology, 10*, 210-224.

HASSAN, Z., DOLLARD, M.F., & WINEFIELD, A.H. (2007) Work-family policy and work-family conflict in the Malaysian private sector; A preliminary study. pp123-129. In Dollard, M.F., Winefield, A.H., & Tuckey, M. (2007). *Better work. Better organisations. Better World.* (Eds). Proceedings 7th Australian Industrial & Organisational Psychology Conference and the 1st Asia Pacific Congress on Work and Organisational Psychology, Melbourne: APS.

HOUTMAN, I., JETTINGHOFF, K., & CEDILLO, L. (2007). *Raising awareness of stress at work in developing countries: A modern hazard in a traditional working environment.* Geneva: WHO (Protecting Workers' Health series No. 6). Geneva: World Health Organisation (WHO).

INTERNATIONAL LABOR ORGANIZATION (2004). *Helping hands or shackled lives? Understanding child domestic labor and responses to it.* Geneva: Author.

INTERNATIONAL LABOUR ORGANISATION (2004). *A fair globalization: Creating opportunities for all-ILO.*

JOHNSON, J.V., & HALL, E.M. (1996). Dialectic between conceptual and causal inquiry in psychosocial work-environment research. *Journal of Occupational Health Psychology, 1*(1), 362-374.

KANG, S.Y., PANNELL, J.C., & DOLLARD, M.F. (2008). *Passenger Service Assistants' job well-being: An organisational report*. Work and Stress Research Group, University of South Australia, Adelaide, Australia.

KARASEK, R.A. (1979). Job demands, job decision latitude, and mental strain: Implications for job redesign. *Administrative Science Quarterly, 24*, 285-308.

KARASEK, R.A., & THEORELL, T. (1990). *Healthy work: Stress, productivity and the reconstruction of working life*. New York: Basic Books.

KELLY, S., & BUNTING, J. (1998). Trends in suicide in England and Wales, 1982-1996. *Population Trends 1998, 92*, 29-41.

KOMPIER, M.A.J., GEURTS, S.A.E., GRUNDEMANN, R.W.M., VINK, P., & SMULDERS, P.G.W. (1998). Cases in stress prevention: The success of a participative and stepwise approach. *Stress Medicine, 14*, 155-168.

KOMPIER, M. & TARIS, T. (2005). Psychosocial risk factors and work-related stress: State of the art and issues for future research. In A. Antoniou & C. Cooper (Eds.) *Research companion to organizational health psychology*. Cheltenham: Edward Elgar Publishing, 59-69.

KOMPIER, M.A.J. (2006). New systems of work organization and worker's health. *Scandinavian Journal of Work Environmental Health, 32*(6, special issue), 1-10.

KRISTENSEN, T.S. (1996). Job stress and cardiovascular disease: A theoretic critical review. *Journal of Occupational Health Psychology, 1*(3), 246-260.

LANDSBERGIS, P.A. (2003). The Changing organization of work and the safety and health of working people: A commentary. *Journal of Organizational and Environmental Medicine, 45*(1), 61-72.

LAZARUS, R.S., & FOLKMAND, S. (1984). *Stress, appraisal, and coping*. New York: Springer.

LEWIS, S. & COOPER, C.L. (1999). The work-family research agenda in changing contexts. Journal of Occupational Health Psychology, 4(4), 382-393.

LOEWENSON, R. (2001). Globalization and occupational health: A perspective from southern Africa. *Bulletin of the World Health Organization, 79*, 863-868.

MULKAY, M. (1979). *Science and the Sociology of Knowledge*. London: George Allen & Unwin.

NATIONAL INSTITUTE OF OCCUPATIONAL SAFETY AND HEALTH (NIOSH). *What is OHP?* Retrieved February 21, 2007, from US Center for Disease Control and Prevention (CDC) Web site: http://www.cdc.gov/niosh/ohp.html#whatis

NATIONAL INSTITUTE OF OCCUPATIONAL SAFETY AND HEALTH (NIOSH) (2002). *The changing organization of work and the safety and health of working people: Knowledge gaps and research directions* (DHHS Publication No. 2002-116). Washington, DC: US Government Printing Office.

Parker, S. (2003). Longitudinal effects of lean production on employee outcomes and the mediating role of work characteristics. *Journal of Applied Psychology, 88*(4), 620-634.

Population Division of the Department of Economic and Social Affairs of the United Nations Secretariat, *World Population Prospects: The 2004 Revision* and *World Urbanization Prospects: The 2005 Revision*, http://esa.un.org/unup, 08 January 2007; 8:18:59 PM.

Quick, J.C. (1996). Advancing public policy, social science, and biomedical inquiry: State-of-the-art reviews IV. *Journal of Occupational Health Psychology, 1,* 347-348.

Quick, J. C. (1999). Occupational health psychology: Historical roots and future directions. *Health Psychology, 18,* 82-88.

Rama, M. (2003). *Globalization and Workers in Developing Countries.* Policy Research Working Paper 2985. Washington, D.C.: World Bank.

Raymond, J.S., Wood, D.W., & Patrick, W.K. (1990). Psychology doctoral training in work and health. *American Psychologist, 45,* 1159-1161.

Sauter, S., & Hurrell, J. J. (1999). Occupational health psychology: Origins, content, and direction. *Professional Psychology: Research and Practice, 30,* 117-122.

Schabracq, M. J., & Cooper, C. L. (2000). The changing nature of work and stress. *Journal of Managerial Psychology, 15,* 227-241.

Schaufeli, W. B. (2004). The future of occupational health psychology. *Applied Psychology: An International Review, 53,* 502-517.

Schnall, P.L., Landsbergis, P.A., & Baker, D. (1994). Job strain and cardiovascular disease. *Annual Review of Public Health, 15,* 381-411.

Semmer, N.K. (2003). Job stress interventions and organization of work. In J.C. Quick and L.E. Tetrick (Eds.) *Handbook of Occupational Health Psychology.* Washington, DC: APA, 325-353.

Semmer, N.K. (2006). Job stress interventions and organization of work. *Scandinavian Journal of Work, Environment and Health, 32,* 515-527.

Siegrist, J. (1998). Adverse health effects of effort-reward imbalance at work: Theory, empirical support, and implications for prevention. In C.L. Cooper (Ed). *Theories of organizational stress, pp. 190-205.* Oxford: Oxford University Press.

Sprigg, C. A. & Jackson, P. R. (2006). Call centres as lean service environment: Job-related strain and the mediating role of work design. *Journal of Occupational Health Psychology, 11,* 197-212

Staniford, A.K., Dollard, M.F. & Guerin, B. (2007). *Stress and Help Seeking for Citrus Growers in the Riverland of South Australia.* Unpublished Manuscript: University of South Australia.

Tan, A. (2008). Village on the edge of time. *National Geographic,* (China: Inside the dragon, Special Issue) May 2008, 102-125.

Taris, T. & Kompier, M. (2003). Challenges in longitudinal designs in occupational health psychology. *Scandinavian Journal of Work, Environment and Health, 29*, 1-4.

Tokyo Declaration, (1999). The Tokyo declaration on work-related stress and health in three postindustrial settings—The European Union, Japan and the United States of America. *Journal of Occupational Health Psychology, 4*(4), 397-402.

Van der Klink, J., Blonk, R., Schene, A., & Van Dijk, F. (2001). The benefits of interventions for work-related stress. *American Journal of Public Health, 91*, 270-276.

Van den Bossche, S., Smulders, P., and Houtman, I. (2006). *Trends and risk groups in working conditions*, Hoofddrop: TNO Work & Employment.

Wallis, A. & Dollard, M. F. (2008). Local and global factors in work stress: The Australian dairy farming exemplar. *Scandinavian Journal of Work Environment and Health* (In Press).

WHO. (2007). *Raising awareness of stress at work in developing countries: A modern hazard in a traditional working environment*. Geneva.

WHO Workers' health: global plan of action; retrieved on 28th June 2008, http://www.euro.who.int/occhealth/20070515_1

Zapf, D., Dormann, C. & Frese, M. (1996). Longitudinal studies in organisational stress research: A review of the literature with reference to methodological issues. *Journal of Occupational Health Psychology, 1*(2), 145-169.

SELF-DETERMINATION THEORY
A THEORETICAL AND EMPIRICAL OVERVIEW IN OCCUPATIONAL HEALTH PSYCHOLOGY

Anja Van den Broeck, Maarten Vansteenkiste and Hans De Witte

CHAPTER OVERVIEW

The present chapter presents Self-Determination Theory (SDT; Deci & Ryan, 2000; Vansteenkiste, Ryan, & Deci, in press) and points at its applicability for occupational health psychology. Over some 40 years of research, SDT has developed into a grand theory of human motivation and optimal functioning. The theory has been applied to various life domains including education, exercising, development, parenting and relationships. Recently, the theory was introduced in the field of occupational health psychology and several empirical contributions have now provided support for its validity (Gagné & Deci, 2005; Sheldon, Turban, Brown, Barrick, & Judge, 2003). Within this chapter, we provide a conceptual overview of SDT and review the empirical findings that have supported its theoretical assumptions. We start with an outline of SDT's meta-theoretical assumptions. We then describe three important themes within SDT, that is, 1) the distinction between qualitative different types of behavioural regulation, labelled as the 'why' of behaviour, 2) the differentiation between qualitative different goal orientations, conceptualised as the 'what' of behaviour and 3) the concept of basic psychological need satisfaction. We furthermore discuss job design and leadership style, which represent two important organisational aspects to which SDT has been fruitfully applied. We conclude with a summary of SDT's most important contributions for occupational health psychology.

META-THEORETICAL ASSUMPTIONS

The starting point for SDT is its organismic dialectic meta-theory. Within this meta-theory it is suggested that individuals are growth-oriented organisms who actively interact with their environment (Deci & Ryan, 2000). SDT maintains that individuals are endowed with an innate striving to actualise their potentials, that is, to elaborate their knowledge, cultivate their interests, seek challenges and explore the world. They strive to integrate and meaningfully organise these new experiences into a harmonious and authentic sense of self. The tendency to extend and organise one's experiences is accompanied by the natural inclination to interconnect with other people. As much as human beings strive for self-development, according to SDT, they aim at a harmonious and authentic integration in the larger social environment. At their best, people give direction and meaning to their behavior and act in a volitional and self-integrated manner (Vansteenkiste, 2005). Within SDT, it is, however, also acknowledged that individuals can become passive and counter-productive (Ryan & Deci, 2000). The assumption that humans are inherently active organisms does not imply that this tendency can be taken for granted or happens automatically. In contrast, SDT maintains that the growth oriented nature of individuals requires fundamental nutrients. The growth oriented nature can only come about if individuals have built sufficient inner resources to nourish this inherent tendency or found the necessary support in the environment. The social context can thus support and nurture or deny and frustrate individuals' inherent growth tendency.

From these assumptions, it becomes clear that SDT takes into account both individuals' optimal functioning (bright side) and malfunctioning (dark side) and studies the conditions which stimulate the former or elicit the latter (Ryan & Deci, 2000). Explicating SDT's meta-theory is not only of theoretical importance. From a practical point of view these assumptions suggest that individuals can best be motivated by supporting their endogenous potential. Thus, according to SDT, employees are likely to display optimal performance and well-being in a context in which their inherent tendency is cherished and encouraged. If the work environment is over-challenging, overly controlling or rejecting, individuals' vulnerabilities will dominate and their dysfunctions will become apparent.

The idea that individuals can act as active agents or passive entities has previously been put forward in psychology. When comparing SDT's viewpoint with the writings of, for instance, the humanistic psychologist McGregor (1960), it is evident that both acknowledge individuals' instances of active engagement as well as their moments of alienation. McGregor (1960) outlined two sets of beliefs about human nature which occupational health psychology scholars and practitioners might hold, that is, Theory X and Theory Y. Within Theory X, employees are considered to dislike work. They are assumed to avoid investing energy and contributing to the organisational goals, unless they are strictly directed and controlled. Within Theory X, coercion is not only considered necessary, the average employee is also assumed to prefer being controlled. The second set of beliefs, Theory Y, holds that work is as natural as rest and play. It assumes that under the right conditions employees want to develop their skills, seek responsibility and take initiative. Within Theory Y, not coercion, but the provision of self-direction is the most important means through which employees contribute to the organisations' objectives.

Although they both acknowledge individuals' optimal and maladaptive functioning, SDT seems to differ from McGregor's point of view in at least two aspects. First, unlike SDT, McGregor considers that both Theory X and Y can be valid depending on employees' level of need satisfaction, as defined by Maslow (1943). If employees lack satisfaction of Maslow's lower needs such as physiological sustainability or safety, McGregor assumes they can best be motivated by the promise of rewards and the threat of punishments, which build on Theory X. If employees have satisfied these lower needs, they are theorised to strive for higher order needs such as self-esteem and self-actualisation (Maslow, 1943). Only, in that case, interventions based on Theory Y are assumed to become applicable (McGregor, 1960). SDT, in contrast, maintains that all individuals are always optimally stimulated if their inherent growth oriented nature is appealed to. The second difference is that humanistic psychology in general and McGregor in particular have refrained from conducting empirical research to examine their theoretical claims, whereas SDT's meta-theoretical framework is, in part, inductively derived from previous empirical research (Deci & Ryan, 2000).

SDT shares its empirical approach and encompassing view on individuals' well-being and behaviour with the general positive psychology movement (Seligman & Csikszentmihalyi, 2000) and positive occupational psychology in particular (Luthans, 2002). Like SDT, positive psychology dissociates itself from a disease model in which the focus is on individuals' weaknesses and the reparation of ill-being. The positive psychology movement is oriented towards the study of positive subjective experiences and individual traits, as well as the social factors that nurture individuals' strengths and development. The positive psychology movement studies various concepts ranging from pleasure and hope to self-efficacy. As SDT's development is coherently guided by its meta-theoretical assumptions, it is argued to provide a coherent framework in which positive psychology can be grounded (Deci & Vansteenkiste, 2004). The following sections deal with SDT's theoretical developments.

THE 'WHY' OF BEHAVIOR

The conceptual development of SDT started off with the empirical examination of the interplay between intrinsic and extrinsic motivation

(Deci, 1975). Subsequent research provided the impulse for a more refined view in which different types of extrinsic motivation are distinguished (Deci & Ryan, 1985). These types of extrinsic motivation are expected to yield different relations with employees' optimal functioning. Intrinsic motivation and the different types of extrinsic motivation all concern particular reasons for engaging in activities or behavioral regulations. Within SDT, they are therefore referred to as the 'why' of behaviour (Deci & Ryan, 2000).

The interplay between intrinsic and extrinsic motivation

Several motivation theories (e.g., Atkinson, 1964; Vroom, 1964) consider intrinsic and extrinsic motivation to be additive, such that both types of motivation would need to be summed up to arrive at individuals' total motivation. Intrinsic motivation is defined as the engagement in an activity for its own sake, that is, for the satisfaction and enjoyment experienced during the course of the activity itself. An intrinsically motivated employee is genuinely interested in his job and experiences enjoyment while working. Extrinsic motivation, in contrast, concerns the engagement in an activity to obtain an outcome that is separable from the activity. Extrinsically motivated employees put effort in their jobs to obtain, for example, a bonus. In the additive view, providing monetary rewards for doing an inherently interesting task would increase individuals' total amount of motivation. If the reward would subsequently be removed, the person's motivation is expected to decrease to the pre-rewarded baseline.

Deci (1971), however, challenged these assumptions. In a set of experiments he showed that individuals who had been paid for working on intrinsically motivating puzzles, subsequently displayed less intrinsic motivation compared to both their own pre-rewarded baseline and compared to a control group of individuals who had never been paid (Deci, 1971). If individuals' behavior was not extrinsically reinforced by financial rewards, but was followed by positive feedback, no such decrease in intrinsic motivation occurred. Numerous follow-up studies confirmed that, in general, external contingencies such as monetary rewards, threats and deadlines undermined intrinsic motivation, whereas verbal rewards (i.e., positive feedback) enhanced one's intrinsic motivation (Deci, Koestner, & Ryan, 1999, 2001). Further studies also pointed at some important moderators. First, it was shown that the interpersonal context in which these external contingencies were administered might alter their average relationship with intrinsic motivation. For instance, if positive feedback is given in a supportive way, it enhances intrinsic motivation, whereas it diminishes intrinsic motivation if it is administered in a controlling way

(Ryan, 1982; Ryan, Mims, & Koestner, 1983). Second, it was shown that tangible rewards only undermine intrinsic motivation if they are expected and made contingent upon task engagement, task completion or performance. Tangible rewards that are not expected or do not require doing the task, completing the task or achieving a particular performance standard, do not undermine intrinsic motivation.

Within SDT these differences are explained by referring to the meaning attributed to these external contingencies. In general, external contingencies, such as monetary rewards and feedback, can serve an informational and a controlling function (Deci, Koestner, & Ryan, 1999). To the extent that they provide individuals with information about how well they performed a task, they enhance intrinsic motivation. The controlling aspect of extrinsic contingencies on the other hand causes a cognitive shift from attributing task engagement to personal interest and enjoyment towards the obtainment of the external reward. The locus of causality for engaging in the activity thus changes from an internal to an external one (deCharms, 1968). The more external contingencies are perceived as controlling, the more intense the shift and the more they forestall intrinsic motivation. Verbal rewards such as praise are typically highly informational and little controlling. Therefore, they enhance intrinsic motivation. Unexpected tangible rewards are not controlling either, as they are only given post hoc and thus can never come to control one's behaviour. Expected tangible rewards, in contrast, are likely to become the reason for doing the activity and hence their controlling function is likely to rule out their informational function. This is especially the case when external contingencies are conditional upon engagement in or completion of the task (Deci, Koestner, & Ryan, 1999). As performance contingent rewards are only given when a normative standard is met, they provide a good deal of competence information and undermine intrinsic motivation less compared to the other reward contingencies (e.g., Luyten & Lens, 1981).

Within occupational health psychology and related fields, the positive effect of feedback on intrinsic motivation has been generally acknowledged (e.g., Hackman & Oldham, 1976). Despite the extensive research within SDT, however, psychologists have been rather reluctant to consider the problematic characteristics of monetary rewards (Sheldon et al., 2003). As findings obtained within the framework of SDT were mainly based on laboratory studies, various psychologists questioned their ecological validity (Rynes, Gerhart, & Parks, 2005). Financial rewards were assumed to be more complex in the occupational health context and to affect employees' functioning differently compared to what had been found in laboratory studies. Payment is indeed a fundamental aspect of employment and compensation specialists tend to link financial rewards with increased individual performance and organisational success (Rynes, Gerhart, & Parks, 2005). Lately, economists and management scholars have, in line with SDT, advocated that the increased effort and performance resulting from raised payment (i.e., price effect) might be counteracted by the decrease in intrinsic motivation following the provision of rewards (i.e., crowding out effect). It has even been suggested that the net effect of both tendencies might turn out negatively for employees' motivation and performance (Frey & Osterloh, 2005). Economists, management scholars and psychologists have increasingly examined the boundary conditions of the motivational effects of compensation systems (Gagné & Forest, in press). Specifically, the negative effects of incentives are now shown to hold for qualitative, but not for quantitative aspect of performance (Jenkins, Mitra, Gupta, & Shaw, 1998), and for complex, interesting tasks which involve intrinsic motivation but not for simple, boring tasks which excite little inherent enjoyment (Stajkovic & Luthans, 2001). Finally, scholars warrant for the hidden costs of compensation systems in terms of decreased mental health (Gagné & Forest, in press). Mental health problems are generally neglected in compensation research, but do represent an economic burden for organisations and the economy as a whole (Groot & van den Brink, 1999). Although more research is needed, these studies might warn HR-professions about the use of merit pay for complex, intrinsically motivating tasks.

In sum, SDT holds a nuanced view on the interplay between intrinsic and extrinsic motivation. Whereas other theories considered intrinsic and extrinsic motivation to be simply additive, SDT points out that financially rewarding individuals for intrinsically motivating tasks might decrease their inherent enjoyment and interest. Within the occupational health psychology context, this assumption might help to understand the influence of incentives on employees' motivation more deeply. The research on the impact of external contingencies on intrinsic motivation stimulated SDT scholars to examine the nature of extrinsic motivation more closely as not all types of extrinsic motivation seemed to be detrimental for individuals' optimal functioning. This led to the formulation of qualitatively different types of extrinsic motivation.

Qualitative different types of extrinsic motivation

Most motivational theories (e.g., Vroom, 1964) consider motivation from a quantitative point of view. The degree to which individuals are motivated (high or low) is considered a critical predictor of their optimal functioning. SDT, however, considers optimal functioning not only to be determined by the strength or quantity of motivation, but also by the type or quality of motivation. More specifically, SDT maintains that extrinsic motivation can vary in the degree to which individuals have internalised and integrated the reason for behavioural engagement, that is, the degree to which they experience the reason for a particular action as part of their self. Within SDT, four different types of extrinsic motivation have been distinguished (Ryan & Connell, 1989). These can be ordered on a continuum from low to full personal endorsement (Deci & Ryan, 2000).

First, external regulation refers to the engagement in an activity to meet external expectations, to obtain rewards or to avoid punishments provided by the environment. The reason for conducting the behaviour is thus situated external to the individual (Deci & Ryan, 2000). The pressuring aspects could be material as well as social. For instance, external regulated employees might work hard to obtain a bonus or to get the recognition of their supervisor. External regulation is the only type of regulation emphasised in operant theory (e.g., Skinner, 1974). Within the second type of extrinsic motivation, labelled introjection, behaviour is guided by internally pressuring reasons. Engagement in an activity is a means to attain personal pride or to avoid guilt or shame. In case of introjection, people thus buttress their behaviour with internally administered rewards and punishments. In contrast to external regulation, the contingencies for introjected behaviour have been partially taken in. Whereas some employees might, for example, work overtime to meet their supervisor's expectations (i.e., external regulation), others might work long hours because they would feel guilty otherwise. Both external regulation and introjection are characterised by an external perceived locus of causality (deCharms, 1968). As no or only a little internalisation has taken place, individuals are likely to feel pressured in executing behaviour out of external or introjected regulation. Therefore, these two types of extrinsic motivation are considered to be controlled (Deci & Ryan, 2000) and are often combined in empirical research to form a controlled composite score (e.g., Vansteenkiste, Zhou, Lens, & Soenens, 2005).

Identified and integrated regulation are the two remaining types of extrinsic motivation (Ryan & Connell, 1989). Both are said to be characterised by an internal perceived locus of causality (deCharms, 1968), that is, individuals perceive the behaviour as their own because they identify with the reason for the activity. For identified regulation, the goal of the behaviour is personally endorsed and considered important. Internalisation is, however, not complete until integration has occurred. Only in the case of integration one engages in an activity because this activity fits one's broader set of values and beliefs. Identified behaviours do not necessarily concord with other aspects of one's self. For instance, a nurse might put effort in her job because she personally values her job which she believes is useful and meaningful (i.e., identified regulation) or because she believes her job as a nurse is in line with her other values referring to helping others (i.e., integrated regulation). In the case of identified and integrated regulation, the reason for performing the behaviour is personally accepted and internalised. The behaviour is said to be enacted with a sense of volition. Therefore, identified and integrated regulation are considered to be autonomous types of motivation (Deci & Ryan, 2000). Note that intrinsically motivated behaviour is the most autonomous type of motivation because people spontaneously and freely follow their interests when being intrinsically motivated (Deci & Ryan, 2000). Within SDT the focus shifted from the distinction between intrinsic and extrinsic motivation towards the differentiation between autonomous versus controlled motivation (Sheldon et al., 2003). According to SDT, extrinsic motivation is not necessarily negative, as long as the reason underlying the behaviour is internalised so that one is autonomously motivated in executing the activity. Importantly, the differentiation between the qualitative types of extrinsic motivation must not be considered as a stage theory (Gagné & Deci, 2005). Individuals can integrate different behaviours to various degrees and can at any point in time internalise behaviours that were not assimilated previously.

According to SDT, adopting an autonomous versus controlled regulation style yields positive effects in terms of higher well-being and better performance (Deci & Ryan, 2000). This assumption has been validated in various sub-domains of I/O psychology such as the work context (Richer, Blanchard, & Vallerand, 2002), the process of career exploration (Guay, Senécal, Gauthier, & Fernet, 2003; Guay, 2005) and unemployment (Vansteenkiste, Lens, De Witte, & Feather, 2005; Vansteenkiste, Lens, Dewitte, De Witte, & Deci, 2004). These findings have been shown when assessing one's regulations for a specific task (Fernet, Sen, Guay, Marsh, & Dowson, 2008), in a specific domain (e.g., Richer, Blanchard, & Vallerand, 2002), or for one's work-related goals (Bono & Judge, 2003).

With respect to the work context, being autonomously compared to controlled regulated for one's job has been found to relate positively to job satisfaction, life satisfaction, feelings of professional efficacy and general mental health, whereas it is negatively related to emotional exhaustion and cynicism (e.g., Fernet, Guay, & Senécal, 2004, Judge, Bono, Erez, & Locke, 2005). Holding a predominantly autonomous job regulation associates positively with self-rated job performance and relates negatively to turnover intentions (Millette & Gagné, 2008; Richer et al.,

2002). Autonomous versus controlled regulation might also be seen as a personal resource that helps one to shape the environment, as highly autonomously motivated employees make use of job control, as defined by Karasek (1979), to reduce the health impairing effect of job demands (Fernet et al., 2004).

Within the context of career exploration, being autonomously instead of controlled regulated is associated with less career indecisiveness and reduced procrastination in job seeking (Guay et al., 2003; Senécal, & Guay, 2000). Within unemployed, autonomous regulation to search for a job is associated with less feeling of worthlessness, meaninglessness and social isolation, and greater general health. Feeling coerced to search for a job is associated with negative feelings and health problems (Vansteenkiste et al., 2004; Vansteenkiste, Lens, et al., 2005). Interestingly, the more unemployed individuals feel coerced to search for a job, the less job search behaviour they reported (Vansteenkiste et al., 2004). Controlled individuals thus do not only feel more negative, they also seem to undertake less action to end the unemployment situation they experience as negative (Vansteenkiste et al., 2004). In line with SDT's assumption regarding the importance of the quality of motivation, autonomous and controlled job-search regulation were found to matter in predicting unemployed individuals' optimal functioning after controlling for the strength of their motivation to search. More specifically, autonomous job search regulations related positively to job search intensity and well-being after taking into account the quantity of unemployed individuals' motivation to find a job as conceptualised within Expectancy-Value Theory (Vansteenkiste, Lens, et al., 2005).

In sum, within SDT different types of extrinsic motivation are distinguished ranging from controlling (i.e., external regulation and introjection) to more autonomous (i.e., identified and integration) types. Intrinsic motivation is assumed to be the most autonomous type of motivation, as individuals follow their personal interests when performing intrinsically motivating activities. The differentiation between these qualitative types of motivation is considered useful to understand why employees could be qualitatively motivated for both intrinsically and extrinsically motivating tasks (Sheldon et al., 2003). Furthermore, the recognition that not all types of extrinsic motivation are necessarily experienced as controlling and alienating implies that there are different avenues for managers and companies to optimally motivate their employees for tasks that are not intrinsically appealing (Sheldon et al., 2003). SDT maintains that individuals can best be extrinsically motivated by stimulating their autonomous instead of controlled motivation. This can be achieved through emphasising the personal importance and significance of tasks, such that employees will begin to identify with these tasks and might integrate them. The provision of rewards, punishments or the appeal to individuals' self-esteem, in contrast, can better be avoided as they are likely to elicit external regulation and introjection and thus result in controlled motivation (Gagné & Deci, 2005).

Both the interplay between intrinsic and extrinsic motivation and the distinction of different types of extrinsic motivation deal with individuals' reasons for acting ('why' of behaviour; Deci & Ryan, 2000). In addition, within SDT, also the content of goal striving is considered important for individuals' optimal functioning which is referred to as the 'what' of behaviour (Deci & Ryan, 2000).

THE 'WHAT' OF BEHAVIOUR

The motivational influences of goals are well-known within occupational health psychology. Goal Setting Theory (Locke & Latham, 2002), which is commonly applied in occupational health psychology, maintains, for instance, that individuals will best be motivated if they pursue specific rather than general goals, goals of optimal difficulty, and self-set rather than other-imposed goals. The specificity, difficulty and origin of goals are thus considered important motivational features. SDT equally suggests optimally challenging goals to be more motivating (Deci & Ryan, 2000). However, SDT also maintains that individuals will be optimally stimulated if they are autonomously instead of controlled motivated to obtain a particular goal (Sheldon et al., 2003). Autonomous motivation to strive for a particular goal is achieved when a self set goal is perceived to emanate from one's true self or when a goal which is set by others aligns with one's personal values.

SDT furthermore focuses on the content or the quality of one's goals (Deci & Ryan, 2000). Specifically, within SDT a differentiation is made between intrinsic goals, such as contributing to the community, affiliation, and self-development, and extrinsic goals, such as accumulating wealth, acquiring fame and pursuing attractive physical looks (Kasser & Ryan, 1996). Working hard as an employee may, for instance, serve an intrinsic goal because a higher ranked job offers new challenges and growth opportunities. It may, however, also serve extrinsic goal attainment because the higher ranked job is likely to provide status and social recognition. As no distinction is made between qualitative different types of goals within Goal Setting Theory, both goals would be assumed equally motivating. In contrast, according to SDT the pursuit of intrinsic goals is likely to yield more adaptive outcomes than the pursuit of extrinsic goals (Kasser & Ryan, 1996; Vansteenkiste,

Lens, & Deci, 2006). Intrinsic goals are theorised to be a manifestation of individuals' organism's growth-oriented nature and to stimulate actualisation of one's inherent potential. Extrinsic goals, in contrast, are characterised by an outward orientation. Extrinsic goal oriented individuals predominantly strive to obtain external signs of worth and might even renounce their intrinsic interests to impress others. Extrinsic goal pursuit is thus likely to detract individuals from their inherent growth orientation. The pursuit of extrinsic goals at the expense of intrinsic goals is therefore hypothesised to be detrimental for employees' well-being and performance.

Various studies focusing on people's intrinsic versus extrinsic life aspirations have validated this claim (see Kasser, 2002 for an overview). Within the context of work, it has been shown that adopting an extrinsic rather than intrinsic work value orientation is negatively related to employees' job satisfaction, dedication, vitality and general well-being and positively related to emotional exhaustion, turnover intentions and the experience of work-home interference (Vansteenkiste et al., 2007).

Goal-content does not only yield implications for employees' well-being and job experiences. Among unemployed individuals, type of goal pursuit has been found to be related to one's attitudes towards the labour market, as indexed by the degree and types of flexibility unemployed individuals are willing to display when searching for a job (Van den Broeck, Vansteenkiste, Lens, & De Witte, 2008). Whereas the pursuit of extrinsic goals associates with a less flexible attitude towards the labour market, the pursuit of intrinsic goals is related to a greater degree of flexibility as well as to more adaptive types of flexibility. Holding an intrinsic goal orientation goes along with more flexibility to follow additional training and more flexibility to accept jobs that are less well paid. As these types of flexibility do not imply the renouncement of the content of one's job, these types of flexibility are likely to result in finding an interesting and stimulating job (Feldman, Leana, & Bolino, 2002).

The pursuit of extrinsic goals might, however, be tempting as its attainment is likely to provide some short-lived satisfaction, a construct tapping employees' superficial positive feelings which follow successful goal attainment (Vansteenkiste et al., 2007). These hedonic feelings of happiness and contentment, however, quickly disappear, such that again extrinsic goals need to set. Extrinsic goal pursuit is therefore likely to lead to a hedonic treadmill, in which one is hardly really satisfied with one's goal attainment (Diener, Lucas, & Scollon, 2006). As mentioned, intrinsic goal pursuit goes along with a deeper and more long-lasting, eudaimonic sense of psychological well-being such as job engagement (Vansteenkiste et al., 2007).

Within the literature on intrinsic and extrinsic goal pursuit, different moderators have been suggested to alter the negative impact of extrinsic over intrinsic goals on optimal functioning (see Vansteenkiste, Soenens, & Duriez, in press). First, it has been suggested that the differential associations between intrinsic versus extrinsic goal orientations and individuals' well-being and behaviour must be attributed to differences in attainability and attainment of these types of goals. However, the negative associations of extrinsic over intrinsic goal pursuit have been found both when goal importance and attainability were assessed (Kasser & Ryan, 1996). Extrinsic goal pursuit was also found to be detrimental for employees who already had attained the extrinsic goal of financial success. For instance, Vansteenkiste and his colleagues (2007) found no interaction between level of income and type of goal pursuit in the prediction of job satisfaction, life satisfaction, and happiness, while extrinsic goals negatively predicted these outcomes. This implies that the pursuit of extrinsic, relative to intrinsic, goals is detrimental for employees with both a high and low income.

Second, within the person-environment-fit literature (Kristof-Brown, Zimmerman & Johnson, 2005) the degree to which one's personal goals match with the values that are promoted in the context is also be assumed to moderate the impact of extrinsic versus intrinsic goal pursuit. In this view, employees holding intrinsic values would benefit from working in an environment in which intrinsic goals are promoted, whereas extrinsic oriented employees would function optimally in a context in which extrinsic goals are advocated. Empirical research, however, fails to confirm this claim (Kasser & Ahuvia, 2002; Vansteenkiste, Duriez, Simons, & Soenens, 2006). More specifically, in line with SDT, business students attaching high importance to a high status and appealing appearance have been found to experience less well-being compared to business students predominately oriented towards self-development and affiliation, although business schools generally promote extrinsic goals over intrinsic goals.

In sum, from a SDT perspective, the content of employees' goals matters and the pursuit of intrinsic goals has been shown to be more strongly associated with optimal functioning than the pursuit of extrinsic goals (Deci & Ryan, 2000). HR-professionals might therefore encourage employees to formulate their personal strivings in terms of intrinsic rather than extrinsic goals. In addition to studying the differential outcomes of intrinsic versus extrinsic goals and autonomous versus controlled motivation, SDT has also focused on the process, that is, basic psychological need satisfaction underlying the 'what' and 'why' of behaviour (Deci & Ryan, 2000).

BASIC PSYCHOLOGICAL NEEDS

The concept of needs has received quite some attention within psychology (Latham & Pinder, 2005). For example, Maslow (1943) postulated the concepts of inborn needs for self-actualisation and social recognition and Murray (1938) started the tradition on socialised needs for achievement, power and affiliation. Empirical evidence, however, failed to support Maslow's theorising (Porter, Lawler, & Hackman, 1975). Attention for the concept of needs waned when cognitive psychology became dominant (Reeve, 2005). Cognitive psychologists consider internal mental processes such as expectations, self-efficacy or attributions rather than needs or desires as the key variables to understand individuals' motivation. SDT scholars, however, assume that both individuals' regulatory style and goal directed behaviour cannot be understood completely without addressing the process that energises and directs behaviour (Deci & Ryan, 2000). Satisfaction of the basic psychological needs is said to represent this process.

Within SDT, basic psychological needs are conceptualised as 'those nutrients that must be procured by a living entity to maintain its growth, integrity and health' (Deci & Ryan, 2000, p. 326). Just as the satisfaction of physical needs (e.g., hunger, shelter) is crucial for one's physical survival, SDT assumes the satisfaction of psychological needs to be crucial for one's optimal psychological functioning. Three innate basic psychological needs are distinguished: that is, the need for Autonomy, the need for Belongingness and the need for Competence, which can be remembered with the acronym of ABC-needs.

The need for autonomy is defined as an inherent desire to act with a sense of choice and volition, that is, to be the author of one's actions and to feel psychologically free (Deci & Ryan, 2000). SDT's concept of autonomy differs from the conceptualisation of autonomy in terms of independence or discretion as it is frequently held in psychological research (Morgeson, & Humphrey, 2006). In fact, the need for autonomy is relatively orthogonal to independence (Soenens et al., 2007; Vansteenkiste, Zhou, et al., 2005). If employees are, for instance, asked to execute a particular task, they might exert little if any discretion about which task to accomplish. If they perceive the task as fun, interesting or meaningful, however, they are likely to engage in them with a sense of volition and psychological freedom (Ryan & Deci, 2006). Although employees do not act independently in such a case, they thus might still act volitionally, indicating that the experience of volition might not only accompany independent acting, but might also be experienced when employees follow their supervisors' requests.

The need for belongingness is conceptualised as the inherent propensity to feel connected to others, that is, to be a member of a group, to love and care and be loved and cared for (Baumeister & Leary, 1995, Deci & Ryan, 2000). The need for relatedness is satisfied if people experience a sense of communion and maintain close and intimate relationships. Employees who feel part of a team and feel free to express their personal concerns and joys are more likely to have their need for belongingness met compared to employees who feel lonely and lack social support. The concept of relatedness is in line with developmental approaches such as attachment theory (Bowlby, 1969) which emphasise the importance of secure and nurturing attachment bonds. The need for belongingness is not controversial within psychology. Its importance is emphasised in concepts such as social support (Viswesvaran, Sanchez, & Fisher, 1999) and loneliness at work (Wright, Burt, & Strongman, 2006).

Finally, the need for competence represents the desire to feel capable to master the environment and to bring about desired outcomes (Deci & Ryan, 2000; White, 1959). It is prominent in individuals' propensity to explore and actively seek out challenges in which one can extend one's physical and psychological skills. Satisfaction of the need for competence helps individuals to develop their skills and adapt to complex and changing environments. Like the need for belongingness, the need for competence is rather uncontroversial within psychology. Similar constructs have been proposed in cognitive oriented models, such as Vroom's (1964) construct of the expectancy to obtain valued outcomes and Bandura's (1997) self-efficacy concept.

The construct of needs as conceptualised within SDT is different from other need conceptualisations such as McClelland's (1965), in which the focus is on individuals' need strength. McClelland maintains that individuals differ in the value they attach to different needs, because they have learned to attach positive and negative feelings to particular situations in their personal socialising processes (McClelland, 1965). In this perspective, the pursuit and attainment of a need will be valued more or less depending on one's developmental trajectory. Inter-individual differences in the importance attached to different acquired needs would determine to what degree a particular need fuels behaviour and the degree in which the satisfaction of that desired need is beneficial. For example, individuals with a high need for achievement are likely to be stimulated by the possibility of successful performance, as these individuals are ambitious and focused on achieving high performance standards. Individuals with a low need for achievement, in contrast, are unlikely to benefit from the eventuality of high performance. Within SDT, needs are, in contrast, postulated to be primary, innate propensities (Deci & Ryan, 2000). As the basic needs for autonomy, belongingness and competence are essential to individuals' functioning, SDT does not focus on need strength, but on need satisfaction. Put differently, not the degree to which individuals express a particular need, but the degree to which one is able to satisfy each of one's basic psychological needs is considered important. The offer of choice and positive feedback, for example, are regarded to be beneficial for all employees, as they satisfy the inborn needs for autonomy and competence respectively. Note that unlike Maslow's (1943) needs, the inborn needs for autonomy, belongingness and competence are not assumed to be hierarchically organised. All three needs are thus considered to be equally important, as it is assumed that none can be ignored to experience well-being and growth (Sheldon & Niemiec, 2006).

Various studies have confirmed the positive versus negative consequences of the satisfaction versus frustration of the basic psychological needs (Deci & Ryan, 2000). Within the occupational health context, need satisfaction has, for instance, been shown to relate positively to employees' work related well-being in terms of task and job satisfaction; their general well-being as indexed by decreased insomnia, anxiety and depression; their attitudes in terms of self-esteem, attitudes towards customers and organisational commitment; and self-rated performance (e.g., Baard, Deci, & Ryan, 2004; Lynch, Plant, & Ryan, 2005, Vansteenkiste et al., 2007). These results have been found across professional levels, sectors and cultures (e.g., Deci, Ryan, et al., 2001), which is in line with the claim that satisfaction of these needs yield universal positive associations. The positive relationship between need satisfaction and employees' optimal functioning also remains significant after controlling for employees' salary and organisational status, with need satisfaction even accounting for more variance in these outcomes compared to salary and status (Ilardi, Leone, Kasser, & Ryan, 1993). Optimal functioning at work is thus not predominately determined by organisational rewards, but also, and even more, by basic need satisfaction. Interestingly, satisfaction of the basic needs for autonomy, belongingness and competence also positively predicts average earnings. Kasser, Davey and Ryan (1992) have shown that employees' level of need satisfaction goes along with work participation, performance and, therefore, monthly wages.

As mentioned, within SDT, the three fundamental needs are not only considered important as such, but also because they represent the underlying mechanism of the 'what' (qualitatively different types of goals) and 'why' (qualitatively different types of motivation) of motivation (Deci & Ryan, 2000). Within SDT, both the need for competence and the need for autonomy are put forward to explain the differential effects of external contingencies such as monetary and verbal rewards on intrinsic motivation

(Deci, Koestner, & Ryan, 2001). More specifically, the informational function of these rewards is said to appeal to individuals' competence, whereas their controlling function is expected to relate to individuals' need for autonomy. The need for belongingness is said to be less prominent in explaining the effects of external contingencies on intrinsic motivation. People indeed do not necessarily need to experience a sense of intimacy and connectedness to engage in intrinsically motivating activities such as reading a book or computer programming (Deci & Ryan, 2000). Feeling connected to others is, however, considered fundamental for the personal endorsement and internalisation of socially prescribed norms and values (Deci & Ryan, 2000). Norms and values are often introduced by others and pursued in an attempt to gain or maintain the love and care of socialisation figures who introduced them. Satisfaction of the need for belongingness may facilitate internalisation of social norms and values to the degree of introjection. The transition from external regulation to introjection, however, also requires some understanding of the meaning of the behaviour and feelings of competence to engage in the activity. Satisfaction of the need for competence thus also represents a necessary condition for introjection to occur. True internalisation in terms of identification and integration requires support for the need for autonomy (Deci & Ryan, 2000). To assimilate activities with one's other values and goals, people need to feel psychologically free in enacting them and to volitionally endorse their importance.

A couple of studies have examined the relationship between need satisfaction and autonomous versus controlled motivation. More specifically, the satisfaction of the needs for competence and relatedness was shown to relate positively to employees' autonomous versus controlled work regulation, which in turn predicted well-being, willingness to follow job training and reduced turnover (Richer et al., 2002; Vansteenkiste, De Witte, & Lens, 2006). Need satisfaction is, however, not only likely to predict, but also to follow from autonomous versus controlled engagement, as it was found to account, at least partially, for the positive relationships between employees' autonomous regulation and optimal functioning (Hendrikx, 2004). Although these results stem from cross-sectional research, it is possible that autonomous regulation and need satisfaction mutually reinforce each other, so that autonomously oriented individuals get involved in an upward spiral of need satisfaction and adaptive regulations over time (Deci & Ryan, 2000).

Besides explaining the 'why' of motivation, the three needs are also considered to be crucial in understanding the 'what' of motivation in terms of intrinsic versus extrinsic goal pursuit (Kasser, 2002; Vansteenkiste, Soenens, & Duriez, in press). Intrinsic goals comprise the pursuit of affiliation and personal development, which are likely to go along with the satisfaction of the needs for belongingness and competence respectively. As intrinsic goals align with the inherent tendency for personal development and affiliation, they are furthermore likely to be executed volitionally and hence satisfy the need for autonomy. Extrinsic goals for status, wealth and power, in contrast, are more likely to be associated with interpersonal comparison and competition, which are likely to forestall the needs for autonomy, belongingness and competence (Vansteenkiste et al., in press). Empirical evidence indeed confirms that need satisfaction is an important process that can account for the relation between intrinsic goal pursuit and employees' functioning (Vansteenkiste et al., 2007).

To summarise, within SDT the satisfaction of the needs for autonomy, belongingness and competence is considered to fuel optimal functioning. It furthermore drives autonomous versus controlled regulations and intrinsic, relative to an extrinsic, work goals. Based on this research (e.g., Ilardi, et al., 1993; Lynch, et al., 2005) employers might be advised not to restrict their motivation policies to monetary rewards, but also to consider subordinates' basic needs satisfaction to enhance their well-being and performance. This can be done by encouraging autonomous rather than controlled regulation and stimulating intrinsic over extrinsic goal pursuit. The job context does also offer a variety of possibilities to enhance employees' need satisfaction, as described in the following section.

ORGANISATIONAL FACTORS STIMULATING MOTIVATION

Within the framework of SDT, various organisational aspects are considered to have a motivational impact. In an exemplary study, Deci and his colleagues (1989) examined the general impact of supportive job design and leadership from one's supervisor and the top-management. This general support related positively to employees' well-being in terms of work engagement, self-esteem and reduced anxiety, which validates SDT's claim that supportive work contexts are beneficial for employees' optimal functioning. In addition to this study, a number of other studies have focused on the motivational effects of organisational aspects (Sheldon et al., 2003). In the following paragraphs we turn to the studies that examined job design and leadership style from a SDT perspective. These domains represent respectively a structural and a social aspect of organisations which can enhance employees' motivation.

Job design

Within occupational health psychology, job design is regarded as an important and effective way to motivate employees. Various job characteristics models have been formulated, such as the Demands-Control model (Karasek, 1979), the Effort Reward Imbalance model (Siegrist, 1996) and the Job Demands Resources model (Demerouti, Bakker, Nachreiner, & Schaufeli, 2001; Schaufeli & Bakker, 2004). Within these models, however, little attention has been paid to the processes underlying the relationships between job characteristics and employees' well-being. Different studies have shown that SDT can help shed light on this issue.

For instance, employees' autonomous versus controlled job regulation was found to account for the positive contribution of task significance, feedback and skill variety to employees' work satisfaction and their negative relation with emotional exhaustion (Richer et al., 2002). Basic need satisfaction was also shown to be useful to understand the motivational impact of job characteristics. Gagné, Senécal and Koestner (1997) showed that meaningfulness, autonomy, impact and competence played an explanatory role in the associations between stimulating job characteristics such as task significance and feedback, and intrinsic motivation. Although these mediating variables were framed in terms of the empowerment concept, they are closely related to SDT's needs for autonomy and competence. Recently, the role of basic need satisfaction as an explanatory mechanism in the relation between resourceful job characteristics (i.e., social support, opportunities for skill utilisation) and employees' well-being was confirmed (Van den Broeck, Vansteenkiste, De Witte, & Lens, 2008). Need satisfaction was also shown to explain the associations between demanding job characteristics (i.e., emotional demands, work-home interference) and employees' functioning in terms of burnout and engagement (Van den Broeck et al., 2008).

Leadership styles

Within SDT, it is assumed that besides structural environmental aspects such as job design, also interactional aspects such as leadership can yield a motivational impact. Within the context of occupational health psychology, leadership is considered a crucial variable in the motivation of employees (Kaiser, Hogan, & Craig, 2008). SDT maintains that supervisors can stimulate employees by adopting an autonomy-supportive supervisory style which comprises a) the acknowledgement of subordinates' feelings, b) the offer choices and c) the provision of rationales for requests (Deci, Eghrari, Patrick, & Leone, 1994). An autonomous leadership style increases subordinates' satisfaction with supervisors, job design, pay, benefits and enhances their trust in the organisation (Deci, Ryan, et al., 1989). Adopting an autonomy-supportive leadership style during organisational change results in more acceptance of these changes from the part of the employees (Gagné, Koestner & Zuckerman, 2000). A controlling leadership style in contrast is likely to yield negative outcomes (Richer & Vallerand, 1995). Controlling leaders direct employees' behaviour and intrude upon their thoughts and feelings. In contrast to autonomy-supportive leaders, they manipulate employees psychological functioning (Soenens, Vansteenkiste, Duriez, & Goossens, 2006). In line with the expectations derived from SDT, controlling supervisors decrease subordinates' motivation (Richer & Vallerand, 1995).

The influence of an autonomy-supportive versus controlling leadership style can be explained by need satisfaction. Richer and Vallerand (1995) showed that autonomy-supportive supervisors stimulate autonomy and competence satisfaction, whereas controlling supervisors thwart subordinates' needs. Further research showed that the positive effects of autonomy support on employees' well-being are mediated by satisfaction of employees' needs for autonomy, competence and relatedness (Baard et al., 2004). In sum, these studies show that supervisors' autonomy-supportive leadership style yields a positive impact on employees' well-being and performance.

CONCLUSION

Within this chapter we provided an overview of SDT and point at its applicability to the context of occupational health psychology. We started with an outline of SDT's meta-theory. As mentioned, SDT scholars assume individuals to be endowed with a natural tendency to grow and develop (Deci & Ryan, 2000). This natural inclination manifests itself in individuals' behavioural regulation (the 'why') and the type of goals they pursue (the 'what'; Vansteenkiste, 2005). Within SDT, individuals are considered to have a natural tendency to spontaneously engage in inherently interesting and enjoyable activities, that is, to be intrinsically motivated (Deci, 1975). This tendency is, however, likely to be thwarted by the provision of external contingencies (Deci & Ryan, 1985). From SDT's point of view, external contingencies, such as bonuses, are to be avoided. Within SDT, individuals are furthermore considered to be inclined to internalise initially external regulated behaviour and to move from more controlled to more autonomous types of behavioural regulation (Deci & Ryan, 2000). Not all types of extrinsic motivation are supposed to yield negative outcomes. Autonomous types of extrinsic motivation (i.e., identified and integrated) in which the reasons for performing is internalised, are likely to foster optimal functioning (e.g., Richer et al., 2002; Vansteenkiste, Lens, et al., 2005). Finally, individuals are presumed to be oriented towards intrinsic rather than extrinsic goal pursuit, which is likely to result in optimal well-being and performance (Kasser, 2002; Vansteenkiste et al., 2007).

Individuals' natural growth orientation must, however, be nurtured for individuals to flourish and to actualise their potential (Deci & Ryan, 2000). More specifically, within SDT it is assumed that the social context must satisfy the inherent basic psychological needs for autonomy, belongingness and competence. Within SDT, satisfaction of these needs is considered as crucial for individuals' thriving as water and sunlight is for plants to flourish (Deci & Ryan, 2000). An important role is thus assigned to social contexts, such as the work environment, to bring out the best in people. This can, for instance, be achieved through autonomy supportive leadership (Baard et al., 2004) and stimulating job design (Van den Broeck et al., 2008). Need satisfaction might thus offer a promising tool to align different HR-practices.

A considerable amount of research has now provided evidence for the usefulness of SDT in occupational health psychology. SDT deals with the 'why' and 'what' of employees' behaviour and considers need satisfaction as the underlying process of optimal functioning (Deci & Ryan, 2000). Therefore, SDT might be considered a coherent grand theory of motivation (Reeve, 2005) and might serve as a general framework for the study and practice of employees' optimal functioning (Deci & Vansteenkiste, 2004).

ACKNOWLEDGMENTS

The first author's contribution was supported by a grant from the Fund for Scientific Research Flanders (FWO-Vlaanderen). We would like to thank Willy Lens, Hein Huyghe and Bart Neyrinck for their comments on a first draft of this chapter.

REFERENCES

ATKINSON, J.W. (1964). An introduction to motivation. Princeton, NJ: Van Nostrand.
BAARD, P., DECI, E. L., RYAN, R. M. (2004). Intrinsic need satisfaction: A motivational basis of performance and well-being in two work settings. *Journal of Applied Social Psychology*, 34, 2045-2068.
BANDURA, A. (1997). Self-efficacy: *The exercise of control*. New York: W.H.

Freeman.

BAUMEISTER, R. & LEARY, M. (1995). The need to belong. Desire for interpersonal attachments as a fundamental human motivation. *Psychological Bulletin*, 117, 497-529.

BONO J. E., & JUDGE, T. A. (2003). Self-concordance at work: Toward understanding the motivational effects of Transformational leaders. *Academy of Management Journal*, 46, 554-571.

BOWLBY, J. (1969). Attachment and loss: Vol. 1. *Attachment*. New York: Basic Books.

deCHARMS, R. (1968). *Personal causation: The internal affective determinants of behavior*. New York: Academic Press.

DECI, E. L, & RYAN, R. M. (1985). *Intrinsic motivation and self-determination in human behavior*. New York: Plenum.

DECI, E. L, & VANSTEENKISTE, M. (2004). Self-determination theory and basic need satisfaction: Understanding human development in positive psychology. R*icherche di psicologia*, 27, 23-40.

DECI, E. L., & RYAN, R. M. (2000). The "what" and "why" of goal pursuits: Human needs and the self-determination of behavior. *Psychological Inquiry*, 11, 319-338.

DECI, E. L., CONNELL, J. P., & RYAN, R. M. (1989). Self-determination in a work organization. *Journal of Applied Psychology*, 74, 580-590.

DECI, E. L., KOESTNER, R., & RYAN, R. M. (2001). Extrinsic rewards and intrinsic motivation in education: Reconsidered once again. *Review of Educational Research*, 71,1-27.

DECI, E. L., KOESTNER, R., RYAN, R. M., (1999), A Meta-Analytic Review of Experiments Examining the Effects of Extrinsic Rewards on Intrinsic Motivation, *Psychological Bulletin*, 125, (6), 627-668.

DECI, E. L., RYAN, R. M., GAGNÉ, M., LEONE, D. R., USUNOV, J., & KORNAZHEVA, B. P. (2001). Need satisfaction, motivation, and well-being in the work organizations of a former Eastern Bloc country. *Personality and Social Psychology Bulletin*, 27, 930-942.

DECI, E. L. (1971). Effects of externally mediated rewards on intrinsic motivation. *Journal of Personality and Social Psychology*, 18, 105-115.

DECI, E. L., EGHRARI, H., PATRICK, B. C., LEONE, D. R. (1994). Facilitating internalization: The self-determination perspective. *Journal of Personality*, 62, 119-142.

DECI, E. L. (1975). *Intrinsic motivation*. New York: Plenum.

DEMEROUTI, E., BAKKER, A., NACHREINER, F., & SCHAUFELI, W. (2001). The job demands-resources model of burnout. *Journal of Applied Psychology*, 86, 499-512.

DIENER, E., LUCAS, R. E., & SCOLLON, C. N., (2006). Beyond the hedonic treadmill - Revising the adaptation theory of well-being. *American Psychologist*, 61, 305-314.

FELDMAN, D., LEANA, C., & BOLINO, M. (2002). Underemployment and relative deprivation among re-employed executives. *Journal of Occupational and Organizational Psychology, 75,* 453-471.

FERNET, C., GUAY, F., & SENÉCAL, C. (2004). Adjusting to job demands: The role of work self-determination and job control in predicting burnout. *Journal of Vocational Behaviour, 65,* 39-56.

FERNET, C., SEN, C., GUAY, F., MARSH, H., & DOWSON, M., (2008). The Work Tasks Motivation Scale for Teachers (WTMST). *Journal of Career Assessment,* 16, 256-279

FREY, B. S., OSTERLOH, M. (2005). Yes, managers should be paid like bureaucrats. *Journal of Management Inquiry,* 14, 96-111.

GAGNÉ, M., & DECI, E. L. (2005). Self-determination theory and work motivation. *Journal of Organizational Behaviour, 26,* 331-362.

GAGNÉ, M., & FOREST, J. (in press). The Study of Compensation Systems through the Lens of Self-Determination Theory: Reconciling 35 Years of Debate. Canadian Psychology.

GAGNÉ, M., KOESTNER, R., & ZUCKERMAN, M. (2000). Facilitating acceptance of organizational change: The importance of self-determination. *Journal of Applied Social Psychology, 30,* 1843-1852.

GAGNÉ, M., SÉNÉCAL, C. B., & KOESTNER, R. (1997). Proximal job characteristics, feelings of empowerment, and intrinsic motivation: A multidimensional model. *Journal of Applied Social Psychology, 27,* 1222-1240.

GROOT, W., & VAN DEN BRINK, H. M., (1999). The price of stress. *Journal of Economic Psychology,* 20, 83-103.

GUAY, F. (2005). Motivations Underlying Career Decision-Making Activities: The Career Decision-Making Autonomy Scale (CDMAS). *Journal of Career Assessment, 13,* 77-97.

GUAY, F., RATELLE, C. F., SENÉCAL, C., LAROSE, S., & DESCHENES, A. (2006). Distinguishing developmental from chronic career indecision: Self-efficacy, autonomy, and social support. *Journal of Career Assessment, 14,* 235-255.

GUAY, F., SENÉCAL, C., GAUTHIER, L., & FERNET, C. (2003). Predicting career indecision: A self-determination theory perspective. *Journal of Counseling Psychology, 50,* 165-177.

HACKMAN, J., & OLDHAM, G. (1976). Motivation through design of work – Test of a theory. *Organizational behavior and human performance,* 16, 250-279.

HENDRIKX, K. (2004) Zelf-concordantie in de werkcontext. De redenen achter werkdoelen, fundamentele behoeftes, werkgerelateerd welbevinden en jobfunctioneren. [Self concordance at work. The reasons behind work goals, fundamental needs and work related well-being and performance] Unpublished Masters' thesis. Katholieke Universiteit Leuven.

ILARDI, B., LEONE, D., KASSER, T., & RYAN, R. (1993). Employee and supervisor ratings of motivation: Main effects and discrepancies associated with job satisfaction and adjustment in a factory setting. *Journal of Applied Social Psychology, 23*, 1789-1805.

JENKINS, G. D., MITRA, A., GUPTA, N., & SHAW, J.D., (1998). Are financial incentives related to performance? A meta-analytic review of empirical research. *Journal of Applied Psychology, 83*, 777-787.

JUDGE, T. A., BONO, J. E., EREZ, A., & LOCKE, E. A., (2005). Core self-evaluations and job and life satisfaction: The role of self-concordance and goal attainment. *Journal of Applied Psychology, 90*, 257-268.

KAISER, R. B., HOGAN, R., & CRAIG, S. B. (2008). Leadership and the fate of organizations. *American Psychologist, 63,*, 96-110.

KARASEK, R. (1979). Job demands, job decision latitude, and mental strain – Implications for job redesign. *Administrative Science Quarterly, 24*, 285-308.

KASSER, T. (2002). *The high price of materialism*. London: The MIT Press.

KASSER, T., & AHUVIA, A. C., (2002). Materialistic values and well-being in business students. *European Journal of Social Psychology, 32*, 137-146.

KASSER, T., & RYAN, R. M., (1996). Further examining the American dream: Differential correlates of intrinsic and extrinsic goals. *Personality and Social Psychology Bulletin, 22*, 280-287.

KASSER, T., DAVEY, J., & RYAN, R. M. (1992). Motivation and employee-supervisor discrepancies in a psychiatric vocational rehabilitation setting. *Rehabilitation Psychology, 37*, 175–187.

KRISTOF-BROWN, A., ZIMMERMAN, R., & JOHNSON, E. (2005). Consequences of individuals' fit at work: A meta-analysis of person-job, person-organization, person-group, and person-supervisor fit. *Personnel Psychology, 58*, 285-342.

LATHAM, G., & PINDER, C. (2005). Work motivation theory and research at the dawn of the twenty-first century, *Annual Review of Psychology, 56*, 485–516.

LOCKE, E., & LATHAM, G. (2002). Building a practically useful theory of goal setting and task motivation – A 35-year odyssey. *American Psychologist, 57*, 705-717

LUTHANS, F. (2002). The need for and meaning of positive organizational behavior. *Journal of Organizational Behavior 23*, 695-706.

LUYTEN, H., & LENS, W., (1981). The effect of earlier experience and reward contingencies on intrinsic motivation. *Motivation and Emotion, 5*, 25-36.

LYNCH, M., PLANT, R., & RYAN, R. (2005). Psychological needs and threat to safety: Implications for staff and patients in a psychiatric hospital for youth. *Professional Psychology – Research and Practice, 36*, 415-425.

MASLOW, A. (1943). A theory of human motivation. *Psychological Review, 50*, 370-396.

McClelland, D. C. (1965). Achievement and Entrepreneurship: A Longitudinal Study. *Journal of Personality and Social Psychology*, 14, 389-92

McGregor, D., (1960). *The Human Side of Enterprise*. New York: McGraw-Hill.

Milette, V., & Gagné, M. (2008). Designing volunteers' tasks to maximize motivation, satisfaction and performance; The impact of job characteristics on the outcomes of volunteer involvement. *Motivation and Emotion*, 32, 11-22.

Morgeson, F. P., & Humphrey, S. E., (2006). The Work Design Questionnaire (WDQ): Developing and validating a comprehensive measure for assessing job design and the nature of work. *Journal of Applied Psychology*, 91, 1321-1339.

Murray, H. (1938). *Explorations in personality*. New York: Oxford University Press.

Porter, L. W., Lawler, E. E., & Hackman, J. R., (1975). *Behavior in Organizations*. McGraw-Hill.

Reeve, J. (2005). Understanding motivation and emotion (4th ed.). Hoboken, NJ: Wiley.

Richer, S. F., & Vallerand, R. J. (1995). Supervisors' interactional styles and subordinates' intrinsic and extrinsic motivation. *Journal of Social Psychology, 135,* 707-722.

Richer, S. F., Blanchard, C., & Vallerand, R. J. (2002). A motivational model of work turnover. *Journal of Applied Social Psychology, 32,* 2089-2113.

Ryan, R. M., (1982). Control and information in the intrapersonal sphere: An extension of cognitive evaluation theory. *Journal of Personality and Social Psychology*, 43, 450-461.

Ryan, R. M., & Connell, J. P., (1989). Perceived locus of causality and internalization: Examining reasons for acting in two domain. *Journal of Personality and Social Psychology*, 57, 749-761.

Ryan, R. M., & Deci, E. L., (2000). The darker and brighter sides of human existence: Basic psychological needs as a unifying concept. *Psychological Inquiry*, 11, 319-338.

Ryan, R. M., Mims, V., & Koestner, R., (1983). Relation of reward contingency and interpersonal context to intrinsic motivation: A review and test using cognitive evaluation theory. *Journal of Personality and Social Psychology*, 45, 736-750.

Rynes, S. L., Gerhart, B., & Parks, L. (2005). Personnel psychology: Performance evaluation and pay for performance. *Annual Review of Psychology*, 56, 571-600.

Schaufeli, W., & Bakker, A. (2004). Job demands, job resources, and their relationship with burnout and engagement: a multi-sample study. *Journal of Organizational Behavior*, 25, 293-315.

SELIGMAN, M., & CSIKSZENTMIHALYI, M. (2000). Positive psychology – An introduction. *American Psychologist*, 55, 5-14.

SENECAL, C., & GUAY, F. (2001). Procrastination in job-seeking: An analysis of motivational processes and feelings of hopelessness. *Journal of Social Behavior and Personality*, 15, 267-282.

SHELDON, K. M., & NIEMIEC, C. P. (2006). It's not just the amount that counts: Balanced need satisfaction also affects well-being. *Journal of Personality and Social Psychology*, 91, 331-341.

SHELDON, K., TURBAN, D., BROWN, K., BARRICK, M., & JUDGE, T. (2003). Applying Self-Determination Theory to organizational research. *Research in Personnel and Human Resources Management*, 22, 357-393.

SIEGRIST, J. (1996) Adverse health effects of high effort-low reward conditions. *Journal of Occupational Health Psychology*, 1, 27–41.

SKINNER, B. F. (1974). *About behaviorism*. New York: Knopf.

SOENENS, B., VANSTEENKISTE, M., DURIEZ, B., et al. (2006). In search of the sources of psychologically controlling parenting: The role of parental separation anxiety and parental maladaptive perfectionism. *Journal of Research on Adolescence*, 16, 539-559.

SOENENS, B., VANSTEENKISTE, M., LENS, W., LUYCKX, K., GOOSSENS, L., BEYERS, W., RYAN, R. (2007). Conceptualizing parental autonomy support: Adolescent perceptions of promotion of independence versus promotion of volitional functioning. *Developmental Psychology*, 43, 633-646.

STAJKOVIC, A. D., & LUTHANS, F. (2001). Differential effects of incentive motivators on work performance. *Academy of Management Journal*, 44, 580-590.

VAN DEN BROECK, A., VANSTEENKISTE, M., DE WITTE, H., & LENS, W. (2008). Extending the job demands resources model: Basic need satisfaction as an explanatory mechanism in the relation between job stressors, job challenges and job resources and job well-being. Submitted for publication.

VAN DEN BROECK, A., VANSTEENKISTE, M., LENS, W., & DE WITTE, H. (2008). Unemployed individual's work values and job flexibility: An exploration from Expectancy Value theory and Self-determination Theory. Resubmitted for publication.

VANSTEENKISTE, M. (2005). Intrinsic versus extrinsic goal promotion and autonomy support versus control. Facilitating performance, persistence, socially adaptive functioning and well-being. Unpublished Doctoral Dissertation, Katholieke Universiteit Leuven

VANSTEENKISTE, M., DE WITTE, H., & LENS, W., (2006). Explaining the negative relationship between length of unemployment and the willingness to undertake a job training: A Self-Determination perspective. In T. Kieselbach, A., Winefield, C., Boyd, & S., Anderson (Eds). Unemployment and Health. International and interdisciplinary perspectives (pp. 199-217). Australian Academic Press.

Vansteenkiste, M., Duriez, B., Simons, J., & Soenens, B. (2006). Materialistic values and well-being among business students: Further evidence of their detrimental effect. *Journal of Applied Social Psychology*, 36, 2892-2908.

Vansteenkiste, M., Lens, W., De Witte, H., & Feather, N. (2005). Understanding unemployed people's job-search behaviour, unemployment experience and well-being: A comparison of expectancy-value theory and self-determination theory. *British Journal of Social Psychology*, 44, 1-20.

Vansteenkiste, M., Lens, W., Dewitte, S., De Witte, H., & Deci, E.L. (2004). The "why" and "why not" of job-search behaviour: Their relation to searching, unemployment experience, and well-being. *European Journal of Social Psychology*, 34, 345-363.

Vansteenkiste, M., Neyrinck, B., Niemic, C., Soenens, B., De Witte, H., & Van den Broeck, A. (2007). Examining the relations among extrinsic versus intrinsic work value orientations, basic need satisfaction, and job experience: A self-determination theory approach. *Journal of Occupational and Organizational Psychology*, 80, 251-277.

Vansteenkiste, M., Ryan, R. M., & Deci, E. L. (in press). Self-determination theory and the explanatory role of psychological needs in human well-being. In L. Bruni, F. Comim, & M. Pugno (Eds.), *Capabilities and happiness*. Oxford, UK: Oxford University Press.

Vansteenkiste, M., Soenens, B., & Duriez, B. (in press). Presenting a positive alternative to materialistic strivings and the thin-ideal: Understanding the effects of extrinsic relative to intrinsic goal pursuits. In Lopez, S. J. (Ed.) (in press). *Positive psychology: Exploring the best in people.* Westport, CT: Greenwood Publishing Company.

Vansteenkiste, M., Zhou, M., Lens, W., & Soenens, B. (2005). Experiences of autonomy and control among Chinese learners: Vitalizing or immobilizing? *Journal of educational psychology*, 97, 468-483.

Viswesvaran, C., Sanchez, J. I., Fisher, J. (1999). The role of social support in the process of work stress: A meta-analysis. *Journal of Vocational Behavior*, 54, 314-334.

Vroom V. (1964). *Work and motivation*. New York: Wiley.

White, R. (1959). Motivation reconsidered: The concept of competence. *Psychological Review*, 66, 279-333.

Wright, S. L., Burt, C. D., & Strongman, K. T. (2006). Loneliness in the workplace: Construct definition and scale development. *New Zealand Journal of Psychology*, 35, 59-68.

SUBJECTIVE OCCUPATIONAL SUCCESS
A RESOURCE IN THE STRESS PROCESS

Simone Grebner[1], Achim Elfering and Norbert K. Semmer

CHAPTER OVERVIEW

While resources such as social support and job control have been widely investigated in the study of work-related stress, the experience of success has not. As a result, very little is known about what kinds of work experiences are perceived as successful. We do not know the extent to which success predicts well-being, health, and job-related behaviour. In addition, little is known about the antecedents of success experiences at work. This chapter presents the *'Success Resource Model'*. Moreover, it deals with the definition, measurement using the *'Subjective Occupational Success Scales'*, and dimensionality of subjective occupational success that is considered a resource in the work-related stress process. Subjective Occupational Success includes four dimensions: goal attainment, pro-social success, positive feedback, and career success. Evidence and considerations concerning selected antecedents and consequences of subjective occupational success are presented. Finally, the chapter outlines future research questions and emphasises methodological concerns.

SUBJECTIVE OCCUPATIONAL SUCCESS

A necessary shift in theory development in occupational health psychology from a traditional disease model to a genuine health model requires inclusion of all relevant resources that act as causal agents for human strengths and optimal functioning (Schaufeli, 2004).

While resources such as social support (Visweswaran, Fisher, & Sanchez, 1999) and job control (e.g., Frese & Zapf, 1994; Kahn & Byosiere, 1992; Karasek 1979) have frequently been conceptualized as resources and investigated within the study of work-related stress, the experience of success has not (cf. Kahn & Byosiere, 1992; Sonnentag & Frese, 2003). Within this context, resources are considered to "refer to conditions within the work situation and to individual characteristics that can be used to

---

[1] Author for correspondence

attain goals" (Sonnentag & Frese, 2003, p. 467). So far, goal attainment or, more generally, success, has not been regarded as a resource in work-related stress research.

Within theoretical accounts, achievements have rarely been considered as resources in the stress process that can have beneficial main effects on well-being and health. Instead, achievements have frequently been investigated in terms of a response to stress (e.g., Kahn & Byosiere, 1992, Sonnentag & Frese, 2003). For instance, direct and indirect negative effects of stressors on performance and performance-related outcome variables have been conceptualized and studied (Sonnentag & Frese, 2003). Nevertheless, there is good evidence that goal attainment and goal progress may lead to positive emotions and are beneficial for well-being (e.g., Carver & Scheier, 1990; Diener & Lucas, 1999; Locke & Latham, 1990; Wiese, 2007).

We take the stance that it is important to conceptualize and investigate the role of subjective success in the occupational stress process because subjective success can act as a causal agent for human strengths and optimal functioning.

Firstly, we describe briefly the *'Success Resource Model'* in the occupational stress process that specifies beneficial main and buffer effects of subjective success on job strain in terms of well-being, health, and recovery. Secondly, we define subjective occupational success experiences. The definition emphasizes the event-character of subjective occupational success experiences. Thirdly, we discuss the subjectivity of success experiences. Forthly, we specify why subjective occupational success is a resource referring to a variety of well-established theoretical accounts. Fifthly, we present briefly a newly developed multidimensional measurement instrument for subjective occupational success (The Subjective Occupational Success Scales, *SUCCESS*, Grebner, Elfering, Achermann, Knecht, & Semmer, 2008a, 2008b). Moreover, we summarize briefly available evidence concerning associations of dimensions of subjective success with well-being indicators. Sixthly, we discuss some examples of factors that seem qualified to promote subjective occupational success experiences (e.g., job control, social support at work, self-efficacy and problem-focused coping) and factors that may act as hindrances for subjective occupational success (e.g., job stressors). Finally, we make some suggestions for required research in the future.

THE SUCCESS RESOURCE MODEL

In order to achieve a better understanding of the work-related stress process, it is suggested that subjective success might be included as a resource in theoretical accounts. The success resource model assumes that subjective occupational success is a resource because it is valued in it's own right, elicits positive emotions, helps to protect other resources (e.g., Hobfoll, 1998, 2001), has beneficial effects on well-being (e.g., Carver & Scheier, 1990), and health and an energizing effect (e.g., Locke & Latham, 1990, 2002), which facilitates recovery from work demands. Moreover, the model presumes that subjective success can facilitate learning (e.g., Frese & Zapf, 1994). Furthermore, the model assumes that subjective success is promoted by situation-related resources such as job control, perceived social support at work and person-related resources such as self-efficacy and problem-focused coping. In addition, the model assumes that subjective success is hampered by job stressors, in particular by hindrance stressors (LePine, Podsakoff, & LePine, 2005). The model also hypothesizes reciprocal effects of well-being, health, and recovery on subjective success. Finally, the model hypothesises a buffering effect of subjective success experiences on the stressor-strain relationship. The assumption is that the more subjective success an individual experiences, the less detrimental the effects of job stressors on well-being, health, and recovery. The assumption is that the more subjective success an individual experiences, the less detrimental are the effects of job stressors on well-being, health, and recovery. Subjective success has an energizing (Locke & Latham, 1990) and, hence, protecting effect on the individual. Moreover, success experiences can help to perceive stressful experiences as less harmful or threatening because success represents gain (e.g., status improvement), which counterbalances experiences of harm, threat and loss. Moreover, subjective success experiences elicit positive emotions, and therefore help to focus on task-relevant and positive self-related cognitions.

Subjective occupational success refers to goal attainment, pro-social success (e.g., successfully supporting others at work, motivating others, settling conflicts), positive feedback by others (e.g., supervisor, coworkers and clients), and career success (e.g., promotion, making useful business contacts). Goal attainment and pro-social success are considered as immediate personal experiences of good performance, whereas positive feedback and career success are regarded as acknowledgement of good performance by others.

DEFINITION OF SUBJECTIVE OCCUPATIONAL SUCCESS

Subjective occupational success can be defined as positive and meaningful experiences at work that are goal-related and salient for an individual or a group, in terms of subjective goal attainment or reasonable movement toward a goal (Grebner et al., 2008). Subjective occupational success can be represented by (1) reaching milestones such as acquiring an important customer, (2) results in terms of actions (e.g., settling a conflict), (3) outcomes (e.g., a report or a product), and (4) consequences in terms of acknowledgement of good performance by others. Acknowledgement by others can occur in the short term for instance as positive feedback by a client and in the long term for example as promotion and receiving more job control and more interesting work tasks (e.g, Grebner et al., 2008a, 2008b; see also Sonnentag, 2002).

One important characteristic of many subjective occupational success experiences is their *event-character* (e.g., Grebner, Elfering, Semmer, Kaiser-Probst, & Schlapbach, 2004; see also the affective events theory of Weiss & Cropanzano, 1996). Specific events, where the meaning 'success' is ascribed, have a defined beginning and an end and can, therefore, be told in terms of a story (e.g., 'some weeks ago I was contacted by a head hunter who tried to recruit me for a well paid job' or 'in a meeting I ensured that the leader could save his face'). Nevertheless, one can certainly also ascribe 'success' to enduring conditions such as achieved occupational status (e.g., self-employed craftsman, team leader, executive consultant) or promotion prospects. We concentrate on success experiences with event-character because events are more salient for the individual. Salience is likely to lead to more attention by the individual compared to enduring conditions. Therefore, salience of an event can promote mental and emotional preoccupation with the experience. For instance, an employee who received a promotion is likely to reflect on what happened and may indulge in the pride and joy elicited by the event.

SUBJECTIVITY OF OCCUPATIONAL SUCCESS

Subjective success refers to an employee's assessment about his or her accomplishments using personal criteria (Dyke & Murphy, 2006). Hence, the meaning of success that people assign to performance outcomes or a work-related event is determined subjectively (Plaks & Stecher, 2007). For instance, one may be successful in the eye of others but not in terms of a subjective judgment. One reason for this might be extremely high aspirations. For instance, an employee whose project proposal was accepted and who subsequently received the congratulations of co-workers may not, however, experience the event as successful if (s)he expected a higher amount of project funding.

Another reason could be that the work environment makes it very easy to achieve a goal, for instance, via very high levels of social support that results in low goal difficulty (cf. Latham & Locke, 1991; Locke & Latham,

1990; 2002). Moreover, one may be successful subjectively but not in terms of outsiders' judgments or other indicators of performance. The reason can be that goal attainment is not visible for others (e.g., 'at the outset of a project I didn't have very relevant knowledge. Nevertheless, I was able to keep to the tight schedule'). Another reason might be that others have extremely high standards.

Therefore, subjective occupational success is not necessarily synonymous with performance, which is defined as meeting organisational goals (e.g., Sonnentag & Frese, 2002). For instance, when a customer service representative gives advice at length and is praised by the customer, the employee might consider the service as very successful. However, a supervisor might assess the service as suboptimal because of the extra time that was needed.

From our point of view, subjectivity in success experiences can be important for employee well-being and health because if an individual or group ascribes 'success', the outcome or event is congruent with the goals of an individual (e.g., receiving attention or positive feedback by important others) or group (e.g., to outperform another group). Overall, subjectively ascribed 'success' implies that an experience is meaningful in the individuals' or groups' own frame of reference.

WHY IS SUCCESS A RESOURCE?

The experience of success requires an internal attribution, where an individual (or a group he or she identifies with – Garcia-Prieto & Scherer, 2006) takes credit for a positive outcome (Pekrun & Frese, 1992; Scherer & Ellsworth, 2003; Lazarus, 1999). Experiencing success (as well as experiencing failure) therefore, is likely to have strong implications for the self-concept. Success induces pride, which is an emotion that has the self as a reference. It shares this self-reference with shame and guilt, which tend to be induced by failure. These emotions therefore have been called self-conscious emotions (Tangney & Fischer, 1995), feelings of self-worth (Brown & Dutton, 1995), or self-feelings (Riketta & Ziegler, 2006). Since maintaining a favourable self-concept may be considered a basic human need (Epstein, 1998), experiences that have strong implications for the self are likely to be especially important and consequential for the individual (cf. the concept of "Stress as Offense to Self"; Semmer, Jacobshagen, Meier, & Elfering, 2007). Experiences that foster a positive self-concept may be considered a valuable resource.

According to the *conservation of resources theory* (Hobfoll, 2001, 2002), resources refer to objects, conditions (e.g., time), personal characteristics (e.g., self-efficacy, optimism, health), or energies that are valued in their own right or that are valued because they act as conduits to the achievement or protection of valued resources. Subjective success is clearly a resource because it is valued in its own right. Most individuals and groups highly value success experiences such as goal progress, goal attainment and consequential appreciation and positive feedback by significant others (e.g., co-workers, supervisor, clients). Moreover, career success such as receiving a promotion is highly valued by most employees. Success-related themes therefore occur several times in Hobfoll's (2001) list of resources.

Furthermore, subjective success experiences such as goal attainment can help to generate or protect other resources (e.g., job experience, approval, autonomy, status, and money) in terms of an upwards spiral that may result in better coping, well-being, and health. For instance, a new-starter who repeatedly deals effectively with difficult clients is gaining job experience, is able to cope in a problem focused manner with difficult clients, might receive as a consequence more autonomy, and might experience a high level of job satisfaction. Hence, goal attainment can help to protect or generate better working conditions and improved well-being. Furthermore, a manager who successfully motivates subordinates (i.e. pro-social success) is capable to reach his or her goals. In case, the good performance is acknowledged by others the manager might receive in the short-term positive feedback that is also experienced as success and elicits feelings of pride. Moreover, in the long term, the manager might be promoted, which represents career success.

Moreover, success experiences can be crucial for work motivation in terms of boosting self-efficacy (see *social cognitive theory*, Bandura, 1982) that in turn can lead to commitment to higher goals and greater effort and persistence (see *goal-setting theory*, Locke & Latham, 1990, 2002). For example, when an insurance salesman has sold a predefined number of automobile insurances he might set himself a higher goal and try to sell even more insurances in the same space of time.

In addition, specific types of subjective success such as goal attainment and positive feedback by other people can facilitate further goal attainment due to learning processes. In particular, feedback processing helps to develop and attain further and higher-order goals (see *action theory*, e.g., Frese & Zapf, 1994). Positive feedback provides the recipient with information about what was right about his or her work behaviour.

The broaden-and-build theory of positive emotions (Fredrickson, 2001) explains why success acts as a conduit to the achievement of other valued resources. Subjective success experiences are likely to elicit positive emotions such as pride and joy that in turn can 'produce flourishing in terms of an upward spiral by broadening momentary thought-action repertoires'. Pride, for instance, creates the 'urge to share news of the achievement with others and to envision even greater achievements in the future'. These achievements in turn serve to build enduring personal resources (i.e., physical, intellectual, social and psychological), and stress resilience (e.g., recovering quickly and efficiently from stressful experiences, Fredrickson & Branigan, 2001, p. 220). For instance, receiving a compliment from a client for outstanding service can make a service representative proud about her work. As a consequence, the service representative might share the news of the achievement with her spouse and envision an even better client service in the future (e.g., communication tailored to the specific needs of clients). According to affective events theory (Weiss & Cropanzano, 1996) goal attainment, contextual performance, positive feedback, and positive career related events can be considered as affective events that positively influence affect and emotions (see also Ilies, de Pater, & Judge, 2007). Finally, subjective success experiences might have an energizing effect in terms of motivating people (e.g., Locke & Latham, 1990). As a consequence, the boost in the energy level of an individual might lead to better recovery from stressful encounters.

Although subjective success experiences can be short-lived (e.g., day-to-day goal attainment; Wiese, 2007) and the effects likewise (e.g., pride after receiving positive feedback or after solving a complex problem), personal resources accrued during states of positive emotions that might follow success experiences are conceptualized as endurable. These resources 'outlast the transient emotional states that led to their acquisition" (Fredrickson, 2001, p. 220). For example, positive feedback by the supervisor or settling a conflict between subordinates might lead in the short-term to pride and might increase the employee's self-efficacy and job satisfaction (see also Locke & Latham, 1990).

SUBJECTIVE SUCCESS: MEASUREMENT AND EVIDENCE

To examine subjective success experiences in the occupational stress process a measurement instrument is needed. Therefore, it is firstly important to investigate what people experience as success and how many dimensions success experiences have. To date, a well-established instrument does not exist. Rather, success has frequently been equated with indicators of well-being such as job satisfaction and career satisfaction (e.g., Ng, Eby, Sorensen, & Feldman, 2005), which may actually better be conceived as consequences of success in terms of well-being indicators. Sometimes success is measured with items that assess not only goal attainment but also satisfaction that leads to a conceptual overlap between the success and satisfaction measure (e.g., Wiese, Freund, & Baltes, 2000) and can, therefore, result in inflated correlations when associations between success and well-being are examined. Moreover, Lyubomirsky, King, and Diener (2005), in a meta-analysis, summarized various types of desirable behaviour and life outcomes under the term success. In the work domain they included beneficial working conditions (e.g., job control), work behaviour (e.g., organisational citizenship behaviour), performance, superior mental health, and well-being (e.g., job satisfaction and a low level of exhaustion). From our point of view well-being should be separately conceptualized from the occupational success experience, because 'individual well-being and performance are distinct concepts' (Sonnentag, 2002, p. 407).

Hence, it is important to disentangle subjective success from its potential antecedents and consequences to specify the concept. For instance, well-being can be an antecedent and a consequence of subjective success experiences. High work engagement in a teacher might lead to more positive feedback by students or the teacher may feel satisfied because most of the students achieved a learning target. Well-being is in both examples either conceptualized as a cause or outcome of the success experience.

Many studies equated subjective career success with well-being using career or job satisfaction as indicators for success (e.g., Dette, Abele, & Renner, 2004; Ng et al., 2005). Other studies measured success using items that overlap with well-being (e.g., Wiese et al., 2000). Even though some individuals might experience their satisfaction as a success, we think it is most important to avoid a conceptual overlap between independent variables (i.e., measures of subjective success) and dependent variables (i.e., well-being indicators; see also Heslin, 2005), to prevent content-related redundancies and consequential inflated correlations.

Consequently, Grebner, Elfering, Achermann, Knecht and Semmer developed and validated the *Subjective Occupational Success Scales* (SUCCESS, Grebner et al., 2008a, 2008b). The SUCCESS measures work-related experiences in terms of events that are perceived as successful. The authors conducted several studies that facilitated the development and validation of the instrument. The first question was what do people experience as occupational success and how many dimensions do subjective occupational success experiences have? Hence, content and dimensionality of subjective occupational success experiences were examined based on 195 critical incidents (Flanagan, 1954) reported by 57 employees of small-, medium-, and large-size organizations (Grebner, et al., 2008a, 2008b). Classification of verbal descriptions of success events resulted in 14 categories. Eleven of the 14 categories could be assigned to 4 content-related dimensions: The most frequent dimension was *pro-social success* that included 4 categories: Supporting others, solving conflicts, preventing negative outcomes for others/causing positive outcomes for others, and being asked for advice. The preponderance of pro-social situations can be attributed to the fact that participants worked mainly in the service sector. Pro-social success can be related to in-role behaviour (e.g., it belongs to the role of leaders to settle conflicts, to give advice, and to motivate subordinates). Moreover, pro-social success can be related to *contextual performance* such as voluntary helping behaviour (cf. Organ, Podsakoff, & McKenzie, 2006) in terms of extra-role behaviour. There exists some evidence that *contextual performance* such as helping others can contribute positively to subjective well-being (e.g., Dovidio, Piliavin, Schroeder, & Penner, 2006; Organ, 2006; Otake, Shimai, Tanaka-Matsumi, Otsui, & Fredrickson, 2006). For instance, prosocial behavior 'can make the helper feel good or feel better in case the helper is feeling bad' (Dovidio et al. 2006, p. 107).

Goal attainment was the second frequent dimension and included 3 categories: Attaining/exceeding goals, goal attainment, despite of adverse conditions, and acting for one's interests/ideas. Goal attainment can be related to *task-performance* such as meeting or exceeding organisational goals. Moreover, we suppose that subjective occupational success also includes attainment of personal goals (e.g., Maier & Brunstein, 2001) that need not necessarily be relevant for the organization (e.g., making business contacts that help to find another job). In general, there is ample evidence that goal progress and *goal attainment* are positively related to positive emotions and well-being in various life domains (e.g., Brunstein, 1993; Carver & Scheier, 1990; Diener & Lucas, 1999; Elliot, Sheldon, & Church, 1997; Emmons, 1986; Koestner, Lekes, Powers, & Chicoine, 2002; Louro, Pieters, & Zeelenberg, 2007; Wiese, 2007). The reason is that goal attainment can result in positive changes in self-perception and life circumstances (Sheldon, Kasser, Smith, & Shore, 2002). In work-related research there is also good evidence that subjective work-related goal progress and goal attainment are important predictors of job satisfaction and organisational commitment (e.g., Locke & Latham, 1990; 2002; Maier & Brunstein, 2001; Wiese & Freund, 2005), and positive affect (Harris, Daniels, & Briner, 2003). Moreover, positive experiences at work predict job satisfaction over and above negative experiences (Elfering, Semmer, Tschan, Kälin, & Bucher, 2007). In addition, goal progress can result in greater well-being, which in turn promotes the setting of more self-concordant goals, which again fosters further goal attainment and well-being enhancement (Sheldon & Houser-Marko, 2001).

Nevertheless, the number of studies that focus on subjective success at work as an antecedent of different indicators of general and work-related well-being, including indicators for impaired well-being, is comparatively small.

Over and above goal attainment, positive *consequences* of pro-social success and goal attainment belong to the concept of subjective success. A possible consequence of goal attainment and pro-social success can be positive feedback. Consequently the authors found a third frequent domain: *positive feedback* by supervisor(s), coworkers, subordinates, and clients. Positive feedback was less frequently reported than pro-social success and goal attainment because not every pro-social success and goal attainment is recognized and acknowledged by others (London, 2003). Hence, positive feedback does not automatically follow goal attainment but depends rather on the willingness of others to provide positive feedback (e.g., supervisor, coworkers, subordinates, clients). The importance of positive feedback - in the sense of acknowledgement of one's behaviour, achievements, or personal worth – has been emphasized in many areas of psychology (e.g., Kluger & DeNisi, 1996; Locke & Latham, 1990; London, 2003). However, the role positive feedback plays in terms of a resource in the occupational stress process is hardly understood because available job analysis instruments usually do not differentiate between positive and negative job-related feedback (e.g., JDS, Hackman & Oldham, 1975). According to social cognitive theory (e.g., Bandura & Locke, 2003) *positive feedback*, that frequently indicates and rewards successful goal attainment, is followed by positive affective states such as satisfaction. However, even though the association of positive feedback with positive emotions is well-known and has repeatedly been emphasized (e.g., Kluger & DeNisi, 1996; London, 2003; Taylor, Fisher, & Ilgen, 1984), the specific role positive feedback plays for general and job-related well-being, in particular for indicators of impaired well-being, is hardly investigated.

A further possible way of acknowledgement of good performance by others is career success. *Career success* was the fourth dimension and comprised 3 categories: promotion/career advancement, making innovations, and outperforming others. It is not a surprise that career success was least frequently reported. Subjective career success consisted of achieving milestones in one's career, such as making innovations or receiving a promotion, which are usually not experienced on a day-to-day level but are infrequent experiences. For instance, a promotion is mostly the result of years of work. Moreover, making innovations takes time to develop ideas and to solve many problems. Furthermore, outperforming others is not done on a day-to-day level but requires, in many cases, hard work over an extended period. Finally, subjective career success does not follow automatically aggregated goal attainment but depends rather on multiple circumstances (e.g., promotion possibilities, available financial resources, organisational politics, etc.).

Since, *subjective career success* was frequently equated with well-being there is little evidence available on the question of whether specific career related positive events contribute positively to different types of well-being. In general, more frequent dimensions are not automatically more important than less frequent dimensions. For instance, events that represent career success occur less frequently compared to goal attainment but are mostly of very high importance.

The items of the SUCCESS questionnaire were formulated based on the 4 categories of subjective success. Hence, the instrument includes 4 dimensions: *Goal attainment* (e.g., 'I achieved good results'), *pro-social success* (e.g., 'I helped others to succeed'), *positive feedback* (e.g., 'I received positive feedback by my supervisor'), and *career success* (e.g., 'I made very useful work contacts', 'I got a promotion'), measured by 16 items. The four-dimensions of the instrument were tested in two studies (Grebner et al., 2008a, 2008b) using Principal Components Analysis (PCA) and were replicated using Confirmatory Factor Analysis (CFA). Overall, the dimensions of subjective occupational success showed satisfying reliability in terms of internal consistency. Each dimension of subjective success correlated positively with well-being (e.g., job satisfaction and work engagement) and negatively with impaired well-being (e.g., exhaustion and feelings of resentment). In both studies, all success indicators were positively related to job satisfaction confirming former results (e.g., Locke & Latham, 1990, 2002; Wiese & Freund, 2005). In addition, work engagement that has been found to predict work performance (Salanova, Agut, & Peiro, 2005) correlated positively with all success indicators. Moreover, pro-social success was positively related to affective commitment, which is also in line with previous evidence (e.g., Locke & Latham, 1990, 2002). Furthermore, in both studies negative associations of goal attainment with resigned attitude toward one's job were found. Resigned attitude toward one's job is a defensive, resentful adaptation to sub-optimal working conditions in terms of lowering one's expectations (Semmer, 2003). Finally, both studies showed negative associations between goal attainment and exhaustion. Overall, subjective success dimensions seem to predict a variety of well-being indicators, especially job-related well-being. Moreover, consistent with the job demands resources model (Demerouti, Bakker, Nachreiner, & Schaufeli, 2001; see also Semmer & Mohr, 2001). success dimensions showed in particular associations with indicators of positive well-being.

SUBJECTIVE SUCCESS: PROMOTING FACTORS AND HINDRANCE FACTORS

To understand the meaning of the subjective success concept within the occupational stress process it is important to know how subjective success is related to situational and person-related resources (e.g., job control, social support and self-efficacy) and job stressors. In general, a wide variety of situational factors can influence subjective occupational success. For instance, goal attainment may depend on macro-level factors (e.g., market situation), meso-level factors (e.g., organisational politics, available financial resources), and micro-level factors such as task characteristics (e.g., job control), social conditions (e.g., social support), and attributes of goals such as goal difficulty (Latham & Locke, 1991; Locke & Latham, 1990, 2002; Seijts, Latham, Tasa, & Latham, 2004). Moreover, characteristics of the individual (e.g., self-efficacy, adaptive coping, perfectionism, optimism) may play an important role in determining the frequency of subjective occupational success experiences. We focus here in a first step on some factors that can promote subjective success. Below, we discuss the role of stressors for subjective occupational success experiences.

Job control may contribute positively to goal attainment because it implies that an employee can either define goals or choose between or modify predefined goals. For instance, a teacher can define learning goals and teaching methods. Moreover, job control means that an employee can make decisions concerning the way a task is conducted, the means used and the timing. For example, a teacher can decide how much time he or she spends on exercises and feedback in class. From a theoretical point of view, job control can have beneficial effects on subjective success – in particular on goal attainment, pro-social success, and career success - because job control might help to avoid or attenuate stressful situations at work (e.g., performing tasks that require a high concentration in times when work interruptions are infrequent), help individuals to cope effectively with work stressors that are conceptualized as barriers to success (cf. action theory, Frese & Zapf, 1994) or provide the time needed to settle a conflict or to make important business contacts. Our own studies provide some supporting evidence for this; for example, in two studies, job control was positively associated with goal attainment and career success (Grebner et al., 2008b). In general, high job control allows decisions to be made that are tailored to situational requirements because every situational aspect that is relevant for a goal is controllable by the individual (Frese & Zapf, 1994).

Perceived social support at work might directly promote subjective success. In particular, goal attainment might be promoted by social support because other people (e.g., supervisor, co-workers) may provide information or tangible help that is necessary for a task (e.g., Viswesvaran et al., 1999). Social support is especially important for goal attainment when tasks are novel or high in complexity (Sonnentag, 2002). For instance, Maier (1996) found increased satisfaction in newcomers who received co-worker and supervisor support for goal attainment. Moreover, social support in general and, in particular, emotional support, can contribute to diffusing stressful situations at work and to returning to task-relevant cognitions and actions after a stressful event (e.g., Dahlen & Ryan, 2005). The process of 'calming down', in turn, can facilitate goal attainment because it allows for the reduction of task-irrelevant and stress-related cognitions. Our own, again, provide supporting evidence for this: perceived social support at work was positively related with goal attainment (Grebner et al., 2008b).

Beyond the characteristics of the work-situation, characteristics of the individual can also determine whether success is experienced. In particular, self-efficacy (Stajkovic & Luthans, 1998) can play an important role in subjective success. For instance, people who perceive themselves as highly efficacious tend to invest sufficient effort and are less likely to cease their efforts prematurely, despite the stressors present in the situation (Bandura, 1982). Furthermore, people high in self-efficacy perceive stressful situations as less threatening (e.g., Jex, & Bliese, 1999; Sonnentag, 2002), 'set higher goals, are more committed to assigned goals, and find and use better task strategies to attain the goals' (Locke & Latham, 2002, p. 706).

Moreover, *problem focused coping* in terms of taking action might play an important role for success. Problem-focused coping helps individuals to cope successfully with stressors (Folkman, 1992, 2008; Lazarus, 1999) such as organisational problems, work interruptions, time pressure, role ambiguity and conflicts. As with social support, problem focused coping can contribute to calming down (Grebner et al., 2004) and returning to task-relevant cognitions and actions after a stressful event. Results supporting this assumption have been reported, for instance, by Forsyth and Compas (1987) and Vitaliano, Dewolfe, Maiuro, Russo, and Katon (1990), Reicherts (1988), Perrez and Reicherts (1992), and Reicherts and Pihet (2000). In a study of our own among service employees, problem-focused coping was found to be positively associated with goal attainment, pro-social success, and career success (Grebner et al., in prep).

Job-related stressors can impede or even thwart successful task fulfilment, and therefore hamper subjective occupational success experiences (Frese & Zapf, 1994), according to the challenge-hindrance stressor framework. In particular *hindrance stressors* such as role ambiguity, role conflict, hassles, and red tape act as success barriers (LePine, Podsakoff, & LePine,

2005). Encountering hindrance stressors at work means that an employee has to overcome obstacles during task fulfilment ,which can be time and energy consuming. Take, for example, the customer service representative who is asked by a customer for updated information concerning a new product that was advertised in the media. If the employee did not receive updated information about the new product he or she has to take action to get the necessary information. As a result, the employee will need to talk a second time with the customer.

The assumed mechanism is that *hindrance stressors* lower employee motivation because "people are likely to believe that no reasonable level of effort will be adequate to meet these types of demands" (LePine et al., 2005, p. 766). For instance, emotional and cognitive effort associated with coping with organisational constraints (e.g., lack of information) can result in fatigue and exhaustion, which reduce energy that could otherwise be used to perform tasks. From our point of view social stressors, in terms of interpersonal conflicts and harassment at work, can also be classified as hindrance stressors. On the other hand, LePine et al. (2005) hypothesize that challenge stressors (e.g., time pressure) can have beneficial effects on success. The meta-analysis of LePine et al. (2005) provides supporting evidence for performance: hindrance stressors were found to be negatively related to performance and challenge stressors were positively related to performance. Our own research has also shown supporting evidence for subjective success (Grebner, Mauch, Zehnder, & Baumgarten, 2008). Challenge stressors (i.e., time pressure) positively predicted career success, while hindrance stressors (i.e., role ambiguity and workplace conflicts) were negatively associated with goal attainment, positive feedback and career success. Hence, challenge stressors can lead to gains while hindrance stressors seem to have preliminarily costs in terms of negative effects on subjective success. However, whether time pressure is really beneficial for success depends heavily on the type of task. For instance, when it comes to tasks that include a risk for employee or client safety (e.g., driving a truck, intensive care), time pressure might rather work as a hindrance stressor.

SUMMARY AND RESEARCH REQUIREMENTS

Our *'Success Resource Model'* points to the importance of examining variables that measure subjective occupational success in occupational health psychology. Subjective success is a resource that deserves more attention in organisational stress research. Using the *Subjective Occupational Success Scales* (SUCCESS, Grebner et al. 2008a, 2008b) that are based on critical incidents (Flanagan, 1954), subjective occupational success can be conceptualized as referring to goal attainment, pro-social success (e.g., successfully supporting others at work), positive feedback by others (e.g., supervisor), and career success (e.g., promotion). Goal attainment and pro-social success are considered as immediate and more frequent types of subjective occupational success, whereas positive feedback and career success are regarded as acknowledgement of good performance by others that are less frequent compared to immediate types of subjective occupational success.

Even though, good evidence exists for specific aspects of the subjective success concept (e.g., goal attainment), only a few studies exist that have investigated the four dimensions of the subjective occupational success concept, and these are cross-sectional. Results show main effects of all subjective occupational success dimensions on well-being indicators - in particular job-related and positive well-being constructs such as job satisfaction. This is in line with previous theoretical accounts and evidence (e.g., Carver & Scheier, 1990, Diener & Lucas, 1999; Locke & Latham, 1990; Wiese, 2007). Moreover, available results demonstrate main effects of potential antecedents (e.g., job control, social support, self-efficacy, problem-focused coping, challenge and hindrance stressors) of subjective occupational success. Available results also show that situation- and person-related resources seem to promote subjective success experiences. Job stressors – in particular hindrance stressors (LePine et al. 2005) - seem to hamper subjective success experiences. However, because results are mainly based on a few cross-sectional studies further research is needed. Findings, therefore, require replication with large and heterogeneous samples using longitudinal designs.

In general, future research should study the success as a resource model extensively using a longitudinal, multi-method, and multi-level approach. Longitudinal studies would allow for the stability and time dynamics of the success dimensions, causation, and reverse causation of the success-strain relationship to be investigated (e.g., Hobfoll, 1998; Locke & Latham, 1990; Lyubomirsky et al., 2005; Sonnentag, 2002).

Because of possible problems of common-method variance in terms of inflated correlations between independent and dependent variables when, for instance, self-reports are exclusively used (e.g., Podsakoff, MacKenzie, Lee, & Podsakoff, 2003; Semmer, Grebner, & Elfering, 2004) a multi-method approach would be desirable for future studies. Such could include, for instance, measurement of day-to-day success experiences by self-observation using event sampling or time sampling.

Effects of success experiences should be measured on multiple levels of job strain, i.e., the psychological level (e.g., well-being indicators), the behavioural level (e.g., other ratings of job performance) and the physiological level (e.g., recovery of physiological stress parameters such as blood pressure decline after work and on days off work).

Moreover, all proposed effects within the success as a resource model, including reciprocal effects and moderator effects of success on the stressor-strain relationship, should be investigated. Whether success ameliorates the harmful effects of stressors on well-being in terms of buffer effects is especially important to investigate in future studies. We think that buffering effects of subjective occupational success on stressor-strain relationships are plausible. For instance, the offences of a coworker may have a less detrimental effect on well-being when an individual attains his or her goals and receives positive and public feedback from a supervisor because the positive feedback assures the position of the employee.

Furthermore, future research should include the systematic investigation of the differential effects of the dimensions of subjective success on well-being, health and recovery, including physiological recovery. To study the differential effects of subjective success dimensions is important because the influence of the employee is greater for immediate success, such as goal attainment and pro-social success, compared to the potential consequences of immediate success (i.e., positive feedback, career success).

Finally, because many employees work in teams with a high degree of interdependence, more evidence is required that examines subjective success at the group level. A further development of the Subjective Occupational Success Scales (SUCCESS) may include, for instance, group-related goal attainment (e.g., 'we achieved good results'), pro-social success (e.g., 'we helped each other to succeed'), and positive feedback (e.g., 'we received positive feedback as a team').

REFERENCES

BANDURA, A. (1982). Self-efficacy mechanisms in human agency. *American Psychologist, 37*, 122-147.

BANDURA, A. & LOCKE, E. A. (2003). Negative self-efficacy and goal effects revisited. *Journal of Applied Psychology, 88*, 87-99.

BROWN, J. D., & DUTTON, K. A. (1995). The thrill of victory, the complexity of defeat: Self-esteem and people's emotional reactions to success and failure. *Journal of Personality and Social Psychology, 68*, 712-722.

BRUNSTEIN, J. C. (1993). Personal goals and subjective well-being: A longitudinal study. *Journal of Personality and Social Psychology, 65,* 1061-1070.

CARVER, C. S., & SCHEIER, M. F. (1990). Principles of self-regulation: Action and emotion. In E. T. Higgins & R. M. Sorrentino (Eds.), *Handbook of motivation and social behavior* (pp. 3–52). New York: Guilford.

DAHLEN, E. R., & RYAN, M. C. (2005). The experience expression and control of anger in perceived social support. *Personality and Individual Differences, 39,* 391-401.

DETTE, D. E., ABELE, A. E., & RENNER, O. (2004). Zur Definition und Messung von Berufserfolg [Definition and measurement of occupational success]. *Zeitschrift für Personalpsychologie, 3,* 170-183.

DEMEROUTI, E., BAKKER, A. B., NACHREINER, F., & SCHAUFELI, W. B. (2001). The job demands-resources model of burnout. *Journal of Applied Psychology, 86,* 499-512.

DIENER, E., & LUCAS, R. E. (1999). Personality and subjective well-being. In D. Kahneman, E. Diener, & N. Schwarz (Eds.), *Well-being: The foundations of hedonic psychology* (pp. 213-229). New York: Russell Sage Foundation.

DOVIDIO, J. F., PILIAVIN, S. A., SCHROEDER, D. A., & PENNER, L. A. (2006). *The social psychology of prosocial behavior.* Mahwah, NJ: Lawrence Erlbaum Associates.

DYKE, L. S., & MURPHY, S. A. (2006). How we define success: A qualitative study of what matters most to women and men. *Sex Roles, 55,* 357-371.

ELFERING, A., SEMMER, N. K., TSCHAN, F., KÄLIN, W., & BUCHER, A. (2007). First years in job: A three-wave analysis of work experiences. *Journal of Vocational Behavior, 70,* 97-115.

ELLIOT, A. J., SHELDON, K. M., & CHURCH, M. A. (1997). Avoidance personal goals and subjective well-being. *Personality and Social Psychology Bulletin, 51,* 1058-1068.

ELLSWORTH, P. C., & SCHERER, K. R. (2003). Appraisal processes in emotion. In Davidson, R., J., Scherer, K. R., & Goldsmith, H. H. (Eds.), *Handbook of affective sciences* (pp. 572-595). New York: Oxford University Press.

EMMONS, R. A. (1986). Personal strivings: An approach to personality and subjective well-being. *Journal of Personality and Social Psychology, 51,* 1058-1068.

EPSTEIN, S. (1998). Cognitive-experiential self-theory. In D. F. Barone, M. Hersen, & V. B. van Hasselt (Eds.), *Advanced personality* (pp. 211-238). New York: Plenum.

FLANAGAN, J. C. (1954). The critical incident technique. *Psychological Bulletin, 51,* 327-359.

FOLKMAN, S. (2008). The case for positive emotions in the stress process. *Anxiety, Stress, & Coping, 21,* 3-14.

FOLKMAN, S. (1992). Making the case for coping. In B. Carpenter (Ed.)

Personal coping: Theory, Research, and Application (pp.31-46). New York: Praeger.

FORSYTHE, C. J., & COMPAS, B. E. (1987). Interaction of cognitive appraisals of stressful events and coping: Testing the goodness of fit hypothesis. *Cognitive Therapy and Research*, 11, 473-485.

FREDRICKSON, B. L. (2001). The role of positive emotions in positive psychology. *American Psychologist*, 56, 218-226.

FREDRICKSON, B. L., & BRANIGAN, C. (2001). Positive emotions. In T.J. Mayne & G.A. Bonnano (Eds.), *Emotions: Current Issues and Future Directions*, (pp. 123-151). New York, NY: Guilford Press.

FRESE, M., & ZAPF, D. (1994). Action as the core of work psychology: A German approach. In M. D. Dunnette, L. M. Hough, & H. C. Triandis (Eds.), *Handbook of Industrial and Organizational Psychology* (Vol. 4, pp. 271-340). Palo Alto, CA: Consulting Psychologists Press.

GARCIA-PRIETO, P., & SCHERER, K. R. (2006). Connecting social identity theory and cognitive appraisal theora of emotions. In D. Capozza & R. Brown (Eds.), *Social identities: Motivational, emotional and cultural influences* (pp. 189-207). Hove, UK: Psychology Press.

GREBNER, S., ELFERING, A., ACHERMANN, E., KNECHT, R., & SEMMER, N. K. (2008a). *Subjective Occupational Success: A resource*. Paper presented at the 7th International Conference on Occupational Stress and Health 2008: Work, Stress, and Health (APA/NIOSH), March 6-8, Washington DC, USA.

GREBNER, S., ELFERING, A., ACHERMANN, E., KNECHT, R., & SEMMER, N. K. (2008b). *Subjective occupational success as a resource: Development and validation of a multidimensional instrument*. Manuscript submitted for publication.

GREBNER, S., MAUCH, I., ZEHNDER, C., & BAUMGARTEN, J. (2008). *Gains and costs of work stressors: Challenge and hindrance stressors predict differentially subjective success*. Paper presented at the XXIX. International Congress of Psychology (ICP) 2008, July 20 – 25, Berlin, Germany.

GREBNER, S., ELFERING, A., & SEMMER, N. K. (in preparation) Adaptive coping promotes subjective occupational success. Unpublished manuscript.

GREBNER, S., ELFERING, A., SEMMER, N., KAISER-PROBST, C., & SCHLAPBACH, M. L. (2004). Stressful situations at work and in private life among young workers: An event sampling approach. *Social Indicators Research*, 67, 11-49.

HACKMAN, J. R. & OLDHAM, G. R. (1975). Development of the Job Diagnostic Survey. *Journal of Applied Psychology*, 60, 159-170.

HARRIS, C., DANIELS, K., & BRINER, R. B. (2003). A daily diary study of goals and affective well-being at work. *Journal of Occupational and Organizational Psychology*, 76, 401-410.

HESLIN, P. A. (2005). Experiencing career success. *Organizational Dynamics*, 34, 376-390.

Hobfoll, S. E. (1998). *Stress, culture, and community: The psychology and philosophy of stress.* New York: Plenum.

Hobfoll, S. E. (2001). The influence of culture, community, and the nested-self in the stress process: Advancing conservation of resources theory. *Applied Psychology: An International Review, 50,* 337 – 421.

Hobfoll, S. E. (2002). Social and psychological resources and adaptation. *General Review of Psychology, 6,* 307-324.

Ilies, R., De Pater, I. E., & Judge, T. (2007). Differential affective reactions to negative and positive feedback, and the role of self-esteem. *Journal of Managerial Psychology, 22,* 590-609.

Jex, S. M., & Bliese, P. D. (1999). Efficacy beliefs as a moderator of the effects of work-related stressors: A multilevel study. *Journal of Applied Psychology, 84,* 349-351.

Kahn, R. L., & Byosiere, P. (1992). Stress in organizations. In M. D. Dunnette & L. M. Hough (Eds.), *Handbook of Industrial and Organizational Psychology* (2nd ed., pp. 571-650). Palo Alto, CA: Consulting Psychologists Press.

Karasek, R. A. (1979). Job demands, job decision latitude, and mental strain: Implications for job redesign. Administrative Science Quarterly, 24, 285-308.

Kluger, A. N., & DeNisi, A. (1996). The effects of feedback interventions on performance: Historical review, a meta-analysis and a preliminary feedback intervention theory. *Psychological Bulletin, 119,* 254-284.

Koestner, R., Lekes, N., Powers, T. A., & Chicoine, E. (2002). Attaining personal goals: Self-concordance plus implementation intentions equals success. *Journal of Personality and Social Psychology, 83,* 231-244.

Latham G. P., & Locke, E. A. (1991). Self-regulation through goal setting. *Organizational Behavior and Human Decision Processes, 50,* 212-247.

Lazarus, R. S. (1999). *Stress and emotion. A new synthesis.* New York, NY: Springer.

LePine, J. A., Podsakoff, N. A., & LePine, M. A. (2005). A meta-analytic test of the challenge stressor-hindrance stressor framework: An explanation for inconsistent relationships among stressors and performance. *Academy of Management Journal, 48,* 764-775.

Locke, E. A., & Latham, G. P. (1990). *A theory of goal setting and task performance.* Englewood Cliffs, NJ: Prentice Hall.

Locke, E. A., & Latham G. P. (2002). Building a practically useful theory of goal setting and task motivation. *American Psychologist, 57,* 705-717.

London, M. (2003). *Job feedback. Giving, seeking, and using feedback for performance improvement.* Mahwah, NJ: Lawrence Erlbaum Associates.

Louro, M. J., Pieters, R., & Zeelenberg, M. (2007). Dynamics of multiple goal pursuit. *Journal of Personality and Social Psychology, 93,* 174-193.

Lyubomirsky, S., King, L. A., & Diener, E. (2005). The benefits of frequent positive affect: Does happiness lead to success? *Psychological Bulletin, 131,* 803-855.

Maier, G. W. (1996). *Persönliche Ziele im Unternehmen* [Personal goals in organizations]. Unpublished Dissertation, University of Munich, Germany.

Maier, G. W., & Brunstein, J. C. (2001). The role of personal work goals in newcomers' job satisfaction and organizational commitment: A longitudinal analysis. *Journal of Applied Psychology, 86,* 1034-1042.

Ng, T. W. H., Eby, L. T., Sorensen, K. L., & Feldman, D. C., (2005). Predictors of objective and subjective career success: A meta-analysis. *Personnel Psychology, 58,* 367-408.

Organ, D. W., Podsakoff, P. M., & MacKenzie, S. B. (2006). *Organizational citizenship behavior. Its nature, antecedents, and consequences.* Thousand Oaks: Sage.

Otake, K., Shimai, S., Tanaka-Matsumi, J., Otsui, K., & Fredrickson, B. L. (2006). Happy people become happier through kindness: A counting kindness intervention. *Journal of Happiness Studies, 7,* 361-375.

Pekrun, R., & Frese, M. (1992). Emotions in work and achievement. *International Review of Industrial and Organizational Psychology 1992, 7,* 153-200).

Perrez, M., & Reicherts, M. (1992). *Stress, coping, and health: A situation behavior approach: Theory, methods, applications.* Bern: Hogrefe & Huber.

Plaks, J. E. & Stecher, K. (2007). Unexpected improvement, decline, and stasis: A prediction confidence perspective on achievement success and failure. *Journal of Personality and Social Psychology, 93,* 667-684.

Podsakoff, P. M., MacKenzie, S. B., Lee, J.-Y., & Podsakoff, N. P. (2003). Common method biases in behavioral research: A critical review of the literature and recommended remedies. *Journal of Applied Psychology, 88,* 879-903.

Reicherts, M. (1988). *Diagnostik der Belastungsverarbeitung* [Diagnosis of coping with stress]. Bern: Huber.

Reicherts, M., & Pihet, S. (2000). Job newcomers coping with stressful situations: A micro-analysis of adequate coping and well-being. *Swiss Journal of Psychology, 59,* 303-316.

Riketta, M., & Ziegler, R. (2006). Self-ambivalence and reactions to success versus failure. *European Journal of Social Psychology, 37,* 547-560.

Salanova, M., Agut, S., & Peiro, J. M. (2005). Linking organizational resources and work engagement to employee performance and customer loyalty: The mediation of service climate. *Journal of Applied Psychology, 90,* 1217-1227.

Schaufeli, W. B. (2004). The future of occupational health psychology. *Applied Psychology: An International Review, 53,* 502-517.

SEIJTS, G. H., LATHAM, G. P., TASA, K., & LATHAM, B. W. (2004). Goal setting and goal orientation: An integration of two different yet related literatures. *Academy of Management Journal, 47*, 227-239.

SEMMER, N. K. (2003). Individual differences, work stress, and health. In M. J. Schabracq, J. A. M. Winnubst, & C. L. Cooper (Eds.), *Handbook of work and health psychology* (2nd ed., pp. 83-120). Chichester: Wiley.

SEMMER, N. K., & MOHR, G. (2001). Arbeit und Gesundheit: Konzepte und Ergebnisse der arbeitspsychologischen Stressforschung [Work and health: Concepts and results of psychological research on stress at work]. *Psychologische Rundschau, 52*, 150-158.

SEMMER, N. K., GREBNER, S., & ELFERING, A. (2004). Beyond self-report: Using observational, physiological, and event-based measures in research on occupational stress. In P. L. Perrewé & D. C. Ganster (Eds.), *Research in occupational stress and well-being: Vol. 3, Emotional and physiological processes and positive intervention strategies* (pp. 205-263). Amsterdam: Elsevier.

SEMMER, N. K., JACOBSHAGEN, N., MEIER, L. L., & ELFERING, A. (2007). Occupational stress research: The „Stress-as-Offense-to-Self" perspective. In J. Houdmont & S. McIntyre, (Eds.), *Occupational health psychology: European perspectives on research, education and practice, Vol. 2* (pp. 43-60). Castelo da Maia, Portugal: ISMAI Publishing.

SHELDON, K. M., & HOUSER-MARKO, L. (2001). Self-concordance, goal attainment, and the pursuit of happiness: Can there be an upward spiral? *Journal of Personality and Social Psychology, 80*, 152-165.

SHELDON, K. M., KASSER, T., SMITH, K., & SHORE, T. (2002). Personal goals and psychological growth: Testing an intervention to enhance goal attainment and personality integration. *Journal of Personality, 70*, 5-31.

SONNENTAG, S. (2002). Performance, well-being, and self-regulation. In S. Sonnentag (Ed.), *Psychological management of individual performance* (pp. 405-423). Chichester: Wiley.

SONNENTAG, S., & FRESE, M. (2003). Stress in organizations. In W. C. Borman, D. R. Ilgen, & J. R. Klimoski (Eds.), *Comprehensive handbook of psychology: Industrial and organizational psychology* (Vol. 12, pp. 453-491). New York: Wiley.

SONNENTAG, S., & FRESE, M. (2002). Performance concepts and performance theory. In S. Sonnentag (Ed.), *Psychological management of individual performance: A handbook in the psychology of management in organizations* (pp. 3-25). Chichester, UK: Wiley.

STAJKOVIC, A. D., & LUTHANS, F. (1998). Self-efficacy and work-related performance: A meta-analysis. *Psychological Bulletin, 124*, 240-261.

TANGNEY, J. P., & FISCHER, K. W. (1995). *Self-conscious emotions: The psychology of shame, guilt, embarrassment, and pride.* New York, NY: Guilford Press.

Taylor, S. M., Fisher, C. D., & Ilgen, D. R. (1984). Individuals' reactions to performance feedback in organizations: A control theory perspective. In K. M. Rowland & G. R. Ferris (Eds.), *Research in Personnel and Human Resources Management, 2*, 81-124.

Viswesvaran, C., Sanchez, J., & Fisher, J. (1999). The role of social support in the process of work stress. *Journal of Vocational Behavior, 54*, 314-334.

Vitaliano, P. P., Dewolfe, D. J., Maiuro, R. D., Russo, J., & Katon, W. (1990). Appraised changeability of a stressor as a modifier of the relationship between coping and depression: A test of the hypothesis of fit. *Journal of Personality and Social Psychology, 59*, 582-592.

Weiss, H. M., & Cropanzano, R. (1996). An effective events approach to job satisfaction. In B. M. Staw & L. L. Cummings (Eds.), *Research in organizational behavior, 18*, pp. 1-74. Greenwich, CT: JAI Press.

Wiese, B. S., Freund, A. M., & Baltes, P. B. (2000). Selection, optimisation, and compensation: An action-related approach to work and partnership. *Journal of Vocational Behavior, 57*, 273-300.

Wiese, B. S., & Freund, A. (2005). Goal progress makes one happy, or does it? Longitudinal findings from the work domain. *Journal of Occupational and Organizational Psychology, 78*, 287-304.

Wiese, B. S. (2007). Successful pursuit of personal goals and subjective well-being. In B. R. Little, K. Salmela-Aro, & S. D. Phillips. (Eds), *Personal project pursuit: Goals, action, and human flourishing* (pp. 301-328). Mahwah, NJ: Lawrence Erlbaum Associate Publishers.

STRESS MODELS: A REVIEW AND SUGGESTED NEW DIRECTION

George M. Mark and Andrew P. Smith

CHAPTER OVERVIEW

This chapter gives an overview of how changes in the nature of many work environments have led to increases in stressful job characteristics, and how these characteristics may be implicated in many stress-related physical and psychological problems. The economic and human consequences of these issues are outlined, and the nature of 'work stress' is defined. Many of the major theoretical models that depict the stress process are described, with particular attention paid to the most influential. It is proposed that while current stress models present fruitful frameworks for stress research, many existing models suffer from being either too narrow in scope and lacking a role for individual differences, or too broad and complex, and lacking in predictive validity. A new approach that combines many of the features of existing models is proposed, which includes strong roles for psychosocial stressors, individual differences, and subjective perceptions. Some research based on this new approach is briefly described, and it is suggested that the proposed model could be a useful new direction for stress research.

THE CHANGING WORK ENVIRONMENT AND ITS EFFECTS

It is a common perception that working life is changing in Britain and across the world, and these changes have led to new challenges and problems for organisations and employees. In recent years this has been characterised by the decline of manufacturing and many forms of industry in the UK, the advance of IT and the service sector, more short-term contracts, outsourcing, mergers, automatisation, trade union declines, globalisation and more international competition (Cox & Griffiths, 1995; Schabracq & Cooper, 2000). The majority of these changes mean that workers are under growing pressure to compete, adapt, and learn new skills in order to meet the demands of their work (Cox & Griffiths, 1995). Schabracq and Cooper (2000) state that the combination of new technology, globalised economies, and new organisational products and processes, have caused unprecedented changes and increasing stakes.

These shifts in the nature of organisations may result in increasingly "stressful" working environments, which can be manifested in many forms. These include a lack of control at work, shorter holidays, longer hours, insufficient rewards, job insecurity, poor promotion prospects, increased time pressure, lack of support, poor feedback, isolation, harassment, role conflict, and work-life balance issues (Griffiths, 1998). The UK Health and Safety Executive (HSE, 2007) has attempted to categorise the key work design factors which may relate to stress-related health issues. These are presented as part of a "Management Standards" framework and include: Demands; Control; Support; Relationships; Role; and Organisational change.

All of the pressures listed above are known as "psychosocial stressors", and these have been implicated as risk factors for many physical and psychological problems, including increased risks of heart disease, gastro-intestinal problems, anxiety, depression, burnout, absence, fatigue, accidents, substance misuse, musculoskeletal disorders, work-family conflict, and many other problems (Cox & Griffiths, 1995; Gianakos, 2002; HSE, 2007). These outcomes can also have serious consequences for employers, potentially leading to high turnover, absence, strikes, decreased productivity, low morale, etc.

THE ECONOMIC AND HEALTH COSTS OF STRESS RELATED ILLNESS

The economic and health costs of stressful work environments may be much greater than many suspect. Cardiovascular illness has been strongly implicated as a potential health outcome for those exposed to stressful work conditions (Karasek, 1979). In Britain, heart disease accounts for a loss of 70 million working days per year and causes 180,000 deaths (Earnshaw & Cooper, 1994). Alcohol misuse, which may be related to work stress in some individuals, costs the UK economy an estimated £2.2 billion from sickness absence and turnover (Earnshaw & Cooper, 1994).

The Confederation of British Industry claims that the average cost to businesses of sickness absence, including musculoskeletal disorders in 2003 was £11 billion (a 3.7% rise over 2002) or £588 per employee. Cox, Griffiths, and Rial-Gonzalez (2000) cite an EU study from 1996 which showed that 29% of surveyed workers believed that work had affected their health, with 23% of respondents claiming to have been absent from work in the previous 12 months due to stress-related issues. The study found that the average number of days absent was 4 days per year, or 600 million working days across the EU. A study of 46,000 US employees by Goetzel, Anderson, Whitmer, Ozminkowski, Dunn and Wasserman (1998) showed that the health care costs of those suffering from high levels of stress were 46% higher than those not suffering stress.

A large body of literature also suggests that work stress is closely related to anxiety and depression (Wang & Patten, 2001) and Tennant (2001) suggests that depression is the most likely adverse psychological outcome of exposure to work stress. A survey by Hodgson, Jones, Elliot, and Osman (1993) found that musculoskeletal disorders, job stress and depression were the three most commonly mentioned problems in a UK sample. Gabriel (2000) found that increased stressors at work were significantly related to increased incidence of depression and anxiety, and states that depression costs the US economy over $47 billion, and 200 million lost working days per year.

Statistics released in 2007 by the UK Health and Safety Executive, stated that from 2005-06 (HSE, 2007) work-related stress, depression, and anxiety, cost the UK economy £530 million, with 530,000 workers thought to have sought medical advice for work-related stress. Overall, 30 million working days were lost due to work related ill-health, with 6 million lost due to workplace injury. Finally, Arnold, Cooper and Robertson stated in 1995 that some estimated the total cost of sickness absence in the UK to be as much as 10% of the Gross National Product.

THE NATURE OF WORK STRESS

Cox and Griffiths (1995) suggest that many believe that there is no consensus as to the definition of the term stress, and Dewe and Trenberth (2004) claim that it is almost a tradition in work stress research to point out the difficulties surrounding the various definitions of stress. However, despite all the hyperbole, Cox and Griffiths (1995) state that, there are really only three different types of conceptions of the nature of stress. First is the "engineering" approach, where stress is seen as a stimulus or characteristic of the environment in the form of level of demand. Second is the physiological approach, where the definition of stress is based upon the physiological or biological changes that occur in the person when they are in a stress state, e.g. as a dependent variable based on neuroendocrine activation. The third view is termed the psychological approach by Cox and Griffiths (1995) where stress is not conceived of as a mere stimulus or response, but is itself the dynamic process that occurs as an individual interacts with their environment (Cox, Griffiths & Rial-Gonzales, 2000; Cox & Mackay, 1981).

The psychological viewpoint is perhaps the most popular conceptualisation today and is considered superior by Cox and Griffiths (1995) as the engineering and physiological approaches treat people as passive vehicles for stimulus and response, and cannot account for the effects of cognitive or situational factors on performance and well-being.

There are many different models of workplace stress which are important in guiding research and practice, and these vary in popularity and empirical support. A selection of key frameworks will be outlined below, including influential models from the past and present, as well as some of the more up-to-date frameworks.

THEORIES AND MODELS OF STRESS AND WELLBEING AT WORK: PERSON-ENVIRONMENT FIT

Lewin (1951) observed that an individual's personal characteristics interacted with their work environment to determine strain, and consequent behaviour and health. This concept was developed into the Person-Environment fit model (French, 1973), which suggests that the match between a person and their work environment is key in influencing their health. For healthy conditions, it is necessary that employees' attitudes, skills, abilities and resources match the demands of their job, and that work environments should meet workers' needs, knowledge, and skills potential. Lack of fit in either of these domains can cause problems, and the greater the gap or misfit (either subjective or objective) between the person and their environment, the greater the strain as demands exceed abilities, and need exceeds supply (Sonnentag & Frese, 2003). These strains can relate to health related issues, lower productivity, and other work problems (French, Caplan & Harrison, 1982). Defence mechanisms, such as denial, reappraisal of needs, and coping, also operate in the model, to try and reduce subjective misfit (Buunk, deJonge, Ybema & deWolff, 1998).

Lazarus (1991) states that the P-E fit model represented an advance in thinking, but that the concept of fit between the person and environment is treated as static, with emphasis on stable relationships rather than the changing process of action and interaction in work contexts. Buunk et al. (1998) state that empirical support for the theory is limited.

THE JOB CHARACTERISTICS MODEL

Hackman and Oldham's (1980) job characteristics model focuses on important aspects of job characteristics, such as skill variety, task identity, task significance, autonomy, and feedback. These characteristics are proposed to lead to 'critical psychological states' of experienced meaningfulness, and experienced responsibility and knowledge of outcomes. It is proposed that positive or negative work characteristics give rise to mental states which lead to corresponding cognitive and behavioural outcomes, e.g. motivation, satisfaction, absenteeism, etc. In conjunction with the model, Hackman and Oldham (1980) developed the Job Diagnostic Survey, a questionnaire for job analysis, which implies key types of job-redesign including combining tasks, creating feedback methods, job enrichment, etc.

Kompier (2003) states that there is an impressive literature relating the outcome variables to the core job characteristics. The model is also well integrated with the Job Diagnostic Survey, however there is limited variety in the core job characteristics, with only a small number of key psychological states considered.

THE VITAMIN MODEL

The Vitamin Model (Warr, 1987) proposes that certain job characteristics have an effect on mental health that is analogous to the way that vitamins work in the human body. Simply put, some job characteristics have "constant effects" where health increases linearly with increasing "dose" up to a threshold, after which increased dose has no positive or negative effect, and these may include salary, safety, and task significance (Buunk et al. 1998). Alternately, some have a curvilinear or "additional decrement" effect, where moderate levels are the most beneficial, but too much or too little can have negative health effects, for example job demands, autonomy, social support, skill utilisation, skill variety, and task feedback (van Veldhoven, de Jonge, Broersen, Kompier, & Meijman, 2002). Affective well-being is expressed in the model on three dimensions of discontent-content, anxious-comfortable, and depressed-pleased and individual characteristics can moderate the effect of job characteristics on health (Buunk et al, 1998).

Despite the interesting premise of the Vitamin model, both Sonnentag & Frese (2003) and Buunk et al. (1998) state that evidence for the model is mixed and inconclusive, and van Veldhoven, Taris, de Jonge, and Broersen (2005) state that the full model has yet to be empirically investigated.

THE MICHIGAN MODEL

The Michigan Model is based on a framework established by French and Kahn at the University of Michigan in 1962, and is sometimes known as the ISR model (Institute of Social Research) the Social Environment Model, or the Role Stress Approach. Like the P-E fit model (French et al., 1982) the Michigan Model (Caplan, Cobb, French, Harrison, Pinneau, 1975) also places much emphasis on the individual's own subjective perceptions of stressors. Environmental stressors, such as role ambiguity, conflict, lack of participation, job security, workload, lack of challenge etc, are subjectively perceived, and personality variables, demographics, and social support moderate these perceptions to lead to health outcomes (Kompier, 2003). Role issues, such as role conflict, role ambiguity, and role expectations are particularly central stressors, hence why it is sometimes known as the Role Stress Approach (Kompier, 2003).

The model was refined by Hurrell and McLaney (1988) from the U.S. National Institute of Occupational Safety and Health to result in what is known as the NIOSH model, which as well as specifying examples of how stressors, individual differences, acute reactions, and illness outcomes occur, also focuses more on the role of objective workplace factors in the aetiology of work stress (Huang, Feurstein, & Sauter, 2002).

Buunk et al. (1998) state that the Michigan model does not have a clear theoretical perspective that easily leads to specific hypotheses, and the model is hard to empirically evaluate due to its complexity. Mixed support was found for aspects of a simplified Michigan Model in regards to the relationship between managerial support and job satisfaction by Jones, Smith, and Johnston (2005), however a general lack of empirical support means it does not have much predictive validity for health outcomes, unlike other models such as the well-known Demand-Control model (Karasek, 1979).

DEMAND CONTROL SUPPORT MODEL

The Demands-Control model (Karasek 1979) is currently perhaps the most influential model of stress in the workplace (Kompier, 2003) and the original model focuses on the two psychosocial job characteristics of job demands and job control. The latter factor is sometimes called decision latitude (Karasek, 1979) and is made up of the sub-factors of decision authority (control over work situation) and skill discretion (possibility of using learnt skills and competencies). Cox and Griffiths (1995) call the demand-control model an "interactional" model, as it focuses on the structural features of an individual's interactions with their environment (as opposed to the process of what is occurring in this interaction).

Karasek's (1979) research showed that those exposed to high levels of demand, as well as having low levels of job control (high-strain situation) were disproportionately more likely to show increased levels of depression, fatigue, and cardiovascular disease and mortality. However, the lowest levels of illness were in individuals with moderate or even high demands, if they also had high levels of job control (challenge situation). Karasek (1979) thus proposed an interaction where high demands and low control would predict high strain, but that high control would buffer the negative effect of demands on outcomes. The model was expanded (Johnson & Hall, 1988) to include social support (DCS) as evidence suggested that support may act as a buffer in high demand situations (Cooper, Dewe, & O'Driscoll, 2001; Karasek & Theorell, 1990; Lim, 1996).

There is significant evidence in a variety of populations associating health outcomes with control, demands, and support (Van der Doef and Maes, 1999). However, there is mixed support for the interactive effects of demands and controls, with some claiming these effects to be largely additive (Warr, 1990).

Despite the later inclusion of social support, the model is limited in the number of job characteristics it considers, which may not reflect the dynamic multi-stressor nature of modern workplaces. While the model has good predictive validity at the macro level, it does not take account of individual differences in susceptibility to stressors, and can't explain why the same levels of demand and control in two individuals may give rise to different behavioural or health outcomes (Perrewe and Zellars, 1999). This issue may be related to the "oversimplification assumption" (Payne, Jick & Burke, 1982) which can arise from too great a focus on environmental demands, and is the notion that the presence of an environmental demand is an indication that the event is demanding, when in some cases for some individuals it is not.

Other criticisms of the DCS model include its definition of demand as based primarily on workload and not other types of demand (Cox et al. 2000) and that the conceptualisation of control is quite a narrow view of this multi-dimensional construct (Carayon, 1993). The DCS model also assumes that high control is always a desirable state (and a positive moderator of negative demands) however it could be argued that some individuals may not see job control as desirable, and may find having control a stressor in itself, for example if they have a low sense of self efficacy.

The implications for job redesign are that healthy jobs ought to have high levels of control without extreme levels of demand, and with wide networks of social support. The efficacy of these measures has been reported by Van der Doef & Maes (1998) Ganster (1995) and Kristensen (1995). The DCS is a popular and influential model of workplace stress with good predictive validity, however it is limited in encapsulating the complexities of the stress process, and could perhaps be most useful when used in conjunction with other models, particularly those that may include individual difference components.

TRANSACTIONAL THEORIES OF STRESS

Cox and Griffiths (1995) make a distinction between two types of psychological model of work stress: interactional or structural approaches, such as the DCS model; and transactional or process models.

Interactional models focus on the structural characteristics of the stress process, i.e. which stressors are likely to lead to which outcomes in which populations, however transactional views are more cognitive, and focus on the dynamic relationship that occurs between individuals and their environment in terms of mental and emotional processes (Cox et al. 2000). Transactional views often place emphasis on the role of subjective perceptions of the environment, and are more likely to acknowledge the possible impact of individual difference factors, such as differences in coping, appraisal, personality, locus of control etc. Some of the main models with these features in the occupational stress literature are described below.

EFFORT-REWARD IMBALANCE

The Effort-Reward imbalance model (ERI: Siegrist, 1996) is a popular view of stress at work, that like DCS model, was developed with a focus on cardiovascular disease (Siegrist, 1996). The ERI model has some key transactional features, as it places emphasis on subjective perceptions of the environment, however the role of individual differences and the explication of internal processes is less developed than in other transactional models, such as those by Folkman and Lazarus (1980) and Cox (1987).

The key concept of ERI is one of reciprocity, where effort at work should be compensated by suitable rewards, and a mismatch between these will lead to stressful experiences (Peter & Siegrist, 1999). Rewards are defined as money, esteem, career opportunities, and security. Effort is proposed to have two components: intrinsic effort, from the personal motivations of the individual, such as a need for control and overcommitment (a tendency to make excessive efforts or be committed to unrealistic goals); and extrinsic motivations, or external pressures, such as workload (similar to the concept of job demands in the DCS model, Kompier, 2003). External demands are also proposed to relate to the status of the labour market and how easily alternative employment can be found.

According to Peter and Siegrist (1999) the DCS model is only concerned with extrinsic factors, whereas the ERI uses extrinsic factors (extrinsic effort) and intrinsic factors (overcommitment). The ERI model also differs from the DCS model in that it is not the "actual" level of mismatch between efforts and rewards that is important, but rather their perceived mismatch (Siegrist, 1996). This implies a role for individual differences, as different subjective perceptions are likely to result from variability between individuals, however how this may happen in practice is not explored in the model.

There is much support for the principles of the ERI model, including Siegrist, Peter, Junge, Cremer and Seidel (1990) and the Whitehall II studies (Bosma, Peter, Siegrist, & Marmot, 1998) which showed significantly elevated risks of heart disease in those exposed to high effort-low reward conditions, compared to low effort and/or high reward. Van Vegchel, de Jonge, Bakker, and Schaufeli (2002) also found strong effects for the reward components relating to self-esteem and job security on psychosomatic complaints and exhaustion, and de Jonge, Bosma, Peter, and Siegrist (2000) found that individuals with high efforts and low rewards were up to 21 times more likely to suffer emotional exhaustion than those with low efforts and high rewards.

The relationship between effort and rewards can be operationalised in different ways, including as a ratio of efforts divided by rewards multiplied by a correction factor (where zero indicates low efforts and high rewards, and values beyond 1 indicating high efforts not met by rewards) and as a multiplicative interaction term. Van Vegchel, de Jonge, Bosma, and Schaufeli (2005) compared results using these different methods and found evidence that the latter ratio term may be better at significantly predicting outcomes.

The ERI expands on the DCS model in several key ways and the predictive validity of the model also appears good, however the role of individual differences is limited to the intrinsic effort dimension, and there are no proposed mechanisms by which individual differences may influence the stress perception process. Kompier (2003) states that ERI doesn't provide a detailed redesign theory, but like the DCS model implies basic design principles. However research has shown that there is some scope for the DCS and ERI models to be used in conjunction, as each can add cumulatively to the explanation of variance in emotional and physical health outcomes (de Jonge et al. 2000).

THE COGNITIVE THEORY OF PSYCHOLOGICAL STRESS AND COPING

Lazarus and Folkman's theory of psychological stress and coping (1980) is perhaps the most theoretically influential transactional theory. Sometimes known as the Cognitive-Relational approach, the individual and their environment are seen as coexisting in a dynamic relationship, where stress is the psychological and emotional state that is internally represented as part of a stressful transaction (Folkman, Lazarus, Gruen & DeLongis, 1986). The two key concepts in this process are appraisal and coping (Cox et al., 2000).

Folkman et al (1986) describe primary appraisal as the first stage of the appraisal process, where encounters are subjectively evaluated to see what is at stake in terms of potential risk (Perrewe & Zellars, 1999) and these assessments allow for the influence of individual differences, because the nature of what is considered stressful is individual-specific (Park & Folkman, 1997).

In later work, Park and Folkman (1997) write that the attribution of meaning that individuals give to events, can be framed by existing beliefs based on their global meaning. These are enduring beliefs and valued goals, based on fundamental assumptions, theories of reality (e.g. religion), self-worth, life experience etc. Park and Folkman (1997) propose that the making of situational meaning is what occurs when an individual's global beliefs and goals interact with the specifics of a particular person-environment transaction which are defined by the processes of appraisal and coping.

If a situation is evaluated as potentially stressful, then secondary appraisal occurs, which is where the individual evaluates if the potential harm can be altered, avoided or prevented (Park & Folkman, 1997), where to assign blame or credit, and what future expectations are. Potential actions or ways of coping are assessed, informed by past coping experience, personality, personal resources (and presumably global meaning). Folkman and Lazarus (1980) described many types of coping behaviours, and suggested that they could be aggregated into two major categories of coping response: problem-focused coping (attempts to cope using more rational problem solving type approaches) or emotion-focused coping (emotional-oriented coping approaches) each of which are suitable in different kinds of situation. While the problem focused/emotion focused distinction has been popular in research, many argue that it is important to split coping into more distinct categories (many based on Folkman and Lazarus' work) such as problem focused coping, seeking social support, blamed self, wishful thinking, and avoidance (Vitaliano, Russo, Carr, Maiuro, and Becker, 1985) and action oriented coping, accommodation, positive thinking, seeking support, self blame and defence (Falkum, Olff, and Aasland, 1997).

Once possible coping methods are assessed and selected, then the final stage of the model occurs, where coping is implemented. Coping has been characterised as (Folkman et al, 1986) "cognitive and behavioural efforts to manage (reduce, minimise, master, or tolerate) the internal and external demands of the person-environment transaction that is appraised as taxing or exceeding the person's resources". Park and Folkman (1997) suggest that coping is the main method by which incongruence between global meaning and situational meaning is managed. A failure to cope successfully (from excessive demands or lack of resources) is likely to lead to stress and negative health and organisational outcomes (Cox et al. 2000).

The cognitive-relational model gives weight to the job situation, subjective perceptions, and the potential influence of various individual differences factors, and indeed Lazarus argues (1991) that many stress management interventions fail because they treat all people as if they were alike, and it is useful to view the individual, the group, and the workplace as a single analytic unit, rather than separate variables which are to be manipulated independently.

The complexity of this model means that it is hard to empirically evaluate, however examples include: Folkman et al. (1986) where personality, primary appraisal, secondary appraisal and coping were investigated in stressful situations in a sample of 150 adults, and support was found for aspects of the model in the prediction of psychological symptoms; and Dewe (1991) who found that primary and secondary appraisal factors, and coping, contributed significantly to the prediction of emotional discomfort in a workplace sample. There has also been a large amount of research on the relationship between coping and health outcomes in a variety of situations. Zeidner (1994) found that emotion focused coping significantly predicted anxiety during university finals, and those with less active coping behaviours showed higher levels of depression, and Haghighatgou and Peterson (1995) found similar results in a sample of Iranian students. Lease (1999) found that avoidance coping significantly predicted role stress in academics. Welbourne, Eggerth, Hartley, Andrew, and Sanchez

(2007) found that problem-solving coping associated with increased job satisfaction, and finally, Tong, Bishop, Diong, Enklemann, Why, Ang and Khader (2004) who found that stress experience was associated with avoidance and re-appraisal coping.

Cooper et al. (2001) and Cox and Ferguson (1991) have stated that despite the widespread use of the term "coping" there are difficulties surrounding its definition, as it can be seen as a process, a behaviour, as a stable trait, or as situation specific, and Briner, Harris and Daniels (2004) have suggested that the conception of appraisal is too simplistic and doesn't include individuals' histories, and anticipated futures. Cox (1987) also states that the processes discussed may not be as rational as presented in transactional theories.

COX'S TRANSACTIONAL MODEL OF OCCUPATIONAL STRESS

Cox's transactional model of work stress (Cox, 1978; Cox & Mackay, 1981; Cox et al, 2000) is closely related to the work of Lazarus and colleagues and many of the processes and stages in the two models are similar, however there are certain important differences in Cox's model, particularly a clarified structure and greater focus on occupational health and individual differences (Cox & Ferguson, 1991).

Cox's framework (1978) has five stages. The first stage represents the demand or job characteristics of the environment, and the second stage represents the individuals' perceptions of these demands relative to their ability to cope (Cox et al., 2000). These two stages could be seen as analogous to the primary appraisal stage of Folkman and Lazarus' model (1981). Stress is conceptualised as being the psychological state that occurs when there is a mismatch between perceptions of the significance of a demand, and beliefs about one's ability to cope with it (Cox et al, 2000). Cox and Ferguson (1991) describe how this primary appraisal process is influenced by the internal and external demands experienced, as well as coping abilities and resources, and support from others.

The third stage of the model is associated with the mental and physical changes that the person undergoes as a result of the recognition of a stress state, and involves secondary appraisal and coping, which are analogous to those in Folkman and Lazarus' model (Cox et al, 2000). Cox and Ferguson (1991) describe the psychological changes that occur in a stress state, including mood change, emotional experience, e.g. tension, feeling worn out, or depressed etc, as the defining feature of the stress state for the individual. Thus the awareness of a stressful problem initiates a cycle of behaviours that are "an adjustment to the situation, or an adjustment of the situation" failure of which leads to negative health outcomes. The fourth stage of the model represents the outcomes or consequences of coping, and finally, the fifth and last stage is feedback which is proposed to occur in relation to all other stages (Cox et al, 2000).

Cox and Ferguson (1991) state that primary appraisal is a continual monitoring process, and secondary appraisal is a distinct decision making process, and that the entire stress process is grounded in a "problem solving" context. Cox (1987) writes that the basic framework for this context involves recognition of a problem, diagnosis, suggestion of possible solutions, evaluation of suggested solutions, implementation, feedback, and learning, and that such a problem-solving approach can also be used as the basis for organisational interventions.

Cox and Ferguson (1991) make a point of stressing the importance of individual differences in this transactional model. Differences in locus of control, hardiness, and coping resources are deemed particularly important, and may exert effects in the model via a mediating role in appraisal, and a moderating role in helping to determine health outcomes.

A clearer structure, the inclusion of a feedback stage, and the emphasis on individual differences which exert an influence by mediation and moderation, represent important steps forward over many other models, however Cox warns that in reality, the problem solving process in a stress setting is unlikely to be so rational (Cox, 1987). For example, appraisal and coping processes may not be open to such conscious evaluation, and may be carried out with bias, insufficient information, to appear irrational or counterproductive, with consideration of a limited number of solutions, and with little or no attention paid to feedback or past learning. However, it could be argued that these problems could be what makes the difference between successful and unsuccessful problem-solving episodes.

Much of the evidence related to the above model is very similar to that related to Folkman and Lazarus' model, for example research on coping and appraisal. However, while there is plenty of supporting research on the main effects of individual difference factors such as hardiness, locus of control, self-efficacy, and their relationship to health outcomes, results into the mediating and moderating roles of these factors are far less conclusive (see Cooper et al., 2001; Spector, 2003; Parkes, 1994). Moreover, like the cognitive-relational approach, the very complexity of Cox's model means that it is hard to empirically capture, unlike the more simple models of Karasek (1979) and Siegrist (1996).

DEMAND-SKILL-SUPPORT MODEL

Recently a newer wave of stress models have emerged that take important aspects of existing models and try to develop them in new ways. Examples of these include the Demand-Skill-Support model, Demand-Induced-Strain-Compensation model, and the Job-Demands-Resources model.
The Demand-Skill-Support model (DSS: van Veldhoven, Taris, de Jonge, & Broersen, 2005) was developed largely based on the DCS model (Karasek and Theorell, 1990) with the aim of specifying a model as parsimonious as possible (i.e., with a minimum number of factors) that still would be able to predict stress in a wide variety of situations and occupations.

On a sample of 37,000 Dutch employees in four branches of industry, van Veldhoven et al. (2005) investigated the relationships between pace and amount of work, physical effort, skill utilisation, task autonomy, quality of social relationships with colleagues, quality of relationships with supervisor, and job security, with the outcome variables of work-related fatigue, task satisfaction, and organisational commitment. The best fit to the data was found to be a model that included the four factors of physical and time demands, skill utilisation, and quality of social relationships (combined for colleagues and co-workers). Task autonomy and job security did not make significant improvements in predicting outcomes over the above four factors.

On the basis of the results, van Veldhoven et al. (2005) proposed that quantitative and qualitative demands were more likely to relate to health outcomes and strain, and skill utilisation, and social support were more likely to relate to attitudinal outcomes and wellbeing. The four-factor solution was also found to be a good fit for the data over four branches of industry, suggesting it could be applied to a range of occupational situations.

While the model was formulated with parsimony in mind, the authors do acknowledge that only a limited number of job characteristics were used, and the model could perhaps be improved with the inclusion of more factors. However they conclude that a general four-factor DCS based model is a good starting point for research.

The sample size used for the development of this model is impressive, however the DSS gives little recognition of the impact of individual differences in the stress process, or subjective perceptions of job demands. This method is in line with the authors' stated aims of a parsimonious model that captures aspects of stressful environments with the minimum of factors, and such a model could be useful as a preliminary screening tool to get a broad view of the levels of stressors in an organisation. However it goes against the popular trend of viewing stress as a relative, subjective, and transactional process (Dewe, 1991; Dewe & Trenberth, 2004; Perrewe & Zellars, 1999; Florio, Donnelly, & Zevon, 1998; Frese & Zapf, 1999; Spector, 2003). The DSS may benefit from further testing with the inclusion of other job characteristics.

DEMAND INDUCED STRAIN COMPENSATION MODEL

De Jonge et al. (2000) found that sub-factors of the Demands-Control-Support and Effort-Reward-Imbalance models had independent cumulative effects in the prediction of emotional exhaustion, job satisfaction, and psychosomatic and physical health complaints. Similar results were found by Rydstedt, Devereaux and Sverke (2007) and both they and de Jonge et al. (2000) conclude that future research should look to refining and combining aspects of these two models.

An approach that attempts to do this is the Demand-Induced-Strain-Compensation model which uses factors from the above models (de Jonge & Dormann, 2003). The model was developed particularly with a focus on stress in service jobs. The central assumption of the model is that there are various types of demands and resources, and that each of these are matched, so that emotional demands at work are most likely to be compensated for by emotional resources, cognitive demands by cognitive resources, and physical demands by physical resources (van Veldhoven et al., 2005). Furthermore the strongest interactions between demands and resources are likely to occur also on these qualitatively matched dimensions, and that each of these interactions is related to a particular type of emotional or affective outcome (Van Vegchel et al., 2005). For example, if high behavioural demands are met with low behavioural resources, high cognitive demands with low cognitive resources, and high emotional demands with low emotional resources, then adverse health is likely to result. However, if high demands in each dimension are met with high resources, then motivation, learning and growth are likely to result. This has been called the "triple match principle" (de Jonge & Dormann, 2003). The model therefore takes the principles of balance, reciprocity, demands, and resources of different types, from the ERI and DCS models. More research is needed on this model, particularly with respect to the interesting hypothesis that resources in a particular domain are best compensated by resources in the same domain, however citing de Jonge and Dormann (2004), Van Vegchel et al. (2005) state that preliminary results are promising.

THE JOB DEMANDS-RESOURCES MODEL

Finally, an interesting new approach that attempts to develop and expand upon existing research is the Job Demands-Resources Model (JD-R: Demerouti, Bakker, Nachreiner & Schaufeli, 2001). The JD-R model takes cues from several of the approaches described above, and categorises psychosocial factors into the global categories of job demands and job resources to see how these may influence illness and organisational commitment (Llorens, Bakker, Schaufeli, & Salanova, 2006). Demands are said to be physical or social aspects of a job that require efforts and thus have physical and mental costs, and resources as workplace or organisational aspects that help with the achievement of work goals, reduce demands, or stimulate growth and development. Demanding and resource providing job conditions influence the key processes of health impairment and motivation. Burnout and work engagement are proposed to be opposing psychological states that lead to health effects (Llorens et al., 2006) e.g. organisational commitment may be damaged by burnout through the health impairment process, or boosted by engagement through the motivation process.

Llorens et al. (2006) maintain that the JD-R is a heuristic, overarching model, the principles of which can be applied to any occupational setting regardless of the particular demands or resources involved. The JD-R model also expands upon the DCS model by stating that many different resources may buffer the impact of many different demands on stress outcomes (Bakker, Demerouti, and Euwema, 2005). Research has supported aspects of the model, for example Llorens et al. (2006) show that burnout mediates a negative relationship between job demands and organisational commitment in Dutch and Spanish samples, and engagement plays a mediating role in the relationship between resources and commitment. Also, Bakker et al. (2005) showed that interactions between demands and resources explained a unique proportion of the variance in exhaustion and cynicism outcomes.

Xanthopoulou, Bakker, Demerouti and Schaufeli (2007) state that despite the support that has been gained for the JD-R model, its basis on a tradition of research derived from the demands-control model of Karasek (1979) means that much research on the JD-R has focused only on the characteristics of the work environment. Xanthopoulou et al. (2007) have attempted to further the research based on the JD-R model, by adding the category of personal resources, i.e., characteristics that contribute to resiliency, such as general self-efficacy, organisational based self-esteem (OBSE), optimism etc, and that these resources should moderate and mediate the relationships between environment and outcomes. Xanthopoulou et al.

(2007) cite past research that has supported a moderating role of efficacy, self esteem, and optimism on outcomes (including Van Yperen & Snijders, 2000, Pierce & Gardner, 2004, and Mäkikangas & Kinnunen, 2003). Unfortunately, Xanthopoulou et al. (2007) found no moderating role for personal resources. However evidence was found that personal resources mediated the relationship between job resources, and work engagement and exhaustion.

Despite the mixed support for a role of personal resources in the JD-R framework, the model represents a theoretical step forward over the JDC and DSS models, and the addition of personal factors into a job demands and resources-based model may well be a fruitful direction for future research.

THE IMPORTANCE OF INDIVIDUAL DIFFERENCES

The sections above describe a range of important stress models that have been influential in the field of work stress research. It is clear that there are models of different types, for example those that mainly focus on job characteristics, such as the DCS and DSS models, and those include a role for subjective perceptions of stressors, such as the Michigan and P-E fit models, and models such as the ERI that combine aspects of these features. There are the models that focus on the psychological processes that may occur in stressful interactions, such as the transactional models of Folkman and Lazarus, and Cox, and finally there are models that try and combine aspects of all of the above models, such as the DISC and JD-R models.

While these distinctions are useful for understanding the development of stress models, there is another feature of stress frameworks that is important. This feature is whether or not the framework takes account or includes a role for individual difference variables. While the possible influence of Individual Differences is implicit in models that treat stressors as subjective (such as the ERI model and others) few models actually have an explicit role for individual difference factors integrated into them. The ERI model has the ID factor of intrinsic effort, but this factor is narrow and its influence on subjective perceptions is not specified. The theories of Folkman and Lazarus (1980) and Cox (1987) pay specific attention to the individual factors of coping styles, and new research on the JD-R model includes a role for self-esteem, efficacy, and optimism, but in other models an explicit role for ID factors is uncommon.

There are a large range of individual difference variables (IDs) that may be involved in the stress process. These include trait anxiety, NA, personality, self esteem, locus of control, coping style, hardiness, type A, attributional style, demographics, expectations, preferences, commitment, health related factors, and abilities and skills (Payne, 1988; Parkes, 1994).

Cox and Ferguson (1991) state that ID factors are often seen to function in the stress process as either "components or mediators of stress appraisal" or as "moderators of the stress-outcome relationship". Mediators are variables that transmit an effect (for example by affecting primary appraisal, Cox & Ferguson, 1991) but do not qualitatively change the effect (Baron & Kenny, 1986) and moderators are variables that change the direction or strength of a relationship between other variables (Cox & Ferguson, 1991) or determine when certain responses to stress will occur (for example affecting secondary appraisal and coping processes).

Parkes (1994) argues that research into individual differences is necessary to clarify their effects in predicting stress, and to implement person and environment focused interventions. Briner, Harris and Daniels (2004) state that individual contexts and behaviour are vital to understand the causes of strain, stress, and coping, and that it may make no sense to consider stressful job characteristics as "out there" without subjective individual perceptions taken into account. Indeed Briner et al. (2004) propose that stressors are not even stressors if the individual does not perceive them as such, a viewpoint echoed in models such as Person-Environment fit, the ERI model, and the transactional models of Folkman and Lazarus and Cox.

A GAP IN THE LITERATURE?

The number of stress models described illustrates how many different viewpoints there are of occupational stress, and show how complex these processes may be, and while the range of stress models in the workplace is impressive, certain viewpoints have historically been more popular. Dewe claimed in 1991 that the primary concern for many years in occupational research had been to explore the relationship between stimulus and response, and that despite the advances in alternate views with a more relational perspective, there had still been no real attempt to actually understand what stress actually is. Dewe (1991) argued that there was a need to develop theoretical and empirically supported transactional frameworks using appropriate measurement strategies. Schaubroeck agreed in 1999 and stated that there was no well-accepted working model of appraisal and coping processes, despite a requirement for one. However, little seemed to have changed by 2004, when Briner, Harris and Daniels claimed that very little stress research makes a new contribution, with only a narrow range of methods used in the study of stress. Further, they claimed that there is little new theory and that a fundamental reappraisal of the field was needed.

Dewe (1991) argued that transactional perspectives were largely accepted at a conceptual level by most researchers, and individual differences and subjective perceptions were seen by many as integral to the entire stress process (for example Parkes, 1994, and Cox & Ferguson, 1991). Indeed, many authors such as Dewe (1991), Dewe and Trenberth (2004), Perrewe and Zellars (1999), Florio, Donnelly, and Zevon (1998), Frese and Zapf (1999), and Spector (2003) suggest that transactional conceptualisations are ecologically valid and theoretically rich, yet empirical research is still more likely to be based on models that focus on environmental stressors, or that largely neglect individual differences.

Jick and Mitz (1985) and Long, Kahn, and Schutz, (1992) write that research that uses multiple-factors (including individual differences) is necessary when a number of possible independent variables may be implicated in an outcome, because without combining them, the relative explanatory power of the different IVs cannot be known, and no interactions between variables can be tested.

TOO LITTLE COMPLEXITY IN STRESS-RELATED RESEARCH

Despite the support of many of the authors for transactional-type models, full-blown transactional theories (i.e., theories that describe the stress process in terms of antecedent factors, cognitive processes, emotional experiences, and health outcomes, Cox, 1978; Cox & Griffiths, 1995; Lazarus, 1991) are complex and difficult to test, and may not be the only way forward. Indeed, job characteristics type models that focus primarily on work conditions may not be the most accurate depiction of the stress process for individuals. However, it is possible that they are "good enough" to capture the range of stress-related factors for most work situations and individuals.

While it is important to avoid falling into the oversimplification assumption (that the presence of an environmental stressor implies that an individual will be "stressed" by it) job characteristics models may be a good way of gaining an initial idea of how healthy a workplace may be, and which roles or departments in an organisation may require further stress audits. Models such as the DCS, DSS, ERI, and DISC may be very useful for this kind of work, and such a view is reflected in the recent development of a measurement tool by the UK Health and Safety Executive, that combines items from DCS and ERI questionnaires (HSE, 2007).

In 1991, Lazarus commented on the vital need to understand individual patterns in stress reactions, however Brief and George (1991) responded by claiming that Lazarus may go too far, and that it is instead useful to try and understand what factors affect most workers exposed to them. Following this, job characteristic models could be described as having a "majority of the people, the majority of the time" approach that works at a macro level, but does not help us to understand much about what stressful encounters are like for individuals with different characteristics, or indeed how to design individually relevant interventions.

TOO MUCH COMPLEXITY IN STRESS-RELATED RESEARCH

The theoretical alternative to job characteristic-based research therefore, might be seen as work that undertakes a transactional perspective, which takes a more individual-centred view, with a role for individual differences and subjective perceptions. However, another key feature of transactional stress models is (according to Cox and Griffiths, 1995) that they focus on the process of the stressful transaction that takes place in the individual when they encounter a stressful environmental stimulus. Such a focus has lead to the development of structured process-oriented frameworks in the models by Folkman and Lazarus and Cox and colleagues, which attempt to explain the processes by which an individual perceives the presence of a threat, analyses its possible effects and ways to cope with it, foresees possible future outcomes, implements coping, experiences actual outcomes, and applies feedback. The complexity of these models means that research aimed at supporting them in entirety is a huge task, and as stated by Cox himself (1987), the actual psychological processes of appraisal and coping are unlikely to be so rational as outlined in transactional theories. Indeed, Briner, Harris, and Daniels (2004) suggest that coping (and perhaps appraisal) processes are significantly more complex than transactional theories suggest, and that personal histories and many individual factors are not accounted for in current theory.

Lazarus (1991) states that many stress interventions fail because they treat individuals as if they were all alike. He also states (as Brief & George noted in 1991) that as stress is an individual and subjective phenomenon, identifying general work conditions that affect most workers is not useful. However, the task of accounting for every factor or individual difference that may be relevant to every individual in any given job situation, or an "all of the people, all of the time" approach is particularly daunting. Of course such complexity is not directly advocated by transactional frameworks, and much work has transactional features without following the entire multiple stage aspects of some models. However, a huge array of variables and personal experiences could become relevant, when one aggregates the mechanics of broad mental processes into discrete stages, and tries to apply the effects of individual difference variables to each.

A MIDDLE GROUND BETWEEN SIMPLICITY AND COMPLEXITY

Therefore, if job characteristic models may have too little complexity to account for individual experiences, and highly structured process-oriented transactional viewpoints may have too much, there may be an approach that sits somewhere between the two. Such an approach would need to not delve too deeply into the actual mental processes that may be occurring in a stressful transaction, but should still acknowledges the input of multiple individual difference variables, while maintaining a role for stressful job characteristics as the primary referent for subjective stress perceptions.

Brief and George (1991) suggested that it was important to try and identify negative conditions that affected most workers. If this were done, but in conjunction with also finding which individual difference characteristics most strongly affected the stress process for most workers (either to predispose individuals to view job characteristics as stressful, to exacerbate the effects of those stressful perceptions, or to buffer individuals from stressors) then this could be a view that could be said to try and consider "most of the people, most of the time".

The latest research on the Job Demands-Resources model (Xanthopoulou et al. 2007) could be said to be an approach that has things in common with this concept, as it attempts to use job characteristics from the DCS model to represent environmental demands, and to investigate the mediating and moderating effects of the personal resources of self-efficacy, self-esteem, and optimism on outcomes. While results for this research are mixed, it represents an important framework for future research, but which could benefit from the inclusion of more individual and work characteristics.

A SUGGESTED APPROACH

On this basis of the issues presented above a new stress framework will be described. This acknowledges the important role played by psychosocial workplace stressors in the stress process, and tries to account for the role of important individual difference factors in the development of subjective experiences of stress, and in influencing the possible health-related outcomes that result from subjective stressful perceptions. This framework aims to represent key aspects of the stress process, without getting bogged down in the minutiae of more complex theories and mental processes.

Mark (2008, in preparation) developed and tested the model shown below (figure 1) which simultaneously compared a number of job characteristics and individual difference variables in the prediction of anxiety, depression, and job satisfaction, in a working population. Independent variables included: job demands, social support, decision authority, and skill discretion from the DCS model; extrinsic effort, intrinsic effort and rewards from the ERI model; 40 coping behaviours (a key feature of the transactional models) which included the categories of problem focused coping, seeking advice, self blame, wishful thinking, and escape/avoidance; attributional/ explanatory styles; and age, gender, and demographic variables. This framework was called the Demands, Resources, and Individual Effects model (DRIVE).

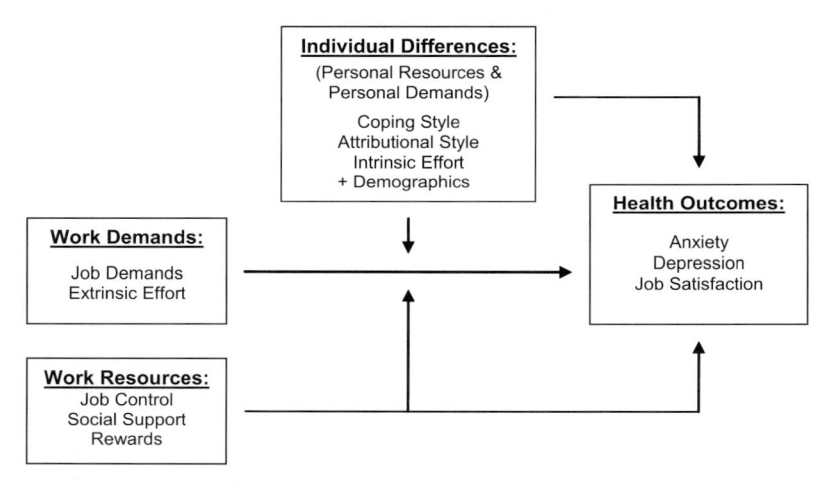

Figure 1: Simple DRIVE Model

In the model (taking a cue from the JD-R), workplace and individual characteristics are conceived of in terms of work demands and resources, and individual demands and resources. Other work demands and resources could include workload, bullying, job security, management style, feedback etc, and other personal demands and resources could include self efficacy, locus of control, personality, home environment, experience, work/life balance, role conflict, etc.

The model proposes that work demands, individual differences, and work resources, all have main effect relationships on anxiety, depression, and job satisfaction (other outcomes could include organizational commitment, musculoskeletal disorders, gastro-intestinal disorders, heart disease, absence etc). It is also proposed that work resources and individual differences may moderate the relationship between work demands and health outcomes. The individual difference variables of positive coping (problem focused coping, etc) and attributional styles can be seen as personal resources, and intrinsic effort, negative coping (self blame, etc) and attributions as "personal demands", as maladaptive behaviours are effectively self-induced demands. This model makes no predictions about the "importance" of the different variables in predicting outcomes, and gives each type of variable (work and individual demands and resources) a theoretical equivalency.

Many aspects of the above model were supported by recent research (Mark, 2008, in preparation) notably the main effect relationships, however there was little support for a moderating effect of individual differences on work demands, and only moderate support for the effect of work resources on moderating demands. In response to the results gained, and to find out more about these relationships, a new model was developed as outlined below.

A MORE COMPLEX DRIVE MODEL

Despite being more complex than the DCS, DSS, and ERI models, the model as shown above is still relatively simplistic in representing the complexities of the workplace-individual stress process, and in particular in one key way. Although hypothesising possible individual effects in the relationship between environment and outcome, this process is described without reference to conscious or affective perceptions of psychosocial stressors, a process which is specified in the appraisal stages of transactional models. While it is implicit in the model above that individuals may not view "stressors" as stressful, this subjective process is buried in the pathway between environment and outcome.

The above model could therefore benefit from some way of representing how individuals subjectively feel about their exposure to potential psychosocial stressors (the presence of which are also subjectively measured) because without inclusion of a specifically affective component, the DRIVE model could fall foul of the oversimplification assumption.

The model shown in figure 2 has similar basic principles to the simpler DRIVE model. However, there is a major change with the inclusion of a "perceived job stress" variable. It is proposed that this variable is measured simply by asking an individual if they feel that their work makes them feel stressed - whatever that may mean to the individual. The use of a single question: "In general, how do you find your job?" with responses indicated on a 5-point likert scale (0 = not at all stressful; 1 = mildly stressful; 2 = moderately stressful; 3 = very stressful; 4 = extremely stressful). Such a measure has been shown to be an accurate indicator of perceived stress, which measures this construct as well as many longer questionnaires (Smith, Johal, Wadsworth, Davey, Smith, & Peters, 2000).

As shown in the new DRIVE model in figure 2, perceived job stress is proposed to mediate the relationship between work demands/work resources and health outcomes. Perceived stress is hypothesised to be the mechanism by which levels of workplace psychosocial demands and resources can affect health outcomes. In other words, a psychosocial stressor won't transmit any stressful potential to lead to negative health outcomes, if the person does not perceive their work conditions to be stressful. Further, it is proposed that individual differences can not only moderate the relationship between environmental factors and perceived stress, but that they can also moderate the relationship between perceived stress and health outcomes. Likewise, individual differences (personal demands and resources) are proposed to have independent main effects on perceived job stress and health outcomes.

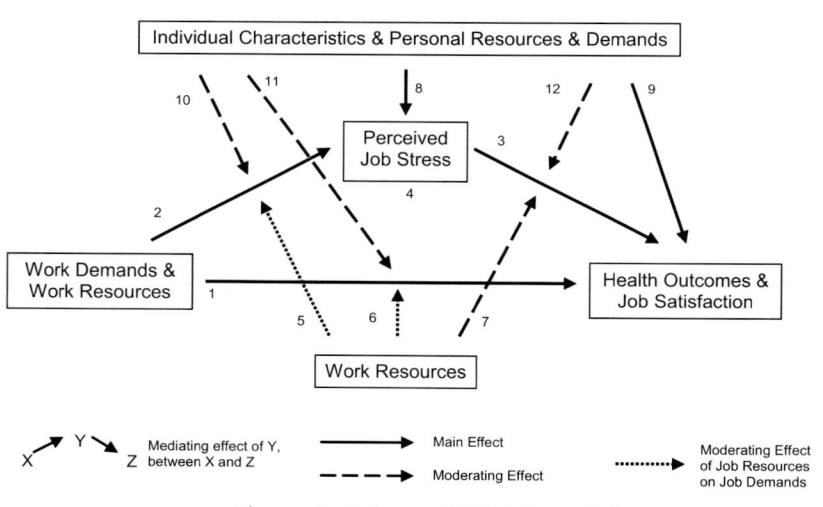

Figure 2: Enhanced DRIVE model

Like the JD-R model (Xanthopoulou et al. 2007) this model is not intended at this early stage to be a predictive model, but rather a theoretical framework into which any relevant variables can be introduced. The nature of what is actually occurring inside the person it terms of mental processes, stages, and rational procedures or analyses of situations is not hypothesised. Rather, this framework is suggested as a way of illustrating which variables and factors may relate, not how or why they relate. Twelve key relationships are proposed in the model, and these are shown below.

1) Work demands and work resources will significantly relate to outcomes.
2) Work demands and resources will significantly relate to perceived job stress.
3) Level of perceived job stress will significantly relate to outcomes.
4) Level of perceived job stress will significantly mediate the relationships between Job Demands/Resources and outcomes.
5) Work resources will significantly moderate the effect of work demands in the prediction of perceived job stress.
6) Work resources will significantly moderate the effect of work demands in the prediction of health outcomes.
7) Job resources will significantly moderate the effect of perceived job stress in the prediction of health outcomes.
8) Individual differences in the form of personal demands and resources, will be significantly related to perceived job stress.
9) Individual differences will be significantly related to outcomes.
10) Individual differences will moderate the effect of job demands on perceived stress.
11) Individual differences will moderate the effect of job demands on outcomes.
12) Individual differences will moderate the effect of perceived stress on outcomes.

FINDINGS AND IMPLICATIONS

The model proposed above was tested by Mark (2008, in preparation) in two working populations of nurses and university employees, with almost 1,200 participants. Using a series of interactive regression analyses and mediation calculations using the software Medgraph (Jose, 2004) all of the proposed relationships in the model in figure 2 above were tested. Strong evidence was found for many of the predictions above, and experimental hypotheses relating to these were supported in regards to predictions 1, 2, 3, 4, 9 and 11 with mixed support for predictions 6 and 8. No support was found for predictions 5, 7, 8, 10 and 12.

As expected from the literature, workplace demands and resources were good predictors of health outcomes, and these factors were also found to be good predictors of perceived work stress. Also, individual difference factors in the form of positive and negative coping and attributional styles (or personal demands and resources) were shown to be important predictors of health outcomes, with intrinsic efforts the most important predictor by standardised beta weight in anxiety and depression, and rewards and attributional behaviours particularly good predictors of job satisfaction.

A large number of interactive effects were found between personal characteristics and work demands and resources, as depicted above by relationship 11. These results support the case for the key role that individual differences can have in moderating the strength or direction of the relationships, between workplace conditions and mental health outcomes and satisfaction.

A key observation from the results was the finding that perceived stress mediated the relationship between work demands and resources and outcomes. While these effects were largely partial (although full mediating effects were found between job demands and depression, and extrinsic effort and satisfaction in a sample of university employees) it is still an important finding that how people feel about the stressful (or not stressful) nature of their work environment, can be just as important a pathway towards health outcomes, as is the direct perception of those work environments. This finding also supports the work of many authors, such as Payne, Jick, and Burke (1982) and Briner et al. (2004) who state that subjective perceptions of the stressful nature of work environments, rather than just the nature of those environments themselves, must be taken into account. Similarly, a key finding was that personal characteristics had main effects on health outcomes, and had moderating effects on the relationship between workplace demands/resources and health outcomes.

The supporting of many aspects of the model shown in figure 2 provides a good basis for the development of future research. Different organisational and personal variables could easily be inserted into the framework and tested, and such research could provide more information on the relative importance of different variables in the prediction of outcomes, and more information about how they may interact. Such research may provide support for the structure of the proposed model, or could be used to revise the model. Longitudinal research could be particularly useful to see if such a model has any predictive validity.

SUMMARY AND CONCLUSIONS

The purpose of this chapter was to outline some of the main issues associated with increasing levels of work-related stress in our society, and the growing awareness of what this may mean for the health of employees, and the economic costs to employers and the UK economy. A brief summary of many of the key models relating to work-related stress was carried out, including a consideration of some of their pros and cons, and common features. It was suggested that many models have failed to include a role for the important effect of subjective perceptions and individual differences (despite some good predictive validity) or otherwise are complex, hard to support, and lack predictive validity. On the basis of these issues a new model was proposed, which attempts to combine features of existing models, including roles for psychosocial job characteristics and individual differences (framed in terms of demands and resources) and to represent the complexities of the stress process, without making hypotheses about the specific details of mental processes. Some supporting research was described, and a key aspect was the inclusion of a subjective perception of job stress variable (included in response to the oversimplification assumption) which predicted health outcomes in some circumstances as well as perceived job characteristics.

It is suggested that the DRIVE model as shown in figure 2, strikes a good balance between integration of aspects of job characteristics models such as the DCS, as well as aspects from the ERI model, and important developments from transactional stress models, while still maintaining a balance between simplicity and complexity. If more data could be provided for the development and support of models such as the DRIVE model, such frameworks could provide a useful guide for organisational interventions, by showing how alteration of one aspect of the model may affect other parts of it, and to help co-ordinate single or multi-level interventions that focus on one or more of primary, secondary, and tertiary levels – something that models that focus only on job characteristics may be limited in their ability to do.

REFERENCES

ARNOLD, J., COOPER, C. L., & ROBERTSON, I. T. (1995). Work psychology. Understanding human behaviour in the workplace (2nd ed.). London: Pitman Publishing.

BAKKER, A.B., DEMEROUTI, E., EUWEMA, M.C. (2005). Job resources buffer the impact of job demands on burnout. Journal of Occupational Health Psychology, 10, 170-80.

BARON, R. M., & KENNY, D.A. (1986). The Mediator-Moderator Variable Distinction in Social Psychological Research: Conceptual, Strategic, and Statistical Considerations. Journal of Personality and Social Psychology, 51, 6, 1173-1182.

BOSMA, H., PETER, R., SIEGRIST, J., AND MARMOT, M.G. (1998). Alternative job stress models and the risk of coronary heart disease. American Journal of Public Health, 88, 68-74.

BRIEF, A.P., & GEORGE, I.M. (1991). Psychological stress and the workplace: A brief comment on Lazarus' outlook. In P.L. Perrewe (Ed.), Handbook on job stress. Journal of Social Behaviour and Personality, 6 (7), 15-20.

BRINER, R.B., HARRIS, C., & DANIELS, K. (2004). How do work stress and coping work? Toward a fundamental theoretical reappraisal. British Journal of Guidance & Counselling., 32, 2, 223-234.

BUUNK, B. P., DE JONGE, J., YBEMA, J.F., & DE WOLFF, C.J. (1991). Psychosocial Aspects of Occupational Stress. In P.J.D. Drenth, H. Thierry & C.J. de Wolff (Eds.), Handbook of Work and Organizational Psychology, 145-182.

CAPLAN, R.D., COBB, S., FRENCH, J.R., HARRISON, R.D. & PINNEAU, S.R. (1975). Job Demands and Worker Health: Main effects and occupational differences. Washington: U.S. Government Printing Office.

CARAYON, P. (1993). Effect of electronic performance monitoring on job design and worker stress: Review of the literature and conceptual model. Human Factors, 35, 385-95.

COOPER, C. L., DEWE, P.J., & O'DRISCOLL, M.P. (2001). Organizational Stress: A Review and Critique of Theory, Research, and Applications. Sage Publications.

COX, T. (1987). Stress, coping and problem solving. Work & Stress, 1, 5-14.

COX, T., & FERGUSON, E. (1991). Individual Differences, Stress and Coping. In C.L. Cooper, & R. Payne (Eds.). Personality and Stress: Individual Differences in the Stress Process. Wiley.

COX, T. & GRIFFITHS, A. (1995). The nature and measurement of work stress: theory and practice. In J.R. Wilson & E.N. Corlett (Eds.), Evaluation of human work: a practical ergonomics methodology, London: Taylor & Francis.

COX, T., GRIFFITHS, A. & RIAL-GONZALEZ, E. (2000). Research on Work-Related Stress, Office for Official Publications of the European Communities: Luxembourg.

COX, T. & MACKAY, C.J. (1981). A Transactional approach to occupational stress. In E.N. Corlett and J. Richardson (Eds.), Stress, Work Design and Productivity. Chichester: Wiley & Sons.

DE JONGE, J., BOSMA, H., PETER, R. & SIEGRIST, J. (2000). Job strain, effort-reward imbalance and employee well-being: a large-scale cross-sectional study, Social Science and Medicine, 50, 1317-1327.

DE JONGE, J., & DORMANN, C. (2003). The DISC model: Demand-induced strain compensation mechanisms in job stress. In M. F. Dollard, H. R. Winefield, & A. H. Winefield (Eds.), Occupational stress in the service professions, 43-74. London: Taylor & Francis.

DEMEROUTI, E., BAKKER, A.B., NACHREINER, F. & SCHAUFELI, W.B. (2001). The job demands-resources model of burnout, Journal of Applied Psychology, 86, 499-512.

DEWE, P. (1991). Primary Appraisal, secondary appraisal and coping: their role in stressful work encounter, Journal of Occupational Psychology, 64, 331-351.

DEWE, P., & TRENBERTH, L. (2004). Work stress and coping: drawing together theory and practice, British journal of guidance & counselling, 32, 143-156.

EARNSHAW, J. & COOPER, C. L. (1994). Employee stress litigation: The UK experience. Work and Stress, 8, 287-295

FALKUM, E., OLFF, M., & AASLAND, O.G. (1997) Revisiting the factor structure of the ways of coping checklist: a three-dimensional view of the problem-focused coping scale. A study among Norwegian physicians. Personality and Individual Differences, 22, 257-267.

FLORIO, G. A., DONNELLY, J.P. & ZEVON, M.A (1998). The Structure of Work-Related Stress and Coping Among Oncology Nurses in High-Stress Medical Settings: A transactional Analysis, Journal of Occupational Health Psychology, 3, 227-242.

FOLKMAN, S. (1984). Personal control and stress and coping processes: A theoretical analysis, *Journal of Personality and Social Psychology*, 46, 839-852.

FOLKMAN, S., & LAZARUS, R.S. (1980). An Analysis of coping in a Middle-Aged Community sample. Journal of Health and Social Behaviour, 21, 219-239.

FOLKMAN, S., LAZARUS, R.S., GRUEN, R.J., & DELONGIS, A. (1986). Appraisal, Coping, Health Status, & Psychological Symptoms, Journal of Personality and Social Psychology, 50, 571-579.

FRENCH, J.R.P. JR. (1973). Person-role fit, Occupational Mental Health, 3, 15-20.

FRENCH, J.R.P. JR, CAPLAN, R.D., & HARRISON, R.V. (1982). *The mechanisms of job stress and strain.* London: Wiley.

FRESE, M., & ZAPF, D. (1999). On the Importance of the objective environment in stress and attribution theory. Counterpoint to Perrewe and Zellars, Journal of Organizational Behavior, 20, 761-765.

GABRIEL, P. (2000). Mental Health in the Workplace, International Labour Office, Geneva.

GIANAKOS, I. (2002). Predictors of Coping with Work Stress: The Influences of sex, gender role, social desirability, and locus of control, Sex Roles, 46, 149-158.

GOETZEL, R.Z., ANDERSON, D.R., WHITMER, R.W., OZMINKOWSKI, R.J., DUNN, R.L. & WASSERMAN J. (1998). The relationship between modifiable health risks and health care expenditures, Journal of Occupational and Environmental Medicine, 40, 843-854.

GRIFFITHS, A. (1998). The psychosocial work environment. In R. C. McCaig and M. J. Harrington (Eds.) The changing nature of occupational health, 213-232.

HACKMAN, J. R., & OLDHAM, G. R. (1980). Work Redesign, Reading, MA: Addison-Wesley.

HAGHIGHATGOU H. & PETERSON C. (1995). Coping and depressive symptoms among Iranian students, Journal of Social Psychology, 135, 175-80.

HEALTH AND SAFETY EXECUTIVE (2007). Workplace Stress Costs Great Britain in Excess of £530 million, Retrieved, March 2008, from, http://www.hse.gov.uk/press/2007/c07021.htm

HEALTH AND SAFETY EXECUTIVE (2007). Managing the risk factors of work-related stress in Home Office headquarters and the Border and Immigration Agency, Retrieved, March 2008, from, http://www.homeoffice.gov.uk/hons/white-hon/hon041-2007.pdf?view=Binary

HEALTH AND SAFETY EXECUTIVE (2007). HSE Management standards indicator tool, Retreived, June 2008, from, http://www.hse.gov.uk/stress/standards/pdfs/indicatortool.pdf

HODGSON, J.T., JONES, J. R., ELLIOT, R.C. & OSMAN, J. (1993). Self-reported Work-related Illness: Results from a Trailer Questionnaire on the 1990 Labour Force Survey in England and Wales. Sudbury: HSE Books.

HUANG, G.D., FEURSTEIN, M., & SAUTER, S.L. (2002). Occupational Stress and Work-Related Upper Extremity Disorders: Concepts and Models, American Journal of Industrial Medicine, 41, 298-314.

HURRELL, J. J. & McLANEY, M. A. (1988). Exposure to job stress -- A new psychometric instrument, Scandinavian Journal of Work Environment and Health, 14, 27-28.

JICK, T. D. & MITZ, L.F. (1985). Sex Differences in Work Stress, Academy of Management Review, 10, 408-420.

JOHNSON, J.V., HALL, E.M. (1988). Job strain, workplace social support and cardiovascular disease: a cross-sectional study of a random sample of Swedish working population, *American Journal of Public Health*, 78, 1336-42.

JONES, M., SMITH, K. & JOHNSTON, D. (2005). Exploring the Michigan model: The relationship of personality, managerial support and organizational structure with health outcomes in entrants to the healthcare environment, Work & Stress, 19, 1-22.

Jose, P.E. (2004). Medgraph. www.victoria.ac.nz/psyc/staff/paul-jose/files/medgraph/download.php.

Karasek, R. (1979). Job demands, job decision latitude and mental strain: Implications for job redesign, Administrative Science Quarterly, 24, 285-306.

Karasek, R.A. (1998). Demand/Control Model: a social, emotional, and physiological approach to stress risk and active behaviour development, In J. Stellman (Ed.). Encyclopaedia of Occupational Health and Safety. Geneva: International Labour Office, 34.6-34.14.

Karasek, R. & Theorell, T. (1990). Healthy work: Stress, productivity and the reconstruction of working life, New York: Basic Books.

Kompier, M. (2003). Job Design and Well-being. In M. Schabracq, J. Winnubst & C.L. Cooper, (Eds.), Handbook of Work and Health Psychology, 429-454.

Kristensen, T.S. (1995). The demand-control-support model: Methodological challenges for future research, Stress Medicine, 11, 17-26.

Kuper, H., Singh-Manoux, A., Siegrist, J. & Marmot, M. (2002) When reciprocity fails: Effort-reward imbalance in relation to coronary heart disease and health functioning within the Whitehall II Study, Occupational and Environmental Medicine, 59, 777-784.

Lazarus, R.S. & Folkman, S. (1984). Stress, appraisal, and coping. New York: Springer.

Lazarus, R.S. (1991). Psychological Stress in the Workplace. In P.L. Perrewe (Ed.). Handbook on job stress, Journal of Social Behavior and Personality, 6, 1-13.

Lease, S. H. (1999). Occupational role stressors, coping, support, and hardiness as predictors of strain in academic faculty: An emphasis on new and female faculty, Research in Higher Education, 40, 285-307.

Lewin, K. (1951). Field theory in social science; selected theoretical papers. New York: Harper & Row.

Lim, V.K.G. (1996). Job insecurity and its outcomes-moderating effects of work-based and non-work based social support, Human Relations, 49, 171-194.

Llorens, S., Bakker, A.B., Schaufeli, W., Salanova, M. (2006). Testing the robustness of the job demands-resources model. International Journal of Stress Management. 13, 378-391.

Long, B.C., Kahn, S.E. & Schutz, R.W. (1992). Causal Model of stress and coping: Women in Management, Journal of Counselling Psychology, 39, 227-239.

Mark, G.M. (2008, in preparation). The relationship between workplace stress and job characteristics, individual differences, and mental health.

Parkes, K.R. (1989). Personal control in an occupational context, In A.

Steptoe, & A. Appels (Eds.), *Stress, personal control and health*, 21-48. Chichester, England: Wiley.

PARKES, K. (1994). Personality and coping as moderators of work stress processes: models, methods and measures, Work & Stress, 8, 110-129.

PAYNE, R. (1988). Individual Differences in the Study of Occupational Stress, New York: Wiley.

PARK, C.L. & FOLKMAN, S. (1997). Meaning in the context of stress and coping, Review of General Psychology, 2, 115-144.

PAYNE, R.A., JICK, T.D. & BURKE, R.J. (1982). Wither stress research?: An agenda for the 1980's. Journal of Occupational Behaviour, 3, 131-145.

PERREWE, P.L., & ZELLARS, K.L. (1999). An examination of attributions and emotions in the transactional approach to the organizational stress process, Journal of Organizational Behavior, 20, 739-752.

PETER R. & SIEGRIST J. (1999). Chronic psychosocial stress at work and cardiovascular disease: the role of effort–reward imbalance, International Journal of Law and Psychiatry, 22, 441-449.

RYDSTEDT, L.W., DEVERAUX, J. & SVERKE, M. (2007). Comparing and combining the demand-control support model and the effort-reward imbalance model to predict long-term mental strain, European Journal of Work and Organizational Psychology, 3, 261-278.

SCHABRACQ, M.J. & COOPER, C.L. (2000). The changing nature of work and stress, *Journal of Managerial Psychology, 3*, 227-241.

SCHAUBROECK, J. (1999). Should the subjective be the objective? On Studying mental processes, coping behaviour, and actual exposures in organizational stress research, Journal of Organizational Behavior, 20, 753-760.

SIEGRIST, J. (1996). Adverse health effects of high-effort/low-reward conditions, *Journal of Occupational Health Psychology*, 1, 27-41.

SIEGRIST J, & PETER, R. (2000). The effort-reward imbalance model. The workplace and cardiovascular disease, Occupational Medicine: State of the Art Reviews, 15, 83-87.

SIEGRIST J., PETER R., JUNGE, A., CREMER, P. & SEIDEL, D. (1990). Low status control, high effort at work and ischemic heart disease: Prospective evidence from blue-collar men, Social Science and Medicine, 31, 1127-34.

SIEGRIST, J., STARKE, D., CHANDOLA, T., GODIN, I., MARMOT, M., NIEDHAMMER, I. & PETER, R. (2004). The measurement of effort-reward imbalance at work: European Comparisons, Social Science & Medicine, 58, 1483-1499.

SMITH, A., JOHAL, S.S., WADSWORTH, E., DAVEY SMITH, G., & PETERS, T. (2000). The Scale of Occupational Stress: the Bristol Stress and Health at Work Study. *HSE Books. Report 265/2000.*

SONNENTAG, S. & FRESE, M. (2003). Stress in Organisations. In W.C. Borman, D.R. Ilgen & R.J. Klimoski (Eds.), Comprehensive handbook of psychology. Hoboken, NJ: Wiley.

SPECTOR, P.E. (1982). Behavior in organisations as a function of employee locus of control, Psychological Bulletin, 91, 482 – 497.

SPECTOR, P.E. (2003). Individual differences in health and well-being in organisations, In D.A. Hoffman L.E. Tetrick (eds). Health and Safety in Organisations: A Multilevel Perspective. in the Society of Industrial and Organizational Psychology. San Francisco, CA: Jossey- Bass, Inc.

TENNANT, C. (2001). Work Related Stress and Depressive Disorders. Journal of Psychosomatic Research, 51, 697-704.

TONG, E.M.W., BISHOP, G.D., DIONG, S.M., ENKELMANN, H.C., WHY, Y.P., ANG, J. & KHADER, M. (2004). Social support and personality among male police officers in Singapore, Personality and Individual Differences, 36, 109-123.

VAN DER DOEF, M. & MAES, S. (1998). The Job Demand-Control (-Support) Model and physical health outcomes: a review of the strain and buffer hypotheses, Psychology and Health, 13, 909-936.

VAN DER DOEF, M. & MAES, S. (1999). The Job-Demand (-Support) Model and psychological well-being: a review of 20 years of empirical research, Work & Stress, 13, 87-114.

VAN VEGCHEL, N., DE JONGE, J., BAKKER, A.B. & SCHAUFELI, W.B. (2002). Testing global and specific indicators of rewards in the Effort-Reward Imbalance Model: Does it make any difference? European Journal of Work and Organizational Psychology, 11, 403-421.

VAN VEGCHEL, N., DE JONGE, J., BOSMA, H. & SCHAUFELI, W.B. (2005). Reviewing the effort-reward imbalance model: drawing up the balance of 45 empirical studies, Social Science & Medicine, 60, 1117-1131.

VAN VELDHOVEN, M., DE JONGE, J., BROERSEN, S., KOMPIER, M. & MEIJMAN, T. (2002). Specific relationships between psychosocial job conditions and job-related stress: A three level analytical approach, Work & Stress, 16, 207-228.

VELDHOVEN, M. VAN, TARIS, T.W., JONGE, J. DE & BROERSEN, S. (2005). The relationship between work characteristics and employee health and well-being: how much complexity do we really need? International Journal of Stress Management, 12, 3-28.

VITALIANO, P.P., RUSSO, J., CARR, J.E., MAIURO, R.D. & BECKER, J. (1985). The Ways of Coping Checklist Psychometric Properties, Multivariate Behavioral Research, 20, 3-26.

WANG, J. & PATTEN, S.B. (2001). Perceived work stress and major depression in the Canadian employed population, 20-49 years old, Journal of Occupational Health Psychology, 6, 283-289.

WARR, P.B. (1987). Work, unemployment, and mental health. Oxford: Clarendon Press.

WARR, P.B. (1990). Decision latitude, job demands, and employee well-being, Work and Stress, 4, 285–294.

WELBOURNE, J.L., EGGERTH, D., HARTLEY, T.A., ANDREW, M.E. & SANCHEZ, F. (2007). Coping strategies in the workplace: Relationships with attributional style and job satisfaction, Journal of Vocational Behavior, 70, 312-325.

XANTHOPOULOU, D., BAKKER, A. B., DEMEROUTI, E. & SCHAUFELI, W. B. (2007). The role of personal resources in the job demands-resources model, International Journal of Stress Management, 14, 121–141.

ZEIDNER, M. (1994). Personal and Contextual Determinants of Coping and Anxiety in an Evaluative Situation: A Prospective Study, Personality and Individual Differences, 16, 899-918.

EDUCATION

THE DEFINITION OF CURRICULUM AREAS IN OCCUPATIONAL HEALTH PSYCHOLOGY

Jonathan Houdmont, Stavroula Leka and Carrie A. Bulger

CHAPTER OVERVIEW

Across the international educational landscape, numerous higher education institutions (HEIs) offer postgraduate programmes in occupational health psychology (OHP). These seek to empower the next generation of OHP practitioners with the knowledge and skills necessary to advance the understanding and prevention of workplace illness and injury, improve working life and promote healthy work through the application of psychological principles and practices.

Among the OHP curricula operated within these programmes there exists considerable variability in the topics addressed. This is due, inter alia, to the youthfulness of the discipline and the fact that the development of educational provision has been managed at the level of the HEI where it has remained undirected by external forces such as the discipline's representative bodies. Such variability makes it difficult to discern the key characteristics of a curriculum which is important for programme accreditation purposes, the professional development and regulation of practitioners and, ultimately, the long-term sustainability of the discipline.

This chapter has as its focus the imperative for and development of consensus surrounding OHP curriculum areas. It begins by examining the factors that are currently driving curriculum developments and explores some of the barriers to such. It then reviews the limited body of previous research that has attempted to discern key OHP curriculum areas. This provides a foundation upon which to describe a study conducted by the current authors that involved the elicitation of subject matter expert opinion from an international sample of academics involved in OHP-related teaching and research on the question of which topic areas might be considered important for inclusion within an OHP curriculum. The chapter closes by drawing conclusions on steps that could be taken by the discipline's representative bodies towards the consolidation and accreditation of a core curriculum.

THE IMPERATIVE FOR A CORE OHP CURRICULUM

The need to identify key topic areas that might be included in an OHP curriculum was recognised by the European Academy of Occupational Health Psychology (EA-OHP) in its strategy document on *The Promotion of Education in Occupational Health Psychology in Europe* (EA-OHP, 2002)[1]. Despite the passing of six years since publication of the strategy document, limited progress has been made in respect to the definition of a core curriculum within and without Europe (Houdmont, Leka and Cox, 2007). The reason for this might reside in the challenges associated with three complex questions that Sinclair (2006) identified as being of central importance to the definition of an OHP curriculum. These concern (i) on what knowledge, skills and abilities should OHP education focus, (ii) how might OHP programmes address the needs and concerns of multiple stakeholder groups including employers, trade unions, practitioners and academics, and (ii) how might and to what extent should OHP integrate knowledge from other disciplines?

A number of imperatives now exist that together highlight the urgency for activities directed at the definition of a core OHP curriculum. Three issues in particular can be identified as responsible for driving current endeavours in this regard. These include (i) problems associated with variability in existing provision across HEIs, (ii) the role of the discipline's representative bodies in supporting, directing and regulating educational provision and, (iii) pan-European structural changes in the delivery of postgraduate education in psychology.

Variability in existing provision

Since the mid 1990s, several HEIs have introduced taught OHP programmes at Masters level (primarily in Europe) or within doctoral and post-doctoral training (mainly in the USA). Most, if not all, of the institutions that offer education and training in the discipline apply an OHP curriculum constructed on the basis of faculty members' understanding of the discipline and the key topics that it addresses. This approach to curriculum design has contributed to the generation of considerable variability in the topics covered within curricula across institutions.

Variability in curricula applied across institutions is not necessarily problematic. Indeed, variability may reflect factors that contribute to the creation of high quality programmes that are fit for purpose in particular

---

[1] A detailed account of the development, content and implications of the EA-OHP strategy document can be found in Houdmont, Leka & Cox (2007)

educational, social, economic and geographical contexts. Such factors may include, among other things, institutional research expertise and the needs of local employers as well as faculty members' understanding of OHP. Curriculum variability only becomes problematic when it exists to such a degree that it becomes difficult to discern the defining characteristics of OHP within a given curriculum.

At the time of writing, numerous HEIs across the globe are known to be undertaking scoping activities to assess the market potential for OHP programmes and some are on the verge of introducing their own programme. It is likely that the curriculum associated with each of these new programmes will be determined by faculty members on the basis of their understanding of the discipline or informed by existing curricula which, in turn, have been developed in the same way. In this climate of rapid expansion of provision it is essential that consensus is achieved on the topic areas that might be considered core to a curriculum; it would be a disservice to the discipline if ten years from now common ground across programmes could not be identified.

The role of the discipline's representative bodies in supporting, directing and regulating educational provision

The bodies that represent OHP on the international stage, EA-OHP (Europe), the Society for Occupational Health Psychology (SOHP: North America) and the International Coordinating Group for Occupational Health Psychology (ICG-OHP), have witnessed a growth in recent years in requests from HEIs for assistance with the design and implementation of OHP programmes. In numerous cases, advice has been elicited on (i) the topics that ought to be included within an OHP curriculum, (ii) issues of programme implementation, (iii) approaches to and avenues for marketing and, (iv) issues of programme accreditation.

At present, none of these bodies is equipped to offer formal programme accreditation or to provide a regulatory facility. This might be considered a matter for regret since programme accreditation offers an important indicator of the quality of a programme that would be of use to academics, prospective students and graduate employers. Accreditation that recognises an achieved standard of competency and adherence to a professional code of conduct would represent an important move towards the professional regulation of OHP practitioners. This in turn would likely serve to boost the discipline's profile among potential employers and clients. The development of consensus on the important and core elements of an OHP curriculum would therefore offer a basis for the possible introduction of programme accreditation criteria.

Although formal programme accreditation may be some way off, the institutions and individuals that contribute their time and energy to the operation of these representative bodies bring with them a wealth of experience in terms of the establishment of OHP programmes and a deep knowledge of the subject area. As such, they are well placed to offer guidance on the introduction of new OHP programmes. Consensus among these subject matter experts on the important and core content of an OHP curriculum would therefore help the discipline's representative bodies to administer consistent and useful advice that will contribute to the international expansion of OHP educational provision within a guiding framework.

Pan-European structural changes in the delivery of postgraduate education in psychology

In Europe, a particularly strong and immediate imperative for the definition of the important and core topics that might be included within an OHP curriculum has arisen out of the emergence of the European Certificate in Psychology (EuroPsy). Equivalent to doctoral-level training and awarded by the European Federation of Psychologists' Associations (EFPA), the EuroPsy certificate:

"is intended to provide a standard of academic education and professional training which informs clients, employers and colleagues that a psychologist can be considered to have gained the necessary competencies for the provision of psychological services. EuroPsy aims to set a common standard of competence in all the countries where it is issued. It promotes the free movement of psychologists across the countries of the European Union" (European Federation of Psychologists' Associations, 2006, p. 9).

The EuroPsy certificate is obtained upon completion of a 3 + 2 + 1 professional training model that comprises a first degree in psychology, a two-year full time Masters degree in a psychological specialty and a minimum of one year's full time supervised practice as a psychologist-practitioner in training. At the time of writing, the EuroPsy was undergoing a pilot roll-out in six European countries ahead of its Europe-wide launch. The introduction of the EuroPsy framework has a series of implications for the evolution of postgraduate OHP curricula, three of which are discussed here.

First, EuroPsy requires that the Masters portion of the training pathway consists of two years full time study. At present, few European HEIs offer this; most Masters degrees operate on a one-year full-time programme of study (or equivalent). The introduction of a two-year full-time programme could bring benefits for OHP programmes: it would allow for a greater number of topic areas to be addressed within a course of study and an in-depth focus on particular topics. However, it will require the modification of existing one-year full-time programmes which will generate attendant resource implications. Furthermore, at most HEIs it is likely that the fee charged for a two-year full-time programme would, by necessity, be higher than that applied to one-year full-time programmes; it is uncertain how such a change might affect student applications.

Second, in its current incarnation, the EuroPsy certificate is available to individuals who have demonstrated professional competence in one of three areas: clinical and health psychology, work and organisational psychology or educational psychology. It remains unclear how Masters-level education in occupational health psychology might be encompassed into the scheme.

Third, EuroPsy requires that students undertake an organisational internship during their Masters programme of study as well as one year of supervised practice. Under EuroPsy provisions the internship usually takes place in the second year of Masters study to provide "an introductory professional field training in order to enable students to: integrate theoretical and practical knowledge, learn procedures related to psychological knowledge, start practicing under supervision, be able to reflect upon and discuss own and other people's activities, begin working in a setting with professional colleagues" (European Federation of Psychologists' Associations, 2006, p. 26). For both the internship and supervised practice element, as they relate to OHP, it is unclear what arrangements will be required in respect of (i) the nature and activities of the organisation(s) in which the internship and period of supervised practice takes place, (ii) the specific tasks that individuals undertake during these periods and (iii) the nature and scope of supervision as well as the qualifications of supervisors. Particularly in Europe, the notion of an internship represents a novel concept that will present a series of implications for Masters level curricula.

As the EuroPsy certificate is rolled out across the Member States of the European Union it is likely to have an increasingly important bearing on the structure and content of European Masters degrees in OHP. As such, it is important that the representative bodies for the discipline have at their disposal a consensus position on the important and core content of an OHP curriculum before entering into discussions with the European Federation of Psychologists' Associations towards the integration of OHP into the EuroPsy framework.

ISSUES OF DEFINITION

Having established the imperative for the identification of important and core topics within an OHP curriculum, this section considers a potential challenge to the achievement of such: disagreement between continents on the definition of OHP. How OHP is defined is not merely a matter of semantics since the definitions adhered to by programme designers will determine, in part, the content of those programmes (Cox, Baldurrson and Rial González, 2000). Thankfully, despite the absence of a shared heritage among the international community of OHP practitioners there exists broad agreement on the definition of the discipline. Nevertheless, there is evidence of divergence between the European and North American perspectives (Cox, 2000), specifically in respect of the subject areas that inform and together comprise OHP. Such divergence may have implications for the topic areas considered within a curriculum.

In Europe, the generally accepted definition of OHP is that used by the EA-OHP. This is based on the definition advanced by Cox et al. (2000), whereby OHP concerns "the contribution of applied psychology to occupational health" (p. 101). Cox et al.'s definition is termed an 'interface' definition since it locates OHP at the interface between occupational health and psychology. Cox and colleagues suggest that the areas of psychology that might be applied in addressing occupational health issues include health psychology, work and organisational psychology and social and environmental psychology (see Figure 1). The contribution of these areas of psychology implies that OHP practitioners have their focus on the psychological, social and organisational aspects of occupational health questions. Taken as a whole, this perspective allows for the following definition:

> *Occupational health psychology involves the contribution of the principles and practices of applied psychology to occupational health issues. It is the study of psychological, social and organisational aspects of the dynamic relationship between work and health.*

This European perspective recognises that occupational health is a multidisciplinary area and that OHP practitioners offer a focused specialisation that they may usefully apply within multidisciplinary teams. In this way, it "requires that European occupational health psychologists are aware of and recognise the contributions that can be made by others, and can appreciate their intellectual positions, knowledge and practical skills" (Cox et al., 2000, p. 103).

```
┌─────────────────────────────────────────────────────────────────────┐
│   ┌──────────────────┐  ┌──────────────────┐  ┌──────────────────┐  │
│   │ Health Psychology│  │ Work and Organisational │ │ Social and Environmental │
│   │                  │  │ Psychology       │  │ Psychology       │  │
│   └────────┬─────────┘  └─────────┬────────┘  └─────────┬────────┘  │
│            └──────────────────────┼─────────────────────┘           │
│                         ┌─────────▼──────────┐                      │
│                         │ Occupational Health Psychology │          │
│                         └────────────────────┘                      │
└─────────────────────────────────────────────────────────────────────┘
```

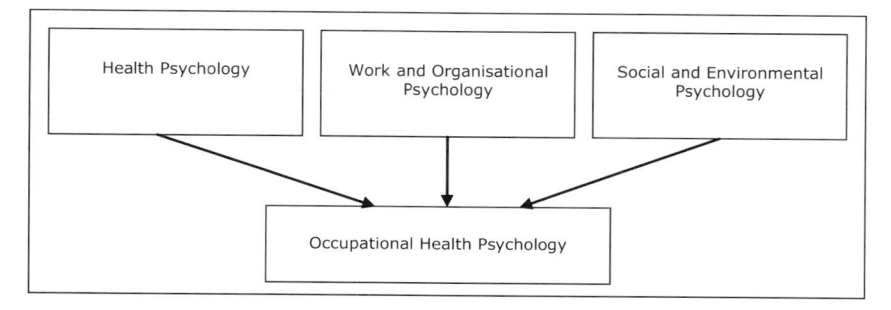

Figure 1: The foundations of European OHP

Some North American perspectives on OHP are entirely consistent with the European approach that conceptualises a discipline which draws on the procedures, practices and methodologies from various fields of applied psychology. The definition proposed by the US National Institute for Occupational Safety and Health (NIOSH), for example, states that OHP concerns "the application of psychology to improving the quality of work life, and to protecting and promoting the safety, health and well-being of workers"[2]. However, other groups of researchers in North America have suggested that OHP might encompass psychological procedures, practices and methodologies alongside those from other occupational health sciences such as occupational and environmental health, organisational behaviour, human factors, sociology, industrial engineering, ergonomics and economics (Chen, Huang & DeArmond, 2005). This multidisciplinary perspective was established at the outset of the discipline's existence in North America. In their seminal article in which the term 'occupational health psychology' was coined, Raymond, Wood & Patrick (1990) called for training in a discipline that "would integrate and synthesise insights, frameworks and knowledge from a diverse number of specialties, principally health psychology and occupational (public) health but also preventative medicine, occupational medicine, behavioural medicine, nursing, political science, sociology and business" (p. 1159). The North American perspective on the foundations of OHP is illustrated in Figure 2.

The multi-disciplinary nature of North American OHP recognises that a wide range of perspectives and disciplines have something to offer in regard to the prevention of workplace illness and injury and the promotion of health under the umbrella of OHP. Each vies for representation on an OHP curriculum, forcing programme designers to make difficult decisions on which to include and which to leave out.

---

[2]See: http://www.cdc.gov/niosh/topics/stress/ohp/ohp.html#whatis

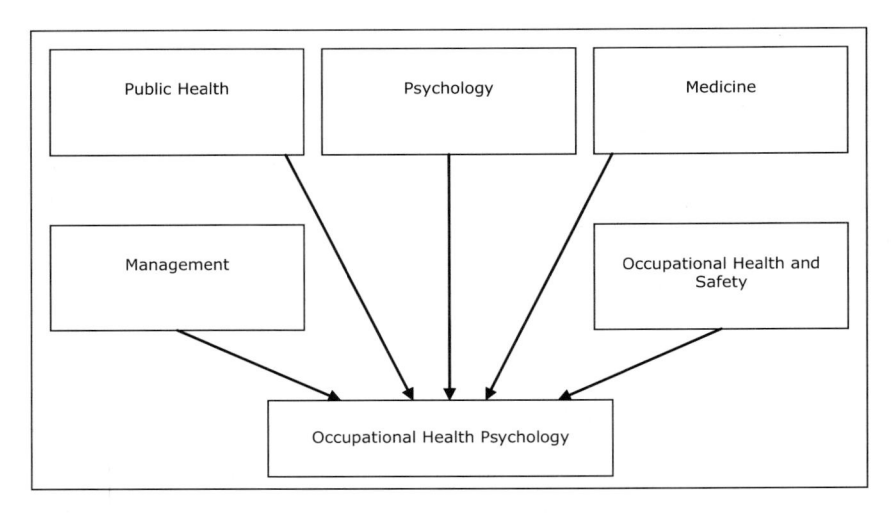

Figure 2: The foundations of North American OHP (From Adkins, 1999. Adapted with permission).

Despite differences in definition that can be identified between the North American and European approaches, OHP practitioners the world over would no doubt unanimously endorse the vision of OHP "to create healthy workplaces in which people may produce, serve, grow, and be valued" (Quick, Camara, Hurrell, Johnson, Piotrkowski, Sauter & Spielberger, 1997, p. 3). Likewise, most would agree with the high-level characteristics that Cox et al. (2000) have suggested appear to define the discipline. These include an acknowledgement that OHP is (i) an applied science, (ii) evidence driven, (iii) oriented towards problem solving, (iv) multidisciplinary, (v) participatory – actively involving students, workers and managers, (vi) focussed on intervention, with an emphasis on primary prevention and, (vii) operational within a legal framework. Nevertheless, the contrast between the European and North American perspectives remains more than a mere matter of wordplay and it remains a possibility that the differing traditions out of which OHP has emerged could present a challenge to the development of international consensus on the important and core topics that might be contained within a curriculum.

RESEARCH ON THE DEFINITION OF OHP CURRICULUM AREAS

The content of most, if not all, extant OHP curricula has largely been informed by faculty members' knowledge and understanding of the discipline. In many cases, programme designers have turned to the published academic literature for guidance on topic areas that ought to be included. Perhaps as a result of this approach, a degree of consistency can be identified across programmes. For example, a review of the content of eleven doctoral-level OHP programmes at North American HEIs revealed that six topic areas appeared consistently (Barnes-Farrell, 2006). These included: (i) survey (overview) of occupational safety and health, (ii) job stress theory, (iii) organisational risk factors for occupational stress, injury and illness, (iv) physical and psychological health implications of stressful work, (v) organisational interventions for the reduction of work-related stress and, (vi) research methods and practices in public/occupational health and epidemiology. This list is broadly consistent with the findings of a recent review of topics addressed in papers published in the Journal of Occupational Health Psychology over an eleven year period which revealed seven broad topic areas: (i) stress, (ii) burnout, (iii) work-family issues, (iv) aggression, violence and harassment, (v) safety, (vi) employment issues and, (vii) health issues (Macik-Frey, Quick & Nelson, 2007).

Analyses such as that of Macik-Frey and colleagues offer an indication of the topics with which researchers have commonly engaged. However, beyond the intrinsic interest or importance of a topic there exists a host of factors that drive research foci and which encourage a focus on particular topics at different points in time across social and economic contexts. As such, it might be considered that key themes evident in the published research provide an indication of some important topics that ought to be included in an educational curriculum; they do not, however, provide guidance on the topics that are fundamental to the discipline nor do they offer a comprehensive account of OHP topics. A curriculum that seeks to reflect the key themes in published OHP research may also be problematic in that it is unlikely to fully address practitioner concerns and interests. OHP is an applied discipline and it is therefore important that curricula do not merely reflect the topics that academics study but encompass the issues faced by its practitioners in their work within organisations. To this end, programme designers on both sides of the Atlantic Ocean have sought to identify the key areas of concern to practitioners and employers.

In the USA, this line of research was initiated with a survey of 1,100 human resource managers, public health professionals and experts in disciplines allied to OHP (Schneider, Camara, Tetrick & Sternberg, 1999). The survey, commissioned by the American Psychological Association (APA) and the U.S. National Institute for Occupational Safety and Health (NIOSH), revealed a need for OHP education and training but stopped short of delineating a curriculum. Schneider and colleagues' study laid the groundwork for the development of OHP curricula in the USA in the late 1990s, including the programme operated as a minor within doctoral-level training at the University of Houston. Keen to ensure that the Houston curriculum met the needs of local employers, the programme directors surveyed 141 human resource managers and 27 trade union representatives on their organisation's concern about various OHP-related topics (Tetrick & Ellis, 2002). Using a 5-point scale, respondents were required to indicate the degree of organisational concern associated with thirty one OHP-related topics derived from the authors' knowledge of the OHP literature and human resource practices in the USA. Results revealed that the top ten concerns of human resource managers included: accidents, attendance, changing technology, education and training, employee commitment, physical well-being, psychological well-being, safety, teamwork and workplace injuries. Overall, trade union representatives generated a similar list of concerns but with an emphasis on issues of concern to individual employees such as job security, occupational stress, retirement and workload.

Subsequently, a survey of US-based health and safety practitioners (n = 67) and OHP academics/researchers (n = 9), conducted at Portland State University, sought to assess both the types of organisations that OHP practitioners work within and the nature of health and safety issues they are charged with addressing (Sinclair, Hammer, Oeldorf Hirsch & Brubaker, 2006). Taking the sample as a whole, the top ten OHP-related issues identified as being most important included: accidents, safety climate, personal protective equipment, compliance with US Occupational Safety and Health Administration regulations, fire safety, repetitive strain injuries, ergonomics, traumatic injuries, workers' compensation and noise/hearing protection. Due to the nature of the sample the results were biased towards the perceptions of practitioners, many of whom worked in safety-related occupations. Thus, the results offer a tentative indication of the topics that might be considered important to an OHP curriculum from the viewpoint of a particular constituency.

Fullagar & Hatfield (2005) conducted an analysis of curriculum areas addressed in US doctoral-level OHP training programmes alongside a knowledge, skills and abilities analysis for jobs related to OHP (e.g., industrial/organizational psychologist, occupational safety and health specialist and occupational safety engineer). Across the twelve curricula examined, only one topic area was taught at each HEI: an introduction to the discipline of OHP. Work-related stress was taught at seven HEIs, making it the second most common topic area. Fullagar & Hatfield's study was important because the results permitted, for the first time, the tentative advancement of an OHP practitioner job description. This conceptualised the practitioner's job as being to:

"Review, evaluate, and analyze work environments and design programs and procedures to promote worker health and reduce occupational stress caused by psychological, organizational and social factors. Apply principles of psychology to occupational health problems. Activities may include policy planning; employee screening, training and development; and organizational development and analysis. May work with management to reorganize the work setting to improve worker health. May be employed in the public or private sector."

In Europe, there have been similar attempts to design curricula around practitioner needs; most notably, at the University of Nottingham which introduced the world's first OHP Masters programme in 1996. Since that time the number of students pursuing the programme has grown year on year and in 2005 an e-learning variant was introduced as an alternative to full-time campus-based study. Despite the success of the programme, alumni feedback revealed that graduates sometimes felt insecure at job interviews in the months following programme completion owing to a lack of real-life work experience within organisations. Alumni asserted that work experience within the Masters programme would help to engender greater depth of knowledge in respect of the occupational health needs of employers and thus better equip graduates for entering the professional world of work. In response, the programme team initiated two activities. Proposals were advanced on the introduction of an internship within the Masters programme and a study was conducted to identify (i) emerging and future occupational health priorities and (ii) occupational health (and safety) practitioner training needs in the British context (Leka, Khan & Griffiths, 2007).

The study consisted of (i) a Delphi interview-based investigation that involved national-level occupational safety and health experts (n = 30) and (ii) a questionnaire that was administered to occupational health and safety practitioners (n = 1,679). Results of the Delphi study showed that subject matter experts' top five emerging and future workplace health priorities included (i) common mental health problems (anxiety, depression and stress), (ii) sickness absence (monitoring, management, return to work, rehabilitation, presenteeism), (iii) musculoskeletal disorders, (iv) engaging and advising small and medium sized enterprises, and (v) the evaluation of workplace health interventions. Survey results revealed that practitioners identified eight priority areas in terms of emerging and future workplace health issues: (i) common mental health problems, (ii) the use of government guidance on the management of work-related stress (the British Health and Safety Executive's Management Standards), (iii) the identification of emerging risks, (iv) planning for major events (e.g., pandemics), (v) work-related driving, (vi) work-life balance, (vii) immigrant and migrant workers, and (viii) non-standard workplaces (e.g., flexiwork and tele-work). In terms of training needs, survey respondents highlighted seven key knowledge areas: (i) persuasion, attitude and behaviour change, (ii) risk perception and communication, (iii) change management, (iv) new legislation and guidance, (v) organizational culture, (vi) ethics and codes of conduct, and (vii) the bio-psycho-social model of health. These findings provided useful guidance on topics that might be covered within the Nottingham curriculum with a view towards preparing graduates for professional practice.

The studies described here share the intention of canvassing stakeholder opinion on topic areas that might be considered important and core to an OHP curriculum. In light of this aim, it is perhaps surprising that the review highlights only one attempt to elicit views from the OHP academic community (Sinclair et al., 2006): an important constituency whose views bring considerable weight to bear in the design and implementation of curricula in HEIs. Sinclair and colleagues' study provided a useful preliminary indication of the views of the academic OHP community; however, care must be taken in generalising results generated from a restricted sample of nine academics all of whom worked in the US higher education system. Thus, the review highlights the need for further research on the definition of an OHP curriculum involving this key constituency whose voice has hitherto been neglected in the debate.

This chapter now turns to an exploratory study that sought to address this shortcoming in the research base. The study involves the elicitation of subject matter expert opinion from an international sample of OHP academics for the purpose of defining important and core topics within OHP curriculum.

THE CURRENT STUDY

In recognition of the imperative for research into the definition of OHP curriculum areas as a pre-requisite for the expansion and consolidation of educational provision, the EA-OHP Education Forum and the SOHP Education and Training Committee together designed and administered the current study. The collaboration represented an important landmark in co-operation between the European and North American representative bodies for the discipline. It is anticipated that the study will signal the beginning of an ongoing set of collaborative activities on the advancement of research, education and professional practice in OHP.

The study had the following aims:

1. To identify the topic areas perceived by OHP academics to be (i) important and (ii) core to an educational curriculum in the discipline
2. To assess whether differences exist between North American and European OHP academics in respect of the topics perceived to be (i) important and (ii) core to an educational curriculum in the discipline

METHOD

Participants

Delegates at the Work, Stress and Health 2008 conference in Washington, DC, USA, comprised the sample of participants in the current study. The event was the latest in the conference series jointly organised by the APA, NIOSH and, more recently, SOHP. The conference was targeted at OHP researchers, educators and practitioners as well as professionals from the allied disciplines.

Data was collected by means of a questionnaire that was included in the information pack issued to each delegate. Delegates were asked to return completed surveys to a box at the conference registration desk or, alternatively, to mail surveys to the lead author. Twenty eight completed and usable surveys were returned.

Table 1 reveals that respondents were drawn from ten countries. The United Kingdom and the United States of America were the most strongly represented countries in numeric terms; these two countries generated four and fifteen responses respectively. Respondents had 14 years mean OHP-related work experience.

Table 1: Respondents' country of residence

Country of residence	Frequency
Germany	1
Ireland	1
Italy	1
Netherlands	2
Norway	1
Russia	1
Spain	1
Taiwan	1
United Kingdom	4
United States of America	15

The questionnaire

The questionnaire presented a list of sixty eight OHP-related topic areas. The topics were selected by the authors on the basis of a review of issues addressed in the two leading international OHP journals: Work and Stress and the Journal of Occupational Health Psychology over a ten-year period from 1997 to 2007. Respondents were required to indicate the importance of each topic to an educational OHP curriculum on a five point scale that ranged from [1] 'not important' to [5] 'extremely important'. The topics within the list were not entirely independent, e.g., 'work design and health' and 'job characteristics and health'. However, such topics were presented separately to capture potentially different perspectives among respondents. Space was provided for respondents to add topics not covered in the list. Data was also collected on respondents' job type, job title, number of years of experience in OHP and country of residence.

An additional set of questions focused on competencies required for professional practice in OHP. Results will be reported in a separate forthcoming publication.

RESULTS

Core topic areas

Topic areas that achieved a mean score of 3 or more were defined as *important* to an OHP educational curriculum. Table 2 reveals that on the basis of responses given by the entire sample of participants, twenty one topics met this criterion. Six participants made suggestions for additional topic areas; however, each topic was advanced by only one participant and no overlap was discernable. This allowed the authors to conclude that the sixty eight OHP-related topics listed in the questionnaire offered a near-comprehensive overview of topics that might be included under the OHP umbrella.

A cut-off of 3.5 was applied for the identification of topics that might be considered essential, or *core*, to a curriculum. Six topic areas met this criterion (indicated by an asterisk in Table 2): (i) interventions to promote health, (ii) organisational research methods, (iii) psychosocial work environment, (iv) stress theory, (v) stress interventions and (vi) work design and health.

Differences between European and North American experts

Data provided by participants working in Russia and Taiwan (n = 2) were excluded for purposes of drawing comparisons between the perspectives of academics working in Europe and North America on the question of which topics might be important and core to a curriculum.

Table 3 reveals that thirty-one topic areas were identified by the European sample (n = 11) as important to an OHP curriculum. Among these, eight topic areas were identified as core. These included: (i) absence, (ii) combating

Table 2: Topic areas identified as important to an OHP educational curriculum (entire sample)

Topic area	Mean score
Accidents	3.1
Ageing	3.1
Attitude and behaviour change	3.1
Bullying and harassment	3.0
Burnout	3.3
Combating psychosocial risks	3.4
Coping	3.1
Design of the work environment	3.4
Health promotion	3.3
Interventions to promote health	3.7*
Mental health	3.1
New ways of working	3.2
Occupational health hazards	3.4
Organisational research methods	3.6*
Psychosocial work environment	3.6*
Relationships at work	3.0
Stress theory	3.7*
Stress interventions	3.7*
Work-life balance	3.4
Work design and health	3.5*
Work schedules	3.1

psychosocial risks, (iii) design of the work environment, (iv) interventions to promote health, (v) organisational research methods, (vi) psychosocial work environment, (vii) stress theory and (viii) stress interventions.

Twenty three topic areas were identified by the North American sample (n = 15) as important to an OHP curriculum. Among these, six topic areas were identified as core to an educational curriculum. These included: (i) interventions to promote health, (ii) organisational research methods, (iii) psychosocial work environment, (iv) stress theory, (v) stress interventions and, (vi) work design and health.

Sixteen topic areas were identified by both North American and European participants as important to an OHP curriculum. These are illustrated in Table 4. Among these, five topics were identified by both groups as core to an OHP curriculum: (i) interventions to promote health, (ii) organisational research methods, (iii) psychosocial work environment, (iv) stress theory and, (v) stress interventions.

Table 3: Topic areas identified as important to an OHP educational curriculum (European and North American samples)

Topic area	Mean score (North American sample) (n = 15)	Topic area	Mean score (European sample) (n = 11)
Accidents	3.2	Absence	3.6*
Burnout	3.3	Accidents	3.1
Combating psychosocial risks	3.1	Ageing	3.2
Coping	3.0	Attitude and behaviour change	3.4
Design of the work environment	3.1	Bullying and harassment	3.2
Development and history of the discipline of OHP	3.2	Burnout	3.3
Ergonomic factors	3	Combating psychosocial risks	3.8*
Health promotion	3.1	Coping	3.4
Interventions to promote health	3.5*	Design of the work environment	3.7*
Mental health	3.0	Employee emotions	3.1
Musculoskeletal disorders	3.0	Health promotion	3.4
New ways of working	3.0	High risk jobs and populations	3.0
Occupational health hazards	3.4	Interventions to promote health	3.9*
Organisational research methods	3.7*	Job insecurity	3.2
Psychosocial work environment	3.5*	Leadership	3.1
Safety climate	3.4	Management competencies	3.0
Stress theory	3.7*	Mental health	3.3
Stress interventions	3.5*	New ways of working	3.4
Training	3.0	Occupational health hazards	3.3
Wellness programmes	3.0	Organisational change	3.4

Table 3: Contd.

Topic area	Mean score (North American sample) (n = 15)	Topic area	Mean score (European sample) (n = 11)
Work-life balance	3.3	Organisational culture	3.1
Work design and health	3.7*	Organisational research methods	3.7*
Work schedules	3.3	Professional competencies	3.0
		Psychosocial work environment	3.8*
		Relationships at work	3.2
		Return to work	3.1
		Risk management	3.2
		Stress theory	3.7*
		Stress interventions	3.9*
		Work-life balance	3.3
		Work design and health	3.3

Table 4: Topic areas identified as important and core to an OHP educational curriculum by European and North American participants (topics identified as core by both groups are identified by an asterisk)

Topic area	Mean score (North American sample) (n = 15)	Topic area	Mean score (European sample) (n = 11)
Accidents	3.2	Accidents	3.1
Burnout	3.3	Burnout	3.3
Combating psychosocial risks	3.1	Combating psychosocial risks	3.8
Coping	3.0	Coping	3.4
Design of the work environment	3.1	Design of the work environment	3.7
Health promotion	3.1	Health promotion	3.4
Interventions to promote health	3.5*	Interventions to promote health	3.9*

Table 4: Contd.

Topic area	Mean score (North American sample) (n = 15)	Topic area	Mean score (European sample) (n = 11)
Mental health	3.0	Mental health	3.3
New ways of working	3.0	New ways of working	3.4
Occupational health hazards	3.4	Occupational health hazards	3.3
Organisational research methods	3.7*	Organisational research methods	3.7*
Psychosocial work environment	3.5*	Psychosocial work environment	3.8*
Stress theory	3.7*	Stress theory	3.7*
Stress interventions	3.5*	Stress interventions	3.9*
Work-life balance	3.3	Work-life balance	3.3
Work design and health	3.7	Work design and health	3.3

DISCUSSION

The exploratory study described here set out to investigate (i) which topic areas might be perceived by OHP academics as important and core to an educational curriculum in the discipline and (ii) whether differences exist between North American and European OHP academics in respect of the above.

The study revealed that it was possible to identify broad consensus among a restricted sample of OHP academics on the topic areas that might be addressed within a curriculum. North American participants identified twenty three topic areas and European academics identified thirty one topics as important to a curriculum. Agreement between the two groups could be found on the importance of sixteen topic areas. Among these, five were held by both groups to be core to a curriculum: (i) interventions to promote health, (ii) organizational research methods, (iii) psychosocial work environment, (iv) stress theory and, (v) stress interventions. In addition to these five areas, North American academics identified work-design and health as an additional core topic. European academics identified an additional three core topics: absence, combating psychosocial risks and design of the work environment. Considerable overlap between these areas can be discerned. It is notable that these findings are not inconsistent with the previously described high level characteristics identified by Cox et al. (2000) as central to defining the discipline.

Differences between North American and European perspectives

European and North American differences in the approach taken to the definition of OHP were discussed earlier in this chapter in the context of possible implications for the selection of topics that might be included in OHP curricula. It was shown that whereas the European perspective conceptualises a discipline that tackles occupational health issues by drawing on principles and practices from various fields of applied psychology, the North American perspective conceptualises OHP in a multidisciplinary fashion whereby knowledge and skills are incorporated from a range of disciplines including, inter alia, psychology, public health, medicine, management and occupational safety and health. It was noted that this difference in perspective might present a barrier to the achievement of international consensus among academics on the topic areas that might be included within an OHP curriculum. The findings of the exploratory study presented here suggest that the contrasting heritage of North American and European OHP may not present a barrier to the achievement of international consensus among academics on the topic areas that are considered (i) important and (ii) core to an OHP curriculum. This conclusion is drawn on the basis of a restricted sample of only twenty eight participants; verification is required through replication of the study with a considerably larger international sample of academics. However, it should be noted that the entire population of OHP academics is limited owing to the youthfulness of the discipline. As such, it may be difficult to secure a sample of a size sufficient to permit inferential statistical analysis of the data.

Curriculum flexibility

It is important to appreciate that the study described here did not set out to identify a list of topic areas that together might be deemed to constitute a comprehensive OHP curriculum. To attempt such would be misguided because, in reality, no single curriculum can prepare an OHP practitioner for every conceivable situation that he or she may face in his or her work. Rather, the objective was to identify those areas that an international sample of OHP academics might consider central to a curriculum while acknowledging that the range of topics taught around this core will be determined by a variety of factors including, inter alia, the needs of the local labour force and faculty members' research expertise.

A flexible approach to curriculume design is advantageous in that it allows for the continual evolution of curricula in response to developments in the challenges to occupational health presented by the changing workforce, changing context of work and changing nature of work. As Adkins (1999) has pointed out,

> "To meet the evolving psychosocial needs of the working community, occupational health psychologists need to adapt and grow with organisational change. Continuing to refine and develop occupational health psychology principles will enable practitioners to confront the challenge of maximizing both workforce and organisational health" (p. 136).

Where flexibility in curriculum design is allied with an emphasis on continual professional development and skills training in (i) the identification of new challenges to occupational health and (ii) the adaptation of existing knowledge and skills to tackle ever-changing challenges, it might be suggested that a generation of OHP practitioners will emerge that is equipped to combat contemporary challenges to occupational health. OHP professionals in this mould would also recognise the limits of their own knowledge and skills and be cognizant of situations when it might be appropriate and necessary to draw in the services of other occupational health professionals.

Limitations

A number of shortcomings can be identified in this study. Largely due to the fact that the survey was administered at a conference in the USA, the majority of survey respondents worked in North America. As such, the findings might over-represent the opinions of North American OHP academics at the expense of the European perspective. In addition, consistent with much previous research on the definition of curriculum areas in OHP, the study involved a numerically small sample that precluded the use of inferential statistical techniques for analysis of the data.

Two anecdotal points may be made in respect of the issue of sample size. First, it might be considered ironic that the study population – academics - who spend much of their time designing and administering surveys, were reluctant to complete and return this particular survey. The low response rate does not appear to be exclusive to this study; it is consistent with that achieved by others which have sought to elicit the opinions of researchers who study work-related psychosocial issues (European Agency for Safety and Health at Work, 2007). It is unclear whether the low completion and return rate reflected distrust of survey-based studies among OHP academics, apathy, fundamental concerns about the research question or other factors. On the basis of informal conversations with colleagues in the OHP academic community, it is the authors' contention that the poor response rate may reflect a lack of recognition of the importance of the research question among the population. Owing to the youthful nature of the discipline, most academics with a professional interest in OHP have come to the discipline already in possession of qualifications and expertise in fields related to but distinct from OHP. As such, the careers of these people are likely to be unaffected by the evolution and professionalisation of OHP. It might be speculated that the growing cohort of OHP graduates in the early stages of their professional OHP careers might have a stronger vested interest in the research question considered here and, by extension, might be more responsive to calls for participation in studies that hold the potential to pave the way for developments in OHP programme accreditation and professional recognition, regulation and support structures.

Second, it waits to be seen whether the combination of a small sample and descriptive statistical analysis of the data is likely to present a barrier to the future publication of this study in a peer-reviewed journal. Among the studies reviewed earlier in this chapter, of those that involved the administration of surveys for the purpose of identifying an OHP curriculum, only one has reached the pages of a peer-reviewed journal (Schneider et al., 1999). That study involved a sample in excess of 1,000 participants, in contrast to most of the remaining studies which used considerably smaller samples. If issues of sample size can explain the paucity of peer-reviewed published research in this area then it might be speculated that attempts to secure publication of the current study in a journal might be fraught with difficulty. That would be a matter of regret for a host of reasons, not least because it could reveal a failure on the part of reviewers to acknowledge that the population of OHP academics remains relatively small and that, as such, survey-based studies that have their focus on this population will inevitably involve small samples. It is important that the dissemination of research on the development of an OHP curriculum is not hampered by the reviewing criteria of academic journals. This situation highlights one of the important roles of the EA-OHP's book series *Occupational Health Psychology: European Perspectives on Research, Education and Practice*: to provide a forum for the communication of research on topics of importance to the development of education and training in OHP where that research might not be suitable for publication via the traditional journal-based route. In addition, by virtue of being distributed free of charge to all delegates at EA-OHP conferences and available for purchase online, the book series has the added benefit of reaching its target market (OHP researchers, educators, students and practitioners) in a way that journal articles cannot always achieve.

In light of these shortcomings the study presented here must be considered exploratory and its results receptive to validation through replication using larger samples. The authors intend to address both these shortcomings by conducting a repeated administration of the survey at the EA-OHP 2008 conference in Valencia.

Future research

As has been described, the definition of the important and core topic areas within an OHP curriculum is of importance in various ways to the development of education and professional practice in OHP. However, while the definition of curriculum areas is important, to develop a curriculum that truly prepares graduates for professional practice it is important that such research activities are augmented with those directed at the delineation of core competencies required in professional practice. The results of such research would have important implications for the content of OHP curricula and the style of learning activities adopted. Perhaps surprisingly, researchers have largely neglected this topic. An exception is that of Adkins (1999) who noted that practice should be: a) grounded in theory, b) informed by a business plan capable of predicting financial and psychological benefits, c) focused at the organisational 'systems' level that recognises the dynamic and complex transaction between people and their environment rather than focussing at the individual level of analysis and, d) open to transcending traditional boundaries and using knowledge and skills derived from a variety of domains. In view of the paucity of research on professional competencies in OHP, the current authors intend to extend the collaborative research between EA-OHP and SOHP initiated by the current study with further investigations into the development of a matrix of core competencies for professional practice.

As mentioned above, the current study represents the beginning of an era of collaborative research between EA-OHP and SOHP. Such activities are to be welcomed because this youthful discipline is unlikely to mature and develop long-term sustainability in the absence of collaboration between its representative bodies. However, collaborative ventures such as that presented here also serve to highlight the contrasting educational structures that operate in Europe and North America. As such, research that may be of immediate importance to one body may offer less short-term utility to the other. This can be seen, for example, in informal conversations surrounding the current study that revealed the immediate imperative to define a core curriculum in the European context where such may usefully contribute to the pan-European debate on the professionalisation of psychologists in respect of the EuroPsy qualification. The expansion of EuroPsy is likely to have an increasingly important bearing on the structure and content of

European Masters degrees. In the USA the picture is quite different; OHP is rarely, if ever, taught at Masters level and, as such, fewer imperatives may exist in the short term for the delineation of a core curriculum. It is inevitable that research will not always have equal pertinence across constituencies. It is a sign of the strength of international relationships between representative bodies that initiatives such as that reported in this chapter should not prevent collaborative endeavours.

CONCLUSIONS

For reasons outlined herein, it is the authors' contention that education and training in OHP must be standardised to some degree if professional practice in the discipline is to sustain in the long term. Part of the standardisation process involves the definition of the central features of an OHP curriculum. This chapter has demonstrated that a host of imperatives exists for the development of consensus surrounding the topic areas that might be considered important to an educational OHP curriculum. Previous studies that have attempted to elicit the views of stakeholders (primarily occupational safety and health practitioners) to this end have been reviewed. The review highlighted the paucity of research involving an important constituency whose views bring considerable weight to bear in the design and implementation of curricula in HEIs: OHP academics. In response to this shortcoming in the knowledge base, the current authors conducted an exploratory study, described in detail here for the first time, which sought to investigate the possibility of achieving consensus among an international sample of OHP academics. Consensus was found on the importance of sixteen topic areas. Among these, five were held by both groups to be core to a curriculum. It was shown that the contrasting heritage of North American and European OHP may not present a barrier to the achievement of international consensus among academics on the topic areas that are considered (i) important and (ii) core to an OHP curriculum. The need for further research involving larger samples is highlighted as a vital next step towards the delineation of the central elements of an OHP curriculum.

ACKNOWLEDGEMENTS

The authors wish to express their gratitude to the EA-OHP for funding the study described herein. The contents of this chapter represent the views of the authors and do not necessarily reflect those of the EA-OHP or the SOHP.

REFERENCES

ADKINS, J.A. (1999). Promoting organizational health: the evolving practice of occupational health psychology, *Professional Psychology: Research and Practice, 30,* 129-137.

BARNES-FARRELL, J. (2006). History of OHP and education of OHP professionals in the United States, In S. McIntyre & J. Houdmont (Eds.), *Occupational Health Psychology: Key Papers of the European Academy of Occupational Health Psychology (Vol. 7),* Maia, Portugal: ISMAI Publishers. ISBN: 972-9048-21-5

CHEN, P. Y., HUANG, Y. H. & DEARMOND, S. (2005). Occupational Health Psychology:Opportunities and Challenges for Psychologists in the 21st Century, *Research in Applied Psychology, 27,* 43-56.

COX, T. (2000). Chair's address: European Academy of Occupational Health Psychology: Present and Future, in T. Cox., P. Dewe., K. Nielsen & R. Cox (Eds.), *Occupational Health Psychology: Europe 2000,* Nottingham: I-WHO Publications. ISSN 1473-0200.

COX, T., BALDURSSON, E. & RIAL-GONZALEZ, E. (2000). Occupational health psychology, *Work & Stress, 14,* 101-104.

EUROPEAN ACADEMY OF OCCUPATIONAL HEALTH PSYCHOLOGY (2002). *The Promotion of Education in Occupational Health Psychology: A Strategy for the European Academy,* Author. (copies of this document may be obtained from the Executive Officer: jonathan.houdmont@nottingham.ac.uk).

EUROPEAN AGENCY FOR SAFETY AND HEALTH AT WORK (2007). *Expert forecast on emerging psychosocial risks to occupational safety and health,* Luxembourg: Office for Official Publications of the European Communities.

EUROPEAN FEDERATION OF PSYCHOLOGISTS' ASSOCIATIONS (2006). *EuroPsy – The European Certificate in Psychology,* Retrieved, 23 April, 2008, from, http://www.efpa.be/doc/EuroPsyJune%202006.pdf.

FULLAGAR, C. & HATFIELD, J. (2005). *Occupational Health Psychology: Charting the Field,* 20th annual SIOP Conference, April 15-17, Los Angeles, CA: USA.

HOUDMONT, J., LEKA, S. & COX, T. (2007). Education in occupational health psychology in Europe: Where have we been, where are we now and where are we going? In J. Houdmont & S. McIntyre (Eds.), *Occupational Health Psychology: European Perspectives on Research, Education and Practice (Vol. 2),* Maia, Portugal: ISMAI Publishers. Pdf available at http://eprints.nottingham.ac.uk/724/

LEKA, S., KHAN, S. & GRIFFITHS, A. (2007). *Exploring Training Needs for Health and Safety Practitioners with Regard to Workplace Health Issues,* report for the Institution of Occupational Safety and Health, Institute of Work, Health and Organisations: University of Nottingham.

MACIK-FREY, M., QUICK, J. AND NELSON, D. (2007). Advances in occupational health: From a stressful beginning to a positive future, *Journal of Management, 33,* 809-840.

RAYMOND, J., WOOD, D. & PATRICK, W. (1990). Psychology training in work and health, *American Psychologist, 45,* 1159-1161.

SCHNEIDER, D.L., CAMARA, W.J., TETRICK, T.E. & STERNBERG, C.R. (1999). Training in occupational health psychology: Initial efforts and alternative models, *Professional Psychology, 30,* 138-142.

SINCLAIR, R. (2006). Decisions and dilemmas in constructing and OHP training program. In S. McIntyre & J. Houdmont (Eds.). *Occupational Health Psychology: Key Papers of the European Academy of Occupational Health Psychology (Vol. 7),* Maia, Portugal: ISMAI Publishers. ISBN: 972-9048-21-5.

SINCLAIR, R., HAMMER, L., OELDORF HIRSCH, A. & BRUBAKER, T. (2006). Do academics and practitioners agree on perceived occupational health priorities? *APA/NIOSH Work Stress and Health conference,* 2-4 March, Miami, FL: USA.

TETRICK, L. & ELLIS, B. (2002). Developing an OHP curriculum that addresses the needs of organizations and labor unions in the USA. In C. Weikert, E. Torkelson & J. Pryce (Eds.), *Occupational Health Psychology: Empowerment, Participation and Health at Work,* Nottingham: I-WHO Publications. ISBN: 0-9539936-2-0

PRACTICE

A PARTICIPATORY APPROACH TO PROMOTING PSYCHOSOCIAL HEALTH AT WORK
DEVELOPING THE INFORMING, COUNSELLING AND ADVISING (ICA) PRACTICES OF OCCUPATIONAL HEALTH PSYCHOLOGISTS

Päivi Jalonen, Sirkku Kivistö and Helena Palmgren

CHAPTER OVERVIEW

Informing, counselling and advising (ICA) in Occupational Health Services (OHS) refers to the educational activities by which occupational health personnel facilitate the learning of individuals and organisations on health and safety issues. The present chapter deals with developing ICA practices by OHS in the context of an action research study conducted in co-operation with six OHS units and their client organisations in 2006-2007. The study consisted of development processes containing learning sessions for the OH personnel and researchers, and the tasks to be carried out in-between the sessions by the OH personnel and their clients. The data emanated from questionnaires and interviews conducted before and after the process, minutes of sessions and the good ICA practice developed in the process. Here we focus on the ICA development process of an occupational health psychologist (OHP) and her client organisation; the nursing staff at a university hospital. During the process, the OHP developed an ICA matrix for planning health education on all levels of the client organisation. The results confirmed that the focus of health education and communication in the work of OHPs is on individual employees, although often the impact of ICA would be more significant if it also reached those organisational stakeholders with authority for decision-making. Action research, as a method, helped the clients to perceive and define their health needs and to understand the role of the OHP.

INTRODUCTION

According to The Occupational Health Service Act in Finland (2002), the mission of Occupational Health Services (OHS) is the primary prevention of illnesses and injuries and overall health promotion. In the Finnish OHS, informing, counselling and advising (ICA) is a form of health education and communication, and it is the central way of promoting health (Palmgren & Turja 2007). ICA can be defined as a process by which OH personnel facilitate the individual and organisational learning of health and safety issues. The goals of ICA in OHS are the development of knowledge, skills, attitudes and behaviours that the clients need for the promotion and maintenance of their own health and well-being, as well as the health and well-being of their work communities and organisations. At present, the majority of ICA activities are focused on individual employees, rather than on other stakeholders within the employing organisation or on the system level of the workplace setting (Palmgren et al. 2008). Still, many issues affecting health and well-being at work are not within the reach of an individual employee. Such things as management and supervisory practices, production processes and their influence on the ways in which work is performed have a significant impact on the well-being of the employees (Sauter et al., 1999). Respectively, the well-being and work ability of employees is related to the performance of the organisation.

By providing relevant information about the relationships between work and health and counselling – not only to individual employees but also to organisational stakeholders with decision-making authority – occupational health psychologists (OHP) are able to support psycho-social health at work. However, the expertise of OHPs has not yet been fully exploited in OHS practice.

The purpose of this chapter is to discuss the contribution of ICA provided by OHPs in promoting health at work. It examines the development of ICA practices by OHPs in the context of an action research study. The aim of the action research was to develop informing, counselling and advising practices in OHS in collaboration with occupational health personnel and the representatives of their client organisations.

HEALTH EDUCATION IN OHS

In spite of the vast amount of research on health education and communication in the field of public health promotion, we still know fairly little about how these activities are carried out in the context of OHS. There are only a limited number of studies and reported projects concerning ICA in OHS despite the consensus among the different stakeholders on the importance of these activities and the promising evidence about their effectiveness (Hulshof et al., 1999, Notkola et al., 1990). Furthermore, most of the empirical studies conducted in OHS focus on health education by occupational health nurses and physicians and how they counsel individuals.

Occupational health physicians spend less time on health education than nurses, even though a doctor's appointment could be an effective context for learning (Hakkarainen, 2000, Palmgren et al., 2007, Mechanic, 1999, Russell et al., 1987). It has been suggested that health education by OH physicians is mostly a transmission of information, whereas nurses tend to emphasise personal empowerment and greater autonomy of clients concerning their own health (Palmgren, 2000, Palmgren et al., 2007, Rantanen, 1993). On the other hand, the methods commonly used by nurses seem to be more suitable for knowledge transfer than for helping the clients develop skills needed in maintaining and promoting health (Palmgren et al., 2008; Rantanen, 1993).

For occupational health nurses and physicians, individual employees are the primary clients of ICA. In their work with individuals, both nurses and physicians concentrate on the traditional topics of health education: personal health and work ability. Mostly, ICA is performed in the context of work ability assessments and health examinations. Also, the impact of educational activities in OHS is mainly considered from the viewpoint of the individual. In their assessments of the effects of health education, nurses and physicians most often perceived positive changes in the health behaviours and lifestyle of employees (Palmgren et al., 2008.)

However, by concentrating mainly on health education by OH nurses and physicians, research on ICA provides us with only a partial picture of health education and communication in OHS. The research on ICA in OHS has seemingly left the contribution of OHPs unexplored. Still, informing, counselling and advising is the responsibility of all OHS professionals; it is an essential part of the work done by OHPs.

To fill the gap in knowledge concerning OHPs' educational activities, we conducted a questionnaire study of ICA in Finnish OHS units (Palmgren et al., 2008). According to our results, OHPs also communicate mainly with individual workers. Yet, unlike other OH professionals, who provide information and advice concerning health and work ability during their encounters with individuals, OHPs concentrate more on collaboration and relationships in the workplace, organisational change, and the ways in which the work is organised at the workplace.

Instead of understanding health education as influencing the knowledge, beliefs and health behaviours of an individual, it can be examined in the wider context of health promotion utilising the concept of health literacy (Kickbusch & Nutbeam, 1998, Nutbeam, 1998, 2001; Kickbush, 2001; Zarkadoolas et al., 2005). In the broad sense, health literacy refers to a range of outcomes for health education and communication activities.

Health literacy refers to the personal, cognitive and social skills which determine the ability of individuals to gain, understand, and use information to promote and maintain good health (Nutbeam 1998). These include improved knowledge and understanding of health determinants and changed attitudes and motivations related to health behaviours (Nutbeam, 2001).

The theories about behavioural change, such as the Theory of Reasoned Action (Fishbein & Ajzen, 1980), Social Learning Theory (Bandura, 1977), and the Transtheoretical Model of Health Behaviour (Prochaska & Velicer, 1997; Prochaska &. Norcross, 2001) have shed light on the complex relationships between knowledge, beliefs, social norms, motivation, and the information transmission of educational programmes in health promotion. In OHS, the efforts to promote knowledge, understanding and the capacity to act should not only be directed at changing personal lifestyle but also to raising awareness about the organisational factors of health and well-being at work. Furthermore, ICA should be directed towards supporting individual and collective actions that can modify these factors.

In work communities and organisations, there is a need for shared knowledge and understanding, for norms and practices that enable organisational members to seek solutions for the challenges to their health and well-being, to utilise OHS and other health supporting services, and to develop work, working environments and work processes that maintain and promote physical and psychosocial health at work. Thus, ICA activities directed only at individual employees are not sufficient. In addition, OH personnel should also consider other organisational members and work communities as their ICA clients.

In spite of their emphasis on educating individual employees, OHPs work more often with work communities and groups than nurses and physicians, who provide information and advice for these clients most often in written form in the context of workplace surveys. OHPs utilise more participative and activating methods, such as case studies, tutoring small groups and practical exercises that not only aim to inform groups and work communities but to enable them to work together to develop a healthy work community. In their assessments of the effectiveness of ICA, OHPs referred most often to changes at the level of work communities; improvements identified included better functioning of work communities, more efficient leadership practices, and new solutions to workplace conflicts (Palmgren et al., 2008.)

In the context of workplace surveys, OHPs have utilised an interactive approach involving all actors in the workplace: employers, foremen, employees, health and safety delegates, and trade union representatives.

In addition to other types of measures, they posed a single question: 'What is your work like from the viewpoint of mental well-being?' The aim of the question was to activate employees and other actors to better recognise their health and safety needs (Kivistö, 2007). OHPs have also developed new ways of providing information to workplaces, such as information letters containing up-to-date information on the specific health challenges of the workplace identified in the workplace surveys (Kivistö et al., 2007, Appendix 1).

Managers, HR staff, and other representatives of the client organisation are only seldom regarded as clients of ICA. OHPs direct even less ICA activities at them than nurses and physicians (Palmgren et al., 2008). However, OHPs possess expert knowledge that is useful for those responsible for decision-making in organisations. In order to prevent occupational stress and promote mental health at work, understanding of the changes of today's work life, as well as their consequences in work organisations, is crucial. For example, organisational downsizing or changes in ownership and management influence role clarity, perceived fairness, and organisational climate that predict sickness absence, job satisfaction and organisational commitment (Väänänen et al., 2004; Head, et al., 2006; Jalonen et al., 2006). The expertise of OHPs should be utilised on a wider scale in the strategic leadership domain within organisations.

There is no systematic planning of ICA activities and no co-ordination of these activities in the OH units (Palmgren et al., 2008). Furthermore, the clients are not engaged in the planning process, even though participative planning would ensure that their needs would be met. Collaborative planning would raise awareness of the potential of ICA by OHS in helping the organisation to solve its health challenges; it would also build commitment to the jointly planned goals and activities and clarify the roles of both parties in promoting health.

Within the scope of occupational health and safety, the needs and expectations of clients have been seldom studied. The customers of OHS appraise informing, counselling and advising as the most important processes in OHS (Dryson, 1995; Reid & Malone, 2003). Opinions about the content of ICA varied among the customers. Dryson (1995) found that in small enterprises, only 15% of employees considered that OHS should provide general health education. Instead, specific occupational health education and informing about local environmental issues were regarded as important. In a study by Talvi et al. (1995), young workers felt they needed information about healthy meals or advice on how to quit smoking, whereas older employees wanted to know more about rheumatic and heart diseases and mental health.

The clients of OHS consist of the management, supervisors, and employees of organisations. In order to be effective, OHS should meet the needs of all these clients, and their opinions should be considered while the services are planned and delivered (Cooper, 1997; Blumenthal, 1996; Macdonald et al., 2000). Furthermore, the needs of special groups, such as young workers and immigrants, should especially be taken into account when planning ICA activities.

THE AIM OF THE STUDY

This action research was the third phase of a research project that aimed to produce new scientific knowledge about health education and communication in OHS and develop good informing, counselling and advising (ICA) practices in OHS. ICA was defined as a process in OHS that facilitates individual and organisational learning of health and safety issues in order to promote the health of individual employees, their work communities, and the entire work organisation. Besides the health education of individual employees, this process also includes educational activities directed to groups, work communities, and representatives of client organisations.

The objective of the action research study was to develop local practices for good ICA and encourage collaboration between OHS and client organisations and within OHS teams. The action research was a collaborative learning process for all participants: the OH personnel, their clients and the researchers. The aim of the research process was also to identify local problems and encourage participants to actively seek solutions to them. In addition, it aimed to identify factors that may facilitate or hinder co-operation between OH personnel and its clients.

Action research provided the context in which the participants could learn together by examining and discussing the health needs of the participating organisations and develop ICA activities to meet these needs. Our theoretical frames were adult learning (Mezirow, 1995) and experiential learning theories (Kolb, 1989) further developed into a model of learning in work communities and organisations (Järvinen et al., 2000) (Figure 1).

MATERIAL AND METHODS

The study was conducted in co-operation with six OHS units and their 11 client organisations between September 2006 and April 2007. It consisted of local development processes containing five learning sessions for the

OH personnel and the researchers and tasks to be carried out in-between the sessions by the OH personnel and the representatives of their client organisations (Fig. 2).

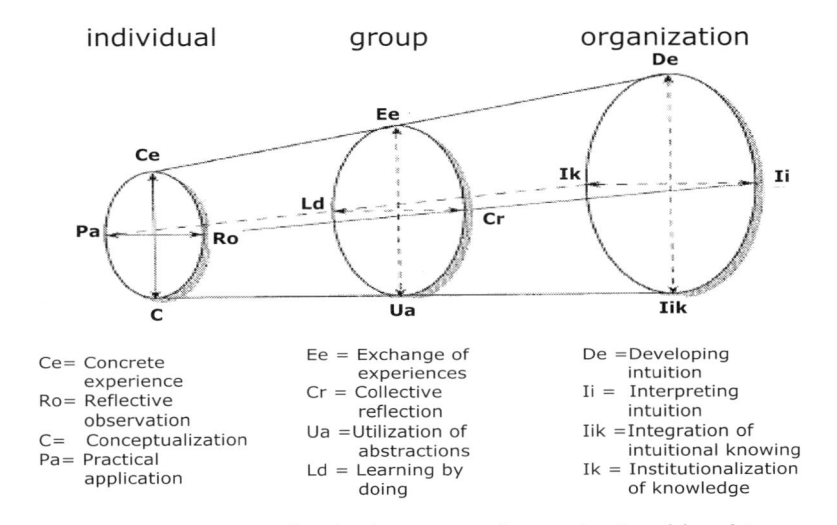

Ce= Concrete experience
Ro= Reflective observation
C= Conceptualization
Pa= Practical application

Ee = Exchange of experiences
Cr = Collective reflection
Ua =Utilization of abstractions
Ld = Learning by doing

De =Developing intuition
Ii = Interpreting intuition
Iik =Integration of intuitional knowing
Ik = Institutionalization of knowledge

Figure 1. Learning at individual, group and organisational level (source Järvinen et al., 2000)

Figure 2. The ICA development process

Each of the local development processes was based on the subjective needs of the participating OH personnel and their clients. The learning sessions built up preconditions for generating good ICA practices; it supported OH personnel's competencies and provided help and advice when needed. In the learning sessions, the OH personnel had opportunities to discuss issues they perceived as important, to reflect jointly on previous ways of conducting ICA and to learn by doing practical exercises and reflecting on them. The development tasks the OH personnel solved in co-operation with their clients provided the context in which OH personnel applied the knowledge and skills they had acquired.

Every learning session had a specific theme that reflected the needs of the participants and the strategic planning process of OHS activities. The development tasks were based on the theme of the previous session. The first learning session oriented the participants to the development process and focussed on the needs of the OH personnel and their client organisation. During the session, the OH personnel specified their own development needs in relation to health education and communication, and set goals for their personal and collective development. After that, they practiced how to apply a collaborative approach to identifying and defining the health and safety needs of the client. In order to plan the ICA process, the participants also needed to be able to set priorities when faced with conflicting needs. The lessons learned in this exercise were transferred into practice in the first development task with the clients.

In the second session, the participants learned how to set measurable, concrete and realistic goals for ICA that were based on the clients' needs. The goals were negotiated and agreed upon with the clients as the second development task. The third session was dedicated to the joint examination of learning as a phenomenon and the means by which learning can be facilitated by ICA. In this session, an action plan of ICA activities for the client organisation was outlined. This tentative plan was discussed and settled with the clients in the third development task. During the fourth learning session, the participants derived good ICA practice from the ICA activities planned with the clients. They also generated guidelines for good ICA practice. The fourth development task was to decide and define the good ICA practice in collaboration with the client. In the concluding session, the utility and practicality of the proposed good ICA practice was discussed. The session ended in a joint evaluation of the process and discussion on what the participants had learned.

Before the process, the researchers had interviewed the participating OH personnel about their views on ICA and learning, their conceptions of how people learn, and expectations concerning the development process. After the process, OH personnel were interviewed about their experiences and what they thought they had learned. The researchers also interviewed the representatives of the client organisations about their experiences, opinions and expectations for OHS. In addition to the interviews, the research data included video recordings and observations of the learning sessions, process evaluation by all participants, and documents, such as ICA action plans, produced in the course of the development process.

In this chapter, we focus on the ICA development process of a psychologist. She worked as an OHP in a multi-professional OH unit of a university hospital. The participatory development process was launched by making a contract between the psychologist and her client; the nursing staff and management of a hospital ward for rheumatism. The former supervisor of the ward had recently retired, and the new head nurse had only brief experience in the ward. The average age of the nursing staff was fairly high, and many were frustrated by the continuous changes in work processes and expected support from the OHS in this stressful situation. The head nurse of the ward was also involved in the development process; she was interviewed before and after the development process. It was in her authority to allow the use of working hours for the development process.

RESULTS

As a result of the development process, the psychologist developed her own model of ICA in the form of an ICA matrix (Table 1). The aim of the matrix is to demonstrate the systematic nature of the ICA process, to emphasise the importance of the need analysis, and to set goals that are concrete, measurable and realistic. The matrix also helps to expand the individually-centred approach in health education and communication to cover all levels of customer: individuals, work communities and organisations.

The psychologist, in collaboration with the participating nursing staff and their supervisor, defined the work ability and well-being of senior workers as the central need of the client. The goals for ICA activities were established as gaining knowledge about how age is related to work ability, knowing where to find help and support when needed, recognising the impact of an ageing worker on the work community and improving the skills needed in interaction and collaboration between workers at different life stages.

The ICA methods utilised by the psychologist included individual counselling sessions, group lectures and the dissemination of information to and discussions with the management of the ward and the hospital. Together with the clients participating in the development process, the psychologist drew up a list of ICA content that helped to generate understanding on the meaning of ageing for work ability and enhance interaction between different generations in the work community. The topics were as follows: 'Health and well-being of an ageing worker',

Components of the matrix	Individual employees	Groups and work communities	Management and other representatives of the client organisation
Need analyses: Focus of ICA: work ability and well-being of a senior worker			
Goals of ICA: Knowledge, abilities, attitudes, and behavioural change of the client	The ageing worker knows and understands influence of age-related changes on health and work ability	Work community understands effects of different cohorts in a working community and on interaction of co-workers	Supervisors understand age-related changes on work ability and can carry out necessary rearrangements regarding working conditions
concrete measurable realistic	He/she knows where to find advice and help for the rearrangements of working conditions		Management knows and understands the significance of the ageing of employees for the organisation
Content of ICA:	Facts about age-related changes on health and work ability	Facts about age-related changes on health and work ability	Facts about age-related changes on health and work ability Workers' thoughts of early retirement as challenges to the HR planning of the organisation
Methods and techniques of ICA	Distribution of information by using discussions, written material, demonstrations	Distribution of information by group discussions, lectures, written material	Informing the management of the hospital via discussions, written material, informing about the sickness absence statistics

Table 1. ICA matrix: ICA activities by OHP concerning ageing workers. Informing, counselling and advising are directed at all three levels of the client: individual employee, groups and working communities and the organisational level.

'Meaning of confidence to collaboration', 'How to give constructive criticism', 'Change as an opportunity', 'Problems and opportunities of multidisciplinary and multi- professional collaboration', and 'Managing sickness absence and return to work'.

During the development process, the psychologist and the other participants realised that it is not easy or self-evident to define the needs of the client and to decide the priorities between them. The clients' needs became easily confused with their expectations towards the OHS. The OHS personnel found it difficult to distinguish the client's needs from the processes of OHS. This was also the case in setting the goals for ICA. In the development process, the OH-personnel learned how to formulate concrete goals in the form of knowledge, skills, attitudes or behaviour of the client.

The main learning experience for the OHP was to perceive the whole organisation as her client. In her previous job as a clinical psychologist, she had worked with psychiatric patients and counselled nurses. She had also worked with work communities, but less so than with individual workers. She had organised counselling sessions for groups of supervisors, but the contacts focussed mainly on stress in the work of an individual supervisor.

During the action research process, the psychologist expanded her sphere of activities to the management of the hospital. Furthermore she was able to consider the hospital from the point of view of organisational psychology. Another, important result to the OHP was that she had opportunities to discuss and reflect on her work with the other OH personnel - at least during the development process.

All of the OH professionals and experts had expected to learn a more co-operative way of working; to work as a unit rather than as separate, individual workers. This object was not realised; everyone had developed their own model of ICA.

The nursing staff and the head nurse were pleased with their experiences in the participatory development process. In particular, they appreciated the interview with the psychologist; the workers really felt that their needs were taken into consideration. Most importantly, the workers reached a deeper understanding of their own needs and how they were related to their health and well-being. They also agreed that the ICA matrix developed by the psychologist was useful and concrete. The nurses had learned about the work and role of the OHP and how she could support the ageing worker and her/his work community. The head nurse, too, was satisfied with the process. She emphasised the importance of active interaction between OHS and the organisation and of informing the management about the health and well-being of the employees.

DISCUSSION

This action research process showed that OHPs still tend to work with individual workers rather than perceive the other stakeholders of the employing organisation as their ICA clients. Yet, many of the psychosocial factors at work, such as the extent to which employees experience time pressure and have too little time to do what is expected of them, and the extent to which employees have opportunities to participate in decision-making, mainly fall within the responsibilities of the supervisor and management. Thus, the ICA by OHPs should be expanded to reach also those responsible for decision-making in organisations.

The finding in which the OHS personnel tended to confuse the needs of the client with the processes of OHS may reflect continuing with the established forms of operation, which may restrict the growth of OHS according to the challenges of work life. Focusing on the OHS's own activities may easily lead OH personnel to ignore the learning of the client.

During the process, OH personnel learned to formulate concrete goals of ICA in forms of knowledge, skills, attitudes or behaviour of the client. Concrete goals direct a person's ICA activities in the right direction, have an effect on methods and help in setting priorities. Further, in order to follow up the results of ICA, it is necessary to have concrete and measurable goals.

The aim of learning to work as a team was not realised. The OH personnel was not able to plan their work together, they failed to design the ICA practices in co-operation, but produced their own, separate ICA models. This result reflects the long tradition of OHS: the occupational health professionals - physicians and nurses - have been responsible for the actual operations of OHS, while psychologists have been perceived as outside consultants rather than permanent or natural members of the team. The influence of this history can be seen in the course of the present study. The participants became aware of their working methods only at the end as they critically reflected on the development process. This finding confirms that behavioural change is a slow process to be achieved one step at a time. It is parallel to the idea of ICA; by it OH personnel can facilitate changes that need a long-term, comprehensive influencing in work organisations.

Providing information and advice about issues related to occupational health and safety are among the key drivers for healthier working life especially in the face of change (Abeytunga, 2000; Mechanic, 1999). In the world of work, employees, organisational leaders, managers and entrepreneurs are in need of information and advice concerning occupational health and safety in their organisation (Abeytunga, 2000; Jouttimäki, 1998; Palmgren et al., 2007; Schulte et al., 2003; Vaaranen et al., 1979). OHS is one of the contributors to health promotion in work organisations and functions as a source of health and safety information and advice to its client organisations. OHPs as members of OHS teams have evidence-based knowledge about psychosocial aspects of work that are related to health. Through sharing this knowledge with their clients on all levels of the organisations, OHPs can have a significant impact on psychosocial health at work.

REFERENCES

ABEYTUNGA, P.K. (2000). *OHS Information on the Internet Today and Tomorrow.* http://www.ccohs.ca/ccohs/speeches/speeches0.html / 4.1.2005

BANDURA, A. (1977). *Social learning theory.* Englewood Cliffs, N.J: Prentice-Hall.

BLUMENTHAL, D. (1996). Quality of health care, *New England Journal of Medicine, 335,* 891-894.

DRYSON, E. (1995). Preferred components of an occupational health service for small industry in New Zealand: health protection or health promotion? *Occupational Medicine, 45,* 31-4.

FIGLEY, C.R. (Ed.) (1995). *Compassion Fatique. Coping with secondary traumatic stress disorder in those who treat the traumatized.* NY: Brunne/Mazel Publishers.

FISHBEIN, M. & AIZEN, I. (1975). *Belief, attitude, intention and behaviour: an introduction to theory and research,* Reading: Addison-Wesley.

HAKKARAINEN, A. (2000). *Health Education in Occupational Health Services,* Unpublished Masters thesis, University of Jyväskylä, Finland.

HEAD, J., KIVIMÄKI, M., MARTIKAINEN, P., VAHTERA, J., FERRIE, J. & MARMOT, M. (2006). Influence of change in psychosocial work characteristics and sickness absence: the Whitehall II study, *Journal of Epidemiology and Community Health, 60,* 55-61.

HULSHOF, C.T.J., VERBEEK, J.H.A.M., VAN DIJK, F.J.H., VAN DER WEIDE, W.E. & BRAAM, I.T.J. (1999). Evaluation research in occupational health services: general principles and a systematic review of empirical studies, *Occupational and Environmental Medicine, 56,* 361-377.

JALONEN, P., VIRTANEN, M., VAHTERA, J., ELOVAINIO, M. & KIVIMÄKI, M. (2006). Predictors of Sustained Organisational Commitment among Nurses, *The Journal of Nursing Administration, 36,* 268-276.

JOUTTIMÄKI, L. (1998). Research on work ability improvement in EU-countries, *Physiotherapist, 6,* 19-22.

JÄRVINEN, A., KOIVISTO, T. & POIKELA, E. (2000). *Learning at Work and Work Communities,* WSOY, Juva, Finland.

KICKBUSCH, I.S. (2001). Health literacy: addressing the health and education divide, *Health Promotion International, 16,* 289-297.

KICKBUSCH, I. & NUTBEAM, D. (1998). *Health Promotion Glossary.* http://whqlibdoc.who.int/hq/1998/WHO_HPR_HEP_98.1.pdf/13.5.2007

KIVISTÖ, S. (2007). Using a single question in the context of workplace mental health promotion. *Occupational Health Psychologist, A publication of the EUROPEAN OF OCCUPATIONAL HEALTH PSYCHOLOGY, 4,* 10.

KOLB, D. (1984). *Experiential Learning. Experience as the Source of Learning and Development,* Englewood Cliffs. N.J.: Prentice-Hall.

MACDONALD, E.B., RITCHIE, K.A., MURRAY, K.J. & GILMOUR, W.H. (2000). Requirements for occupational medicine training in Europe: a Delphi study, *Occupational Environmental Medicine, 57,* 98-105.

MECHANIC, D. (1999). Issues in promoting health. *Social Science & Medicine 48,* 711-718.

MEZIROW, J. (1995). *Recurrent learning. A critical reflection in adult education.* UNIV. OF HELSINKI. HELSINKI, FINLAND.

NOTKOLA, V., HUSMAN, K., TUPI, K., VIROLAINEN, R. & NUUTINEN, J. (1987). Farmers' occupational health programme in Finland 1979-1987, *Social Science and Medicine, 30,* 1035-1040.

NUTBEAM, D. (1998). Health promotion glossary, *Health Promotion International, 13,* 349-364.

NUTBEAM, D. (2001). Health literacy as a public health goal: a challenge for contemporary health education and communication strategies into the 21st century, *Health Promotion International, 15,* 259-267.

PALMGREN, H. (2000). *Supporting, counselling or informing? Conceptions of occupational health nurses about health education - dissecting awareness of health education,* Unpublished Masters thesis, University of Helsinki, Finland.

PALMGREN, H., JALONEN, P., KALEVA, S., LEINO, T. & ROMPPANEN, V. (2007). Informing, counselling and advising (ICA) in Occupational Health Services - a case study of ICA - practices in promoting health of young employees. *People and Work, Research Reports 33.* Institute of Occupational Health, Helsinki Finland.

PALMGREN, H., JALONEN, P., KALEVA, S. & TUOMI, K. (2008). Informing, counselling and advising (ICA) in Occupational Health Services. Institute of Occupational Health, Helsinki Finland. *(in press 1.4.2008).*

PALMGREN, H. & TURJA, J. (2007). *Informing, Counselling and Advising. Good Occupational Health Practice: A Guide for planning and follow-up of Occupational Health Services*. Ministry of Social Affairs and Health and Finnish Institute of Occupational Health. Helsinki; 141-148.

The Occupational Health Service Act in Finland (2002).

PROCHASKA, J.O. & NORCROSS, J.C. (2001). Stages of change, *Psychotherapy, 38*, 443-448.

PROCHASKA, J.O. & VELICER, W.F. (1997). The transtheoretical model of health behavior change, *American Journal of Health Promotion, 12*, 38-48.

RANTANEN, L. (1993). *Health Education, profiling by an occupational health nurse*. Unpublished thesis in licentiate's degree. University of Turku, Finland.

RATZAN, S.C. (2001). Health Literacy: Communication for the Public Good, *Health Promotion International, 16*, 207-214.

REID, A. & MALONE, J. (2003). A cross-sectional study of employer and employee occupational health needs and priorities within the Irish Civil Service, *Occupational Medicine, 53*, 41-45.

RUSSELL, L. B. (1986). *Is Prevention Better than Care*, The Brookings Institution. Washington.

SAUTER, S.L., HURREL, J., FOX, H.R., TETRICK, L.E. & BARLING, J. (1999). Occupational Health Psychology: An Emerging Discipline. *Industrial Health 37*, 199-211.

SCHULTE, P.A., OKUN, A., STEPHENSON, C.M., COLLIGAN, M., AHLERS, H., GJESSING, C., LOOS, G., NIEMEIER, R. W. & SWEENEY, M.H. (2003). Information dissemination and use: critical components in occupational safety and health, *American Journal of Industrial Medicine, 44*, 515-31.

STRINGER, E.T. (1999). *Action research. Second edition*. Thousand Oaks: Sage Publications.

TALVI, A., JÄRVISALO, J., KNUT, L-R., KAITANIEMI, P. & KALIMO, R. (1995). Health promotion of working population: Needs for health education identified by the occupational health services in Neste Inc. 1988-91, *The Finnish Journal of Physicians, 50*, 2193-2198.

VAARANEN, A., KOLIVUORI, T., ROSSI, K., TOLONEN, M. & HASSI, J. (1979). Need for job-related health counselling in small workplaces, *Scandinavian Journal of Work and Environmental Health, 5 Suppl.*, 18-20.

VÄÄNÄNEN, A., KALIMO, R., TOPPINEN-TANNER, S., MUTANEN, P., PEIRO, J., KIVIMÄKI, M. & VAHTERA, J. (2004). Role clarity, fairness, and organisational climate as predictors of sickness absence, *Scandinavian Journal of Public Health, 32*, 426-434.

VIRTANEN, M., KIVIMÄKI, M., ELOVAINIO, M., LINNA, A., PENTTI, J. & VAHTERA, J. (2007). Neighbourhood socioeconomic status, health and working conditions of school teachers, *Journal of Epidemiology and. Community Health, 61*, 326-30.

WILLIAMS, N., SOBTI, A. & AW, T.C. (1994). Comparison of perceived occupational health needs among managers, employee representatives and occupational physicians, *Occupational Medicine, 44,,* 205-208.

ZARCADOOLAS, C., PLEASANT, A. & GREER, D.S. (2005). Understanding Health Literacy: an expanded model, *Health Promotion International, 20,* 195-203.

APPENDIX 1.

One example of ICA methods created by OHPs is the Occupational Health Letter. It was developed in the research and development project, 'Healthy mind at work 2005 - 2008' (ESR S01914). The aim of the project was to improve workplace surveys to promote mental well-being in workplaces.

Workplace surveys usually produce plenty of material for assessment of health conditions at work. For the maximum benefit in developing working conditions, the material should be studied carefully. Knowledge of occupational health psychology is a helpful tool in conceptualising the discovered features. In different contexts, the mental load at work can be hazardous. For example, there are professions in which the worker is exposed to secondary stress while working with vulnerable residential or workplace groups. Virtanen et al. (2007) found that neighbourhood socioeconomic status is associated with the working conditions and health of school teachers. An independent association was found between low socioeconomic status of school neighbourhoods and mental health problems and alcohol use among teachers. It is important that the hazardous working conditions are addressed and the workers protected and supported in the recovery process (Figley, 2002). The Occupational Health Letter can be used in the feedback phase of the workplace surveys to provide information about the specific stressors discovered during the workplace survey and to help the different stakeholders of the workplace to understand their significance and what could be done about them. The following Occupational Health Letter was developed to support the control of secondary stress load in social work.

> Dear social workers,
>
> Thank you for your excellent co-operation during the workplace survey process. We appreciate your important work in looking after the working conditions of your staff. The well-being of personnel also benefits your customers. At this point, we would like to share with you the following thoughts on a particular aspect of your work called secondary stress or compassion fatigue.
>
> Stress from compassion
>
> '....some things are just too personal, they affect you', '...after a really difficult case, you cannot recover at once...', '...you start to become numb, nothing gets to you and things slip your notice...'. The

emotional overload at work may evolve quickly or as a long-term process, and it is a remarkable risk factor in the care professions. It is clear from the above fragments that paying attention to secondary stress or compassion fatigue in your work is worthwhile.

The relationships in work life are multiple and interaction is many-sided. The sympathetic skills are essentially important in safety and service branches. Feelings of compassion and identification with the patient emerge when helping people who suffer from great losses or reactions after a traumatic incident. The sympathetic attitude of the police on the scene of an accident helps the victims to begin restoring their sense of safety. The elderly patients in wheel chairs are comforted by the compassionate approach of their carers. A businesslike manner at the car repair shop calms down the traffic entrepreneur facing a sudden setback in a busy trade.

Employees in the service sector must regulate their emotional reactions so that the customer, even in a difficult situation, will calm down and gets his or her own resources back into use. The service provider must, in a way, produce double effort: to deliver the service and help the client with utilizing her/his own emotional work. Compassion skills are necessary in many professions. Becoming familiar with the client's situation requires engagement and dedication, and many times this means that the difficult feelings are also transmitted to the helper.

Preventing compassion fatigue

Compassion fatigue may affect the job control and confidence in personal competence, and can make life seem less meaningful. To prevent this, it is good to get training in this phenomenon, to decrease exposure to traumatic situations, and monitor the situation of the workers. Increasing the amount of recreational activities helps alleviate stress. Moreover, the role of social support is important: taking a break from the role of helper and accepting help from others may prove to be beneficial.

Often, the person suffering from compassion fatigue is not aware of the situation him/herself or does not find the way to alleviate the stress. The situations are too binding, perspectives are narrowed and perceiving other options may become difficult. Therefore, other people at the workplace must recognise the situation and broaden the perspective. To support and build trust prevents the isolating effects of compassion fatigue. Appreciation and looking after the well-being of helpers is highly significant.

We can discuss the secondary traumatic effects of your work. We can help you to recognize the pull of the demanding situations and to find ways to prevent compassion fatigue. If you wish, a representative of the OHS unit can join your workplace meetings and discuss this further.

Sirkku Kivistö, Eila Kallio, Greta Turunen
OHS, occupational health psychologists

UNDERSTANDING THE PERCEPTION OF OCCUPATIONAL PSYCHOSOCIAL RISK FACTORS IN DEVELOPING COUNTRIES: SETTING PRIORITIES FOR ACTION

Evelyn Kortum, Stavroula Leka and Tom Cox

CHAPTER OVERVIEW

Major national and international developments that concern processes of globalization and structural changes of work have had an impact on the global world of work in the last few decades in high-income, as well as in low-income countries. There is an international trend to shift production to developing countries, which entails a trend to 'transfer' hazardous work and work practices from industrialized to developing countries with wide variations in working conditions and exposure to occupational hazards. These developments have also rendered the reality of psychosocial hazards and the issue of work-related stress a growing global concern. However, whereas there is an abundant body of research in industrialized countries, psychosocial occupational risks have not yet appeared on the horizon of the majority of the developing countries' research and practice agendas.

The research described in this chapter is 'exploratory' and focuses on similarities and differences in the nature and conceptualization of work-related stress and psychosocial risks in industrialized and developing countries and identifies preliminary priorities for action in developing countries. This research does not claim to find ultimate solutions, but it is a first step to prepare the ground for focused awareness-raising activities, for stimulating research and policy development, for collecting best practice examples as they exist in developing countries, for adapting existing tools, for creating, field testing and evaluating new ones.

This study uses a combination of both qualitative and quantitative approaches including interviews and the Delphi method. Knowledge was drawn from a group of multi-disciplinary professionals with expertise in, or related expertise to, occupational health.

Key findings are presented relating to the understanding of work-related stress and psychosocial hazards and whether these are of concern in participants' respective countries, participants' understanding of related health outcomes, interventions applied that address psychosocial risks, and lastly, the most affected occupational sectors.

THE CHANGING NATURE OF WORK, GLOBALIZATION AND PSYCHOSOCIAL RISK FACTORS IN DEVELOPING COUNTRIES

Changes in the nature of work and new occupational risks

During the last few decades many changes have occurred in the world of work. Cooper writes that without being too gloomy, it is safe to say that we have, at the start of this millennium, all the ingredients of corporate stress: an ever-increasing workload with a decreasing workforce in a climate of rapid change and with control over the means of production increasingly being exercised by bigger bureaucracies (Cooper, 2006). The greatest change for the working population concerns the psychosocial working environment, that is the way work is designed, organised and managed. Failures of work design and management (Cox, Griffiths, Rial-Gonzalez, 2000), often associated with the content and context of work, constitute examples of psychosocial hazards in the working environment. The 2005/06 survey of the Health and Safety Executive (HSE) of self-reported work-related illness prevalence estimate indicated a significant increased risk of work-related stress, depression and anxiety for those reporting higher workloads, more tight work deadlines, lack of support at work and being physically attacked or threatened at work (HSE, 2007).

In addition, the Third European Survey of Working Conditions found that from a sample of 21000 workers, 25-33% reported musculo-skeletal problems and 28-29% of workers reported stress (Paoli and Merllie, 2001) as their primary work-related health problems. Ample evidence now shows that stress at work, especially when it is chronic, is a risk for psychological and physical health (Semmer, 2006) and a body of epidemiological evidence indicates the working conditions that lead to work-related stress is constantly growing.

Changes at a global level that impact on the nature and conditions of work include liberalisation of labour markets, a shift towards more insecure forms of employment, reduced control in trade, reduction in public spending in real wages, and problems of reduced regulation and lack of enforcement of regulation of working conditions. For example, in South Africa surveys of occupational health practice have also found that workers are exposed to new chemical, psychosocial and physical hazards that are emerging from new forms of industrial processes and work organization (Loewenson, 1998).

In addition, the use of more sophisticated information and communication technology is affecting work life in several ways. One is through globalisation, since companies are operating increasingly in global markets and often practice cross-border division of labour. The second is through the operation of networks based primarily on knowledge as their primary resource. Growing dependence on computer technology, which once was thought to improve working life, has in the experience of many workers led to greater workload and performance pressure, although this may be mainly due to the way the work process is organized, and not be an inherent facet of the new technology itself (Worklife, 2000).

These rapid changes of the modern working life are associated with increasing demands of learning new skills, the need to adapt to new types of work, pressure of higher productivity and quality of work, time pressure and hectic jobs and with growing psychological workload and stress among the workforce. Such developments require higher priority to be given to the psychological quality of work and the work environment, and more attention to psychosocial aspects of work (WHO, 1995).

In addition, work life is often intertwined with 'private' life, which may cause spill-over effects. The erroneous belief that work and non-work activities are unrelated in their psychological, physiological and health effects, has been described as the 'myth of separate worlds' by Kanter (1977). On the one hand, effective interventions in the workplace will yield positive repercussions and benefits for both the workers and their families, and for companies. And on the other hand, interventions that go beyond the workplace and embrace the community setting, will ensure higher impact and sustainability of positive intervention results.

Addressing psychosocial occupational risks in industrialized countries

The current situation in high-income or industrialized countries indicates that traditional occupational risks have largely been mastered. However, there is still a struggle, and a quite extensive one, to address psychosocial risk factors at work which cause a high prevalence of work-related stress and occupational diseases in the working population as found by the European Working Conditions Survey conducted in 2000. It also needs to be noted that mental health problems and stress-related disorders are the biggest overall cause of early death in Europe (WHO, 2001a). But they are not only a matter of premature mortality, since according to the same report, mental ill health and related disorders are among the major health concerns in Europe today. In particular, depression, suicide and other stress-related conditions together with destructive life-styles and psychosomatic diseases, cause immense suffering to people and their

Table 1. Psychosocial risk factors
(including excerpts from: Work Organization and Stress, PWH series no. 3. 2005)

Organizational and workplace level

Work Content:

Job Content: Monotonous, under-stimulating, meaningless tasks; lack of variety; unpleasant tasks

Workload and Work pace: Having too much *or* too little to do; working under time pressures

Working Hours: Strict and inflexible working schedules; long and unsocial hours; unpredictable working hours; badly designed shift systems

Participation and Control: Lack of participation in decision making; lack of control (for example, over work methods, pace, hours, environment)

Work Context:

Career Development, Status and Pay: Job insecurity; lack of promotion prospects; under-promotion or over-promotion; work of 'low social value'; piece rate payments schemes; unclear or unfair performance evaluation systems; being over-skilled or under-skilled for the job

Role in the Organisation: Unclear role; conflicting roles within the same job; responsibility for people; continuously dealing with other people and their problems

Interpersonal Relationships: Inadequate, inconsiderate or unsupportive supervision; poor relationships with co-workers; bullying, harassment and violence (incl. sexual harassment); isolated or solitary work; no agreed procedures for dealing with problems or complaints

Organisational Culture: Poor communication; poor leadership (including downsizing); lack of clarity about organisational objectives and structure

Home-Work Interface: Conflicting demands of work and home; lack of support for domestic problems at work; lack of support for work problems at home

Physical Work Environment: Unsafe procedures; no or limited information available to protect oneself; risk of injury of death

Employment Conditions: Precarious jobs; lack of job security; lack of health insurance and other protective measures.

---

families, as well as placing "a great economic cost on society". As also noted above, the report states that trends indicate public health impact beyond Europe.

There are several reasons for the lack of addressing these issues effectively that seem to relate to the slow translation of existing knowledge into action. This is despite the fact that psychosocial risk factors have been well researched and defined in industrialized country contexts. They refer to the organization of work, to the context and content of work and also wider issues that concern work-life balance. Table 1 gives a comprehensive account of psychosocial risk factors.

Findings from occupational stress research are consistent with the more general life event stress literature showing that specific acute work-related stressful experiences contribute to 'depression' and, more importantly perhaps, that enduring 'structural' occupational factors, which may differ according to occupation, can also contribute to psychological disorders. There are significant implications for employees, their families, employers and indeed the wider community (Tennant, 2001). In Europe, social dialogue has been effective in the establishment of framework agreements among social partners on work-related stress and also harassment and violence at work. This is a first significant step towards taking targeted action at the policy level.

The global workforce

Major national and international developments have changed the global world of work in the last few decades in high-income, as well as in low-income countries. These include the process of globalisation and structural changes of work. Globalisation is largely an intensification of the processes of interaction involving travel, trade, migration and dissemination of knowledge that have shaped the progress of the world over millennia (Sen, 2000). Considering the impact of globalisation in the developing world, it seems often connected to higher productivity at a lower cost. This adversely produces a high cost for workers in developing countries in terms of their mental and physical health and for economies at large. The process of globalization has generally driven manufacturing to the developing world; however, there is also an emerging trend, even in the developing nations, in the growth of service industries. This growth has been associated with an increase in musculoskeletal disorders from repetitive and forceful movements and stress-related diseases (Wegman, 2006).

Today, approximately 75% of the global work force resides in the developing world (WHO, 2007a). The majority of workers are employed in unhealthy and unsafe working conditions and this includes 350 million children 5-17 years of age. Approximately 30-50% of workers report hazardous physical, chemical or biological exposures or overload of unreasonably heavy physical work or ergonomic factors that may be hazardous to health and to working capacity; an equal number of working people report psychological overload at work resulting in stress symptoms (WHO, 1995). Many individuals spend one-third of their adult life in such hazardous work environments. About 120 million occupational accidents with 200,000 fatalities are estimated to occur annually and some 68-157 million new cases of occupational disease may be caused by various exposures at work (WHO, 1995). Although the workplace is a hazardous environment, a structured system to prevent occupational risks rarely exists in developing countries and often minimum standards are not adhered to.

There is an international trend to shift production to developing countries, which is based on considerations of low-cost production and also entails a trend to 'transfer' hazardous work from industrialized to developing countries given the undeveloped industrial base in developing country contexts. Another trend is characterized by the growth of large multinational companies that has been accompanied by greater decentralization, outsourcing and flexible work environments, with wide variations in the conditions of work and in exposure to occupational hazards (Rantanen, 1999). Developing countries have a low standard of living, and a low per capita income. They are also characterized by widespread poverty and high unemployment. In general, the informal economic sector, a flexible working environment without any worker protection, is very large and can attain up to 95% such as, for example, in Benin, Chad and Mali. This is also visible through statistics such as those in Zambia, which has a population of 10 million and only 400 000 official jobs.

Countries with more advanced economies among the developing nations but those that have not yet fully demonstrated the signs of a developed country, are called Newly Industrialised Countries which include India, China, Russia and Brazil. For example in China, the rich-poor gap is largely an urban-rural one, which is still growing. Earnings in rural areas are less than one-third than in urban areas and hundreds of millions of people earn less than $1/day. There are 24 million job-seekers in cities and towns every year, including the new additional urban workforce and the people carried over from the previous year who did not find work. But there are only a little more than 12 million jobs available in cities and towns every year. Approximately 8 million additional rural labourers move into cities and towns every year (China Economy Watch, 2008).

Albeit a very thin research base in developing countries, some research has been conducted and some trends have been identified with respect to psychosocial risk factors and work-related stress. For example, in the P.R.

of China a study shows that 37.3 % of men and 27.5% of women reported high or very high levels of work stress, and 39% of workers reported feeling burnt out by their work (Li in GOHNET Special 07). Other trends have been observed in Bangladesh where since the late 1990s there has been an increase in work-related stress in the banking business, which started growing rapidly (Ahsan, 2005). And since the mid-1990s in the Republic of Korea, researchers have observed a significant increase in work-related cerebrovascular and cardiovascular diseases. In addition, since the year 2000 a dramatic increase in work-related musculo-skeletal disorders caused by psychosocial factors, awkward working postures and repetitive body movements has been observed (Park, 2005).

Moreover, research has shown an increasing risk of work-related diseases and accidents in Southeast Asian countries which have experienced rapid industrialization (Haratani and Kawakami, 1999). Specific phenomena, such as Karoshi (death by overwork) have become social issues in Korea, and have been so in Japan for some time now. Prognostics indicate that in 2020, India will be the 3rd largest economy in the world after the US and China. Information technology is the fasted growing sector resulting in increased work-related stress (Aziz, 2003), thus confirming the trend towards the growth of the service industry accompanied by its related consequences on the physical and mental health of workers.

Dr Estrella-Gust stresses that in the Philippines the prevalence of occupationally-induced psychosocial disorders is still virgin territory. A data gap exists, suggesting the need to put a high priority on information gathering. The Philippines Occupational Health and Safety Centre in Quezon City believe this is important because of the rapid development of technology putting immense strain on workers, but THIS IS also due workplaces where episodes of epidemic hysteria have occurred due to SARS (Several Acute Respiratory Syndrome) or due to exposure to chemicals causing death and severe disability. Dr Estrella-Gust furthermore states that these incidences caused severe anxiety and reluctance to return to work, as well as decrease in productivity. In addition, there is a growing concern about an increase of child labourers and young workers in the Philippines. Exploitation occurs not only in the form of low wages and long working hours, but also in the inadequacy of welfare and health facilities. Children and young people have a lower attention span than adults and are more prone to accidents at work. Many of those may return to school suffering physical and psychological complications of hazardous work, which often causes delays in catching up at school and often results in dropping out (Estrella-Gust, 2003).

The situation as concerns addressing occupational psychosocial risk factors is very different in developing countries when compared to industrialized countries. Stress in developing countries is one of the areas which have not yet been quantified owing to lack of data on exposure or causality, important exposures and outcomes (Concha-Barrientos et al., 2004). The lack of research in this field and the struggle with other well-known and traditional occupational risks (chemicals, biological and physical hazards) may present barriers that prevent developing countries from developing awareness, addressing and controlling emerging health concerns such as work-related stress and its consequences. This also implies lack of resources allotted to deal with this modern phenomenon, since rarely policies or legislation address these issues in developing countries. In addition, such issues may not be immediately visible. This problem of 'invisibility' (something is happening within the person stimulated by outside adverse working conditions) may be an additional barrier to administering interventions. So is the fact that not all stress-related disorders are disabling.

It can furthermore not be assumed that the existing body of research including available intervention methods can be extrapolated without additional consideration of aspects specific to the working, living and cultural contexts of developing countries. For example, in developing country contexts, the nature of occupational psychosocial hazards cannot always be separated from the community environment. This is for example the case, where many workers suffer from HIV/AIDS or other infectious diseases, which have potential effects on other workers who need to assume additional tasks often over prolonged periods of time. This may also be the case where commuting from and to work is difficult or even dangerous, and where gender inequalities are blatant. Other pressing issues take priority over addressing occupational risks, such as unemployment, wars, famine and natural catastrophes.

Professionals and experts in developing countries have started to address these new and increasing risks. Although this is certainly a challenge when other priorities prevail as stated above, given our knowledge about physical and psychological consequences on the individual, effects on productivity and performance of individuals and organizations and lastly, economies at large, it is worthwhile including occupational psychosocial hazards in the research and political action agendas. To take this direction, the current magnitude of the problem has to be analysed so as to convey the necessary awareness, build a solid research base, and find a forum for the adaptation or the development of new intervention tools. Eventually this action should influence or support the development of occupational health legislation or regulations to include aspects that address psychosocial hazards and work-related stress.

In summary, the phenomena of globalization and the changing nature of work have rendered the reality of psychosocial hazards and the issue of work-related stress a growing concern in industrialized and developing countries, as well as those experiencing rapid social and economic transition. The difference is, however, that industrialized countries have an abundant body of research available on the basis of which they start to address these issues, whereas psychosocial occupational risks have not yet appeared on the horizon of the majority of the developing countries' research and practice agendas.

THE CURRENT RESEARCH

Aim and objectives

The current research can be coined as 'exploratory' as it examines the level of understanding and prevalence of psychosocial hazards and work-related stress in developing countries. In addition, the research aims at exploring action taken in countries to address occupational hazards, and in particular psychosocial occupational risk factors.

The specific objectives of the study are to increase our understanding of these issues in developing countries, to explore similarities and differences in the nature and conceptualization of work-related stress and psychosocial risks in industrialized and developing countries, and to determine preliminary priorities for action. It should also start to prepare the ground for focused awareness-raising activities, for stimulating research and collecting best practice examples as they exist in developing countries, for adapting existing tools, create new ones, field test and evaluate these. This exploratory research should in the long run have an influence on policy development in developing countries.

The project involves the drawing of knowledge from multi-disciplinary professionals with related expertise in occupational health issues across the six global regions as delineated by the World Health Organization and spanning 20 countries in total. The research is being conducted in several phases:

Phase I: recruiting of participants from developing countries;
Phase II: a series of semi-structured interviews;
Phase III: a Delphi survey conducted in two rounds; and
Phase IV: a series of focus groups.

Key findings from Phases I, II and III are presented in this chapter.

Methodology

A mixed methodology was used including both qualitative and quantitative research. This section will describe the procedure, sample and methods in more detail.

Phase I: *Identifying and recruiting participants*

Experts from developing countries, familiar with issues concerning the psychosocial work environment and work-related stress, were identified via an existing network of occupational health and safety specialists. Individuals joined the "Network" through completion of an online registration form. Criteria for inclusion were: (a) expertise in a field related to occupational health; psychology, sociology, epidemiology, medicine, psychiatry, etc.; (b) number of years of experience in their respective field; (c) basic knowledge on workplace interventions and/or legalisation on psychosocial risks at work; and (d) a degree of practical experience in the application of methods or interventions that concern psychosocial risks at work. In addition, it was tapped into other existing networks of experts, who also participated.

Participants were actively recruited from all global regions as proposed by the WHO categorization[1] to collect a suitable breadth of data, and yield a holistic representation of the developing world context. 79 experts who responded satisfactorily to the criteria were identified from inside and outside the 'Network' and included in Phases II and III of the research.

Phase II: *Expert interviews*

The interview schedule was developed based on a scientific literature review and included ten questions in total. This chapter presents key findings in relation to six questions. Two questions explore the respondents' understanding and conceptualization of work-related stress and psychosocial hazards (Questions 1 and 2). A third question assessed the level of concern attributed to these issues within the context of the developing world (Question 3). The fourth question asked about effects on health of psychosocial risks and work-related stress (Question 4), a fifth question probed about knowledge of interventions that address psychosocial risks and work-related stress (Question 9), and a last question

---

[1] The Americas (AMRO), the African (AFRO), Eastern-Mediterranean (EMRO), European (EURO), South-East Asian (SEARO), and Western-Pacific (WPRO) regions

discussed here explored how these pertain to particular occupational sectors (Question 7).

Participants

A total of 29 individuals from developing countries previously recruited were interviewed representing all of the global regions. Table 2 below outlines the participants' demographics, i.e. the countries represented by the participants. The participants' background is multi-disciplinary. The main disciplines represented in the group are psychiatry, social work, medicine, advocacy in public health, education in psychology, epidemiology, occupational health and safety, industrial psychology, management and human resources, neuropsychology, and ergonomics.

Table 2. Participant demographics

Global region	N	Countries discussed
AFRO	8	Namibia (4), Nigeria, South Africa (2), Zambia
AMRO	5	Trinidad and Tobago, Chile , Colombia, Mexico, Puerto Rico
EURO	2	Albania, Macedonia
EMRO	5	Iran (3), Tunisia, Pakistan
SEARO	6	India (3), Malaysia, Thailand (2)
WPRO	3	China, Federated State of Micronesia, Vietnam

Procedure

Following the selection of participants, e-mails were sent proposing a date and time for a telephone interview. The questions were forwarded to participants prior to the interview since the same was conducted in English, a second or even third language to most participants, thus allowing sufficient time for preparation. A telephone interview was conducted with 27 participants and two face-to-face interviews were conducted with participants from Malaysia and Albania.

Participants were called by telephone at the previously agreed-upon day and time. Ethical issues were outlined, assuring them of confidentiality and anonymity. They were provided with a brief overview of the aim and objectives of the study. Probing questions were used to clarify ambiguous answers or to ask participants to elaborate. At times, due to language barriers or poor telephone connections, participants were asked to repeat their answers and some connections needed to be re-established after recurrent problems. Participants were thanked for their participation.

Following the interviews, the data gathered were summarized and transcribed. Thematic analysis was used to analyse the data (Braun & Clarke, 2006). Emerging themes were identified across all participants, thus yielding a holistic perspective across the developing world. The purpose was to reveal potential parallels or inconsistencies in participant perceptions of the situation in their country. The region of origin and the occupational expertise of each participant were included as additional information. A thematic grid was produced through this process and was subsequently used to develop the Delphi survey.

Phase III: Delphi survey

The survey conducted was a two-tiered investigation based on the Delphi survey methodology. It aimed at further exploring key issues identified in Phase II in order to complement the empirical exploratory data. The Delphi is a structured group interaction process that is directed in "rounds" of opinion collection, which is achieved by conducting a series of surveys using questionnaires (Turoff & Hiltz, 1996). Because the study involves 'experts' it is assumed that some reasonable quality information will be inputted, and because it is an iterative system, it is assumed that good quality knowledge will evolve. The goal of the Delphi process is to systematically facilitate communication of information via several stages and to define priorities with respect to the research area.

Participants

Of the previously recruited 79 individuals from developing countries, 74 individuals responded to the first online survey in December 2007. Participants covered multiple areas of expertise from the areas of psychiatry, social work, medicine, epidemiology, sociology, ergonomics, but the largest number had expertise in occupational health and psychology. In February 2008, 53 experts out of the 79 respondents to the first round responded to the second round of the survey. Their areas of expertise were comparable to the first sample.

Procedure

An e-mail message explaining the purpose and providing an overview of the study was sent to all previously recruited experts providing a link to the first online Delphi questionnaire. The online questionnaire requested demographic and background information, and contained seven questions covering: understanding of psychosocial risks, most affected occupational sectors, prevention and intervention approaches, as well as gender and priority areas of action. Respondents were asked to rank their answers in the order of most important to least important.

Before the second round, the survey answers were analyzed and a choice of ten answers for each question retained, which represented the highest results yielded from the first round study. These were used to design the questionnaire for the second round of the Delphi study and respondents were asked to rank their answers to the same number of questions as in the first phase in the order of most important to least important. The ten choices provided were prioritized and the five highest results were retained for data analysis and development of graphs. The analyzed results yielded indications for priorities for research as identified by the participants.

Ethics

Participants participated in the research voluntarily and gave verbal consent for the interview to be undertaken. Participants were free at anytime during, or post interviews to terminate or withdraw their testimonies. They were assured that their identity would remain confidential and not be linked to the responses provided during the several study phases.

KEY FINDINGS FROM SELECTED THEMES OF THE STUDY

General understanding of, and concerns for workers' health through exposure to, psychosocial risk factors

In this section key findings from questions 1 and 2 (understanding work-related stress and psychosocial hazards), question 3 (whether these are of concern in participants' respective countries), question 4 (related health outcomes), question 9 (interventions applied that address psychosocial risks), and lastly, question 7 (most affected occupational sectors) will be presented first based on the exploratory interviews, and second on the findings from the two Delphi rounds. They will be discussed with reference to the literature.

Expert interviews

In general all respondents understood the concepts of work-related stress and psychosocial hazards and could explain these well. One issue that emerged is that they were interchangeable and that participants did not make significant distinctions of the two concepts, although they provided more information for psychosocial hazards than for work-related stress for all categories, and work-related stress was more brought up in connection with adverse health outcomes. For example, to question no. 1 (what does work-related stress mean to you?) one participant said *'For me work-related stress and psychosocial hazards are combined. Stress is a body response; there is an external and an internal stimulus, adverse effects at the workplace. People are unable to control the situation, the work content, the work organization, conflicting roles, etc.'*. Another one reiterated it *'is stress related to the organization of work and activities, the people, the surroundings, ambiance. The psychosocial and physical environment is important. Risks around work are also important. Getting to work by transport, getting to work, and home safely. The stress is whatever changes in your body take place in relation to all the hazards that are around; feeling of uneasiness'*.

To both answers (concerning understanding of work-related stress and psychosocial hazards) interviewees referred to the context and content of work. Extra-work interferences or wider societal issues were more related to psychosocial hazards than to work-related stress, but mentioned frequently. The potential for psychosocial risks to cause physical and psychological harm was also mentioned. A participant said that stress is the *'consequence of lack of balance, and high demand. Stress has physical and psychological consequences, lack of support'*. Another said, it is the *'harmful physical & emotional response when demands don't match abilities, needs. It is a serious problem which threatens workers' health'*.

In terms of work content mostly mentioned were issues pertaining to the work environment, the equipment available, task design, workload and high work pace, high pressure and demands, as well as work schedule (e.g. shiftwork or long working hours). One participant put it more generally: *'In the workplace environment psychosocial hazards are any characteristics in the workplace capable of undesirable and unwanted effects on a person. Psychosocial hazards are aspects of the working environment and can have negative impacts'*.

Work context issues included organizational culture and function, physical safety provisions, career development opportunities, interpersonal relationships, physical violence, psychological and sexual harassment, and the work atmosphere. Issues of decision latitude and control over the work processes, lack of social support, job insecurity and precariousness of work were also seen to be psychosocial hazards within the work context. There was a good understanding of psychosocial hazards by most for example:

'... stress, violence at the workplace, abuse of substances... demands of work, co-worker relationships, amount of work and control over work'.

As concerns the social environmental context, participants mentioned issues that pertain to work-life balance, involvement, respect, dignity, restraints of societal expectations and norms, as well as the prevalence of HIV/AIDS (especially mentioned by the African participants). For example on African participants said: 'Psychosocial problems, such as stress, HIV/AIDS, alcohol... hinder from being productive at work. There is no policy in place, and if there is it is not implemented. It has a hiding status'.

Although the question was general and not necessarily related to work, participants related the social environmental contexts back to work.

With respect to the question if these issues are of concern to workers' health, participants responded that psychosocial hazards are of concern. They referred to the processes of globalization and the intensification of work, increased westernization and no time for the country to adapt to rapid changes (e.g., changes in the employment market), the labour market, high unemployment, job insecurity, global changes and high competition. Also mentioned were a focus on traditional and not on psychosocial hazards, lack of awareness in defining/identifying psychosocial hazards and in understanding and defining stress. Working conditions issues such as working time and shift work as well as reorganization in the work context were also reported. Additional issues that were mentioned were the lack of a comprehensive legislative framework (including psychosocial hazards and stress), the lack of focus on primary prevention and a larger focus on secondary or tertiary prevention, lack of solutions and the lack of an action framework. The work, home and community interface (spill-over effect not just home, but community, and society at large) received special mention as well as low standards at the workplace since there are low standards outside the workplace, and the impact of socio-environmental issues (social, economic, political problems) that affect the work environment and that have a direct and indirect effect on employees' health.

In terms of health outcomes all participants mentioned adverse health outcomes through exposure to work-related stress and psychosocial hazards based on their knowledge, perception or working experience. Reference was made to psychological, physical, and behavioural harm. Psychological and physical working conditions were mentioned as inflicting psychological and physical harm. In terms of behavioural consequences especially alcohol abuse was mentioned, as well as social consequences such as increased divorce. There were concrete ideas about the potential of psychosocial hazards to cause harm in terms of stress, depression, burnout and suicidal behaviour.

E. KORTUM et al.

The knowledge collected portraits well the current literature available from industrialized countries. The themes that emerged and related to physical health outcomes included heart and circulatory effects, gastro-intestinal problems, musculo-skeletal disorders, headaches, migraines, fatigue, and skin effects and respiratory symptoms. In addition, responses related to psychological health in terms of depression, anxiety and burnout, unhealthy behaviours related to alcohol and drug abuse, and smoking were mentioned. Participants stressed the lack of research data from developing countries to complement their experiences and knowledge from the scientific literature of industrialized countries.

DELPHI findings

Considering the context of developing countries, what doe you understand by the term psychosocial risk(s)?

Category	Delphi I (74)	Delphi II (53)
Time pressure & high job demands	36	64
Discrep betw abil., skills, job dem., expect.	39	60
Poor management practices	36	55
Poor physical conditions	27	55
Lack of part. In decision-making	33	53
Job insecurity	42	51
Conflict in interpers. Relationships	24	38
Percvd imbalance; abilities, res.; support	28	34
Precarious employment	22	34

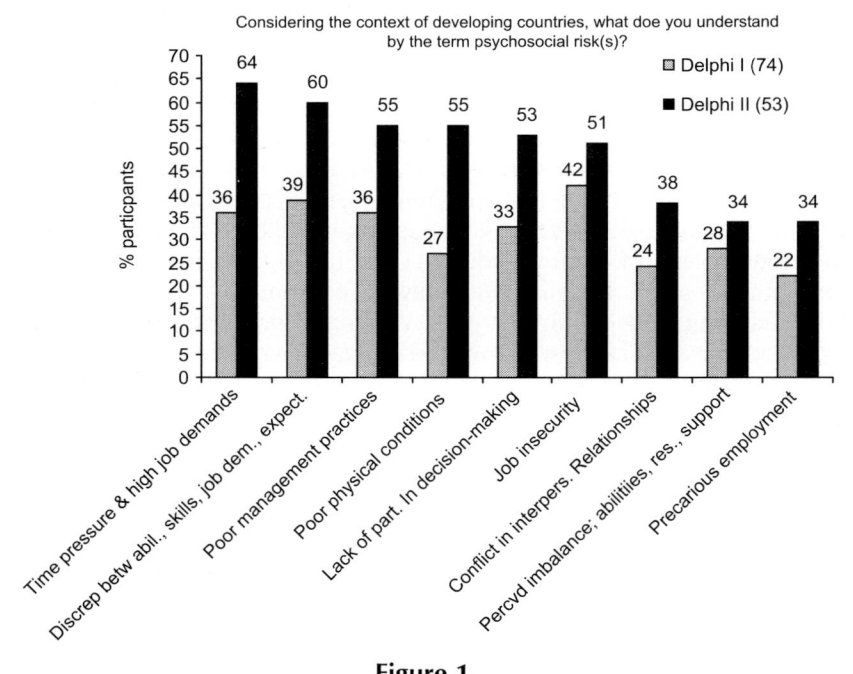

Figure 1.

Results from the Delphi survey reiterate issues of work content and context as obtained from the interviews. As concerns work content the priorities identified pertain to time pressure and high job demands (36/64); discrepancies between abilities, skills, job demands and expectations (38/60); poor management practices (36/55); lack of participation in decision-making (33/53). There is high consensus on job insecurity (42/51), which has been identified as a global psychosocial risk. Precarious employment is related to job insecurity, which has resulted in a relatively high consensus (22/34) as well. Furthermore, high consensus has been reached on a perceived imbalance of abilities, resources and support. Conflict in interpersonal relationships has also been identified as a priority (24/38).

Discussion of findings

At international level, the World Health Organization (2007) defines work-related stress as a *pattern of physiological, emotional, cognitive and behavioural reactions to some extremely taxing aspects of work content, work organization and work environment*. The response may be experienced when workers encounter demands and pressures at work that do not match their knowledge and abilities and which may challenge their ability to cope (WHO, 2005).

This definition refers to issues mentioned in the interviews and to priorities identified in the Delphi. They include aspects of work content and context and the mismatch between a worker's abilities, skills and knowledge with job requirements and expectations.

In studies of occupational stress, a leading theoretical model is the 'Job Demand-Control-Support' model (Karasek and Theorell, 1990). The core contributing factors to work-related stress and resulting fatigue - and those that have mostly been studied - are embedded in the work content and work context. They include low levels of control over work and high demands (decision latitude), shiftwork (particularly nightshift and rapidly rotating shifts), lack of social support, and the level of exposure to occupational violence. There is empirical evidence that asymmetric effort-reward job perceptions are associated with cardiovascular disease, poor self-perceived health, and several mental disorders (Siegrist and Marmot 2004). Where more of the contributing factors are present, increased levels of stress are likely to result. In particular, low levels of control and high job demands are associated with increased stress. Overall, employment relations, their ensuing physical and psychosocial hazards, and various forms of economic compensation affect the health status of workers (WHO, 2007b).

The main components of Karasek and Theorell's model are visible throughout the answers provided during the interviews and identified in the Delphi rounds. They are mentioned with reference to the work content and work context in the interviews and the Delphi findings state that the priority psychosocial risks are inherent in most adverse job-related strain reactions and are to be expected in jobs characterized by high job demands, low control and low worksite support.

Job insecurity and precarious employment are two more priorities identified in the expert interviews and particularly in the Delphi. The study found that job insecurity and precarious employment were within the top ten psychosocial risks in developing countries. These results do not seem surprising given that effects of globalization and the emergence of new and insecure sectors and working arrangements are global and are not restricted to industrialized countries. A recent European survey identified the ten most important emerging psychosocial risks for Europe (European Risk Observatory Report, 2007). The most prevalent psychosocial risks, which resulted from the survey are precarious contracts in the context of the unstable labour market, increased vulnerability of workers in the context of globalization, new forms of employment contracts and the feeling of job insecurity (see Figure 2 below).

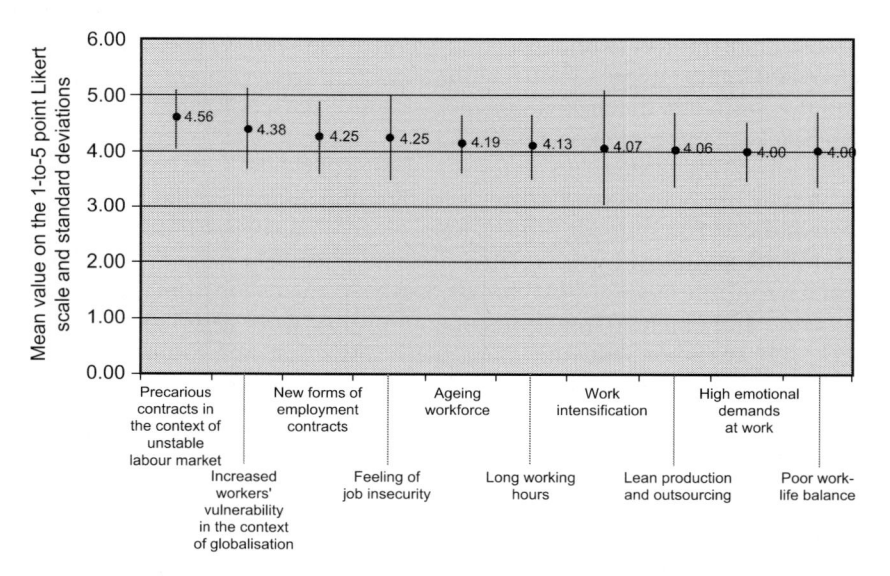

The 10 most important emerging psychosocial risks identified in the survey
NB: MV > 4: risk strongly agreed as emerging; 3.25 < MV ≤ 4: risk agreed as emerging

Figure 2. The 10 most important emerging psychosocial risks

The literature informs that while unemployment has well-known and significant effects on health and psychological well-being, insecure jobs also appear to have health consequences. Even if the effects on individuals are not as serious as unemployment - and this is yet to be demonstrated - the overall effect of precarious employment appears to be negative (Quinlan, 2001). Poverty and economic insecurity, in turn, have multiple effects on exposure and vulnerability, mediated by housing, working conditions, and access to nutrition and education (Labonte and Schrecker, 2006).

The experience of job insecurity has been associated with poorer physical and mental health outcomes (Ferrie, 1998). A study has shown that self-perceived job insecurity was the single most important predictor of a number of psychological symptoms such as mild depression (Dooley et al. 1987). Another study found that workers exposed to chronic job insecurity are more likely to report minor psychiatric symptoms as compared to those with secure jobs (Ferrie et al., 2002). Workers exposed to chronic job insecurity had the highest self reported morbidity, indicating that job insecurity acts as a chronic stressor. Among those who regained job security, adverse effects, particularly in the psychological sphere, were not completely reversed by removal of the threat, indicating the gravity of the threat.

Considering other results from the study discussed above, workers under situations of precarious employment may face greater demands or have lower control over the work process, two factors which have been associated with higher levels of stress, higher levels of dissatisfaction, and more adverse health outcomes. For example, workers with temporary contracts are twice as likely to report job dissatisfaction even after adjusting for various individual- and country-level variables (Benach et al., 2004). Non-permanent workers enjoy less job autonomy and control over working time than workers on permanent contracts and are likely to be occupied in less skilled jobs (Paoli and Merllie, 2001) and they have worse health outcomes as compared with permanent workers (Benavides et al. 2006). Related to these working conditions is participation in decision-making and particularly the lack of it. The Delphi results also show high relevance of this issue as a psychosocial risk.

In this context, downsizing, which can lead to increased job insecurity, has also been shown to be a risk to the health of employees. Thus, a significant linear relation between the level of downsizing and long periods of sick leave, attributable to musculoskeletal disorders and trauma, has been observed (Vahtera et al. 1997). Overall, research on self-reported job insecurity and workplace closure presents consistent evidence that they have significant adverse effects on self-reported physical and mental health (Marmot et al., 2001), as well as produce detrimental psychological and physio-pathological changes leading to poorer health outcomes. These adverse factors may also increase the risk of developing negative health-related behaviours.

Community or work-external issues play a large role in developing countries, which is why the social environmental context crystallized itself from the interview answers, in particular in terms of the prevalence of HIV/AIDS, which is a very important issue to consider in many African countries. The lack of policies to address these issues was also mentioned. In addition, work-life balance issues and spill-over effects, involvement, respect, dignity, societal expectations and norms were included under the social environmental context.

In terms of health outcomes, the scientific literature indicates that stress may significantly contribute to the development of physical illnesses, including asthma, coronary heart disease, skin diseases, and certain types of arthritis, migraine, peptic ulcers, ulcerative colitis and diabetes. There is also evidence that people impaired by stress engage in fewer health promoting behaviours.

The most widely studied physical health outcome is cardiovascular disease, along with its risk factors, such as hypertension, cigarette smoking, and diabetes (Schnall et al., 2000a; Belkic et al., 2004; Kivimäki et al., 2006). Hypertension is primarily a disease of industrial societies, with a very low prevalence in non-market agricultural communities (Waldron et al., 1982). The rising prevalence of hypertension in developed countries parallels the transformation of working life during the past century, away from agricultural work and relatively autonomous craft-based work toward machine-based (including computer-based) labour, characteristic of the assembly line and mass production (Schnall et al., 2000b). The development of hypertension as a global epidemic has occurred in parallel with urbanization and industrialization, and more recently, economic globalization (Graziano, 2004).

Also in the INTERHEART study undertaken with 11 119 patients in Asia, Europe, Middle East, Africa, Australia, North & South America, it could be shown that psychosocial stressors are associated with increased risk of acute myocardial infarction suggesting that approaches aimed at modifying these factors should be developed (Rosengren et al, 2004). Interviewees had a good understanding of these health outcomes and related them back to psychosocial hazards and work-related stress.

A psychological health outcome mentioned frequently was depression. Depression is one of the most common mental disorders found in the general community and in the workplace. Depression can be difficult to diagnose and can manifest as physical symptoms, such as headache, back pain, stomach problems, or angina. Work stressors have also been associated with psychological disorders, such as depression and anxiety (Stansfeld and Candy, 2006; Van Der Doef and Maes, 1999). Depression has been linked to occupational stress (Tennant, 2001), and 8% of depression has been attributed globally to the environmental factors, in particular occupational stress (WHO, 2006). One consequence of long-term exposure to stress may be burnout.

Unhealthy behaviours related to psychosocial hazards and stress at work, that were mostly mentioned were substance abuse as well as smoking. Alcohol is the most commonly used substance in most regions of the world, although prevalence varies. Alcohol is a major contributor to disease burden, accounting for 1.5% of all deaths and 3.5% of the total disability-adjusted life years (WHO, 2001b). There is some evidence that temporary employment is associated with increased death from alcohol-related causes and smoking-related cancers (Kivimäki, et al, 2003). For example, sustained job insecurity due to precarious labour market position is also linked with poor health behaviours by way of declines in specific coping mechanisms. WHO estimates that 400 million people around the world suffer from mental or neurological disorders or from psychosocial problems such as those related to alcohol and drug abuse (WHO, 2000).

Economic stress within a community may exacerbate tensions between social groups, magnify workplace stressors, and induce 'maladaptive' coping behaviours, such as smoking and alcohol use (Brenner, 1995). A relation has been demonstrated between stress at work and smoking; the decision to stop smoking, in particular, has been shown to be negatively related to various job stressors (Schar et al., 1973; Shirom, 1973).

Given the parallels provided through this era of globalization and the changing nature of work, there is hardly any doubt that developing countries experience at least similar health outcomes from exposure to psychosocial risks than those we find in the industrialized world. At most they are amplified given the export of hazardous machinery and work practices, considering the large populations in hazardous jobs and without any protection to their physical, psychological health, neither covered by health insurance, nor by unemployment insurance, and situated in the vast informal economic sector. The results of the interviews confirm at least the existence of these health outcomes, even if they cannot be quantified at this stage.

INTERVENTIONS TO MANAGE PSYCHOSOCIAL RISKS

In this section selected findings from question 9 (awareness of interventions that address psychosocial hazards) will be presented based on the exploratory interviews and the findings from the two Delphi rounds. They will be discussed with reference to the literature.

Expert interviews

The results of the interview in relation to question 9 and workplace interventions were categorized as suggested by the literature in primary, secondary and tertiary level.

Generally, although interventions are not very frequent, secondary intervention methods prevail while primary interventions are mentioned in all regions, i.e. not all countries. Primary prevention approaches mentioned by participants include organization-focused interventions, such as improvement of the work culture and organizational climate, special working arrangements (including teleworking), awareness-raising campaigns, participation in problem solving, active support provided by managers, and early identification of risk factors through application of the risk management cycle.

Secondary prevention approaches focus mainly on stress management and wellness programmes, employee assistance programmes, relaxation opportunities, medical examinations, lifestyle issues, but also training programmes for managers or to enhance team work. One Latin American participant said that *'the most popular programme is work groups to train people to relax, rest breaks'*. Another participant from South-East Asia had a similar experience: *'...teaching of relaxation training, promotion of physical exercises during break time and socialising'*. Whereas primary prevention seems more geared towards organizational action, secondary interventions are primarily focused on individuals, their physical fitness and abilities to relax.

It is noteworthy that, although primary prevention approaches were mentioned for all regions, most countries did not state any known intervention at primary level (South Africa, Zambia, Colombia, Mexico, Chile, Iran, Pakistan, Trinidad and Tobago, Tunisia, Malaysia, India, Viet Nam and Micronesia). For example the participant of Zambia stressed that s/he is *'...not aware of any major programmes. Primary prevention exists on HIV/AIDS....There is a profound lack of knowledge'*. A participant from Iran mentioned that stress management training is specifically offered to managers in some organizations: *'The purpose is to increase productivity and concentrate only on managers and not the rest of the organization.... Information is needed on what psychosocial issues are, and how to manage these'*. The Indian participants explained that there are few interventions, and that they are mostly confined to well-organized and private sectors.

Another participant from Iran stated that *'...many other factors are important to pay attention to, such as the economic level, low wages, culture, and tradition. There is no continuity, no job security. Very high unemployment, close to 30%, although official numbers say 15%'*. Also the participant from Pakistan stresses that *...there is very little in terms of intervention... there is no research or training for occupational health specialists... basic human rights are perceived differently and are limited, ...and when human* *rights are not there, how can we talk about occupational health?'*. The acknowledgement that occupational health considerations are not strictly a priority when a country is experiencing transition stands in line with some existing literature (Nuwayhid, 2004).

Overall, it appears that the participants in this study exhibited similar – and at times encouraging – levels of awareness and understanding of interventions (and most acknowledged that there is a pressing need for more research), although some interviewees considered questionnaires, surveys and legislation to be interventions when in practice these are better considered as informational frameworks on which interventions can develop or improve (Briner, 1996). However, legislation can be considered as an intervention at the policy level.

DELPHI findings

The Delphi results (Figure 3) indicate that secondary interventions are favoured in developing countries. Figure 3 shows seven intervention methods at secondary level: health promotion programmes (46/61);

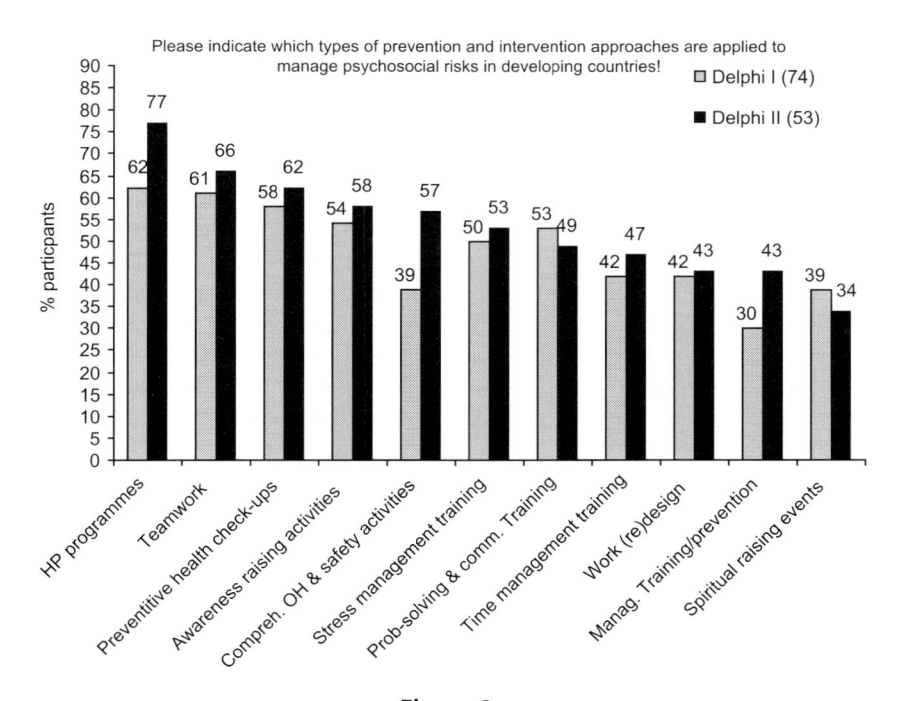

Figure 3.

preventive health check-ups (43/49); problem solving and communication training (39/37); stress management training (37/40); time management training (31/36); and spiritual raising events in some Asian communities (29/28). Those interventions that are located at primary level include teamwork (45/54); awareness-raising activities (40/41), work redesign (31/32); and preventive management training (29/34). One of the most interesting interventions identified is the comprehensive occupational health and safety policy (29/45). None of the interviewees mentioned such a comprehensive policy as being in place. It seems that this issue may be regarded as one of the priorities required to address psychosocial hazards together with traditional hazards to ensure workers' health and safety. The results to question 10 (identify three main priorities for action in relation to occupational health and safety) show that one priority pertains to policy and legislation development and another to implementation and enforcement of workplace occupational health and safety policies and standards. Hence, this may indicate rather a priority than an existing intervention. Further investigation into this finding may be worthwhile.

Discussion of findings

Research on intervention recommendations in occupational health and psychosocial risks in particular is accumulating. Unfortunately there are few evidence-based evaluative studies despite a pressing need for this if genuine progress is to be made (Caulfield et al., 2004). The topic remains particularly scarcely addressed in developing countries and those undergoing transition. In some cases, occupational health is neglected due to competing social, economic and political challenges occurring in the country (Nuwayhid, 2004). It is important to recognize that researchers should aim at conducting their investigations into occupational safety and health with sensitivity to the broader climate of social justice and national circumstances of their target country, and ideally in collaboration with researchers from other disciplines. However, that is not to say that some lessons with respect to interventions cannot be shared. As Rosenstock and colleagues suggest, workers around the world - despite differences in their environments - experience broadly the same categories/types of workplace hazards: chemical, biological, physical and psychological. Disturbingly, though, workers in developing countries (which comprise 80% of the global workforce) face a disproportionate burden of occupational disease and injury (Rosenstock, Cullen and Fingerhut, 2006). The parallels that seem to exist in developed and developing country contexts are important to identify. Once this is done, it seems a feasible approach to apply and modify, as necessary, or develop intervention strategies for developing country contexts.

It is estimated that work-related stress costs the developing and developed world between 5 and 10% of Gross National Product each year in sickness absence, premature retirement due to ill health and lost productive value (Cooper, 2006). The magnitude of the problem makes it difficult to ignore the necessity of interventions that can reduce, if not eliminate and prevent, psychosocial hazards and minimise workers' exposure to such hazards. From an organizational perspective, interventions are desirable not least to help improve worker well-being and productive effectiveness, but also to maintain a positive organizational reputation (Cooper, 2006).

As discussed earlier, it is generally agreed that work-related stress is closely related to work characteristics including overly high or low job demands, fast work pace, isolation, lack of control, harassment, lack of opportunity for growth and irregular work schedules. Broader factors such as poor home-work balance, job insecurity and deprived living conditions are also known to contribute (WHO, 2007a). Consequently, measures which focus exclusively on only one of these levels tend to be ineffective in the long term.

Work-related stress interventions are commonly categorized in terms of primary, secondary and tertiary interventions (Cooper, 2006). Primary intervention aims to reduce or eliminate hazards, through risk assessment and *preventative* measures such as work/task design and promotion of a supportive organizational culture, and raising awareness of workplace risks. Essentially, this stage strives towards achieving an appropriate "fit" between the work environment and its employees. The interventions at this level are less frequent than secondary interventions in developing countries according to the interview and survey results.

Secondary interventions strive to provide 'damage limitation' once hazards and signs of stress may have emerged. This can include stress management training, further information about psychosocial (as well as traditional) hazards, and encouraging self-initiative, and workplace health promotion activities. According to participants' views, health promotion activities are rather frequently applied in developing countries. One reason may be that health promotion can be very largely defined and has seen important developments during the last few decades, which may give an indication about their application in developing countries in terms of comprehensiveness.
Finally, tertiary interventions intend to support the recovery and rehabilitation of employees once they have been exposed and negatively affected by hazards and work-related stress: measures may include counselling or therapy. Some authors argue that the secondary and tertiary methods represent 'band-aid' approaches since they are reactive rather than preventative. Interestingly,

only one participant from the Western-Pacific region mentioned a tertiary intervention in terms of *'individuals receive help from mental health services once they have established symptoms'*.

At the highest level, the ground is set for intervention by delineating policy and legislation with respect to occupational health and safety. This may include policy with respect to working hours, compensation, employee rights and codes of conduct (Semmer, 2006). It is recognized that the existence of a national, legislative framework with government commitment is critical before interventions lower down can be truly regulated. This is problematic for many industrializing countries who try to work with governments that do not fully support their occupational health programmes (Dollard and Winefield, 2002). Moreover, in many developing countries it is difficult to put in place any control strategies specifically for psychosocial risks since there is either inadequate or simply a lack of policy in relation to these types of risk (WHO, 2007).

The findings from the interviews have some important and general implications. Firstly they suggest that interventions are – on a global scale – still limited, or at least very inconsistent. Secondly, where interventions do exist, they tend primarily to focus on the individual, and on one stage (usually secondary), rather than take a comprehensive approach. This raises some concern over how effectively the roots of psychosocial hazards and of work-related stress are actually being addressed, given that participants expressed a lack of basic information about what psychosocial risks at work are and what can be done to deal with them.

Another implication is that, even if research in industrialized countries indicates the scale of problems associated with psychosocial hazards and work-related stress, occupational health is not necessarily a priority for countries currently undergoing transition, or countries where broader social, economic or political challenges demand urgent attention (Nuwayhid, 2004). This unfortunately poses a challenge for gathering funding and resources for occupational health research in these countries, without which it is not possible to develop and implement appropriate, evidence-based interventions (Caulfield et al., 2004).

The finding that, in some countries, psychosocial hazards remain neglected in comparison to traditional (physical, chemical and biological) hazards is problematic for the well-being of millions of employees. The implication of this may be that there is an ever-present need for information sharing between developed and developing countries, context-specific research where possible, and joint efforts to build capacity of these countries to tackle occupational hazards in a holistic manner.

OCCUPATIONAL SECTORS THAT SEEM MOST AFFECTED BY PSYCHOSOCIAL RISKS AND WORK-RELATED STRESS

In this section selected findings from question 7 (which sectors are most affected by psychosocial hazards) will be presented based on the exploratory interviews and the findings from the two Delphi rounds. They will again be discussed with reference to the literature.

Expert interviews

The interviews indicate that the most affected occupational sector is the informal sector, which includes temporary and manual workers (primary sector). Agriculture and mining are part of this sector and present high risk occupations in terms of high accident rates, high labour turnover, and high job uncertainty. In Zambia '*...new mines are coming up and many are multi-nationals from Canada, Australia, South Africa, India, and so on. Some are good and some are in-between. There is very high anxiety in mines and danger of silicosis.*' The participants added that '*multi-nationals use gaps in occupational health and safety legislation with the result of mining disasters*'. The Nigerian participant noted that '*informal sector workers are not even aware of basic concerns*'. Participants confirm the high percentage of workers active in the informal economic sector. For example, Iran counts 10 million traditional weavers who are exposed to straining positions, bad lighting and ergonomic insufficiencies (Borojeny, 2007). An Iranian participant reiterated the statement and added '*Nobody cares about them*'.

The situation in Pakistan is also marked by a large informal sector that includes mainly women and child workers, as expressed by one participant: the majority of workers are women and children, who work long hours for very little money in poor working conditions, and the psychosocial hazards are very high. The Mexican participant noted that '*in most sectors across there is a problem of job insecurity and demands for higher production. Enterprises are linked to the production chain, like most of the maquiladora*', indicating that they have no control over the pace of working processes and that production is very tight.

The secondary sector includes manufacturing, processing and construction. Manufacturing was reported to be result-driven, monotonous and marked by shiftwork in Namibia. Many entrepreneurs of small-and medium enterprises were reported to meet minimum standards with respect to traditional hazards in Zambia. A North African participant said about the manufacturing industry that in the '*textile industry are bad working conditions, many psychological and physical problems*'.

Participants also mentioned the tertiary sector (services to the general population and to businesses) and the quaternary sector (government, culture, information technology), but to a lesser degree. In the tertiary sector mainly health professionals, call centre staff, police officers and security staff were reported to be exposed to psychosocial hazards. Health professionals generally were described as being vulnerable and easily affected by various kinds of diseases. *'They do shift work which produces stress; also people have high expectations of the health professionals who are overworked, have a high labour turnover are understaffed, underpaid and the result is burnout'*. One participant added that healthcare workers, in particular nurses, are aware that any wrong-doing results in loss of registration, which increases stress. Another participant underlined that healthcare workers are exposed to infectious diseases (hepatitis C, tuberculosis, HIV/AIDS, SARS, and bird flu) and that violence and harassment is a problem - mostly in mental health hospitals.

In addition, participants mentioned tourism as an affected occupation since *'...multi-nationals set up lodges and hotels...and due to high unemployment people are desperate to be employed...the result is unconducive working conditions, low pay and no proper transport'*.

In the quaternary sector especially teachers found mention as having problems with discipline, violent outbursts and frustrations (Namibia), and were also reported to be exposed to ever-changing evolutions of teaching materials, multi-tasking, high burden of job demands and a low decision-making level. Another area emerging from newly-industrializing countries is the IT sector, which is characterized by high demands and pressure, and long working days (India).

DELPHI findings

The Delphi findings (Figure 4) support the previous findings as well as the occupational sector research. As concerns the primary sector, the informal sector is one of ten priority areas to be addressed (31/46), agriculture (22/29), and mining (19/30). The secondary sector covers construction (25/35) and the manufacturing and industrial professions (37/59). The tertiary sector includes as priority sectors healthcare (46/58), police, security forces, and law enforcement (35/38), service sector (31/37), and catering and hospitality (20/18). The latter is the only occupation which decreased in the second Delphi round.

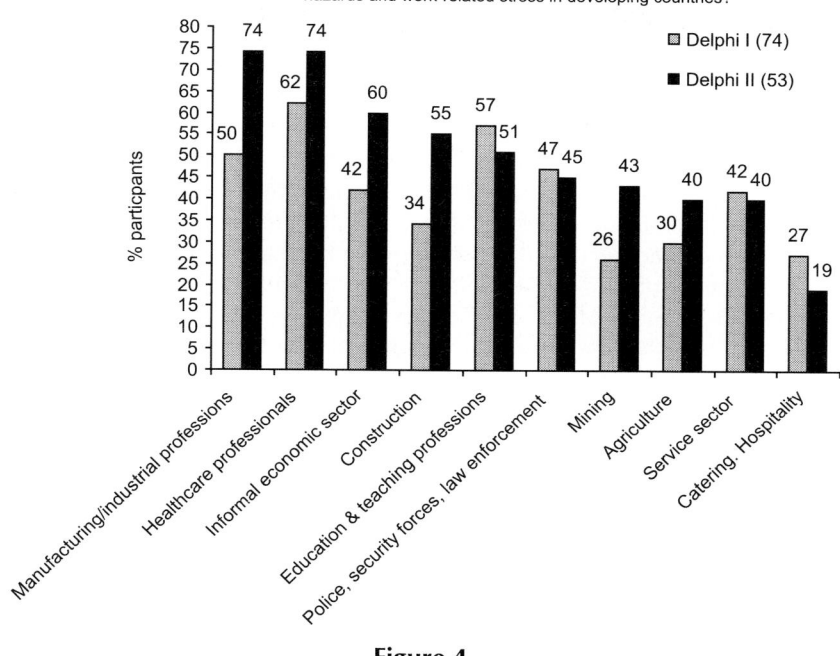

Which occupational sectors do you think are most affected by the impact of psychosocial hazards and work-related stress in developing countries?

Sector	Delphi I (74)	Delphi II (53)
Manufacturing/industrial professions	50	74
Healthcare professionals	62	74
Informal economic sector	42	60
Construction	34	55
Education & teaching professions	57	51
Police, security forces, law enforcement	47	45
Mining	26	43
Agriculture	30	40
Service sector	42	40
Catering, Hospitality	27	19

Figure 4.

Discussion of findings

In general, the literature concurs with the findings of the most affected occupational sectors, which are drawn out in the Delphi figure as being healthcare workers, manufacturing and industrial professions, and the informal sector.

The healthcare sector

Healthcare workers have been in the centre of study in Europe and other industrialized countries. One of the most extensive studies in Europe is the NEXT study. In this study, more than half of healthcare workers complained about the lack of psychological support with respect to the emotional demands of their job, ethical aspects, violence etc. The risks identified are exposure to emotional involvement, stress, work constraints, role uncertainty, dissatisfaction about the quality of care that they have the opportunity to give to patients (61% in Germany, 58.1% in Poland, 40.2% in UK), worrying about making mistakes, dissatisfaction with work prospects and with physical work conditions varies widely by country, dissatisfaction with actual pay relative to necessary income (for decent standard of living), skin, blood, musculoskeletal, accident-related, mental disorders, and violence (with psychiatry, older patients with Alzheimer's).

Due to recent discussions of the brain drain from developing to industrialized countries, a WHO report (WHO, 2004) reiterates the problems healthcare workers face. The research studied the migration patterns of health professionals in six countries in Africa. Healthcare workers leave due to unfavourable macroeconomic conditions, physical strain, and low pay including stressful working conditions. For example, the prevalence of HIV/AIDS is high in Africa. South Africa (57.5%), Uganda (61.5%), and Zimbabwe (58.4%) are among the countries with the highest prevalence of HIV/AIDS. Reasons for leaving included dealing with dying patients. Healthcare workers reported that they find it stressful to care for HIV patients. In addition, the stresses caused by handling several HIV/AIDS-related deaths every day takes its toll on nurses, many colleagues of whom also suffer from the disease (Stilwell, 2001).

The manufacturing sector

In Europe the manufacturing sector employs over 2.5 million workers, many of them women. In some states, women form the majority of workers in the sector.

The textile and clothing sector in Europe is changing as a result of developing technology and economic conditions, with businesses restructuring, modernising, and adapting to technological change. There is a trend of moving away from mass production of simple products towards a wider variety of products with a higher added value. The technical and industrial product subsector in particular is an area where European producers are world leaders. These developments have also had an impact on employment in the sector, with changes in employment models (e.g. subcontracting), and as a result of the techniques involved, on the hazards and risks to which workers are exposed (EASHW, 2008). Several hazards and risks can be encountered in the textile industry, including exposure to noise and chemical agents, to manual handling, working with dangerous machinery, and psychosocial hazards.

Manufacturing including textile production is one of the largest sectors in the developing world and is also perceived by respondents in the interviews and the survey as one that is most affected by psychosocial risks. For example, in Central America a large part of the industry is called maquiladora, and elsewhere the assembly industry or export-processing zones. These are duty free assembly plants and products are destined for export. Maquiladora today denotes factories that employ sweatshop labour from Central America to the Far East. Originally the system was set up by United States of America along the Mexico border by multinational corporations seeking to reduce labour costs. The working conditions resemble those of the 19th century. The trend is that these industries are growing globally, but mostly in developing nations and emerging industries.

In addition to unfavourable working conditions, in developing countries also the living conditions in the housing areas are characterised by lack of basic infrastructure. Families live in single rooms, without proper plumbing or electricity.

Characteristically, in this industry, 90% of employees are women or children between 15 and 24 years of age. Workplaces are often characterized by unstable jobs, low wages, long working hours, sexual harassment, temporary contracts and subcontracting (Gutierrez, 2000). Working conditions are characterized by noise, dust, bad posture, exposure to constant vibration, toxic exposures and industrial accidents. In addition, there is lack of adequate training, lack of safety equipment provision, intimidation of those who try to protest against prevailing conditions, violation of human rights, and different discriminatory actions, for example enforced urine/pregnancy testing of women, who can then get fired when pregnant (Human Rights Watch, 1996).

The informal economic sector

The informal economic sector poses a special challenge in terms of addressing any kind of occupational health and safety issues. The population is hard to identify, to research and to capture due to the fast changing, temporary and precarious working situations. Being in informal business and informal employment may cause mental distress and psychological diseases, because of job insecurity, i.e., the threat to lose long-term stable jobs (WHO, 2007b). Being in the informal sector means that workers are not recognized, recorded, protected or regulated by the public authorities. The work is often similar to the work performed in the formal sector, but by contrast there is an absence of workers rights and protection, including access to health insurance, pension schemes and protection under federal labour and health laws.

The lack of official statistics about workers in the informal economy, the scattered spatial distribution of shops and workers, and the uniqueness of workplaces such as domestic employment, indicate difficulties of access, which is the reason why this sector is ill-researched. Informal sector research indicates a need for a gender-sensitive approach. Psychosocial stressors also reported in informal workplaces are violence, sexual abuse and discrimination (Iriart et al., 2006). These are reported for domestic employed women (Sales and Santana, 2003). The available evidence consistently shows that workers in the informal economy or having informal employment have less favourable health indicators as compared to those in the formal economy or holding formal jobs (Hernandez et al., 1996).

While these new industries of the informal economic sector make an important contribution to the national economy, such working conditions are likely to have a negative impact on the mental health of employees and their families. Without effective international interventions the process of globalization would be used to take advantage of vulnerable people (Voyi, 2006). Hence, based on the available literature on the informal economic sector and the impact of occupational psychosocial risks, it seems reasonable that this sector has received attention in the interviews and the survey results.

SOME LIMITATIONS OF THE STUDY

Some important limitations of this research demand attention. Firstly, the sample used in this study is small and non-randomized, hence it cannot claim either representativeness or generalisability; both in terms of regional and country sub-groups (these did not contain comparable numbers of countries, and some countries had two or more participants whilst others only had one) and in terms of occupational health expertise. It is possible that perceptions and understanding would differ considerably if a different set of professionals was chosen, depending on their personal expertise and level of experience. Moreover, participant awareness of certain interventions does not necessarily translate into the scale or reality of the existence of many interventions; the actual intervention landscape, presumably, could only be reliably explored with national, rigorous and representative research.

It is, however, a first time exploratory attempt to reach experts in developing countries and to ask them to express their views on the different issues discussed. The response rates show great interest in the exploration of the issues at hand. It is also felt to be very positive, that the sample was multi-disciplinary and, therefore, less biased and broader minded than participants from the same or similar background.

THE WAY FORWARD

As indicated, this research is 'exploratory'. It does not claim to find solutions, but it does claim to be one of the first to enter into virgin territory. As much as psychosocial hazards are ill-addressed in many industrialized countries, it is still important to keep the world in our view in these times of the changing nature of work which also affects workers in developing countries through the diverse processes of globalization and the liberalization of the markets. The study claims further that it attempts to examine the level of understanding and prevalence of psychosocial hazards and work-related stress in developing countries, and the perception of needs in the area of addressing psychosocial risks. The research provides the first building blocks for researchers to increase the understanding of these issues in developing countries, to explore similarities and differences in the nature and conceptualization of work-related stress and psychosocial risks in industrialized and developing countries, and lastly to determine preliminary priorities, which are the basis for action.

In the short-term, it is hoped that this research will provide a basis for interaction and interchange of information with researchers and practitioners from developing countries. This chapter clearly outlines that the world, and especially the world of work, has changed. It is increasingly globalized and professionals should capture the tremendous opportunities for bringing multi-disciplinary expertise to developing countries. This is especially important, if workplace hazards, and in particular new and emerging hazards such as those related to the psychosocial working environment, can be addressed in a timely manner in order to have a preventive effect.

In the long-term it is hoped that results obtained facilitate the proposal to include issues concerning psychosocial hazards in national policies and legislatory frameworks of occupational health and safety, and that they are also considered when designing occupational health services, how basic they may be.

ACKNOWLEDGEMENTS

Special thanks for support in this study go to Juliet Hassard and Kasia Rezulska.

REFERENCES

Ahsan J. (2005). Stress among bankers, a study of bankers in Bangladesh.

Second ICOH International Conference on Psychosocial Factors at Work. *Book of Abstracts.* P.027, p. 144.

ALLEN J, DWYER S. (1994). The workplace project-organisational change in QLD workplaces. In Chu C., Simpson R, editor. *Ecological public health: from vision to practice.* Brisbane: joint publication of Centre for Health Promotion, University of Toronto and Institute of Applied Environmental Research, Griffith University, 195-203.

AZIZ, M. (2003). Asian-Pacific Newsletter on Occupational Health and Safety (July 2003), Volume 10, no.2.

BELKIC K, LANDSBERGIS P, SCHNALL P, BAKER D. (2004). Is job strain a major source of cardiovascular disease risk? *Scand J Work Environ Health.* 30(2):85-128.

BENACH J, GIMENO D, BENAVIDES FG, MARTÍNEZ JM, TORNÉ MM. (2004). Types of employment and health in the European Union: changes from 1995 to 2000. *Eur J Public Health.* 14:314-321.

BENAVIDES FG, BENACH J, MUNTANER C, et al. (2006). Associations between temporary employment and occupational injury: what are the mechanisms? *Occup Environ Med.* 63:416-421.

BOROJENY SB (2007). Occupational stressors in carpet weavers in Iran. *GOHNET Special Newsletter.* World Health Organization.

BRAUN V. AND CLARKE V. (2006). Using thematic analysis in psychology. *Qualitative Research in Psychology.* 3: 77-101.

BRENNER MH. (1995). Political economy and health. In: *Society and Health*

BRINER, RB. (1996). Paper presented at the Annual British Psychological Society.

CHINA ECONOMY WATCH. The Third Industrial Revolution (2008). Monday, March 17, 2008; Too Little Pork, Too Much Money, Or Both of These Plus Too Few People To Work The Land, To Grow The Pork, To Move The Money.......? http://chinaeconomywatch.blogspot.com/2008/03/chinese-stocks-and-yuan.html

CAULFIELD, N., CHANG, D., DOLLARD, M. F. AND EISHAUG, C. (2004). A Review of Occupational Stress Interventions in Australia. *International Journal of Stress Management.* 11 (29): 149-166

CHEN M. (1988). Organisational resources for worksite health promotion: a selective national directory. *Health values: achieving high level wellness.* 12(1):36-40.

CHU C. An integrated approach to workplace health promotion. (2004). In: Chu C, Simpson R, editor. *Ecological public health: from vision to practice.* Brisbane: A joint publication of Centre for Health Promotion, University of Toronto.

CONCHA-BARRIENTOS M et al. (2004). Selected occupational risk factors. In: Ezzati M et al., eds. *Comparative quantification of health risks: global* and regional burden of diseases attributable to selected major risk factors. Geneva: World Health Organization. 1651-801

COOPER, C.L. (2006). The changing nature of work: workplace stress and strategies to deal with it. International Congress on Occupational Health. *La Medicina del Lavoro*, Volume 97, n. 2. 29th

COX T, GRIFFITHS A, RIAL-GONZALEZ E. (2000). *Work Stress*. Luxembourg: European Commission.

DOLLARD, M. F. AND WINEFIELD, A. H. (2002). Mental Health: overemployment, underemployment, unemployment and healthy jobs. *Australian E-Journal for the Advancement of Mental Health*. 1 (3): 1-26.

DOOLEY D, ROOK K, CATALANO R. (1998). Job and non job stressors and their moderators. Journal of Occupational Psychology. 60:115–32.

ESTRYN-BEHAR, M. (2005). *Health and Satisfaction of Healthcare Workers in France and in Europe* [results of the PRESST-NEXT study] http://www.next.uni-wuppertal.de/download/BrochurePRESSTNEXTEN2005.pdf

EUROPEAN AGENCY FOR SAFETY AND HEALTH AT WORK. (2008). Occupational Safety and Health in the textiles sector. *E-Fact 30*.

FERRIE JE, SHIPLEY MJ, DAVEY SG, STANSFELD SE, MARMOT MG. (2002). Change in health inequalities among British civil servants: the Whitehall II study. J *Epidemiol Community Health*. 56(12): 922-6.

FERRIE JE, SHIPLEY MJ, MARMOT MG, et al. (1998). An uncertain future: the health effects threats of employment security in white-collar men and women. *Am J Public Health*. 88(7): 1030-6.

GUTIERREZ E (2000). Workers' health in Latin America and the Caribbean: looking to the future. *Perspectives in Health*, 5(2) available at www.paho.org.

HARATANI T. AND KAWAKAMI N. (1999). Work, Stress and Health Conference. Organization of work in a global economy. Baltimore Convention Center, March 11-13.

HEALTH AND SAFETY EXECUTIVE. (2007). Survey on self-reported work-related illness (SWI05-06).

GRAZIANO J. (2004). Global burden of cardiovascular disease. In: Zipes D, Libby P, Bonow R, Braunwald E, editors. *Heart disease*. London: Elsevier; 2004, p. 1-19.

HERNANDEZ P, ZETINA A, TAPIA M, ORTIZ C, SOTO IA. (1996). Childcare needs of female street vendors in México city. *Health Policy and Planning*. 11(2):169-178.

HUMAN RIGHTS WATCH. 1996. Sex Discrimination in Mexico's Maquiladora Sector. Available at www.hrw.org/hrw/summaries/s.mexico968.html

IRIART JAB, Oliveira RP, Xavier S, Costa AM, Araújo GR, Santana, V. (2006). Representações do trabalho informal e dos riscos à saúde entre trabalhadoras domésticas e trabalhadores da construção civil. *Ciência & Saúde Coletiva*.

KANTER R.M. (1977). World and family in the United States: a critical review and agenda for research and policy. *Russell Sage Foundation*, New York.

KARASEK R, THEORELL T. (1990). Healthy work. Stress, productivity, and the reconstruction of working life. New York: Basic Books.

KIVIMAKI M, VIRTANEN M, ELOVAINIO M, KOUVONEN A, VAANANEN A, VAHTERA J. (2006). Work stress in the etiology of coronary heart disease-a meta-analysis. *Scand J Work Environ Health. 32*(6, special issue):431-42.

KIVIMÄKI M, VAHTERA J, VIRTANEN M, et al. (2003). Temporary employment and risk of overall and cause specific mortality. *Am J Epidemiol. 158*:663-8.

LABONTE, R., SCHRECKER, T. (2006). Globalization and social determinants of health: Analytic and strategic review paper. On behalf of the Globalization Knowledge Network.

LOEWENSON, R. (1998). Situation analysis and issues in occupational health and safety in the SADC region. OATUU Health and Safety and Environment Programme. For SADC Employment and Labour sector meeting, Mauritius, April.

MARMOT M, FERRIE J, NEWMAN K, et al. (2001). The contribution of job insecurity to socioeconomic inequalities. *Research Findings: 11.* Health Variations Programme.

NUWAYHID, (2004). *Am J. Public Health. 94*:1916-1921.

PAOLI AND MERLLIE. (2001). Third European Survey of Working Conditions. Dublin: European Foundation.

QUINLAN, M. (2001/2002). Global Occupational Health Network Newsletter, No. 2. World Health Organization.

ROSENGREN A, HAWKEN S, ÔUNPUU S, SLIWA K, ZUBAID M, ALMAHMEED WA, BLACKETT KN, SITTHI-AMORN C, SATO H, YUSUF S (2004). Effect of potentially modifiable risk factors associated with myocardial infarction in 52 countries (the INTERHEART study): case-control study. *Lancet, 364*: 953–62.

SEMMER, N. (2006). Job stress interventions and the organization of work. *Scand J Work Environ Health; 32*(6, special issue).

ROSENSTOCK L, CULLEN M, FINGERHUT M. (2006). Occupational health. In: Jamison DT, Breman JG, Measham AR, Alleyne G, Claeson M, Evans DB, Jha P, Mills A, Musgrove P, eds. *Disease Control Priorities in Developing Countries*. 2nd ed. New York: Oxford University Press. Pp. 1127–1145.

SALES EC, SANTANA VS. (2003). Depressive and anxiety symptoms among housemaids. *American Journal of Industrial Medicine, 44*:685-691.

SCHAR M, et al. (1973). Stress and cardiovascular health: an international cooperative study: II The male population of a factory at Zuerich. *Social Science and Medicine, 7*:585-603.

SEMMER, N.K. (2006). Job stress interventions and the organization of work. *Scandinavian Journal of Work Environ Health.* 32 (6): 1-13.
SHIROM A, et al. (1973). Job stresses and risk factors in coronary heart disease among five occupational categories in kibbutzim. *Social science and medicine.* 7:875-892.
SEN, A K: Global doubles (2000). The 349th commencement of Harvard University, June 9.
SIEGRIST J & MARMOT M. (2004). Health inequalities and the psychosocial environment – two scientific challenges. *Social Science & Medicine;* 58:1463-1473.
STANSFELD S, CANDY B. (2006). Psychosocial work environment and mental health -- a meta-analytic review. *Scand J Work Environ Health;*32(6 (special issue):443-62.
STILWELL, B. (2001). Health worker motivation in Zimbabwe" internal report, Department of Organization of Health Care Delivery, WHO, Geneva.
TENNANT C. (2001). Work-related stress and depressive disorders. *Journal of Psychosomatic Research,* 51(5):697-704.
TUROFF, M. & HILTZ, S. R. (1996). Computer Based Delphi Processes; in Adler, M. & Ziglio, E. (eds) Gazing into the Oracle: The Delphi Method and Its Application to Social Policy and Public Health, Jessica Kingsley Publishers, London.
VAHTERA J, KIVIMÄKI M, PENTTI J. (1997). Effect of organisational downsizing on health of employees. *Lancet;350*:1124–8.
VAN DER DOEF M, MAES S. (1999). The job demand-control(-support) model and psychological well-being: a review of 20 years of empirical research. *Work & Stress;13*(2):87-114.
VOYI K. (2006). Is globalisation outpacing ethics and social responsibility in occupational health? *Med Lav;* 97,2 : 376-382.
WALDRON I, NOWATARSKI M, FREIMER M, HENRY JP, POST N, WITTEN C. (1982). Cross-cultural variation in blood pressure: A qualitative analysis of the relationship of blood pressure to cultural characteristics, salt consumption and body weight. *Soc Sci Med;16*:419-30.
WEGMAN, D H. Aging and globalization (2006). *Med Lav;* 97,2: 137-142.
WORK LIFE 2000, European conference 22-25 January 2001. Workshop summary, No. 18, February 1999.
WHO. (2007a). Raising awareness of stress in developing countries: a modern hazard in a traditional working environment. *Protecting Workers' Health Series no. 6*
WHO. (2007b). Employment Conditions and Health Inequalities. Final Report to the WHO Commission on Social Determinants of Health (CSDH).
WHO (2006). Preventing disease through health environments. *Towards*

an estimate of the environmental burden of disease. Authored by A. Prüss-Ustün and C. Corvalan.

WHO (2005). Health Policies and Programmes in the Workplace. *Mental Health Policy and Service Guidance Package.*

WHO, Regional Office for Africa, Brazzaville. (2004). Migration of health professionals in six countries: a synthesis report.

World Health Organization. (2001a). *Mental Health in Europe.* WHO, Copenhagen.

World Health Organization. (2001b). *The World Health Report.* Geneva.

WHO. (2000). Executive Board 107th Session. Mental Health 2001. Report by the Secretary).

WHO (1995). Global strategy on occupational health for all: The way to health at work. http://www.who.int/occupational_health/publications/globstrategy/en/index.html.

MANAGEMENT COMPETENCIES FOR PREVENTING AND REDUCING STRESS AT WORK

Emma Donaldson-Feilder, Joanna Yarker and Rachel Lewis

CHAPTER OVERVIEW

This chapter summarises applied research presented in two research reports for the UK Health and Safety Executive (Yarker et al, 2007; Yarker et al, 2008) and explores its implementation in practice. The research set out to identify the management behaviours associated with the effective prevention of stress at work. The research, made up of three studies, had the following aims: to build a management competency framework for preventing and reducing stress at work; to develop a questionnaire to measure the behaviours covered by the competency framework; and to explore the ways in which the research findings can be used in practice. In the first study, a qualitative approach was taken, involving structured one-to-one interviews with managers and employees, plus focus groups with HR professionals. This initial study developed a management competency framework consisting of 19 competencies. The second study employed a combined quantitative and qualitative approach to: refine the competency framework into 4 broad management competencies relating to the prevention of stress in employees; and develop a questionnaire measure of the competencies. The third study, run in parallel with study 2, explored the usability of the research outputs and determined the range of its practical applications. The implications for practitioners are explored.

INTRODUCTION

Until recently, research in occupational health psychology has largely examined fairly 'global' work design constructs such as demands, control and support or effort and rewards. Less attention has been given to the role that managers could play in managing work stress in their team. However, managers are important for many reasons: they can cause (or conversely prevent) stress by their behaviour towards their staff (Tepper, 2000; Hogan, Curphy & Hogan, 1994); their behaviour is likely to impact on the presence or absence of psychosocial hazards in their staff's working environment (van Dierendonck, Haynes, Borrill, & Stride, 2004; Cherniss, 1995); if an individual suffers from stress, their manager will need to be involved in designing and implementing solutions (Thomson, Rick & Neathey, 2004); and they have been shown to 'hold the key' to work redesign initiatives (Saksvik, Nytro, Dahl-Jorgensen & Mikkelsen, 2002). In recognition of this, recently there has been more research investigating the impact of manager behaviours and styles on employee stress (e.g., van Dierendonck et al., 2004; Gilbreath, 2004; Nyberg, Bernin, & Theorell, 2005).

Impact of manager behaviour on employee stress

Much of the research looking at the impact of manager behaviour on employee stress focuses on one of two prominent management/leadership theories: task- and relationship- leadership styles (e.g., Duxbury et al., 1984; Seltzer & Numerof, 1988; Sheridan & Vredenburgh, 1978); and transactional and transformational leadership styles (e.g. Alimo-Metcalfe & Alban-Metcalfe, 2001; Sosik & Godshalk, 2000; Arnold, Turner, Barling, Kelloway & McKee, 2007; Nielsen, Randall, Yarker & Brenner, 2008). A number of studies using measures developed from these theoretical stances have demonstrated that management/leadership behaviours are empirically linked to employee stress. For a detailed review of these approaches and an overview of their associations with stress and performance outcomes see Yarker, Donaldson-Feilder, Lewis, & Flaxman (2007) and Yarker, Donaldson-Feilder and Lewis (2008).

Some occupational stress authors have recently noted the limitations of simply adopting prominent management/leadership theories and measures (e.g., Gilbreath, 2004; Gilbreath & Benson, 2004; Nyberg et al., 2005), and have developed and employed manager behaviour scales more reflective of research into work design and occupational health psychology. These studies confirm that manager behaviour is a contributing factor in determining employee stress levels. For example, Gilbreath and Benson (2004) developed a management behaviour scale and found that a range of specific management behaviours were significantly related to employees' mental health, even after accounting for the effects of the other non-management variables: their manager behaviour scale explained an additional 5% of the variance in employees' mental health. A longitudinal study, by van Dierendonck, et al. (2004), suggests that management behaviour and employee stress are linked in a 'feedback loop': more effective manager behaviour was related to better employee mental health at one of the measurement time points, and higher levels of employee mental health led to more favourable perceptions of leader behaviour at another time point.

While the studies outlined above provide evidence that managers contribute to determining employee stress levels, the diversity and range of manager behaviour measures and stress outcome measures used presents three significant limitations for both practice and research: first, it is unclear which behaviours, or combinations of behaviours, are relevant for particular work characteristics or stress outcomes, thereby making practical intervention based on research difficult; second, the range of leadership and management measures used makes it difficult to conduct cross-study comparisons; and third, research to date has largely drawn from existing leadership models developed for performance management purposes, rather than explicitly exploring the behaviours relevant to managing employee stress and well-being. To extend understanding of this area, there is need to understand better the full range of manager behaviours that are significant for employee stress and to develop a framework of those behaviours for use in both practice and research in this field. To do this, we suggest adopting a behavioural competency approach, an approach widely used in areas of assessment, selection and development.

Taking a competency approach

Competency frameworks refer to a complete collection of skills and behaviours required by an individual to do their job (Boyatzis, 1982). Competency frameworks are frequently used to guide human resources interventions, particularly training and development, selection and assessment, and performance management/appraisal (Briscoe & Hall, 1999; Rankin, 2004). There is an extensive literature on management competencies and within this a range of competency frameworks have been developed: for example for nurse managers (Sherman, Bishop, Eggenberger, & Karrden, 2007), social workers managers (e.g., Wimpfheimer, 2004), and General Practitioners (Patterson, Ferguson, Lane, Farrell, Martlew & Wells, 2000). In addition, studies have identified managerial competencies for managers engaged in a range of job roles, for example those working in cross-functional relationships (Rodriguez, 2007), in virtual teamwork (Hertel, Konradt, & Voss, 2006) and for managers of international corporations or global bodies (Brownell, 2006). While there has been some criticism of leadership competency models (e.g. Hollenbeck, McCall & Silzer, 2006), there is evidence that they remain popular with employers and human resources professionals (Whiddett & Hollyforde, 2007).

The competencies included within existing management frameworks are predominantly performance driven, and competency approaches have largely been analysed in relation to their relationship with individual and organisational performance (Goldstein, Yusko & Nicolopoulos, 2001; Levenson, van der Stede & Cohen, 2006), and career development (Dulewicz & Herbert, 1996). The authors are unaware of any research to date that has examined the extent to which they incorporate the behaviours required by managers to manage the stress of others. It is therefore possible that, while existing frameworks may include those behaviours relevant for the prevention and reduction of stress at work, discrete sets of behaviours relevant to this particular context may have been omitted from the existing performance-focussed frameworks. In order to develop a competency framework that identifies the full range of manager behaviours relevant to the prevention and reduction of stress in staff, research needs to explore manager behaviours from this perspective.

Practical application of manager behaviour research findings

From a practitioner perspective, research that clarifies the manager behaviours that are relevant for the prevention and reduction of stress at work needs to generate outputs that can support the development of interventions that help managers behave in the ways identified. In many cases, individuals are promoted or recruited into management positions on the basis of their technical skills and may not have developed the behavioural approaches required to manage staff in a way that prevents stress. These managers need support and guidance to help them adopt the relevant behaviours and, in some cases, may need persuading of the value of doing so. There is therefore a need to clarify how research findings that identify key manager behaviours can best be used in practical interventions in organisational settings. The perspectives of end-users and subject-matter-experts/practitioners working in the field are needed to provide an insight into what will be the best ways of integrating research findings and behavioural models into interventions.

Aims and overview of the research programme

The aims of this research programme were: to build a management competency framework for preventing and reducing stress at work; to develop a questionnaire to measure the behaviours covered by the competency framework; and to explore the ways in which the research findings can be used in practice. The research programme was made up of three studies. In the first study, a qualitative approach was taken, involving structured one-to-one interviews with managers and employees, and focus groups with HR professionals, in order to develop a management competency framework. The second study involved a combined quantitative and qualitative approach to refine the competency framework and develop a questionnaire measure of the competencies. The third study, run in parallel with study 2, explored the usability of the research outputs to establish their practical applications.

STUDY 1 – QUALITATIVE RESEARCH TO DEVELOP A COMPETENCY FRAMEWORK

Study 1: Aims

The aim of this initial study was to develop a competency framework identifying the manager behaviours required to prevent and reduce stress at work. The objective was to start from the basis of managing stress at work, in order to develop an a-posteriori model. In order to do this, a behavioural competency approach was taken, using a critical incident technique interview process.

Study 1: Method

Managers and employees took part in structured one-to-one interviews incorporating the critical incident technique; and HR professionals took part in focus groups. This multi-method, multi-perspective approach has been recommended and successfully employed previously to develop competency frameworks (Graham & Tarbell, 2006; Patterson et al., 2000; Robinson, Sparrow, Clegg & Birdi, 2005). Furthermore, this approach allows for the triangulation and preliminary validation of the findings.

Participants

Participants included 216 employees, 166 managers and 54 HR professionals working in 31 organisations across five sectors: Education, Healthcare, Central Government, Local Government and Finance. All three participant groups were split equally across the five sectors, such that each sector was represented by at least 40 employees, 24 managers and 10 HR professionals. In order to collect a sample that was representative of a number of organisations, rather than being over-represented by one organisation, no more than 20 interviews (manager and employee) were held at any one organisation.

Employee and manager interviews

Two interview proformas were developed to elicit information about specific manager behaviours relevant to stress management. They were piloted with two employees and two managers respectively and minor improvements made. Both interviews incorporated critical incident techniques (Flanagan,

1954) to capture data concerning managers' behaviours that impacted upon the stress of their direct reports. All participants were sent an e-mail two days before the interview prompting them to think about specific incidents in which managers' behaviour impacted upon the stress of their direct reports.

At the start of the interview, participants were asked how they defined work-related stress. A brief discussion with the interviewer ensured that the interviewee's definition was aligned with the established UK Health and Safety Executive (HSE) definition *'stress is the adverse reaction people have to excessive pressures or other types of demand'* (HSE, 2004). This ensured that all participants drew from the same frame of reference (Chell, 1998). Employees were then asked to describe a situation when they had been managed effectively and one when they had been managed ineffectively at a time of pressure and demand. Managers were asked to describe a situation when their action as a manager was effective and one when their action as a manager was less effective at a time of pressure and demand.

HR focus groups

The HR perspective on stress management behaviours was gained through a focus group exercise, in which participants were asked to identify manager behaviours that they felt prevented, caused or alleviated stress.

Data analysis

Each interview was recorded and transcribed. 13 interviews were rejected due to a recording error leading to a lack of audibility. As a result, 369 interviews were suitable for analysis, 209 employee interviews and 160 manager interviews. Behavioural indicators were extracted from each interview transcript using content analysis (Miles & Huberman, 1984). In order to achieve inter-rater reliability in behaviour extraction, two researchers independently highlighted behaviours from three randomly chosen transcripts on the basis of the definition 'all managerial behaviours associated with the management of stress'. An acceptable level of 85% agreement on the three transcripts was achieved (Currell et al., 1999).

Two impartial observers, blind to the aims of the study (Dasborough, 2006), were asked to sort the cards into manager behavioural competency themes, with the following instructions: 'Develop piles of behaviours you think reflect the same competency. Both positive and negative behaviours can be included in the same piles'. Six broad themes with 22 sub-themes were identified. These were used to create the initial coding structure, which was then employed to conduct the content analysis on the remaining transcripts. Inter-rater reliability was tested again at an early stage of content analysis and an agreement level of 76% was achieved. In addition, the researchers met during and at the end of the coding process to ensure that the coding system was precise and each theme mutually exclusive. Three competencies were merged with other competencies during these meetings as a consequence of finding the themes were not exclusive, so the emergent framework included 19 competencies. At this point, the researchers took each competency separately and allocated behavioural indicators to positive and negative examples of behaviours relating to each competency.

The data generated in the focus group exercises with HR professionals were transcribed. Content analysis was used to fit the data into the existing coding framework using the approach described above.

Study 1: Results

4,764 behavioural indicators were extracted from the 369 transcripts, equating to an average of 12.91 behaviours per transcript. 19 competencies emerged from the behavioural coding, theming and content analysis. This initial framework is provided in the appendix.

Study 1: Discussion

This first study identified 19 behavioural competencies that can help managers prevent and reduce stress in those they manage. Interestingly, the data also showed that the same behavioural indicators were mentioned by managers, employees and HR professionals and also across the five different sectors from which participants were drawn, suggesting broad agreement on the manager behaviours that are relevant in this context (see Yarker et al. (2007) for more detail). While the comparison between different groups of participants and different methodologies (interviews versus focus group exercises) allowed for some preliminary validation of the findings, the framework emerging from this study still required full validation. The value of a management competency framework for preventing and reducing stress at work is that it provides a guide for managers and allows integration of stress management into people management interventions and vice versa. However, 19 competencies is a rather unwieldy framework on which to base interventions, so some refinement was also required to ensure that the research findings were of practical value. In addition, practical application of the framework would, in many circumstances, benefit from the ability to measure the degree to which specific managers show the relevant behaviours. A further study was therefore required to validate and refine the findings from this first study and to develop a questionnaire to measure the behaviours covered by the competency framework.

STUDY 2 – REFINING THE COMPETENCY FRAMEWORK

Study 2: Aims

The aims of the second study in this programme were: to validate and refine the behavioural competency framework that emerged from study 1; and to develop a questionnaire to measure the behaviours covered by the competency framework. Whilst ad hoc feedback following publication of the findings from study 1 showed that practitioners were already finding the management competency framework useful, there was still a need to test and refine the model to ensure both full practical benefit and scientific rigour.

Study 2: Method

A questionnaire was developed from the manager behaviours found, in study 1, to be relevant for the prevention and reduction of stress at work; this was piloted qualitatively and quantitatively before being used in a questionnaire survey. The questionnaire generated data that was analysed statistically to explore the factorial structure of the competency framework and to provide initial reliability and validity data relating to the questionnaire. The refined framework and questionnaire underwent further qualitative scrutiny by subject-matter-experts to ensure the findings generated a robust model and usable measure. In addition, feedback from manager participants in the questionnaire was used to explore whether there were any irrelevant questions or gaps in the questionnaire.

Development of the draft questionnaire and initial piloting

Behavioural statements were extracted from the data collected in study 1 in order to develop a questionnaire that measured the behaviours identified as relevant to the prevention and reduction of stress at work. The initial questionnaire, consisting of 156 questions, was tested qualitatively with stakeholders and experts (n = 21). This stage allowed four questions to be removed. The resulting 152 item questionnaire was tested quantitatively with a snowball sample of employees (n = 292). The data generated from this quantitative pilot was analysed using reliability analysis, as described by Rust and Golombok (1999), to revise and refine the questionnaire in preparation for the questionnaire survey.

Questionnaire survey and analysis of direct report data

Following reliability analysis, the revised questionnaire, consisting of 112 items, was used as a self-report and upward feedback measure in a questionnaire survey. Survey participants included managers and their direct reports working within 21 organisations from the same five sectors as for study 1 (Education, Healthcare, Central Government, Local Government and Finance), plus one 'Other' organisation. Managers responded to the questionnaire with their perceptions of their own behaviour, and direct reports responded with their perceptions of their manager's behaviour. The sample included 152 managers and 656 direct reports.

Direct report data was analysed using reliability analysis and exploratory factor analysis in order to establish the psychometric properties of the questionnaire and provide information on the factorial structure of the competency framework. Reliability analysis was conducted following the steps suggested by Rust and Golombok (1999). This analysis allowed 13 questions to be excluded, creating an item pool of 99 questions. In order to establish the psychometric properties of the questionnaire, and to provide information about the factorial structure of the competency framework, the data was then subjected to Exploratory Factor Analysis. Exploratory Factor Analysis has traditionally been employed in the field of leadership and management to determine the number of underlying dimensions in quantitative data (e.g. Kouzes & Posner, 1990). In order to ensure that a rigorous approach was taken to the Factor Analysis, the guide by Ferguson and Cox (1993) was used.

Further qualitative testing of the model and questionnaire measure

To further validate the refined competency framework and questionnaire, two workshops of stress experts (n = 38) explored the research findings, named each factor and identified sub-clusters. The outcomes of these workshops were scrutinised by an independent observer. In addition, structured interviews were conducted with a sample of the manager participants in the questionnaire survey (n = 47) and a sample of stakeholders (health and safety, occupational health and human resources professionals, n = 6) from the participating organisations, to explore whether the questionnaire contained any irrelevant questions or gaps.

Study 2: Results

Exploratory Factor Analysis of the direct report survey data revealed four factors. As a result of the validation exercise with workshop participants, and input from the independent observer, each factor was grouped into three sub-clusters, providing a refined competency framework of four competencies and 12 sub-competencies, as shown in table 1 (with brief descriptions of the competencies).

Table 1. Refined 'Management competencies for preventing and reducing stress at work' framework, including brief descriptions for each sub-competency

Management Competency	Sub-competency	Description of sub-competency
Respectful and Responsible: Managing emotions and having integrity	Integrity	Respectful and honest to employees
	Managing Emotions	Behaves consistently and calmly
	Considerate approach	Thoughtful in managing others and delegating
Managing and communicating existing and future work	Proactive work management	Monitors and reviews existing work, allowing future prioritisation and planning
	Problem solving	Deals with problems promptly, rationally and responsibly
	Participative/ empowering	Listens and consults with team, provides direction, autonomy and development opportunities to individuals
Reasoning/managing difficult situations	Managing conflict	Deals with conflicts fairly and promptly
	Use of organisational resources	Seeks advice when necessary from managers, HR and occupational health
	Taking responsibility for resolving issues	Supportive and responsible approach to issues

Table 1. Contd.

Management Competency	Sub-competency	Description of sub-competency
Managing the individual within the team	Personally accessible	Available to talk to personally
	Sociable	Relaxed approach, such as socialising and using humour
	Empathetic engagement	Seeks to understand the individual in terms of their motivation, point of view and life outside work

Following analysis of the direct report survey data, and feedback from managers, stakeholders and experts, the final number of questions in the 'Stress management competency indicator tool' (questionnaire measure) was 66, as shown in table 2.

Table 2. Items included in the refined 'Stress management competency indicator tool' (questionnaire measure). Upward feedback version - all items would be preceded by 'My Manager'.

Competency	Sub-competency	Items
Respectful and responsible: Managing emotions and having integrity	Integrity	Is a good role model
		Says one thing, then does something different
		Treats me with respect
		Is honest
		Speaks about team members behind their backs
	Managing emotions	Is unpredictable in mood
		Acts calmly in pressured situations
		Passes on his/her stress to me
		Is consistent in his/her approach to managing
		Is consistent in his/her approach to managing

239

Table 2. Contd.

Competency	Sub-competency	Items
	Managing emotions (contd)	Takes suggestions for improvement as a personal criticism
		Panics about deadlines
	Considerate approach	Makes short term demands rather than allowing me to plan my work
		Creates unrealistic deadlines for delivery of work
		Seems to give more negative than positive feedback
		Relies on other people to deal with problems
		Imposes 'my way is the only way'
		Shows a lack of consideration for my worklife balance
Managing and communicating existing and future work	Proactive work management	Communicates my job objectives to me clearly
		Develops action plans
		Monitors my workload on an ongoing basis
		Encourages me to review how I organise my work
		When necessary, will stop additional work being passed on to me
		Works proactively
		Sees projects/tasks through to delivery
		Reviews processes to see if work can be improved
		Prioritises future workloads
	Problem solving	Is indecisive at decision making
		Deals rationally with problems
		Follows up problems on my behalf
		Deals with problems as soon as they arise

Table 2. Contd.

Competency	Sub-competency	Items
	Participative/ empowering	Gives me the right level of job responsibility
		Correctly judges when to consult employees and when to make a decision
		Keeps me informed of what is happening in the organisation
		Acts as a mentor to me
		Delegates work equally across the team
		Helps me to develop in my role
		Encourages participation from the whole team
		Provides regular team meetings
		Gives me too little direction
Reasoning/ Managing difficult situations	Managing conflict	Acts as a mediator in conflict situations
		Acts to keep the peace rather than resolve conflict issues
		Deals with squabbles before they turn into arguments
		Deals objectively with employee conflicts
		Deals with employee conflicts head on
	Use of organisational resources	Seeks advice from other managers when necessary
		Uses HR as a resource to help deal with problems
		Seeks help from occupational health when necessary
	Taking responsibility for resolving issues	Follows up conflicts after resolution
		Supports employees through incidents of abuse
		Doesn't address bullying
		Makes it clear he/she will take ultimate responsibility if things go wrong

Table 2. Contd.

Competency	Sub-competency	Items
Managing the individual within the team	Personally accessible	Prefers to speak to me personally than use e-mail Provides regular opportunities to speak one to one Returns my calls/e-mails promptly Is available to talk to when needed
	Sociable	Brings in treats Socialises with the team Is willing to have a laugh at work
	Empathetic engagement	Encourages my input in discussions Listens to me when I ask for help Makes an effort to find out what motivates me at work Tries to see things from my point of view Takes an interest in my life outside work Regularly asks 'how are you?' Treats me with equal importance to the rest of the team Assumes, rather than checks, I am OK

Note: some of the questions are negatively worded. The scores given on these items would be reversed before calculating overall scores.

Study 2: Discussion

This study refined the competency framework, initially developed in study 1, into four broad management competencies relating to the prevention of stress in employees, with 12 sub-competencies. It also developed a questionnaire measure, consisting of 66 questions, which can be used to explore the extent to which a particular manager shows the behaviours identified in the framework. The two outputs from this second study, the competency framework and questionnaire measure, are designed to be applied in organisational settings in order to help managers show the behaviours identified as relevant for preventing and reducing stress at work. However, further research was needed to clarify the best approaches and interventions for applying the competency framework and questionnaire in organisational settings.

STUDY 3 – EXPLORING THE USABILITY OF THE RESEARCH FINDINGS

Study 3: Aims

The aim of this third study, run in parallel with study 2, was to explore the ways in which the research findings from studies 1 and 2 could best be used in practice. While anecdotal feedback following publication of the findings of study 1 suggested that the management competency framework and questionnaire measure had a range of applications in practical settings, there was a need to understand how these tools were perceived by end-users and subject-matter-experts. The aim was therefore to get specific feedback on how best to use the research findings to intervene in organisational settings.

Study 3: Method

A qualitative approach was employed, using structured interviews and workshops, to explore the usability of both the competency framework and the questionnaire measure within organisations.

Structured one-to-one interviews were conducted with 47 managers and six stakeholders working within the same five sectors as for studies 1 and 2 (Education, Healthcare, Central Government, Local Government and Finance), plus one 'Other' organisation. Both managers and stakeholders were asked: how easy the questionnaire was to answer; whether it was accurate in terms of identifying development needs; and what would be the best use of the questionnaire (self report without feedback, self report with feedback, upward feedback and 360 degree feedback). Stakeholders were additionally asked: in what ways the competency framework would fit into their existing human resources (HR) policies and practices; and how they saw the questionnaire fitting into existing HR/Health and Safety (H&S) policies and practices.

Two workshops were conducted with 38 stress experts, comprising independent stress practitioners, Human Resources, Occupational Health and Health and Safety professionals. Participants were asked: in what ways the competency framework would fit into existing HR/H&S policies and practices; and how they saw the questionnaire fitting into existing HR policies and practices.

Interview and workshop data was transcribed and content analysis was used to extract themes.

Study 3: Results

Feedback from managers and stakeholders on the questionnaire showed that: 91% found the questionnaire 'easy' or 'very easy' to answer; and 82% felt that the questionnaire was accurate in terms of identifying key management development areas. About three-quarters (73%) of manager respondents and five of the six stakeholders felt that a 360 degree feedback questionnaire would be the best format for the questionnaire, while the remainder (27% of managers and one stakeholder) felt that upward feedback would be preferable.

Responses from stakeholders and workshop participants, regarding how the competency framework would fit into existing HR/H&S policies and processes, fell into two themes: firstly, in a stress management context, to review and develop policies, to inform the development of action plans for stress management at an organisational level, and to integrate with existing policies; and secondly, in a management/leadership development/ training context, to dovetail into existing frameworks and programmes, to develop new training programmes, or as a guiding structure or checklist for training.

Stakeholders and workshop participants also saw a dual use for the questionnaire measure. Firstly, in a stress management context, the questionnaire could be used to provide information at the local level, potentially as a logical next step following a stress risk assessment (such as the UK Health and Safety Executive's Management Standards approach, HSE, 2004); this could help 'tie-in' managers to the process and address specific scenarios, for example, where a particular line manager was seeking help with stress-related issues. Secondly, in a more general management/ leadership development or appraisal context, to hep managers identify their development needs and, thereby, develop the relevant behaviours. In this latter case, the feedback suggested that the tool should be used in conjunction with follow-up support or coaching, or as part of an overall development programme, rather than as a stand-alone exercise.

Study 3: Discussion

The usability findings from this third study provide an endorsement for the use, in organisational and individual interventions, of both the competency framework and the questionnaire developed in research studies 1 and 2. The vast majority of end-users found the questionnaire easy to use and accurate in identifying development needs. It would appear that 360 degree feedback or upward feedback would be preferred format in which to use the questionnaire. The findings suggest that these research outputs could prove useful in both stress management and leadership/management development domains: interventions that use the competency framework and/or questionnaire measure as a basis could therefore provide a means of integrating stress management into people management and vice versa.

OVERALL CONCLUSIONS

This research programme set out to build a management competency framework for preventing and reducing stress at work, to develop a questionnaire to measure the behaviours and to explore the ways in which the research findings can be used in practice. As a result of the qualitative and quantitative research in studies 1 and 2, a management competency framework for preventing and reducing stress was produced, comprising four behavioural competencies and 12 sub-competencies. A questionnaire was developed in study 2, comprising 66 questions, which can be used to explore whether specific managers show the behaviours identified in the competency framework. The end-user, stakeholder and subject-matter-expert feedback provided in study 3 suggests that both competency framework and questionnaire have two potential domains of usability: stress management interventions; and management/leadership development programmes. This suggests that these research outputs provide a mechanism for the integration of stress management and people management domains.

IMPLICATIONS FOR PRACTITIONERS: HOW TO USE THE RESEARCH FINDINGS

The development of a framework identifying the behavioural competencies required by managers to prevent stress in employees, together with a questionnaire measure of the relevant behaviours, has a number of advantages for occupational health psychology practitioners. Firstly, the framework puts stress management into a language and format that is accessible to HR professionals and line managers: this means that guidance and interventions based on the research findings are likely to be acceptable to these client and end-user populations. Secondly, the research outputs can form the basis for a number of interventions that help managers behave in ways that will prevent and reduce stress at work.

And thirdly, because they are applicable in both stress management and management/leadership development domains, the research outputs can be used to integrate these two areas in organisational settings.

In terms of interventions that can be developed based on the outputs from this research, occupational health psychology practitioners may find it useful to be guided by the usability findings detailed in study 3 above. We consider these firstly from a stress management intervention perspective and then from a management/leadership development perspective.

Where practitioners are developing workplace stress management programmes, the research outputs can be used as follows:

- The competency framework can help develop or update an employer's stress management or well-being policy. It can be used alongside organisational level statements about the prevention of stress, such as the UK Health and Safety Executive's Management Standards for stress, to make explicit the manager behaviours expected in order to achieve the standards set.
- The competency framework can be integrated into other organisational policies that have a link with work-related stress, such as attendance/absence management, welfare and dignity at work.
- The competency framework, together with the questionnaire measure, can be used to develop proactive interventions providing guidance, development and support for managers to help them prevent and reduce stress for their teams.
- The competency framework, together with the questionnaire measure, can be used as part of a reactive programme responding to particular stress-related issues in work setting. For example, where a stress risk assessment has been conducted (using the UK Health and Safety Executive's Management Standards approach or other methodology) and identified specific stress risks or particular high-risk departments or teams, the competency framework, together with the questionnaire measure, can be used to help managers reflect on their own behaviour and develop behavioural approaches that reduce the risk to their staff.

The usability findings suggest that the research outputs can help achieve manager 'buy-in' to stress management activities as they provide clear guidance to managers on the behaviours they need to show (without adding additional process or procedural requirements).

Where practitioners are helping organisations with management/leadership development processes, the research outputs can be used as follows:

- The competency framework can be used to explore whether existing management/leadership development frameworks and programmes cover all the behavioural competencies relevant to preventing and reducing stress in staff – and to guide the addition of extra modules if gaps are identified.
- The competency framework can be used as a basis from which to develop new management/leadership development programmes.
- The competency framework can be used to design induction programmes for new managers or be integrated into existing induction programmes.
- The competency framework can be integrated into manager training courses in other relevant skills areas, such as communication, delegation and managing conflict.
- By embedding the competencies set out in the framework into management/leadership development, particularly manager inductions, and also by using it to encourage senior managers to role model the behaviours required, it can help to bring about a culture change in which the behaviours specified become the organisational norm for management approach.
- The questionnaire measure can be used as a part of interventions in any of the above management/leadership development or training contexts. Using the questionnaire measure in a 360 degree or upward feedback format allows the production of a feedback report that will help a manager understand how their behaviour is perceived by others. This can be compared with the manager's perception of their own behaviour. Any discrepancies between self and other perceptions and any areas where the manager is seen not to be behaving in ways that prevent and reduce stress in their staff may highlight development needs for that manager. Clarity about their development needs, together with support (in the form of coaching, training or other development intervention), can help the manager develop the relevant behaviours.

The usability feedback suggests that the questionnaire measure should be used in conjunction with follow-up support or coaching, or as part of an overall development programme, rather than as a stand-alone exercise.

Thus, whether approaching the issue of manager behaviour from a stress management angle or from a management/leadership development angle, the research outputs can support practitioners in designing and implementing interventions that help managers behave in ways that prevent and reduce stress in their staff.

OTHER IMPLICATIONS

Implications for employers

Employers can use the competency framework emerging from this research in a range of ways: indeed, feedback suggests that a number of organisations are already doing this. At an individual level, the framework can be provided to managers to give guidance about behaviours they should be displaying. At a group/organisational level, it can be used to guide the design of training programmes and interventions, as described under 'implications for practitioners' above. In addition, questionnaire measure can enhance both individual and organisational applications of the framework by providing specific feedback on the degree to which individual managers are showing the behaviours identified: the vast proportion of managers who used the questionnaire measure found it 'easy' or 'very easy' to answer, relevant to their roles, and accurate in terms of identifying key management development areas.

The competency framework and questionnaire measure can be used both from a stress management perspective and from a management/leadership development perspective, broadening the utility of this research beyond stress to wider aspects of good people management and healthy organisational cultures. The potential uses for both framework and questionnaire measure are explored in more detail in the 'implications for practitioners' section above. The usability study suggests that the research outputs would be best used in a management/leadership development and/or stress management context rather than in a manager selection or performance assessment context. The aim is to enable employers to support managers better.

Implications for line managers

For line managers, the benefit of defining the management behaviours that prevent and reduce stress in their staff is that it shows that stress management is a part of general management activities, not an additional set of processes and procedures. The findings suggest that there is no single behaviour needed to prevent and reduce stress: instead managers need to consider using a complementary set of behaviours. The competency framework aims to provide managers with a clear specification of the relevant behaviours, so that they can identify which are already in their management repertoire and which they need to develop in order to prevent and reduce stress for their staff. The questionnaire measure, used as a self-assessment, upward feedback or 360 degree feedback, can help this latter process of identifying strengths and development needs; in the case of upward feedback or 360 degree feedback, it can give managers clarity about how their behaviour is perceived by others. Managers who are involved in other stress management activities, can use the framework (and the questionnaire measure if appropriate) as a starting point from which to approach solutions.

Implications for national policy

The research findings provide a vehicle for encouraging employers to tackle stress in the workplace, together with mechanisms to help them do so. Promulgation of the findings can be used to show employers how to develop interventions to ensure managers can prevent employee stress effectively. Such interventions can be promoted not only within stress management policies, but also in policies focused on management/leadership development processes. In addition, the research has links with, and therefore provides a potential platform for integration across, national initiatives relating to health and safety, health at work, workplace skills, and people management. These links could be forged even better if effective interventions could be developed to improve employee well-being by improving manager skills/behaviour.

Implications for future research

Research is currently being undertaken to design and test interventions to help managers behave in the ways identified in the competency framework. Further data is also being gathered to test the criterion-related validity, and further assess the construct validity of the competency framework and the questionnaire measure, in order to develop a sound psychometric measure. There is a need for further usability data to provide longitudinal case studies of organisations integrating the framework and the questionnaire measure into their existing processes, in order to support other employers to do the same.

REFERENCES

Alimo-Metcalfe, B., & Alban-Metcalfe, R.J. (2001). The development of a new transformational leadership questionnaire. The Journal of Occupational & Organizational Psychology, 74, 1-27.

Arnold, K, A., Turner, N., Barling, J., Kelloway, K., E & McKee, M., C., (2007). Transformational Leadership and Psychological Well-Being: The Mediating Role of Meaningful Work. Journal of Occupational Health Psychology, 12, (3), 193-203.

BOYATZIS, R. E. (1982). *The competent manager: A model for effective performance*. Chichester: John Wiley & Sons.

BRISCOE, J.P., & HALL, D. T. (1999). Grooming and picking leaders using competency frameworks: Do they work? An alternative approach and new guidelines for practice. *Organizational Dynamics, 28*, 37-52.

BROWNELL, J., 2006, "Meeting the Competency Needs of Global Leaders: A Partnership Approach", *Human Resource Management*, 45 (3), 309-336.

CHELL, E. (1998). Critical Incident Technique. In G. Symon and C. Cassell (eds.). *Qualitative Methods and Analysis in Organisational Research: A practical Guide*. London: Sage.

CHERNISS, C. (1995). *Beyond Burnout: Helping teachers, nurses, therapists & lawyers recover from stress and disillusionment*. NY: Routledge.

CURRELL, S. C., HAMMER, T. H., BAGGETT, L. S., & DONIGER, G. M. (1999). Combining qualitative and quantitative methodologies to study group processes: An illustrative study of a corporate board of directors. *Organizational Research Methods, 2*, 5-36.

DASBOROUGH, M. T. (2006). Cognitive asymmetry in employee emotional reactions to leadership behaviours. *The Leadership Quarterly, 17*, 163-178.

DULEWICZ, V., & HERBERT, P. (1996). General management competencies and personality: A 7-year follow-up study. *Working Paper Series 9621*, Henley Management College, Oxfordshire, United Kingdom.

DUXBURY, M. L., ARMSTRONG, G. D., DREW, D. J., & HENLY, S. J. (1984). Head nurse leadership style with staff nurse burnout and job satisfaction in neonatal intensive care units. Nursing Research, 33, 97-101.

FERGUSON, E. & COX, T. (1993). Exploratory Factor Analysis: A user's guide. *International Journal of Selection and Assessment*, 1(2), 84-94.

FLANAGAN, J. C. (1954). The critical incident technique. *Psychological Bulletin, 51*, 327-358.

GILBREATH, B. (2004). Creating healthy workplaces: The supervisor's role. *International Review of Industrial and Organizational Psychology, 19*, 93-118.

GILBREATH, B., & BENSON, P. G., (2004). The contribution of supervisor behaviour to employee psychological well-being. *Work & Stress, 18*, 255-266.

GRAHAM, & TARBELL (2006). HRM 45 – full ref needed

GOLDSTEIN, H. W., YUSKO, K. P., & NICOLOPOULOS, V. (2001). Exploring black-white subgroup differences of managerial competencies. *Personnel Psychology*, 54: 783-807.

HEALTH AND SAFETY EXECUTIVE (2004). *Management Standards for Work Related Stress*. Web document: www.hse.gov.uk/stress.

HERTEL, G., KONRADT, U., & VOSS, K. (2006). Competencies for virtual teamwork: Development and validation of a web-based selection

tool for members of distributed teams. *European Journal of Work and Organizational Psychology,* 15 (4), 477-504.
HOGAN, R., CURPHY, G. J., & HOGAN, J. (1994). What we know about leadership. *American Psychologist, 49,* 493-504.
HOLLENBECK, G.P., MCCALL, M.W., & SILZER, R.F. (2006). Leadership competency models. *The Leadership Quarterly,* 17, 398-413.
KOUZES, J. M., & POSNER, B. Z. (1990). *Leadership Practices Inventory (LPI): A self assessment and analysis.* University Associates.
LEVENSEN, A. R., VAN DER STEDE, W.A., & COHEN, S. G. (2006). Measuring the relationship between managerial competencies and performance. *Journal of Management, 32,* 360-380.
MILES, M. B., & HUBERMAN, A. M. (1984). *Qualitative data analysis: A sourcebook of new methods.* Beverley Hills: SAGE.
NYBERG, A., BERNIN, P., & THEORELL, T. (2005). *The impact of leadership on the health of subordinates.* The National Institute for Working Life.
NIELSEN, K., RANDALL, R., YARKER, J., & BRENNER, S-O. (2008). The effects of transformational leadership on followers' perceived work characteristics and psychological well-being: A longitudinal study. *Work & Stress,* 22, 16-32.
PATTERSON, F., FERGUSON, E., LANE, P., FARRELL, K., MARTLEW, J., & WELLS, A. (2000). A competency model for general practice: implications for selection, training, and development. *British Journal of General Practice, 50,* 188-193.
RANKIN, N. (2004). *The new prescription for performance: the eleventh competency benchmarking survey. Competency & Emotional Intelligence Benchmarking Supplement 2004/2005.* London: IRS.
ROBINSON, M. A., SPARROW, P. R., CLEGG, C., & BIRDI, K. (2005). Design engineering competencies: future requirements and predicted changes for the forthcoming decade. *Design Studies, 26,* 123-153.
RODRIGUEZ, C. M. (2007). A commentary on undergraduate eductation: The implications of cross-functional relationships in business marketing – the skills of high-performing managers. *Journal of Business-to-Business Marketing,* 14 (1), 95-102.
RUST, J., & GOLOMBOK, S. (1999). *Modern Psychometrics: The science of psychological assessment.* Routledge:Taylor Francis Group.
SAKSVIK, P. O., NYTRO, K., DAHL-JORGENSEN, C., & MIKKELSEN, A. (2002). A process evaluation of individual and organisational occupational stress and health interventions. *Work & Stress, 16,* 37-57.
SELTZER, J., & NUMEROF, R.E. (1988). Supervisory leadership & subordinate burnout, Academy of Management Journal, 31, 439-446.
SHERIDAN, J. E., & VREDENBURGH, D. J. (1978). Usefulness of leadership behavior and social power variables in predicting job tension, performance, and turnover of nursing employees. *Journal of Applied Psychology, 63,* 89-95.

SHERMAN, R. O., BISHOP, M., EGGENBERGER, T., & KARDEN, R. (2007). Development of a leadership competency model. *Journal of Nursing Administration,* 37 (2), 85-94.

SOSIK, J. J., & GODSHALK, V. M. (2000). Leadership styles, mentoring functions received, and job-related stress: A conceptual model and preliminary study. Journal of Organizational Behavior, 21, 365-390.

TEPPER, B. J. (2000). Consequences of abusive supervision. *Academy of Management Journal, 43,* 178-190.

THOMSON, L., RICK, J. & NEATHEY, F. (2003). *Best Practice in Rehabilitating Employees following Absence due to Work Related Stress.* Sudbury: HSE Books.

VAN DIERENDONCK, D., HAYNES, C., BORRILL, C., & STRIDE, C. (2004). Leadership behavior and subordinate well-being. *Journal of Occupational Health Psychology, 9,* 165-175.

WIMPFHEIMER, S. (2004). Leadership and management competencies defined by practicing social work managers: An overview of standards developed by the National Network for Social Work Managers. *Administration in Social Work,* 28(1), 45-56.

WHIDDETT, S., & HOLLYFORDE, S., (2007). Competencies. Wimbledon: Chartered Institute of Personnel and Development.

YARKER, J., DONALDSON-FEILDER, E., LEWIS, R. & FLAXMAN, P.E. (2007). Management competencies for preventing and reducing stress at work: Identifying and developing the management behaviours necessary to implement the HSE Management Standards. Sudbury: HSE Books.

YARKER, J., DONALDSON-FEILDER, E. & LEWIS, R. (2008). Management competencies for preventing and reducing stress at work: Identifying and developing the management behaviours necessary to implement the HSE Management Standards: Phase 2. Sudbury: HSE Books.

Appendix. Management Competency framework (with positive and negative behavioural indicators) resulting from study 1 – NB this framework was refined and updated in study 2 – see table 1

Competency	Positive examples of Manager Behaviour	Negative examples of Manager Behaviour
Managing workload and resources	• Bringing in additional resource to handle workload • Aware of team members ability when allocating tasks • Monitoring team workload • Refusing to take on additional work when team is under pressure	• Delegating work unequally across the team • Creating unrealistic deadlines • Showing lack of awareness of how much pressure team are under • Asking for tasks without checking workload first
Dealing with work problems	• Following through problems on behalf of employees • Developing action plans • Breaking problems down into manageable parts • Dealing rationally with problems	• Listening but not resolving problems • Being indecisive about a decisions • Not taking issues and problems seriously • Assuming problems with sort themselves out
Process Planning and Organisation	• Reviewing processes to see if work can be improved • Asking themselves 'could this be done better?' • Prioritising future workloads • Working proactively rather than reactively	• Not using consistent processes • Sticking too rigidly to rules and procedures • Panicking about deadlines rather than planning
Empowerment	• Trusting employees to do their work • Giving employees responsibility • Steering employees in a direction rather than imposing direction	• Managing 'under a microscope' • Extending so much authority employees feel a lack of direction • Imposing a culture of 'my way is the only way'

Appendix. Contd.

Competency	Positive examples of Manager Behaviour	Negative examples of Manager Behaviour
Participative approach	• Provides opportunity to air views • Provides regular team meetings • Prepared to listen to what employees have to say • Knows when to consult employees and when to make a decision	• Not listening when employee asks for help • Presenting a final solution rather than options • Making decisions without consultation
Development	• Encourages staff to go on training courses • Provides mentoring and coaching • Regularly reviews development • Helps employees to develop within the role	• Refuses requests for training • Not providing upward mobility in the job • Not allowing employees to use their new training
Accessible/Visible	• Communicating that employees can talk to them at any time • Having an open door policy • Making time to talk to employees at their desks	• Being constantly at meetings/away from desk • Saying 'don't bother me now' • Not attending lunches or social events with employees
Health and Safety	• Making sure everyone is safe • Structuring risk assessments • Ensuring all Health and Safety requirements are met	• Not taking Health and Safety seriously • Questioning the capability of an employee who has raised a safety issue
Feedback	• Praising good work • Acknowledging employees efforts • Operating a no blame culture • Passing positive feedback about the team to senior management	• Not giving credit for hitting deadlines • Seeing feedback as only 'one way' • Giving feedback employees are wrong just because their way of working is different

Appendix. Contd.

Competency	Positive examples of Manager Behaviour	Negative examples of Manager Behaviour
Individual Consideration	• Provides regular one-to-ones • Flexible when employees need time off • Provides information on additional sources of support • Regularly asks 'how are you?'	• Assuming everyone is OK • Badgering employees to tell them what is wrong • Not giving enough notice of shift changes • No consideration of worklife balance
Managing Conflict	• Listening objectively to both sides of the conflict • Supporting and investigating incidents of abuse • Dealing with conflict head on • Following up on conflicts after resolution	• Not addressing bullying • Trying to keep the peace rather than sort out problems • Taking sides • Not taking employee complaints seriously
Expressing and managing own emotions	• Having a positive approach • Acting calmly when under pressure • Walking away when feeling unable to control emotion • Apologising for poor behaviour	• Passing on stress to employees • Acting aggressively • Loosing temper with employees • Being unpredictable in mood
Acting with Integrity	• Keeps employee issues private and confidential • Admits mistakes • Treats all employees with same importance	• Speaks about employees behind their backs • Makes promises, then doesn't deliver • Makes personal issues public
Friendly Style	• Willing to have a laugh and a joke • Socialises with team • Brings in food and drinks for team • Regularly has informal chats with employees	• Criticises people in front of colleagues • Pulls team up for talking/ laughing during working hours • Uses harsh tone of voice when asking for things

Appendix. Contd.

Competency	Positive examples of Manager Behaviour	Negative examples of Manager Behaviour
Communication	• Keeps team informed what is happening in the organisation • Communicates clear goals and objectives • Explains exactly what is required	• Keeps people in the dark • Holds meetings 'behind closed doors' • Doesn't provide timely communication on organisational change
Taking Responsibility	• 'Leading from the front' • Steps in to help out when needed • Communicating 'the buck stops with me' • Deals with difficult customers on behalf of employees	• Saying 'its not my problem' • Blaming the team if things go wrong • Walking away from problems
Knowledge of Job	• Able to put themselves in employees' shoes • Has enough expertise to give good advice • Knows what employees are doing	• Doesn't have the necessary knowledge to do the job • Doesn't take time to learn about the employee's job
Empathy	• Takes an interest in employee's personal lives • Aware of different personalities and styles of working within the team • Notices when a team member is behaving out of character	• Insensitive to people's personal issues • Refuses to believe someone is becoming stressed • Maintains a distance from employees 'us and them'
Seeking Advice	• Seeks help from occupational health when necessary • Seeks advice from other managers with more experience • Uses HR when dealing with a problem	• n/a

A CASE OF TEACHER BURNOUT

Pedro R. Gil-Monte

CHAPTER OVERVIEW

The purpose of this study is to present and discuss a case of burnout in a teacher. The subject is a 56-year-old woman dedicated to teaching for thirty-four years. At the time of the diagnosis she had been on sick leave for three years due to a set of symptoms characterised by intense anxiety, depressive disorders, cognitive and affective alterations, and negative attitudes and behaviours toward the job and her students. A description of the subject's symptoms is presented, as well as the evolution of the case over a ten-year period. Her symptoms are discussed in light of the literature, and the conclusion drawn that this case represents an example of burnout.

INTRODUCTION

Work-related stress is one of the greatest professional risks that employees face in the contemporary world of work. Studies carried out in the European Union (EU) have concluded that work-related stress is a major problem in Europe and one that costs business and society dearly. Stress is the fourth most common health symptom reported by Europe's workers (Parent-Thirion, Fernández, Hurley & Vermeylen, 2007). In the United States, work-related stress constitutes a problem similar to that in the EU. According to the National Institute for Occupational Safety and Health (NIOSH, 1999), the percentage of workers who report their job is stressful ranges from 28 % to 40 %, and 26 % of workers report they are "often or very often burned out or stressed by their work". Moreover, workers affected by anxiety, stress, and neurotic disorders experience much greater work loss than those with all other nonfatal injuries or illnesses: 25 days away from work compared to 6 in 2001 (NIOSH, 2004).

Workers in the education sector are a high-risk population with a high prevalence rate for work-related stress (Parent-Thirion et al., 2007). Working in contact with the users or clients of the organisation may frequently expose workers feel to stressors such as aggression and interpersonal conflicts, overload, role conflict and ambiguity, perception of imbalance in the social interchanges, absence of control over results, etc. These work conditions favor the development of burnout (Maslach, Schaufeli & Leiter, 2001). According to a report by the European Agency for Safety and Health at Work (2007) on emerging psychosocial risks related to occupational safety and health, burnout, job-induced tension and depression are consequences of new forms of employment, new types of contracts and job insecurity.

Burnout is a psychological response to chronic work-related stress of an interpersonal and emotional nature that appears in professionals in service organisations who work in direct contact with the clients or users of the organisation. Edelwich and Brodsky (1980) have defined burnout as "a progressive loss of idealism, energy, and purpose experienced by people in the helping professions as a result of the conditions of their work". It is a process that progresses from enthusiasm to stagnation, frustration and, finally, apathy. Price & Murphy (1984) define burnout as a disordered or unsuccessful process of adaptation to a stressful work situation that progresses from shock and disorganisation to volatile emotions (e.g., irony), guilt and loneliness.

The currently most widely used definition of burnout is the one elaborated by Maslach & Jackson (1981), who define it as a syndrome characterised by the appearance of low personal accomplishment (feelings of incompetence and a lack of achievement in one's work with people), emotional exhaustion (feelings of being emotionally over-extended and depleted of one's emotional resources) and depersonalisation (impersonal, negative, callous, or excessively detached response toward the recipients of one's care or service). The Maslach Burnout Inventory-Human Services Survey (MBI-HSS) (Maslach & Jackson, 1981) assesses these three aspects of burnout. It is the most commonly used measure of burnout, and has dominated research in the field (Densten, 2001).

On the basis of this conceptualisation, the literature offers several models that describe the process of burnout as a temporal sequence. The model of Golembiewski, Munzenrider and Carter (1983) states that burnout progresses from depersonalisation through lack of personal accomplishment to emotional exhaustion. A second model was developed by Leiter and Maslach (1988). This model states that burnout progresses from emotional exhaustion through depersonalisation to lack of personal accomplishment. A third model, developed by Lee and Ashforth (1993a, 1993b), states that burnout progresses from emotional exhaustion to depersonalisation, and from emotional exhaustion to lack of personal accomplishment. They proposed that elevated levels of emotional exhaustion directly evoked decreases in personal accomplishment rather than indirectly through depersonalisation. All three models have been tested extensively, but previous research has failed to provide convincing evidence for any of the three models (Taris, Le Blanc, Schaufeli, & Schreurs, 2005). Based on appraisal models of stress, Gil-Monte, Peiró and Valcárcel (1998) proposed a model to explain the relationships between the MBI-HSS dimensions. According to this model, burnout progresses in a parallel way from personal accomplishment to depersonalisation and from emotional exhaustion to depersonalisation. The model has been tested, and some cross-sectional studies have provided evidence for the development of burnout proposed by the model (Durán, Extremera & Rey, 2001; Manassero, García, Vázquez, Ferrer, Ramis & Gili, 2000; Manzano & Ramos, 2000).

Diverse studies have suggested that the core of the burnout phenomenon is feeling worn out, or the combination of emotional exhaustion and physical fatigue as an affective state (Moore, 2000; Shirom & Ezrachi, 2003).

Depersonalisation is a feeling and an impersonal response towards recipients of one's service, care, treatment, or instruction (Maslach & Jackson, 1981). In human service professions, recipients can be a source of frustration (e.g., students who do not collaborate), which creates aggression that is generally directed towards the source of frustration (Berkowitz, 1969). Those professionals who behave insidiously towards recipients use depersonalisation to escape from guilt feelings (Bandura, 1986).

Guilt is conceptualised as the unpleasant and remorseful feelings associated with the recognition that one has violated, or is capable of violating, a moral standard (Jones & Kugler, 1993). In contrast to shame, where the focus of attention involves a negative evaluation of the global self, guilt involves a negative evaluation of a specific behaviour (Tangney, Stuewing, & Mashek, 2007). It draws attention to the wrongfulness of the precipitating event and to injury suffered by the victim (Quiles & Bybee, 1997).

From an interpersonal perspective (Baumeister, Stillwell & Heatherton, 1994), guilt is described as a social emotion linked to the communal relationships (intimate or close relationships in which the individual responds to the needs of the other person) and not to an exchange in which reciprocity is expected. The origins, the functions and the process of guilt have important interpersonal aspects, as it is a variable that reinforces ties in relationships (Tangney et al., 2007). Guilt has the symbolic role of reaffirming commitment toward the other person and the responsibility of taking care of him or her. It is used as a strategy to gain influence over others, and it makes it possible to alleviate the stress produced by the lack of balance in the emotional states that results from social exchanges. Guilt has prosocial effects, as it motivates people to make amends to others, correct their errors and apologise. These interpersonal actions reduce the feelings of guilt, so that the expression of guilt and remorse is a way of recovering a relationship after committing some type of transgression. For Hoffman (1982), the stress derived from empathy and a self-attribution of responsibility for the causes that have produced suffering in other individuals intervene in the appearance of guilt; Berndsen and Manstead (2007) have concluded that responsibility is best regarded as an elaborated appraisal generated by guilt, rather an antecedent of guilt.

However, excessive or inappropriate levels of guilt can produce a dysfunctional and disruptive experience, and in some cases clinical alterations (Lewis, 1971). Some studies have concluded that the association between guilt and psychopathology is accounted for by shame (Pineles, Street & Koenen, 2006). However, other studies have found positive and significant relationships between guilt and depression (Harder & Zalma, 1990; Ghatavi, Nicolson, MacDonald, Osher & Levitt, 2002; Mitchell, Goodwin, Johnson & Hirschfeld, 2008; O'Connor, Berry, Weiss & Gilbert, 2002), anxiety, somatisation and psychoticism (Harder, Cutler & Rockart, 1992). Quiles and Bybee (1997) obtained positive and significant correlations between guilt and depression, anxiety, somatisation and psychoticism, and they concluded that chronic feelings of guilt could be an indicator of the use of inappropriate coping strategies and the failure of the individual to regulate his emotions. Ghatavi et al. (2002) found that individuals with depression problems had a history of feelings of guilt, and in their conclusions they suggest the possibility that guilt represents a variable that predisposes individuals to illness.

Guilt appears to be involved in the burnout syndrome (Ekstedt & Fagerberg, 2005; Farber & Miller, 1981; Freudenberger, 1974; Gil-Monte, 2005; 2008; Maslach, 1982; Price & Murphy, 1984). One of the frequent causes of feelings of guilt in professionals is the existence of negative thoughts about others and the negative and cynical way they have treated them (Maslach, 1982). Some professionals feel they are becoming cold and dehumanised, and this experience leads them to reaffirm their commitment toward other people and the responsibility of taking care of them (Baumeister et al., 1994; Tangney et al., 2007). In such a situation, they feel higher levels of burnout. As a result, they develop a sense of failure and loss of self-esteem, which can lead to a state of depression (Maslach, 1982). The clinical alterations produced by feelings of guilt (e.g., depression) can cause an increase in the rate of absenteeism (Baba, Galperin, & Lituchy, 1999). In a cross-sectional study Gil-Monte (2008) obtained empirical evidence for the influence of guilt in the relationships between depersonalisation and absenteeism (i.e., number of work days missed in the past year). Those professionals who presented high levels of depersonalisation showed more absenteeism, but only when they felt high levels of guilt about their attitude/behaviour at work.

CONSEQUENCES OF BURNOUT

Outcomes associated with burnout are numerous. Statistical evidence has been obtained to draw conclusions about the significant relationships between burnout -or some dimensions of the MBI- and physical symptoms (Honkonen et al., 2006; Leiter, 2005; Melamed, Shirom, Toker, Berliner & Shapira, 2006; Pines & Keinan, 2005; Tang, Au, Schwarzer & Schmitz, 2001; Toppinen-Tanner, Ojajärvi, Väänänen, Kalimo & Jäppinen, 2005), such as gastroenteritis (Mohren, Swaen, Kant, Amelsvoort, Borm, & Galama, 2003), musculoskeletal system diseases (Toppinen-Tanner et al., 2005), sleep quality (Grossi, Perski, Evengard, Blomkvist & Orth-Gomér, 2003; Vela-Bueno et al., 2008), etc.; and psychological symptoms, such as depressive mood (Grossi et al., 2003; Hätinen, Kinnunen, Pekkonen & Aro, 2004; Mohren et al., 2003), anxiety (Bruce, Conaglen & Conaglen, 2005; Grossi et al., 2003), and cognitive failures that lead to increased distraction, poor performance and inhibition errors (Van der Linden, Keijsers, Eling & Schaijk, 2005). Ahola et al. (2008) have concluded that severe burnout is associated with an increased probability of having a medically certified episode of sickness absence.

Empirical evidence is available to suggest that these psychosomatic alterations may be related to alterations in the immune and defensive system of the organism (Bargellini et al., 2000; Nakamura, Nagase, Yoshida & Ogino, 1999), to alterations of a physiological nature related to cortisol levels (Grossi et al., 2005; Melamed et al., 1999; Moch, Panz, Joffe, Havlik & Moch, 2003; Pruessner, Hellhammer & Kirschbaum, 1999), and inflammation biomarkers (Toker, Shirom, Shapira, Berliner & Melamed, 2005).

On the other hand, clinical observations indicate that chronic burnout is associated with impaired cognitive functioning. Sandström, Rhodin, Lundberg, Olsson and Nyberg (2005) found statistical evidence leading to the conclusion that significant decreases in performance were present in chronic burnout patients on nonverbal memory in association with the slowing of performance on attention measures. These cognitive impairments may have originated because chronic stress can have profound effects on neuronal functions, notably hippocampal cells. Moreover, stress can also affect the functions of the frontal cortex. On the other hand, the authors state that most of the patients in the study reported sleeping problems, with frequent awakenings during the night as well as early wakening.

Alterations in sleep might thus influence cognition. Another explanation offered by the authors for these results is that some recent data also suggest that increased activity in the hypothalamic-pituitary-adrenal axis can be an important link to cognitive dysfunction after chronic stress.

Bibeau, Dussault and Larouche (1989) have proposed a series of subjective and objective criteria for making a clinical diagnosis of burnout. The main subjective indicator is a general state of severe fatigue that is accompanied by: (a) loss of self-esteem resulting from a feeling of professional incompetence and low job satisfaction, (b) diverse physical symptoms related to the stress without there being any organic cause, and (c) problems of concentration, irritability and negativism. The main objective indicator is a progressive and significant reduction in performance at work as the months go by. The symptoms must not be the result of the professional incompetence of the individual, who had previously done his work well for a reasonable period of time. It must not be the result of a previous psychopathology either, or caused by family problems.

In the EU, there is a climate of sensitivity toward psychosocial risks on the job that can produce the appearance of work-related stress and health disorders (European Agency for Safety and Health at Work, 2007). Due to this climate, some countries in the EU have paid legal attention to the burnout syndrome, considering it a psychological problem stemming from work. In Spain, from a legal point of view, an occupational illness is one stemming from an employee's work in the activities specified in the framework approved by Royal Decree 1995/78 of the 12th of May. Burnout is not included in this list of illnesses, so it cannot legally be considered a work-related illness, even though it meets the characteristics for being considered a work-related pathology (Masiá, 2001).

Due to these legal restrictions, burnout has been considered a work-related accident (Martínez de Viergol, 2005) by the Spanish Supreme Court (October 26th, 2000, Recourse Num: 4379/1999). Other judicial decisions in Spain have also recognised burnout as a work-related accident in trade union delegates (Social Court number 3 of Vitoria-Gasteiz, decision 14/02, from the 27th of March, 2002), teachers (Social Court number 16 of Barcelona, proceedings 751/2001), healthcare professionals (Social Court of Alicante, proceedings 188/2004; Superior Court of Justice of Cataluña, 5367/2003), and food services professionals (Superior Court of Justice of Galicia, 2537/2002), etc. There has also been a recognition of the right of professionals working with the mentally disabled to earn an extra risk bonus for being exposed to work conditions susceptible to causing burnout (Social Court number 1 of Vigo, proceedings 24/1999; Superior Court of Justice of Galicia, 5302/2001).

TEACHING AND BURNOUT

Burnout has been recognised as an important stress-related problem for people working in education (Guglielmi & Tatrow, 1998; Vandenberghe & Huberman, 1999). In this occupational sector the relationship between professionals and clients is central to the job, and the nature of the work is highly emotional (Näring, Briët & Brouwers, 2006). Providing affective, instructional and moral services to pupils makes emotional demands. These demands take place within a complex network of interactions with students and their parents, colleagues, principals, inspectors and the administration of the organisation or centre. A literature review makes it clear that teacher burnout is a function of the quality of life in the workplace. Kyriacou (2001), summarising a number of international studies, found ten main stressors for teachers. These include: teaching students who lack motivation, maintaining discipline, time pressures and workload, coping with change, being evaluated by others, dealings with colleagues, self esteem and status issues, problems dealing with administration/management, role conflict and ambiguity and poor working conditions.

In the last few decades, there has been a series of changes that have affected organisations, jobs and workers. Some of these changes have contributed to the development of burnout. In the case of education, the changes in social structures such as the family have caused educational responsibilities to be transferred to the school. Teachers complain that parents too often withdraw and delegate the education of their children to them, so that they have to fulfill the role of parents, sexual advisors, social workers, socio-cultural cheerleaders, pedagogues and psychologists. Globalisation has contributed to an increase in the population and the ethnic and cultural heterogeneity of the population in certain geographic areas (e.g., countries of the EU), without a proportional increase in the number of educational organisations or the number of workers in these centres. As a result, there has been an increase in the levels of work overload for these teachers, who carry out a fragmented activity in which they must fight simultaneously on different fronts: maintain enough discipline while remaining kind and affectionate, individually attend to high achieving students who would like to go faster but also to those who have to go slower, take care of the class environment, programme, evaluate, orient, receive parents and keep them up to date on the progress of their children, organise diverse activities for the centre, frequently take care of bureaucratic problems, etc. (Antoniou, Polychroni & Vlachakis, 2006; Forlin, 2001). The list of demands seems endless. Teachers have cited work overload as a major stressor in their job (Byrne, 1999). Empirical findings have shown work demands to be significantly related to emotional exhaustion (Dorman, 2003; Peeters & Routers, 2005). Moreover, only highly motivated individuals can burnout (Pines, 1993).

For some teachers, the government, with its changes in laws and norms, is one of the principal sources of burnout, as it has favored the development of a greater number of undisciplined and unmotivated students (Antoniou et al., 2006). Furthermore, the news media present inappropriate models, and the system has not been able to substitute authoritarianism for democratic authority, which means the students are aware of their rights but not their obligations. There are an increasing number of students who make unreasonable requests, citing their rights as citizens, but far from any minimum norms of education and courtesy. In some cases, students have been known to tell the teacher to be quiet, arguing that "my father is paying you". Empirical studies have found significant relationships between discipline problems with students and burnout (Ben-Ari, Krole & Har-Even, 2003; Friedman, 1995; Kokkinos, 2007). The teachers perceive that education has become a consumer product. A result of this culture is the loss of respect and prestige for teachers who feel excluded from making the decisions that affect educational reform and changes in their workplace. Schwab, Jackson & Schuler (1986) found that the lack of participation in decision-making explained 14% of the variance in the attitudes of depersonalisation in a sample of teachers.

According to some teachers, students and their parents see teachers as *slackers* who work in education because they don't have anywhere else to work and, furthermore, have many vacations and a good salary. Demands made by the parents constitute one of the main causes of burnout in education (Friedman, 2002). Many parents simplify what is wrong with the educational system and find teachers responsible for everything that doesn't work right. The lack of social recognition leads to many emotional and physical problems, deprives the individual of the possibility of finding meaning in his work, and favors the development of burnout.

Studies on the prevalence and incidence of burnout in teachers have yielded inconsistent findings. According to estimations by Shirom (1989), the prevalence of burnout in teachers can be situated between 10% and 30%. Unda, Sandova and Gil-Monte (2007/08) concluded that the prevalence of burnout in a sample of Mexican teachers was 17%, and Farber (1991) estimated that 5% to 20% of American teachers are truly burned out.

Regarding demographic characteristics, in previous studies on teacher burnout, a great deal of attention has been paid to the influence of personal characteristics, such as gender, age, and length of teaching experience. Gender is a strong predictor for depersonalisation, which appeared to be higher for male teachers than female teachers (Anderson & Iwanicki, 1984; Greenglass, Burke & Ondrack, 1990; Lau, Yuen & Chan, 2005).

With regard to emotional exhaustion, some studies have found that female teachers reported greater burnout than male teachers (Antoniou et al., 2006; Byrne, 1999; Lau et al., 2005), but other studies found the reverse to be true, and still others have reported no significant differences (Byrne, 1999). Regarding personal accomplishment, the studies have yielded inconsistent findings. Explanations for the differences have been attributed to the socialisation of the masculine and feminine roles (Anderson & Iwanicki, 1984; Greenglass et al., 1990; Maslach & Jackson, 1985; Schwab, 1986).

Some studies have found that younger teachers reported higher levels of burnout compared to older colleagues (Antoniou et al., 2006; Meadow, 1981; Mor & Laliberte, 1984). For emotional exhaustion (Antoniou et al., 2006; Meadow, 1981; Mor & Laliberte, 1984), and depersonalisation (Mor & Laliberte, 1984), the frequency in the perception of the symptoms is low between the ages of 20-25 years, higher between 25-40 years of age, (Mor & Laliberte, 1984), and minimal from 40 (Mor & Laliberte, 1984) or 50 years of age onwards, approximately (Antoniou et al., 2006). According to Huberman and Vandenberghe (1999), older teachers with more than ten years experience are more at risk of burnout. The relationship between the levels of burnout and age has been explained considering the chronic nature of the pathology, and the process, acquired with age, of learning the mechanisms to deal with stress. As professionals –e.g., school psychologists- become older, they may develop a variety of behavioural and attitudinal patterns that reduce the likelihood of burnout (Huberty & Huebner, 1988). However, Maslach et al. (2001) conclude that among younger employees the level of burnout is reported to be higher than it is among those over 30 or 40 years old.

The purpose of this study is to analyse the case of a burned out female teacher. Taking the clinical history of the patient as a reference point, the main symptoms that characterise burnout in teachers, their evolution, and their link to social interaction are examined, in order to contribute to a proper diagnosis of this psychological disorder.

CASE PRESENTATION

The subject in this case is a 56-year-old Caucasian woman. She worked as a primary school teacher for thirty-four years, and at the time of the diagnosis presented a three-year disability leave, attributed to a group of symptoms characterised by intense anxiety, depressive disorders, cognitive and affective alterations, negative attitudes toward the job and students and a deterioration in student behaviour.

The patient began her professional activity as a teacher at the age of 21. Due to her dedication to her work, she was appointed as Director of the Centre after two years of professional work. She carried out this job with very few resources, so that she developed states of exhaustion at the end of the teaching periods. However, after resting between these periods, she went back to work with more energy and enthusiasm.

According to her clinical record, at the age of 34, and after thirteen years of professional activity, there progressively began to appear symptoms of permanent exhaustion, muscle pain, sleep alterations and different types of somatisation, which caused a progressive reduction in her job performance. At the same time, her vocational commitment diminished. She also developed a behaviour pattern characterised by exclusive dedication to her job during the school week, complete rest on the weekends, and loss of interest in social activities and quality of life. Around this time, she saw that she could not get through the working week, and she sought a solution to the problem by consulting different medical specialists. She presented short periods of absence from work with increasing frequently.

Nine years later, at the age of 43, after twenty-two years of professional activity, the set of symptoms continued and worsened with the appearance of numbness, fears, phobias, irritability, dysthymias, migraines and crises of insomnia. Furthermore, cognitive blocks appeared while giving class, she made graphic inversions, had difficulty speaking, and committed errors while giving explanations in the classroom. These symptoms increased the anxiety crisis, the exhaustion, and the need to rest on the weekend. Upon doctor's orders, she began treatment with anxiolitic drugs and analgesics. Her state of mind worsened, and she developed a negative attitude toward her work and toward the students, who she perceived as being the direct cause of her psychological deterioration.

Two years later, at the age of 45, and ten years before the definitive diagnosis, she was diagnosed with "Depressive Syndrome" in the neurology service of the Public Health Service. Given the persistence of the symptoms, she consulted a private psychiatric clinic, where a psychometric evaluation was carried out, and she was diagnosed with "extreme anxiety, depression and a high degree of neuroticism". Treatment was recommended with anxiolitics and disability leave from work, which improved her symptomatology.

However, upon returning to teaching activity, the symptoms reappeared. During the next two years, and after various attempts to return to work, the patient developed feelings of guilt and low self-esteem, due to the perception of job incapacity. She went through psychotherapy treatment without obtaining positive results. Diagnostic tests were performed with a scanner and electroencephalogram, which appeared normal, leading to organic causes for her disorder being ruled out, and she was diagnosed with "Generalized Anxiety Disorder" (DSM-IV, 300.02) (APA, 1994). This diagnosis is ratified by professionals (doctors, psychologists and psychiatrists) from different health centres and organisations that, in some cases, also incorporate the diagnosis of "Conversion Disorder" (DSM-IV, 300.11).

In spite of psychological treatment consisting of therapy and pharmacological treatment with anxiolitics and anti-depressives, symptoms persisted, so that the patient remained in a chronic state for about a decade. During this time, she continued with programmed visits to the psychiatrist and occasionally visited the emergency room owing to the appearance of anxiety crises. The diagnosis referred to above was maintained. The clinical record states that every time the patient tried to go back to work, there was a worsening in the process that would only improve if she stopped her professional activity.

After a decade, when the patient was 55 years old, the psychiatrist following her progress decided that the symptoms she has been showing all these years could constitute a *"Personal Exhaustion Syndrome"*, leading to a change in diagnosis. Eleven months later, this psychiatrist omitted the diagnosis of burnout, reporting that in the chronicity of the symptoms the only stressor that appeared was job activity, and that the patient presented a personality characterised by a high level of self-demand, which, together with her professionalism, led her to take on a large number of responsibilities. He added that although the patient initially had a high performance capacity, this was gradually reduced as the psychosomatic and cognitive symptomatology began.

DISCUSSION AND CONCLUSIONS

In the case described, there are enough indications to conclude that the set of symptoms developed fits a case of burnout. The patient worked in one of the main occupational groups where this disorder appears as a result of chronic work-related stress (Guglielmi & Tatrow, 1998; Vandenberghe & Huberman, 1999). She presented a chronic situation with a progressive onset, characterised by an emotional impairment resulting from interpersonal relationships on the job, a cognitive impairment that negatively affects her self-evaluation of her professional capacity, a deterioration in her attitude toward the clients of the organisation - the students-, and the appearance of guilt feelings. The symptoms are closely related to her professional activity, and no organic cause of the problem was identified. The characteristics of the case fit the subjective and objective criteria formulated by Bibeau et al. (1989) for making a diagnosis of burnout.

A feeling of being emotionally over-extended and depleted of one's emotional resources, i.e., emotional exhaustion, is the core of burnout (Maslach et al., 2001; Moore, 2000; Shirom & Ezrachi, 2003). The patient initially presented states of exhaustion at the end of teaching periods that stopped during rest periods. However, at the age of 34, when she had been working in the profession for thirteen years, symptoms of permanent fatigue appeared progressively. At the age of 43, after twenty-two years of professional practice, the exhaustion and need for rest increased as exhaustion intensified due to job activity. These symptoms are characteristic of burnout, and they are included in the most widely used questionnaires for evaluating the syndrome (MBI, Maslach & Jackson, 1981; BM, Pines & Aronson, 1988).

At this age, 43, the increase in levels of exhaustion were accompanied by cognitive blocks while classes were going on, with the subject experiencing graphic inversions, difficulty in speaking, and errors in explanations in the classroom, which caused and increased the anxiety crises. As a consequence of these symptoms, and due to the perception of job incapacity they produced, the patient developed low self-esteem. Similar symptoms are described in cases of chronic burnout patients. Van der Linden et al. (2005) found that the level of burnout was significantly related to inhibition errors and poor performance; and Sandström et al. (2005) found statistical evidence to conclude that significant decreases in performance were present for chronic burnout patients on nonverbal memory in association with slowing of performance on attention measures. The cognitive impairment suffered by the patient is a characteristic of burnout, and the symptoms are linked to the practice of the work activity. The symptoms reappeared, and a worsening of the process occurred when she tried to go back to work after a period of disability leave.

The loss of self-esteem and the deterioration in the self-evaluation of the capacity to perform the job is one of the symptoms that characterize the appearance of burnout (Cherniss, 1993; 1995; Gil-Monte, 2005; Maslach et al., 2001). Perlman and Hartman (1982), in one of the first review studies of the symptoms that characterize the syndrome, concluded that it should include symptoms such as low morale and negative self-concept. In studies with teachers, the loss of self-esteem has been proposed as an antecedent of low personal accomplishment (Byrne, 1999), and as a symptom related to the development of burnout due to the perception of professional failure (Kelchtermans, 1999).

The patient also developed a negative attitude toward the job and toward the students, whom she saw as the direct cause of her psychological deterioration. This symptom is widely included in the literature as a characteristic symptom of burnout. According to Maslach et al. (2001), a key dimension of burnout involves feelings of cynicism and detachment from the job. The cynicism or depersonalisation "represents the interpersonal context dimension of burnout. It refers to a negative, callous, or excessively detached response to various aspects of the job" (p. 399).

In the appearance of depersonalisation, blaming clients for problems that are perceived as the cause of personal and professional failure plays an important role (Bandura, 1986; Cherniss, 1995; Maslach, 1982). When behaviour is reproachable, some moral justification is needed in order to carry it out. Individuals perform cognitive restructuring to achieve socially acceptable behaviours and to justify performing certain behaviours without feeling guilty. According to Bandura (1986), among these mechanisms are found attribution of blame and dehumanisation. A cognitive strategy for acting aggressively toward people without suffering self-condemnation is dehumanisation or depersonalisation.

Burnout is a prolonged response to chronic emotional and interpersonal stressors on the job (Maslach et al., 2001). In the case presented here, the process did not begin with the working life of the patient. According to the medical records, it was after thirteen years of professional activity, at the age of 34, when the symptoms of permanent fatigue, muscle pain, sleep alterations and various types of somatisations began to appear, which caused a progressive reduction in her job performance and a loss of professional commitment, although the first symptoms of exhaustion were detected after two years on the job. According to Maslach et al. (2001), younger employees feel higher levels of burnout than those over 30 or 40 years old. However, other studies have concluded that the highest levels of burnout appear between twenty-five and forty years of age (Antoniou et al., 2006; Mor & Laliberte, 1984), or between twenty-seven and thirty (Meadow, 1981). According to Huberman and Vandenberghe (1999), teachers with more than ten years of experience are more at risk of burnout.

The levels of emotional exhaustion and burnout in the patient in this case may also have increased and been maintained over time due to gender. Some studies have found that female teachers reported greater burnout than male teachers (Antoniou, 2006; Byrne, 1999; Lau et al., 2005).

Another variable that may intervene in the chronicity of the burnout process is guilt. The patient mentioned that after various attempts to return to work she developed feelings of guilt. The theoretical model elaborated by Gil-Monte (2005; 2008) integrates guilt into the burnout development process. According to this model, it is possible to distinguish two patterns in the development of burnout. In both patterns, depersonalisation can be understood as a coping strategy that arises to handle emotional exhaustion (Lee & Ashforth, 1990) and the perception of low personal accomplishment (Edelwich & Brodsky, 1980; Price & Murphy, 1984). However, while for a series of professionals this coping strategy is sufficient and allows them to manage the levels of strain (Bandura, 1986), other professionals find this manner of proceeding to be inadequate, and they develop feelings of guilt (Gil-Monte, 2008; Jones & Kugler, 1993). Therefore, these professionals become more and more involved in order to reduce their feelings of guilt (Baumeister et al., 1994), so as to diminish the stress arising from the self-attribution of responsibility regarding the causes that have produced the suffering of other individuals (Hoffman, 1982).

One personality characteristic of the patient that is associated with high levels of burnout is perfectionism (Stoeber & Rennert, 2008), and the high level of self-demand that led her to take on a large number of responsibilities and become excessively involved in the practice of her profession (Edelwich & Brodsky, 1980; Heifetz & Bersani, 1983; Pines, 1993). Heifetz and Bersani (1983) have pointed out that the commitment to the job precedes the appearance of burnout, in such a way that the process of burnout will not begin unless there are high levels of motivation toward the work activity. This commitment is enhanced by the desire to induce a positive change in the students. According to Maslach (1978), burnout is a process that appears because helping professionals lack preparation for coping with the unique emotional stresses of their work. These professionals are unable to maintain the care and commitment they initially brought to the job. Pines (1993), concludes that a person with no initial motivation can experience other psychological disorders, i.e., stress, depression, fatigue, etc., but not burnout. On the other hand, Farber (1990; 2000) proposes the existence of three types of teacher burnout (worn-out, classic burnout, and under-challenged types of burnout). The case presented here would fit the classic burnout subtype, "an individual who works increasingly hard, to the point of exhaustion, in pursuit of sufficient gratification or accomplishment to match the extent of stress experienced" (Farber, 2000, p. 677).

The patient presents a range of somatisations and psychic alterations that at some moments caused the incapacitation of her professional practice. These symptoms appear significantly associated with the development of burnout (Bruce et al., 2005; Golembiewsky & Munzenrider, 1988; Hätinen et al., 2004). Some studies have concluded that these somatisations may be associated with physiological alterations of an immunological (Bargellini et al., 2000; Nakamura et al., 1999) or metabolic (Melamed et al., 1999; Moch et al., 2003; Pruessner et al., 1999; Toker et al., 2005) nature produced by the burnout. In the case presented here, there have been no studies of this type carried out that could contribute to establishing a more precise diagnosis.

The process began with the emotional deterioration of the patient, which was accompanied by exhaustion and maintained with different levels of intensity. Later, after twenty-two years of professional practice, she referred to the appearance of cognitive deterioration, which increased the affective and attitudinal impairment. Using the results of these studies as a reference, it is possible to conclude that in the process of developing burnout, the attitudinal deterioration , i.e., depersonalisation, appeared as a result of the cognitive impairment, i.e., low personal accomplishment, and the emotional deterioration, i.e., exhaustion. Currently, one of the lines of research open in the study of burnout is establishing the sequential order of the appearance of its symptoms when evaluated with the MBI (Cordes, Dougherty & Blum, 1997; Gil-Monte et al., 1998; Taris et al., 2005). Due to the limitations of the empirical studies, it has been recommended that qualitative studies be carried out that can contribute to clarifying this relationship (Ashforth & Lee, 1997). In this sense, this study contributes to better understanding the process of the development of burnout.

In the case presented, the time that passed from the onset of the symptomatology to diagnosis is noteworthy. After eleven years of evolution, the patient received the diagnosis of "Depressive Syndrome"; two years later, thirteen since the beginning of the problem, the clinical picture was diagnosed as "Generalized Anxiety Disorder" (DSM-IV, 300.02), and "Conversion Disorder" (DSM-IV, 300.11), and eight years later, twenty-one since the onset, the symptoms were again diagnosed as *"Personal Exhaustion Syndrome"* and burnout. At least a couple of circumstances may have contributed to this situation. On the one hand, numerous professionals lack sufficient knowledge about this pathology. On the other hand, there is no specific category in the DSM-IV (APA, 1994) manual that makes it possible to identify and define burnout.

Using the DSM-IV manual as a reference, some authors prefer to include burnout in the category of "Adjustment Disorders" (Bibeau et al., 1989). According to these criteria, the category that most closely approaches the symptoms and development of burnout is "Adjustment Disorder Unspecified, Chronic (309.9)". Another diagnostic option would be to consider burnout as a work-related problem and include it in Axis I, which groups the "Clinical Disorders and other conditions that may be a focus of Clinical attention", codifying it as an "Occupational Problem" (V62.2). This category can be used when the focus of clinical attention is an occupational problem that is not due to a mental disorder or, if it is due to a mental disorder, is sufficiently severe to warrant independent clinical attention. It includes problems like job dissatisfaction. However, burnout as a pathology presents some symptoms that are much more serious and incapacitating for the individual and for the practice of the job activity than the lack of job satisfaction.

In order to more fully understand the relationships between burnout symptoms, future studies should consider the single case and use qualitative research to examine the generalisability of the current results.

Implications for practitioners

The current study may advance knowledge about burnout. Regarding the practical contributions, it should be pointed out that this case contributes to clinical knowledge about the phenomenon. The study may be an important point of reference for facilitating diagnosis and treatment by professionals who treat subjects with burnout, and it may also contribute to its prevention.

The study provides a useful addition to the tools for the diagnosis of burnout, which currently rely mainly on questionnaires. Diagnosis in the initial stages of burnout could avoid the increase in intensity of the symptoms and make possible earlier recovery. The results of the present study point towards recommending the incorporation of the evaluation of guilt as a symptom of burnout in order to carry out a more complete diagnosis, discriminate among subjects affected by the syndrome, and recognise its influence on disorders of health, and job absenteeism. It could also be useful in detecting the need for intervention programmes that eliminate sources of stress and detecting the need to train teachers in techniques for dealing with stress.

Although the case discussed here concerned a teacher, burnout affects members of other helping professions. The health deterioration process described above may operate when professionals have to do their work in extreme situations, such as taking care of victims of natural disasters, e.g., hurricane Katrina, or terrorist attacks, e.g., the September 11, 2001, attacks to the towers of the World Trade Centre in New York City; the 11 March, 2004, Madrid train bombings; the 7 July, 2005, attack on London's public transport system.
Courtroom expertise is an emerging area of practice for occupational health

psychologists. Carrying out assessments, managing workplace violence and conducting independent medical evaluations are among the professional activities of these experts (DeAngelis, 2008). The case presented here is a source of information for occupational health psychologists whose work takes them into the judicial context. The development of work-related illnesses or accidents as a result of exposure to psychosocial risks grants workers the right to some type of economic compensation. In these cases, occupational health psychologists may have an important role to perform in terms of diagnosis and evaluation for the Justice Department (or equivalent), and in recommending measures to prevent burnout.

ACKNOWLEDGMENTS

This research is supported by a grant from the Spanish Ministry of Science and Technology (SEJ2006-12095/PSIC)

REFERENCES

Ahola, K., Kivimäki, M., Honkonen, T., Virtanen, M., Koskinen, S., Vahtera, J., & Lönnqvist, J. (2008). Occupational burnout and medically certified sickness absence: a population-based study of Finnish employees. *Journal of Psychosomatic Research, 64*, 185-193.

Anderson, M., & Iwanicki, E. (1984). Teacher motivation and its relationship to burnout. *Educational Administration Quarterly, 20*, 109-132.

Antoniou, A. S., Polychroni, F., & Vlachakis, A. N. (2006). Gender and age differences in occupational stress and professional burnout between primary and high-school teachers in Greece. *Journal of Managerial Psychology, 21*, 682-690.

APA (1994). *Diagnostic and statistical manual of mental disorders* (4th ed.). Washington, DC: APA.

Ashforth, B. E., & Lee, R. T. (1997). Burnout as a process: commentary on Cordes, Dougherty and Blum. *Journal of Organizational Behavior, 18*, 703-708.

Baba, V. V., Galperin, B. L., & Lituchy, T. R. (1999). Occcupational mental health: a study of work-related depression among nurses in the Caribbean. *International Journal of Nursing Studies, 36*, 163-169.

Bandura, A. (1986). *Social foundations of thought and action.* New Jersey: Prentice-Hall.

Bargellini, A., Barbieri, A., Rovesti, S., Vivoli, R., Roncaglia, R., & Borella, P. (2000). Relation between immune variables and burnout in a sample of physicians. *Occupational Environmental Medicine, 57*, 453-457.

Baumeister, R. F., Stillwell, A.M., & Heatherton, T. F. (1994). Guilt: an interpersonal approach. *Psychological Bulletin, 115*, 243-267.

Ben-Ari, R., Krole, R., & Har-Even, D. (2003). Differential effects of simple frontal versus complex teaching strategy on teachers' stress, burnout, and satisfaction. *International Journal of Stress Management, 10*, 173–195.

Berkowitz, L. (Ed.) (1969). *Roots of aggression.* New York: Atherton.

Berndsen, M., & Manstead, A. (2007). On the relationship between responsibility and guilt: antecedent appraisal or elaborated appraisal?. *European Journal of Social Psychology, 37*, 774-792.

Bibeau, G., Dussault, G., & Larouche, L. M. (1989). *Certain aspects culturels, diagnostiques et juridiques du burnout: pistes et repères opérationnels.* Montreal: Confédération des Syndicats Nationaux.

Bruce, S. M., Conaglen, H. M., & Conaglen, J. V. (2005). Burnout in physicians: a case for peer-support. *Internal Medicine Journal, 35*, 272-278.

Byrne, B. M. (1999). The nomological network of teacher burnout: a literature review and empirically validated model. In R. Vandenberghe, & A. M. Huberman (Eds.), *Understanding and preventing teacher burnout: a sourcebook of international research and practice* (pp. 15-37). Cambridge: Cambridge University Press.

Cherniss, C. (1993). The role of professinal self-efficacy in the etiology of burnout. In W. B. Schaufeli, C. Maslach, & T. Marek (Eds.), *Professional burnout: recent developments in theory and research* (pp. 135-149). London: Taylor & Francis.

Cherniss, C. (1995). *Beyond burnout.* London: Routledge.

Cordes, C. L., Dougherty, T. W., & Blum, M. (1997). Patterns of burnout among managers and professionals: a comparison of models. *Journal of Organizational Behavior , 18*, 685-701.

De Angelis, T. (2008). Psychology's growth careers. *Monitor on Psychology, 39*(4), 64-71.

Densten, I. L. (2001). Re-thinking burnout. *Journal of Organizational Behavior, 22*, 833-847.

Dorman, J. P. (2003). Relationship between school and classroom environment and teacher burnout: a LISREL analysis. *Social Psychology of Education, 6*, 107-127.

Durán, M. A., Extremera, N., & Rey, L. (2001). Burnout en profesionales de la enseñanza: un estudio en Educación Primaria, Secundaria y Superior [A study of burnout in teacher in primary, secondary, and college education]. *Revista de Psicología del Trabajo y de las Organizaciones, 17*, 45-62.

Edelwich, J., & Brodsky, A. (1980). *Burn-out: stages of disillusionment in the helping professions.* New York: Human Science Press.

Ekstedt, M., & Fagerberg, I. (2005). Lived experiences of the time preceding

burnout. *Journal of Advanced Nursing, 49*, 59–67.
EUROPEAN AGENCY FOR SAFETY AND HEALTH AT WORK (2007). *Expert forecast on emerging psychosocial risks related to occupational safety and health*. Luxembourg: Office for Official Publications of the European Communities.
FARBER, B. A. (1990). Burnout in psychotherapists: incidence, types, and trends. *Psychotherapy in Private Practice, 8*, 35-44.
FARBER, B. A. (1991). *Crisis in education: stress and burnout in the American teacher*. San Francisco: Jossey-Bass.
FARBER, B. A. (2000). Treatment strategies for different types of teacher burnout. *Psychotherapy in Practice, 56*, 675-689.
FARBER, B. A., & MILLER, J. (1981). Teacher burnout: a psycho-educational perspective. *Teacher College Record, 83*, 235-243.
FORLIN, C. (2001). Inclusion: identifying potential stressors for regular class teachers. *Educational Research, 43*, 235-245.
FREUDENBERGER, H. J. (1974). Staff burn-out. *Journal of Social Issues, 30*, 159-165.
FRIEDMAN, I. A. (1995). Student behavior patterns contributing to teacher burnout. *Journal of Educational Research, 88*, 281-289.
FRIEDMAN, I. A. (2002). Burnout in school principals: role related antecedents. *Social Psychology of Education, 5*, 229-251.
GHATAVI, K., NICOLSON, R., MACDONALD, C., OSHER, O., & LEVITT, A. (2002). Defining guilt in depression: a comparison of subjects with major depression, chronic medical illness and healthy controls. *Journal of Affective Disorders, 68*, 307-315.
GIL-MONTE, P. R. (2005). *El síndrome de quemarse por el trabajo: una enfermedad laboral en la sociedad del bienestar* [Burnout: an occupational illness in the well-being society]. Madrid: Pirámide.
GIL-MONTE, P. R. (2008). Magnitude of relationship between burnout and absenteeism: a preliminary study. *Psychological Reports, 102*, 465-568.
GIL-MONTE, P. R., PEIRÓ, J. M., & VALCÁRCEL, P. (1998). A model of burnout process development: an alternative from appraisal models of stress. *Comportamento Organizacional e Gestao, 4*, 165-179.
GOLEMBIEWSKI, R. T., & MUNZENRIDER, R. F. (1988). *Phases of burnout: developments in concepts and applications*. New York: Preager.
GOLEMBIEWSKI, R. T., MUNZENRIDER, R., & CARTER, D. (1983). Phases of progressive burnout and their work site covariants: critical issues in OD research and praxis. *Journal of Applied Behavioral Science, 19*, 461-481.
GREENGLASS, E. R., BURKE, R. J., & ONDRACK, M. (1990). A gender-role perspective of coping and burnout. *Applied Psychology: An International Review, 39*, 5-27.
GROSSI, G., PERSKI, A., EKSTEDT, M., JOHANSSON, T., LINDSTRÖM, M., & HOLM, K.

(2005). The morning salivary cortisol response in burnout. *Journal of Psychosomatic Research, 59*, 103-111.

GROSSI, G., PERSKI, A., EVENGARD, B., BLOMKVIST, V., & ORTH-GOMÉR, K. (2003). Physiological correlates of burnout among women. *Journal of Psychosomatic Research, 55*, 309-316.

GUGLIELMI, R. S., & TATROW, K. (1998). Occupational stress, burnout, and health in teachers: a methodological and theoretical analysis. *Review of Educational Research, 68*, 61-99.

HARDER, D. W., CUTLER, L., & ROCKART, L. (1992). Assessment of shame and guilt and their relationships to psychopathology. *Journal of Personality Assessment, 59*, 584-604.

HARDER, D. W., & ZALMA, A. (1990). Two promising shame and guilt scales: a construct validity comparison. *Journal of Personality Assessment, 55*, 729-745.

HÄTINEN, M., KINNUNEN, U., PEKKONEN, M., & ARO, A. (2004). Burnout patterns in rehabilitation: short-term changes in job conditions, personal resources, and health. *Journal of Occupational Health Psychology, 9*, 220–237.

HEIFETZ, L. J., & BERSANI, H. A., JR. (1983). Disrupting the cybernetics of personal growth: toward a unified theory of burnout in the human services. In B. A. Farber (Ed.), *Stress and burnout in the human services professions* (1985, 2nd ed., pp. 46-62). New York: Pergamon Press.

HOFFMAN, M. L. (1982). Development of prosocial motivation: empathy and guilt. In N. Eisenberg (Ed.), *The development of prosocial behavior* (pp. 281-313). San Diego, CA: Academic Press.

HONKONEN, T., AHOLA, K., PERTOVAARA, M., ISOMETÄ, E., KALIMO, R., NYKYRI, E., AROMAA, A., & LÖNNQVIST, J. (2005). The association between burnout and physical illness in the general population-results from the Finnish Health 2000 Study. *Journal of Psychosomatic Research, 61*, 59-66.

HUBERMAN, A. M., & VANDENBERGHE, R. (1999). Introduction- burnout and teaching profession. In R. Vandenberghe, & A. M. Huberman (Eds.), *Understanding and preventing teacher burnout: a sourcebook of international research and practice* (pp. 1-11). Cambridge: Cambridge University Press.

HUBERTY, T. J., & HUEBNER, E. S. (1988). A national survey of burnout among school psychologists. *Psychology in the Schools, 25*, 54-61.

JONES, W. H., & KUGLER, K. (1993). Interpersonal correlates of the Guilt Inventory. *Journal of Personality Assessment, 61*, 246-258.

KELCHTERMANS, G. (1999). Teaching career: Between burnout and fading away?. Reflections from a narrative and biographical perspective. In R. Vandenberghe, & A. M. Huberman (Eds.), *Understanding and preventing teacher burnout: A sourcebook of international research and practice* (pp. 176-191). Cambridge: Cambridge University Press.

KOKKINOS, C. M. (2007). Job stressors, personality and burnout in primary school teachers. *British Journal of Educational Psychology, 77,* 229-243.

KYRIACOU, C. (2001). Teacher stress: directions for future research. *Educational Review, 53,* 27–35.

LAU, P. S. Y., YUEN, M. T., & CHAN, R. M. C. (2005). Do demographic characteristics make a difference to burnout among Hong Kong secondary school teachers?. *Social Indicators Research, 71,* 491-516.

LEE, R. T., & ASHFORTH, B. E. (1990). On the meaning of Maslach's three dimensions of burnout. *Journal of Applied Psychology, 75,* 743-747.

LEE, R. T., & ASHFORTH, B. E. (1993a). A further examination of managerial burnout: toward an integrated model. *Journal of Organizational Behavior, 14,* 3-20.

LEE, R. T., & ASHFORTH, B. E. (1993b). A longitudinal study of burnout among supervisors and managers: comparisons between the Leiter and Maslach (1988) and Golembiewski et al. (1986) models. *Organizational Behavior and Human Decision Processes, 54,* 369-398.

LEITER, M. P. (2005). Perception of risk: an organizational model of occupational risk, burnout, and physical symptoms. *Anxiety, Stress, and Coping, 8,* 131-144.

LEITER, M. P., & MASLACH, C. (1988). The impact of interpersonal environment on burnout and organizational commitment. *Journal of Organizational Behavior, 9,* 297-308.

LEWIS, H. B. (1971). *Shame and guilt in neurosis.* New York: International Universities Press.

MANASSERO, M. A., GARCÍA, E., VÁZQUEZ, A., FERRER, V. A., RAMIS, C., & GILI M. (2000). Análisis causal del burnout en la enseñanza [Causal analysis of teaching burnout]. *Revista de Psicología del Trabajo y de las Organizaciones, 16,* 173-195.

MANZANO, G., & RAMOS, F. (2000). Enfermería hospitalaria y síndrome de burnout [Hospitable infirmary and burnout syndrome]. *Revista de Psicología del Trabajo y de las Organizaciones, 16,* 197-213.

MARTÍNEZ DE VIERGOL, A. (2005). La consideración del síndrome del «Burn out» como constitutivo de la contingencia profesional del accidente de trabajo origen de la declaración de incapacidad permanente absoluta [The consideration of burnout as constitutive of the professional contingency of the work-related accident leading to the declaration of permanent total disability]. *Revista del Ministerio de Trabajo y Asuntos Sociales, 59,* 213-224.

MASIÁ, J. (2001). *El estrés laboral y el burnout en el mundo judicial: hacia un nuevo enfoque de la cuestión* [Job stress and burnout in the judicial world: toward a new perspective of this topic]. Retrieved May 15, 2008, from http://www.prevencionintegral.com/Estudios/Burnoutjudicial/default.htm

MASLACH, C. (1978). The client role in staff burn-out. *Journal of Social*

Issues, 34, 111-124.
MASLACH, C. (1982). *Burnout: the cost of caring.* New York: Prentice Hall Press.
MASLACH, C., & JACKSON, S. E. (1981). *Maslach Burnout Inventory. Manual.* Palo Alto, CA: Consulting Psychologists Press.
MASLACH, C., & JACKSON, S. E. (1985). The role of sex and family variables in burnout. *Sex Roles, 12,* 837-851.
MASLACH, C., SCHAUFELI, W. B, & LEITER, M. P. (2001). Job burnout. *Annual Review of Psychology, 52,* 397-422.
MEADOW, K. P. (1981). Burnout in professionals working with deaf children. *American Annals of the Deaf, 126,* 13-22.
MELAMED, S., SHIROM, A., TOKER, S., BERLINER, S., & SHAPIRA, I. (2006). Burnout and risk of cardiovascular disease: evidence, possible causal paths, and promising research directions. *Psychological Bulletin, 132,* 327-353.
MELAMED, S., UGARTEN, U., SHIROM, A., KAHANA, L., LERMAN, Y., & FROOM P. (1999). Chronic burnout, somatic arousal and elevated salivary cortisol levels. *Journal of Psychosomatic Research, 46,* 591-598.
MITCHELL, P. B., GOODWIN, G. M., JOHNSON, G. F., & HIRSCHFELD, R. M. (2008). Diagnostic guidelines for bipolar depression: a probabilistic approach. *Bipolar Disorders, 10,* 144-152.
MOCH, S. L., PANZ, V. R., JOFFE, B. I., HAVLIK, I., & MOCH, J. D. (2003). Longitudinal changes in pituitary-adrenal hormones in South African women with burnout. *Endocrine, 21,* 267–272.
MOHREN, D. , SWAEN, G., KANT, I., AMELSVOORT, L., BORM, P., & GALAMA, J. (2003). Common infections and the role of burnout in a Dutch working population. *Journal of Psychosomatic Research, 55,* 201-208.
MOORE, J. E. (2000). Why is this happening?. A causal attribution approach to work exhaustion consequences. *Academy of Management Review, 25,* 335 –349.
MOR, V., & LALIBERTE, L. (1984). Burnout among hospice staff. *Health and Social Work, 9,* 274-283.
NAKAMURA, H., NAGASE, H., YOSHIDA, M., & OGINO, K (1999). Natural killer (NK) cell activity and nk cell subsets in workers with a tendency of burnout. *Journal of Psychosomatic Research, 46,* 569-578.
NÄRING, G., BRIËT, M., & BROUWERS, A (2006). Beyond demand-control: emotional labour and symptoms of burnout in teachers. *Work & Stress, 20,* 303-315.
NIOSH (1999). *Stress...at work.* Publication No. 99–101. Retrieved May 15, 2008, from http://www.cdc.gov/niosh/pdfs/stress.pdf
NIOSH (2004). Worker Health Chartbook 2004. Cincinnati, OH: NIOSH. Retrieved May 30, 2008, from: http://www.cdc.gov/niosh/docs/chartbook/
O'CONNOR, L. E., BERRY, J. W., WEISS, J., & GILBERT, P. (2002). Guilt, fear,

submission, and empathy in depression. *Journal of Affective Disorders, 71*, 19-27.
PARENT-THIRION, A., FERNÁNDEZ, E., HURLEY, J., & VERMEYLEN, G. (2007). *Fourth European Working Conditions Survey*. Luxembourg: Office for Official Publications of the European Communities. Retrieved May 30, 2008, from http://www.eurofound.europa.eu/pubdocs/2006/98/en/2/ef0698en.pdf
PEETERS, M. A., & RUTTE, C. G. (2005). Time management behavior as a moderator for the job demand-control interaction. *Journal of Occupational Health Psychology, 10*, 64-75.
PERLMAN, B., & HARTMAN, E. A. (1982). Burnout: summary and future research. *Human Relations, 35*, 283-305.
PINELES, S. L., STREET, A. E., & KOENEN, K. C. (2006). The differential relationships of shame-proneness and guilt proneness to psychological and somatisation symptoms. *Journal of Social and Clinical Psychology, 25*, 688-704.
PINES, A. M. (1993). Burnout: an existential perspective. In W. B. Schaufeli, C. Maslach, & T. Marek (Eds.), *Professional burnout: recent developments in theory and research* (pp. 33-51). London: Taylor & Francis.
PINES A. M., & ARONSON, E. (1988). *Career burnout*. New York: The Free Press.
PINES, A. M., & KEINAN, G. (2005). Stress and burnout: the significant difference. *Personality and Individual Differences, 29*, 625-635.
PRICE, D. M., & MURPHY, P. A. (1984). Staff burnout in the perspective of grief theory. *Death Eucation, 8*, 47-58.
PRUESSNER, J. C., HELLHAMMER, D. H., & KIRSCHBAUM, C. (1999). Burnout, perceived stress, and cortisol responses to awakening. *Psychosomatic Medicine, 61*, 197-204.
QUILES, Z. N., & BYBEE, J. (1997). Chronic and predispositional guilt: relations to mental health, prosocial behavior, and religiosity. *Journal of Personality Assessment, 69*, 104-126.
SANDSTRÖM A., RHODIN, I. N., LUNDBERG, M., OLSSON, T., & NYBERG, L. (2005). Impaired cognitive performance in patients with chronic burnout syndrome. *Biological Psychology, 69*, 271–279.
SHIROM, A. (1989). Burnout in work organizations. In C.L. Cooper & I. Robertson (Eds.), *International Review of Industrial and Organizational Psychology* (p. 25-48). New York: Wiley & Sons.
SHIROM, A., & EZRACHI, Y. (2003). On the discriminant validity of burnout, depression and anxiety: a re-examination of the Burnout Measure. *Anxiety, Stress and Coping, 16*, 83-97.
SCHWAB, R. L. (1986). Burnout in education. In C. Maslach, & S. E. Jackson (Eds.), *Maslach Burnout Inventory: Manual* (2nd ed, pp. 18-22). Palo Alto: Consulting Psychological Press.
SCHWAB, R. L., JACKSON, S. E., & SCHULER, R. S. (1986). Educator burnout:

sources and consequences. *Educational Research Quarterly, 10,* 14-30.

STOEBER, J., & RENNERT, D. (2008). Perfectionism in school teachers: relations with stress appraisals, coping styles, and burnout. *Anxiety, Stress, & Coping, 21,* 37-53.

TANG, C. S., AU, W., SCHWARZER, R., & SCHMITZ, G. (2001). Mental health outcomes of job stress among Chinese teachers: role of stress resource factors and burnout. *Journal of Organizational Behavior, 22,* 887-901.

TANGNEY, J. P., STUEWIG, J., & MASHEK, D. J. (2007). Moral emotions and moral behavior. *Annual Review of Psychology, 58,* 345-372.

TARIS, T. W., LE BLANC, P. M., SCHAUFELI, W. B., & SCHREURS, P. J. (2005). Are there causal relationships between the dimensions of the Maslach Burnout Inventory?. A review and two longitudinal tests. *Work & Stress, 19,* 238-255.

TOKER, S., SHIROM, A., SHAPIRA, I., BERLINER, S., & MELAMED, S. (2005). The association between burnout, depression, anxiety, and inflammation biomarkers: C-reactive protein and fibrinogen in men and women. *Journal of Occupational Health Psychology, 10,* 344-362.

TOPPINEN-TANNER, S., OJAJÄRVI, A, VÄÄNÄNEN, A., KALIMO, R., & JÄPPINEN, P (2005). Burnout as a predictor of medically certified sick-leave absences and their diagnosed causes. *Behavioral Medicine, 31,* 18-27.

UNDA, S., SANDOVAL, J. I., & GIL-MONTE, P. R. (2007/2008). Prevalencia del síndrome de quemarse por el trabajo (SQT) (burnout) en maestros mexicanos [A study about the prevalence of burnout in Mexican teachers]. *Informació Psicológica, 91/92,* 53-63

VAN DER LINDEN, D., KEIJSERS, G. P. J., ELING, P., & SCHAIJK, R. (2005). Work stress and attentional difficulties: an initial study on burnout and cognitive failures. *Work & Stress, 19,* 23-36.

VANDENBERGHE, R., & HUBERMAN, A. M. (Eds.) (1999). *Understanding and preventing teacher burnout: a sourcebook of international research and practice.* Cambridge: Cambridge University Press.

VELA-BUENO, A., MORENO-JIMÉNEZ, B., RODRÍGUEZ-MUÑOZ, A., OLAVARRIETA-BERNARDINO, S., FERNÁNDEZ-MENDOZA, J., DE LA CRUZ-TROCA, J. J., BIXLER, E. O., & VGONTZAS, A. N. (2008). Insomnia and sleep quality among primary care physicians with low and high burnout levels. *Journal of Psychosomatic Research, 64,* 435-442.

THE RELATIONSHIP BETWEEN ORGANISATIONAL JUSTICE AND JOB STRESS: INSIGHTS, ISSUES AND IMPLICATIONS

Andrew J Noblet and John J Rodwell

CHAPTER OVERVIEW

Management scholars have long been interested in the impact of injustice on attitudes and behaviours that are critical to organisational functioning, including job satisfaction, organisational commitment, absence behaviour, in-role performance and citizenship behaviours (e.g., Adams, 1965; Colquitt, Greenberg, & Zapata-Phelan, 2005; Walster, Walster, & Berscheid, 1978). However this research has tended to overlook the relationship between justice perceptions and health — especially the more serious, chronic indices of strain such as psychological distress (Judge & Colquitt, 2004; Tepper, 2001). Although empirical assessments of the justice-health relationship are rapidly emerging (28 articles published between 2001 and 2007, compared to two prior to the year 2000), there are elements of this relationship that remain unclear (Fujishiro & Heaney, 2007). For example, the health impact of justice variables in comparison to more traditional work-based sources of employee health (e.g., social support and job control) is under-researched and there is some uncertainty regarding the unique contributions that justice perceptions can make to the work-health relationship. Similarly, studies examining interactions between perceptions of justice and traditional work-based sources of well-being are relatively recent and little is known about the extent to which working conditions moderate justice perceptions and vice versa. Despite these limitations, the considerable body of literature involving organisational justice concepts provides important insights into the pervasiveness of justice in modern worklife. This literature can not only help inform future justice-health research, but also has significant implications for strategies aimed at preventing and/or reducing the stress and dissatisfaction associated with injustice.

The purpose of this chapter is three-fold. First, we aim to review the literature documenting the effects of organisational justice, not just in terms of worker health but also in relation to broader measures of organisational functioning (commitment, absenteeism, performance), and to establish the extent to which (in)justice should be considered a source of stress and ill-health along-side the more established psychosocial working conditions (e.g., excessive job demands, low job control). The second aim is to identify the issues that need to be addressed in future justice-health research and, in particular, to highlight those areas where greater conceptual and empirical clarity is required. The final aim of this chapter is to build on the existing body of knowledge regarding the sources and effects of organisational justice and identify the implications this knowledge has for practice. Many of these implications sit firmly within the remit of managers and supervisors, while others are particularly relevant to organisational health professionals (including occupational health psychologists).

Before examining the impact of organisational justice it is first necessary to clarify what is meant by this term and to recognise the different forms of justice.

WHAT IS ORGANISATIONAL JUSTICE?

Concepts of justice can be framed within a prescriptive or a descriptive context. Philosophers dating as far back as Aristotle have discussed what constitutes fairness in the distribution of resources and have debated over principles and standards that must be followed in order to achieve a just society (Colquitt, Greenberg, & Zapata-Phelan, 2005). Whilst this normative approach still dominates the broader justice literature today (e.g., Rawls 2001), contemporary justice accounts have been supplemented by the more descriptive approach of social scientists. The latter group were not so interested in rights, liberties and other 'categorical imperatives' (Rosen, 1993), but more about what people perceive to be fair. Individual perceptions play a major role in shaping attitudes and behaviours and hence understanding perceptions can provide important insights into explaining and predicting human behaviour.

The term organisational justice is used to describe people's perception of fairness in organisations (Greenberg, 1988). The concept of justice, or fairness as it is also referred to, is not a uni-dimensional construct and there are different forms of justice that have been found to be both factorially separate and to have different effects on employee-level outcomes (Bies & Moag, 1986; Colquitt, Conlon, Wesson, Porter, & Ng, 2001). The four main forms of justice referred to in recent justice research are distributive, procedural, informational and interpersonal justice (Colquitt, Conlon, Wesson, Porter, & Ng, 2001).

Distributive justice involves an individual's subjective evaluation of the fairness of resource distributions (Cropanzano, Goldman, & Benson III, 2005). These 'resources' could be in the form of pay, promotions, work roles, physical working conditions (such as office space) or the outcomes of organisational change programs. When assessing the fairness of resource allocations, people consider both equity and equality criteria (Adams, 1965; Walster, Walster, & Berscheid, 1978). That is, employees compare the outcomes they receive relative to the contributions made (in the form of effort, experience, education) (i.e., the equity criterion). They then make an assessment of their input-output ratio in relation to the input-output ratios of referent others, such as co-workers in similar roles or those with comparable experience and qualifications (i.e., the equality criterion). Individuals are therefore likely to become concerned about a lack of distributive fairness when the outcomes are not commensurate with their contributions and when they feel their colleagues are receiving more but giving less.

Employee perceptions of organisational fairness are not just a result of the distribution of resources, but are also based on the procedures used to make resource allocation decisions. This form of organisational fairness is referred to as procedural justice and takes into account the extent to which the processes leading to the decision were clear and transparent, incorporated accurate information, were impartially applied across individuals, and provided employees with the opportunity to contribute to the decision-making process — sometimes referred to as process control or 'voice' (Leventhal, 1976). In accordance with the 'fair process effect' (Folger, Rosenfield, Grove, & Corkran, 1979), studies have found that high levels of procedural fairness can off-set the negative effects of unfavourable distributive outcomes (e.g., Greenberg & Folger, 1983; Shapiro & Brett, 1993). These results are consistent with the view that people do not expect that every resource allocation decision will favour them, however they do expect that appropriate procedures will be followed and that the processes used to make the decision will be fair (Cropanzano, Bowen, & Gililand, 2007).

The importance of the 'means' and not just the 'ends' of resource allocation decisions is further reinforced by the literature involving interactional justice. The term interactional justice is used to describe the perceived fairness of the interactions with authority figures both during and after justice-related decisions have been made (Bies & Moag, 1986). This form of justice is sometimes divided into two categories: (1) informational justice; the extent to which employees receive timely and accurate information about the decision-making processes, or the outcomes of those processes, and (2) interpersonal justice; the respect and dignity with which employees are treated during and after the decision-making process (Colquitt, 2001). While interpersonal and informational justice are relatively new concepts, emerging evidence suggests that they can buffer the ill-effects of unfavourable justice-related outcomes (Judge & Colquitt, 2004).

WHAT ARE THE EFFECTS OF JUSTICE?

Perceptions of justice can have far-reaching effects on the attitudes and behaviours of individual employees as well as the functioning of work groups and entire organisations. While much of the research examining the effects of fairness perceptions has focused on the negative effects of injustice, a growing body of evidence supports the beneficial outcomes associated with fair resource-allocation decisions, processes and treatment.

Perceptions of injustice have been associated with a range of health-related measures including higher self-reported morbidity (Elovainio, Kivimäki, Steen, & Vahtera, 2004), lower wellbeing (Kivimaki et al., 2004), reduced job satisfaction (Schmitt & Dorfel, 1999), increased maladaptive coping such as smoking and alcohol consumption (Elovainio, Kivimäki, Vahtera, & Keltikangas-Jarvinen, 2003), and increased emotion-related responses including anger, depression and anxiety (Harlos & Pinder, 1999; Kivimäki, Elovainio, Vahtera, Virtanen, & Stansfield, 2003; Ylipaavalniemi et al., 2005). Injustice has also been linked to burnout with several studies showing that employees who indicated that they invested more in their relationships with the organisation or clients than they received in return had higher levels of burnout (Bakker, Schaufeli, Sixma, Bosveld, & Van Dierendonck, 2000; Van Horn, Schaufeli, & Enzmann, 1999). In relation to physiological outcomes, a study involving health-care workers found that negative changes in blood pressure were reported when participants were working under an unfair leader when compared to a fair leader (Wager, Fieldman, & Hussey, 2003). Other research shows that more specific forms of fairness, namely distributive and procedural fairness, are closely associated with stress-related outcomes, including psychosomatic health complaints and emotional exhaustion (De Boer, Bakker, Syroit, & Schaufeli, 2002; Schmitt & Dorfel, 1999; Tepper, 2001).

The health effects of injustice suggest that fairness perceptions would also impact on the ability of employees to perform roles central to organisational functioning. Indeed, perceptions of justice are associated with in-role performance (Cropanzano, Bowen, & Gililand, 2007), extra-role performance such as citizenship behaviours (Moliner, Martínez-Tur,

Peiró, Ramos, & Cropanzano, 2008), commitment to the organisation (Ambrose, 2002), and withdrawal behaviours such as a lack of effort, absenteeism and turnover (Conlon, Meyer, & Nowakowski, 2005; Elovainio, Kivimaki, & Vahtera, 2002). In the case of extra-role behaviours, Moliner et al (2008) surveyed 317 hotel workers and found that procedural and interactional justice predicted engagement which inturn predicted extra-role customer service behaviours. Counterproductive (e.g., tardiness, lack of cooperation) and retaliatory (e.g., theft, sabotage) behaviours are also potential outcomes of injustice (Ambrose, Seabright, & Schminke, 2002; Fox, Spector, & Miles, 2001; Greenberg, 1990). For example, Fox et al (2001) found that perceptions of procedural and distributive justice were associated with increased counter-productive behaviour including arriving late, avoiding work and criticising the organisation.

Just as unfair treatment can lead to negative outcomes for individuals and organisations, there is also evidence linking fair treatment to worthwhile benefits. For example, supervisors and managers who are regarded as fair, both in the way they allocate resources and the processes used to make justice related decisions, may strengthen their credibility and power-base in the eyes of employees. A reputation for fairness is particularly valuable when important decisions are to be made, and employees are uncertain about the outcomes (Greenberg 1988). In such situations, employees may accept the manager's decision more readily and be more committed to taking the required actions. The positive benefits of fairness have also been found in studies focusing on leader-member exchanges where perceptions of justice improved the quality of leader-member relationships (Masterson, Lewis, Goldman, & Taylor, 2000; Rupp & Cropanzano, 2002).

CONCEPTUAL AND EMPIRICAL LINKS BETWEEN JUSTICE AND STRESS

The individual and organisational effects of justice perceptions suggest that organisational justice should be regarded as a key source of employee stress in much the same way as excessive workloads, unsupportive leadership styles, ambiguous or conflicting work roles and other adverse psychosocial working conditions. However it is possible that the justice dimensions are masking the effects of other work-based conditions (e.g., supervisor support) and when these other conditions are taken into account the justice-stress relationship is negligible. The primary aim of the following section is to determine the extent to which organisational justice should be considered a unique and significant contributor to employee stress. We will do this by, first, examining the conceptual connections between stress and justice and determining the theoretical relationship between the constructs. We will then identify the major pathways through which justice can impact on job strain and draw on previous job stress research to compare the influence of the justice variables with the more traditional work-based antecedents of job strain.

From a conceptual perspective, there are a number of important similarities between organisational justice and job stress that suggest that justice would play a prominent role in the onset and severity of stress-related outcomes. According to the person-environment fit definition of job stress, stress is a result of a misfit between environmental demands and resources, on the one hand, and individual needs and capacities on the other (French, Caplan, & Harrison, 1982). Within this definition, stress can result from situations where the demands of the situation exceed the capacities of the individual or when they fail to meet his/her needs. This P-E fit definition of job stress closely matches the discrepancy model of organisational justice whereby there is a discrepancy between what one feels they deserve and what one gets (Vermunt & Steensma, 2005). Perceptions of deservingness can relate to the allocation outcomes, the procedures used to decide on those outcomes and the treatment received during and after the justice decision. In any of these cases, what is considered unfair may also be considered stressful. For example, assigning an employee to a new project may create a sense of injustice (distributive) because the employee feels over-qualified for the position. The sense of injustice is exacerbated because the person was not consulted in the decision making process leading to the new assignment (procedural justice), was not given adequate justification for the change (informational justice) and was upset by the impersonal, undignified way s/he learnt of the decision (interpersonal justice). From a job stress perspective, the same situation may generate considerable stress due to the under-utilisation of skills and the person's strong need for growth and development (which have been unfulfilled). In both instances, the discrepancy/misfit leads to feelings of injustice and distress.

Access to resources is another area where there are strong conceptual links between stress and justice. According to Lazarus and Folkman's (1984) stress appraisal model, stress is the result of the way in which events and situations are appraised and the resources available to deal with these situations. In this model, two appraisals occur with the first (the 'primary appraisal') involving an assessment of whether events or situations have implications for individual wellbeing (i.e., whether the event constitutes loss/harm or the potential for loss/harm). Events deemed as threatening trigger a 'secondary appraisal' whereby the individual assesses whether they have the coping capacities for effectively dealing with the event. Internal (self-esteem, physical stamina, problem solving capabilities) and external resources (ability to influence or control event, social support networks) are taken into account when assessing the ability to cope and a negative assessment (where coping resources are insufficient) will result in stress and a positive assessment (where coping resources are adequate) will neutralise the potential threat.

Experiences of injustice may be reflected in the Lazarus and Folkman (1984) model at both the primary and the secondary appraisal points. In relation to primary appraisals, the unfair distribution of outcomes (pay, benefits, working conditions) are likely to be deemed a threat, especially in terms of the loss or potential loss of rewards. At the secondary appraisal stage justice-related procedures that lack clarity or deny individual decision-making input, reduce the external resources employees have to minimise uncertainty, gain greater control over the outcomes and generally practice the more positive problem-focused coping strategies (consistent with the instrumental explanation of procedural justice, Lind & Van den Bos, 2002; Thibaut & Walker, 1975). Furthermore, the lack of equity and poor interpersonal treatment may provide negative feedback regarding the employee's status in the organisation, resulting in a loss of self-confidence and self-efficacy (consistent with non-instrumental explanations such as group value theory Lind & Tyler, 1988). To summarise, Lazarus and Folkman's (1984) model indicates that injustice may not only be evaluated as an actual or potential threat, but the unfair processes and treatment may diminish the individual's ability to effectively deal with the threat. According to this model, injustice is therefore likely to be a key contributor to job stress.

The conceptual overlap between justice and stress constructs suggests that there are three major pathways through which fairness perceptions can impact on stress and wellbeing. Although these are not the only ways that justice may lead to job stress, they appear to have received the most empirical support.

1. Pathway 1: 'injustice as stressor'. The first pathway linking fairness to health is a direct one whereby injustice or unfair behaviour from authority causes strain. The 'injustice as stressor' model (Cropanzano, Goldman, & Benson III, 2005) is consistent with the P-E fit definition of job stress and is supported by studies showing that one or a combination of justice variables have direct and additive (in the case of multiple justice forms) relationships with stress-related measures such as increased psychological distress, reduced job satisfaction (Judge & Colquitt, 2004). Within this pathway, injustice contributes to stress in the same way as other adverse working conditions (monotonous work tasks, unrealistice deadlines, lack of autonomy).

2. Pathway 2: 'justice as moderator'. The second pathway parallels the Lazarus and Folkman (1984) stress appraisal model, as well as several resource-based models of job stress such as conservation of resources theory (Hobfoll, 1989) and Karasek and Theorell's (1990) demand-control-support (DCS) model. These models suggest that the mechanisms for achieving justice (e.g., process control, information support), as well as the perceptions of justice themselves, represent valuable resources that can be used to control potentially stressful work characteristics and/or buffer the impact of these stressors. Perceptions of injustice can reduce internal (self-esteem, self-efficacy) and external (control, information, support) resources that may be used to deal with the threat posed by injustice, as per the earlier discussion of the Lazarus and Folkman (1984) model. Tepper (2001) elaborates on the stress-buffering potential of interpersonal and informational justice by recognising that the resources offered by these forms of justice can reduce harm by helping individuals identify and correct distorted thoughts, reaffirm their professional and personal capacities, provide direction for problem-focused coping and generally promote 'hope-sustaining' beliefs.

3. Pathway 3: 'injustice as mediator'. Research involving this pathway has focused almost exclusively on the mediating roles of procedural and relational justice in the relationship between job control and employee health (Brockner & Wisenfeld, 1996; Elovainio, Kivimaki, & Helkama, 2001; Robertson, Moye, & Locke, 1999). Participatory decision making or 'voice' is considered to be a vital ingredient in procedural justice (Leventhal, 1980; Thibaut & Walker, 1975) and hence a lack of job control can lead to violations in procedural justice that then lead to distress. Fully and partially mediated models have been supported in studies investigating job satisfaction (Robertson, Moye, & Locke, 1999), stressful emotions (Elovainio, Kivimäki, & Helkama, 2001) and sickness absence (Elovainio, Kivimäki, Steen, & Vahtera, 2004).

The other pathways linking justice to stress are variations on the above routes. In a variation to Pathway 2, Zohar (1995) proposes that stressful working conditions (including justice and non-justice stressors) produce a sense of injustice with the injustice then producing strain. Hence the impact of any stressor could be intensified if the employee felt the condition involved unfair elements. The second alternative pathway is an extension of Pathway 1 and according to Fujishiro and Heaney (2007), is where stress mediates the relationship between an aversive event and justice. That is, the employee is exposed to the aversive event and experiences stress. The employee then asks, "do I deserve this much stress" and if the answer is "no" then a sense of injustice will develop (Fujishiro & Heaney, 2007, p.5).

DOES JUSTICE MAKE A UNIQUE CONTRIBUTION TO JOB STRESS?

The conceptual overlap between justice and stress theories, in addition to the associated empirical support for direct and indirect pathways between justice and stress, indicates that justice can make significant contributions to employee stress. However our review so far has not considered whether these contributions are independent of other psychosocial work characteristics or whether justice constructs are simply markers for non-justice antecedents of job stress (e.g., job control and social support). On face value, there appears to be strong similarities between the resources that underpin the moderating effects of procedural, interpersonal and informational justice and existing resources that have been traditionally thought to moderate the effects of aversive working conditions. For example, employee voice or 'process control' is a major source of procedural justice, whilst also being a central dimension of job control (Bies & Shapiro, 1988; Conlon, Meyer, & Nowakowski, 2005; Elovainio, Kivimäki, & Helkama, 2001). Similarly, support from supervisors and authority figures is an important feature of interpersonal and informational justice while also being the hallmark of social support (House, 1981).

There are two key limitations in the justice-stress research that make it difficult to make a firm assessment of the extent to which organisational justice can add value to work stress research: (1) there are relatively few organisational fairness studies that have assessed the effects of injustice on job strain and even fewer have considered these effects in the presence of other stressors (Francis & Barling, 2005; Judge & Colquitt, 2004), and (2) there are some major differences in the way stress- and justice-related concepts have been operationalised thus hindering efforts to draw consistent conclusions from this research (Fujishiro & Heaney, 2007).

In terms of those studies that have tackled the question of whether perceptions of justice make unique contributions to job strain, the findings from these studies are generally supportive of this proposition. Using moderated multiple regression analysis with a sample of 1,083 government employees, Francis and Barling (2005) found that interactional, procedural, and distributive injustice were all unique predictors of psychological strain that account for significant unique variance beyond that explained by job insecurity. Similarly, De Boer et al (2002) compared the effects of fairness perceptions with common stressors (job demands and a lack of control) on psychosomatic health complaints and found that fairness was predictive even after controlling for other stressors. Kivimaki, Elovainio and colleagues found that procedural and relational justice were independent predictors of a range of stress-related outcomes including self-rated health (Kivimaki et al., 2004), CHD risk scores (Kivimäki et al., 2005), minor psychiatric disorders (Elovainio, Kivimaki, & Vahtera, 2002), sickness absence (Kivimaki, Head, & Ferrie, 2003) and depression (Ylipaavalniemi et al., 2005). Importantly, these predictive relationships remained after adjusting for well recognised psychosocial work stressors (such as job demand, job control and, to a lesser extent, social support and effort-reward imbalance), as well as demographic (age, income) and behavioural risk factors (smoking, alcohol consumption).

One of the shortcomings of previous research comparing the effects of injustice with more traditional stressors is that none have examined the influence of all four organisational justice variables in relation to the additive and interaction components of well established job stress models, such as Karasek and Theorell's (1990) DCS model. The DCS is one of the most widely used models underpinning occupational research on employee outcomes (Fox, Dwyer, & Ganster, 1993) and predicts that high levels of stress will be experienced when the demands of the situation are not matched by adequate levels of decision-making authority and/or support from supervisors and colleagues. Support for demand-control-support interactions is mixed (Belkic, Landsbergis, Schnall, & Baker, 2004; van der Doef & Maes, 1999), although research has consistently demonstrated that the DCS component variables - particularly job control and social support - predict health and work performance outcomes across a range of organisational settings (Bond & Bunce, 2003; Marmot, Bosma, Hemingway, Brunner, & Stansfeld, 1997). The strong performance of the full DCS (including interactive and additive hypotheses) suggests that this model would provide an appropriate reference point for testing the degree to which organisational justice can explain job stress over and above that provided by traditional work stress models.

Recent research undertaken by the current authors (Noblet & Rodwell, in press; Rodwell & Noblet, 2008) sought to examine the unique contributions made by all four justice dimensions (distributive, procedural, interpersonal and informational), in comparison to the full DCS. In the first study, two samples of Australian-based public servants (2466 police officers and 1010 occupationally-diverse employees working in a State Government authority), were surveyed using a questionnaire consisting of the DCS variables, psychological contract breach (a measure of unmet expectations) and organizational fairness (Noblet & Rodwell, in press). The results of hierarchical regression analyses involving both samples indicated that the additive effects of the DCS variables accounted for the vast majority (>80% for the police sample and >76% for cross-occupational sample) of the explained variation in all three outcome measures - intrinsic and extrinsic job satisfaction and psychological health. The PC breach and organizational fairness variables still captured significant portions of variance in both forms of job satisfaction, although the contribution for these predictor variables was considerably smaller than that attributed to the DCS. Similar research by Rodwell and Noblet (2008), this time involving the DCS and the justice variables only (i.e., without PC breach), again found that while the variance accounted for by the four justice variables was significant, the majority of the variance in explained strain was attributed to the additive effects of the DCS.

Although the Noblet and Rodwell studies (in press; 2008) support the inclusion of organisational justice variables in job stress research, the strong performance of the DCS relative to justice variables does raise questions regarding the potential size of the justice contribution. However, there are important operational distinctions between these and some of the previous justice-stress studies, particularly those undertaken by Kivimaki, Elovainio and colleagues, which makes it difficult to accurately assess the unique contribution made by justice. First, the Noblet and Rodwell studies incorporated scales of justice that assessed participants' perceptions regarding relatively discrete justice-related decisions (e.g., promotions, performance reviews, allocation of tasks). This context-specific approach is consistent with other justice-stress research (e.g., Judge and Colquitt 2004), however it is in contrast to the more global, context-free measures used by Kivimaki, Elovanio and colleagues. The latter (and others, e.g., Tepper 2001) argue that people's overall assessment of the extent to which they are treated fairly by the organisation has a more pervasive effect than the discrete, event-specific perceptions of fairness. This macro approach has strong intuitive appeal, especially as the DCS variables are generally operationalised according to a context-free perspective. Yet, in defence of the context-specific perspective, modern worklife is characterised by fast-paced, unpredictable change and hence the events/conditions that are the subject to justice-decisions (including change itself), are perhaps not as discrete or 'one-off' as they once were (Korsgaard, Sapienza, & Schwieger, 2002; Sidle, 2003). The need to include context-specific and/or context-free measures of justice in job stress research is clearly one area that warrants further examination.

The second operational distinction between the Noblet and Rodwell studies and previous justice-stress research is the approach taken to social support. In the case of the Australian-based studies, a disaggregated measure of social support was used that tapped into the commonly recognised forms (emotional, instrumental, informational and appraisal) and sources (supervisors, colleagues, subordinates) of support at work. This approach is consistent with the support matching hypothesis whereby the employee is able to match the form and source of support with the specific needs activated by the stressor (Cutrona, 1990; Sarason, Sarason, & Pierce, 1990). In comparison, other justice-stress studies that have incorporated social support have tended to use measures that focused solely on emotional support (Elovainio, Kivimaki, & Vahtera, 2002; Kivimaki, Elovainio, Vahtera, & Ferrie, 2003; Kivimaki, Elovainio, Vahtera, Virtanen, & Stansfeld, 2003). Social support was predictive of all of the outcome variables in both the Noblet and Rodwell (in press) and Rodwell and Noblet (2008) and this strong result may have been attributed, at least in part, to the disaggregated, multi-source measure of support used in these studies.

On balance, the results involving the justice variables and the more traditional antecedents of job stress suggest that justice dimensions can make significant contributions to job stress that are independent of other psychosocial characteristics. However the magnitude of the contributions made by justice is still in doubt and further research is required to determine the role justice dimensions play in the aetiology of job stress. More specifically, these studies need to assess the relative influence of discrete and more global measures of justice while also comparing the effects of disaggregated and aggregated measures of social support.

CAN THE 'JUSTICE AS MODERATOR' HYPOTHESIS BE EXTENDED TO NON-JUSTICE STRESSORS?

There is considerable support in the literature for the 'fair process' effect whereby perceptions of procedural justice can off-set the negative consequences of unfavourable distributive outcomes (Brockner & Wisenfeld, 1996). While this effect was thought to be the result of procedural justice, more recent research suggests that interactional (and their sub-categories, interpersonal and informational justice) can also moderate the negative influence of distributive justice (Bies & Moag, 1986; Colquitt, 2001). Although the precise mechanisms through which procedural, interpersonal and informational justice can impact on stress are unclear, there are instrumental and non-instrumental explanations for this buffering influence (Lind & Tyler, 1988; Lind & Van den Bos, 2002).

The moderating capacity of justice variables raises the question, can these variables moderate other sources of stress? This possibility is based on the premise that justice dimensions represent valuable resources (process control, information and guidance, respect and dignity) that could be used to prevent or buffer the impact of a range of job stressors, not just distributive injustice. Support for this possibility has come from research focusing on the moderating relationship of justice on job demands. A study involving 134 low to mid-level Dutch managers found that participants were more satisfied in response to higher levels of job demands when they perceived their efforts to be fairly rewarded by the organization (Janssen, 2001). In a similar study involving 170 non-management employees, perceptions of effort-reward fairness were found to moderate the relationship between job demands and innovative work behaviors (Janssen, 2000). It is noteworthy that while the latter study supported the moderating influence of fairness, this study did not support a two-way interaction between demand and job control.

The results of the Janssen (2000; 2001) studies bring into question the relevance of Karasek's demand x control interactive term and back calls for researchers to explore contextual factors other than control that may influence the demands-response relationship (Fletcher & Jones, 1993). However, findings from the Noblet and Rodwell study (in press) indicate that there was some support for a demands x control interaction, but not for the demand x fairness interactions. Notably, the moderating influence of job control was only present in one of the regressions (extrinsic job satisfaction) and the authors could not make a firm assessment on the moderating influence of organizational fairness and job control. Nevertheless, the lack of a consistent relationship does raise doubts about the efficacy of the moderating interactions, both for control and fairness.

ISSUES TO ADDRESS IN FUTURE JUSTICE-STRESS RESEARCH

Although researchers examining the justice-stress relationship have made considerable gains in a relatively short period of time, there are clear issues that need to be addressed in order to fully understand the mechanisms through which justice impacts on job stress and the role that justice-related resources can play in moderating job stressors (beyond distributive injustice). Teasing out these mechanisms has important practical implications, especially in terms of identifying the conditions to target when developing strategies aimed at building fairer and less stressful working environments. One of the primary aims of the following section is therefore to highlight the problematic issues that have been identified in the justice-stress research and suggest ways in which these issues could be addressed. This section will also seek to identify new directions in justice-stress research and suggest areas where future investigations could make significant advancements.

Operational overlap between key antecedents

There is strong empirical evidence that justice dimensions can make unique contributions to job stress, independent of other psychosocial working conditions such as job control and social support. However, the magnitude of this contribution is still in doubt, partly as a result of the uncertainty regarding global versus discrete justice measures and also due to the heavy overlap in the way potential antecedents are operationalised (e.g., work-based support). The former issue has been discussed in the previous section and there is a clear need to assess the relative influence of these different levels of justice (and the inter-play between them). In terms of the operational overlap between antecedents, this appears to be related to the numerous conceptual similarities between the justice dimensions and other psychosocial determinants of health (e.g., job control and process control; interpersonal justice and social support).

The lack of separation between the relational justice items (interpersonal and informational) and social support appears to be a particularly problematic issue. Not only are these constructs conceptually similar, but some researchers have used this conceptual overlap to justify taking items from a social support scale and using them to measure relational justice (Kivimaki et al., 2004). The lack of distinction between the antecedent measures creates uncertainty regarding the independent contribution of each construct and, ultimately, raises doubts over how job stress should be tackled and which psychosocial conditions should be the target of job stress prevention/reduction interventions.

Interactions between psychosocial work characteristics

The broader organizational justice literature has focused heavily on the ability of procedural justice to moderate the effects of distributive justice. For example, Brockner and Wisenfeld (1996) reviewed research involving 45 independent samples of employees and found that, generally, procedural justice buffered the negative effects of unfair distribution of resources. In contrast, there are very few justice-stress studies that have considered the two- or three-way effects of procedural, distributive and interactional justice on job strain. Francis and Barling (2005) is one of the few to have assessed these interactions and neither the two- (procedural x distributive justice) or three-way interactions (distributive x procedural x interactional) were supported. These results are consistent with the results of our own research (Noblet & Rodwell, in press; Rodwell & Noblet, 2008) where hypothesised interactions between the justice variables were not supported in the results of multiple regression analyses.

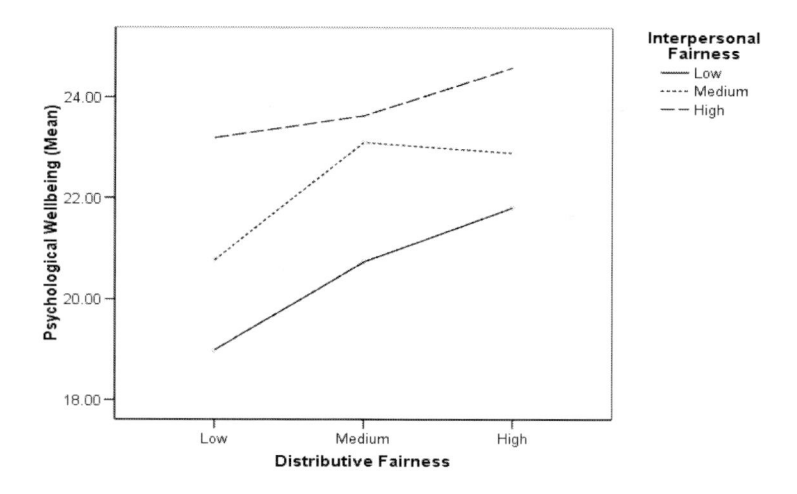

Figure 1. Results of two-way analysis of variance showing association between psychological wellbeing (as measured by the General Health Questionnaire 12-Item version), distributive fairness and interpersonal fairness

Despite the lack of published support for the justice interactions, there are indications in the unpublished literature that two- and three-way multiplicative terms should still be factored into data analyses involving organisational justice and other psychosocial working conditions (Rodwell & Noblet, 2007). This latter research was based on responses from a large sample of Australian-based public servants. The results indicate that low-low combinations of distributive and interpersonal fairness were associated with low levels of wellbeing and organizational commitment (see Figures 1 and 2). Conversely, higher levels of one or both of these justice measures were associated with increased levels of wellbeing and commitment. Further analyses, this time involving three-way analysis on variance, found that there were significant correlations between interpersonal fairness, job control and social support when assessed against job satisfaction (see Figure 3). These latter results indicate that the group recording high levels of social support, job control and interpersonal fairness were also likely to report high levels of job satisfaction. The converse was also true; employees with low levels of control, support and interpersonal fairness were more likely to have low job satisfaction.

The unpublished research involving the two- and three-way interactions indicates that there is some promise in examining the moderating influence of justice and non-justice related working conditions. The conditions

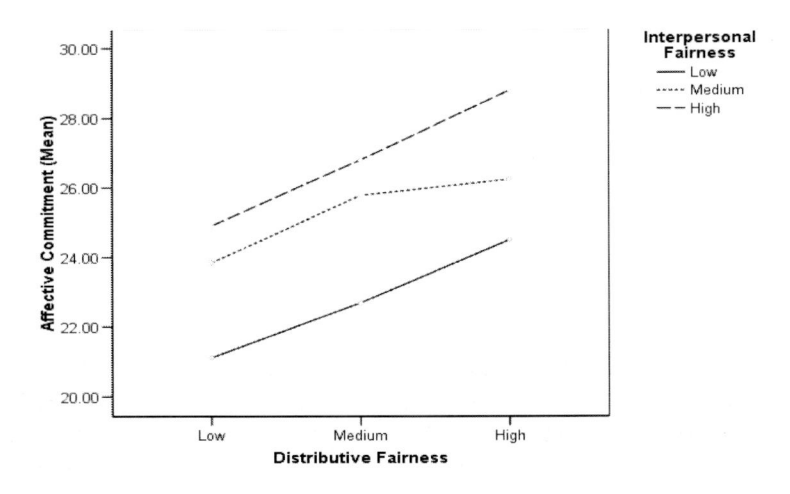

Figure 2. Association between affective commitment, distributive fairness and interpersonal fairness

represented in these interactions are amenable to action and hence further research in this area could play an important role in identifying the conditions that need to be addressed in order to offset the negative effects of unfavourable distributive justice decisions and other sources of stress.

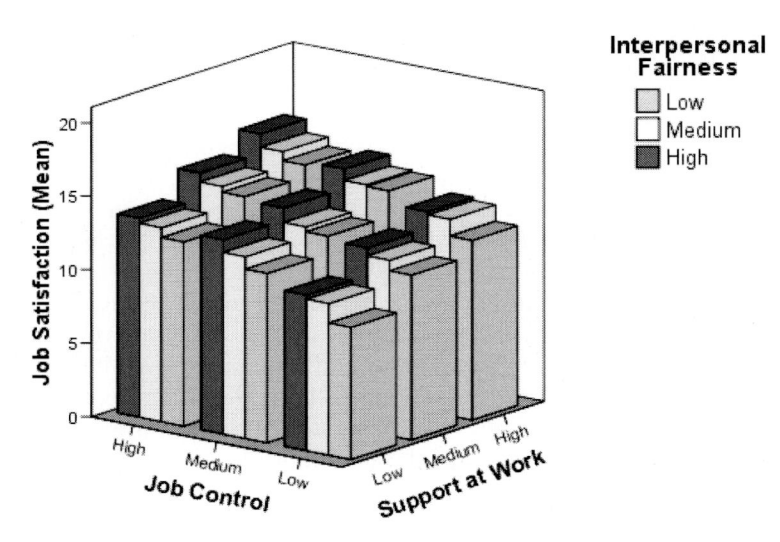

Figure 3. Results of three-way analysis of variance showing the interactions between job control, support at work and interpersonal fairness for job satisfaction

Curvilinear and non-curvilinear effects

A further aim of future justice-stress research should be to test for linear and non-linear relationships of the stress and justice dimensions on the outcome measures. A common criticism of research focusing on the work-stress relationship is that where individual variables are found to have a direct effect on the outcome measures, these relationships are assumed to be linear (Rydstedt, Ferrie, & Head, 2006). That is, the impact of the work characteristic increases in proportion to the duration or intensity of the condition under investigation. In contrast, there is evidence suggesting that an under- or over-supply of a particular working condition can harm health (De Jonge, Reuvers, Houtman, Bongers, & Kompier, 2000; Warr, 1990; Xie & Johns, 1995). For example, significant curvilinear relationships have been found between job demands on the one hand, and job satisfaction, job-related anxiety, and job-related depression on the other (Warr, 1990).

Although the negative effects of unfair perceptions are well documented, support for their curvilinearity would suggest that, at the very least, the positive effects may be attenuated at high levels or, at worst, that health and satisfaction would deteriorate when perceptions of justice are high. Organisational justice scholars have rarely considered the possibility that people can receive too much justice (Janssen, 2001). However, consistent with models of job stress such as Warr's Vitamin model (1987), receiving large quantities of information, guidance and decision-making input - whether related to justice or not - could be as toxic as receiving too little. This being the case, practitioners would need to monitor employees' justice perceptions and ensure that the justice they receive is neither inadequate or excessive.

The potential effects of an under- or over-supply of justice-related resources indicate that this is another important area for future justice-stress research. Job stress research investigating the non-linear effects of working conditions has found that contextual factors (such as the nature of the tasks undertaken and the homogeneity of the workforce) can influence the presence of curvilinearity and hence these factors would need to be taken into account when developing studies designed to assess non-linear justice effects (Janssen, 2001).

DEVELOPING AND IMPLEMENTING JUSTICE-BASED STRESS PREVENTION PROGRAMS

Despite the uncertainty regarding the size of the independent contributions of justice, and the lack of clarity regarding the extent to which justice-related measures can moderate the strain associated with injustice and other workplace stressors (e.g., job demands), there is sufficient evidence to conclude that injustice is a potential source of stress that needs to be considered when developing strategies to prevent stress and enhance wellbeing. Further, the adverse effects of injustice strongly suggest that the unfair allocation of resources, in terms of their distribution and/or procedures, can be as debilitating for the organisation as they are for individuals. These individual and organisational costs also indicate that if injustice is addressed effectively, all parties – employees, employers and clients – stand to gain from efforts to build fairer and more equitable work environments. There is therefore a strong need to consider the steps that organisations can take to enhance organisational justice.

Justice-based interventions hold considerable potential for preventing or reducing job stress (Vermunt & Steensma, 2005), however for these improvements to be realised, there are a number of general guidelines that need to be considered. The guidelines included in this final section do not relate to specific justice-related decisions (performance reviews, promotions, dispute resolution, organisational change), as practical advice on how to effectively deal with these decisions is covered in detail elsewhere (e.g., Cropanzano, Bowen, & Gililand, 2007; Posthuma & Campion, 2008; Sidle, 2003). Instead this final section will concentrate more on how organisations and their members can plan and implement comprehensive justice management programs that can prevent or reduce the stress associated with unfair treatment. Although the emphasis will be on strategies that are designed to promote high levels of fairness in the organisation, we will also discuss how these justice-specific initiatives can be integrated with more generalised stress prevention strategies. This latter point is consistent with the views of organisational justice scholars who have advocated for justice dimensions to be incorporated in comprehensive stress-reduction programs (Cropanzano, Goldman, & Benson III, 2005).

Processes for developing justice-based stress prevention/reduction strategies

A recurring theme in the organisational justice literature is that 'means' are as important as 'ends'. That is, the processes used to make resource allocation decisions, and the way in which employees are treated during and after the decision has been made, are as central to building a fair workplace as the outcomes of the decisions themselves. Ambiguous selection criteria, inaccurate or incomplete performance assessment data, unclear procedures, disrespectful treatment and other breaches of procedural and interactional justice, not only have the potential to lead to poor distributive decisions, but can amplify the negative effects of unfavourable outcomes. Organisations aiming to prevent or reduce the stress associated with injustice and other adverse psychosocial conditions therefore need to carefully consider the processes (administrative and interpersonal) they use to plan and develop strategies aimed at enhancing fairness and reducing stress.

One area where the 'fair process effect' could provide significant benefits is in the identification of policies and practices that are considered unfair or stressful. The attitudes and behaviours that contribute to unfair treatment and other psychosocial stressors are often firmly embedded in the policies, practices and cultures of organisations. Irrespective of whether injustice is operationalised at the discrete or the global level, managers and organisational health personnel need to develop processes and methods that can help them identify the needs and perceptions of their workers. Moreover, they need to use these processes to identify, from the perspective of employees, where current practices are unjust or are contributing to worker stress (Cropanzano, Bowen, & Gililand, 2007).

Although developing stress management programs that are able to identify and respond to employee perceptions are considered important, such programs appear to be the exception, rather than the norm. For example, a review of workplace health promotion programs revealed that only 25% were implemented in response to employees' explicit needs and views and only 14% included employees as partners in planning and implementing programs (Harden, Peersman, Oliver, Mauthner, & Oakley, 1999). It is therefore important that employees have input into promotion policies, performance appraisal programs, grievance procedures and other systems and policies that involve justice related decisions. Providing employees with input into decision-making processes can not only enhance 'voice' and perceptions of procedural justice, but can also help ensure managers and supervisors have an accurate understanding of what their employees consider to be just/unjust (Fujishiro & Heaney, 2007). In addition, these participatory mechanisms can provide a vehicle for identifying broader sources of stress (beyond injustice) and can be used as a general workplace stress diagnostic strategy (i.e., identifying problematic conditions or events).

Another area where it is important to carefully consider processes is when developing strategies aimed at addressing the sources stress and injustice. There is a tendency for stress management programs to focus on individual employees and to be preoccupied with helping them to cope better with stressful working conditions (e.g., through relaxation programs) rather than addressing the work-based sources of job stress (Giga, Noblet, Faragher, & Cooper, 2003; Murta, Sanderson, & Oldenburg, 2007). When coupled with research indicating that employees are rarely involved in planning workplace health promotion programs (Harden, Peersman, Oliver, Mauthner, & Oakley, 1999), there is clear potential for stress prevention and health enhancement initiatives to be seen as a source of distrust and injustice, rather than as an important avenue for building fairer and more satisfying working environments. A key to minimising this possibility, while also developing more effective, needs-based strategies, is to involve all levels of the organisation in the development of appropriate interventions. The people most affected by the stress and injustice-related issues – employees themselves – are especially important in this process, as they are more likely to have a detailed understanding of the reasons why the issue is considered stressful or unjust and how the problem could be addressed. Relevant researchers and government authorities should still be seen as important sources of information on how to tackle workplace stress, however this information should represent a starting point for developing interventions. The effectiveness of job stress interventions is heavily dependent on the social (e.g., cultural values and assumptions), organisational (e.g., level of centralization and formalisation), political (e.g., distribution of power and influence) and economic (e.g., budgetary guidelines) environments in which health and justice-related issues are located (Griffiths, 1999; Saksvik, Nytro, Dahl-Jorgensen, & Mikkelsen, 2002). Ultimately, the people most familiar with these contexts (the organisation's members) need to have a large say in which strategies are adopted.

Adopting a comprehensive justice-stress management program

The specific strategies that need to be implemented to prevent and/or reduce the stress associated with injustice, need to recognise and build on the prescriptive approach to organisational justice. The prescriptive elements of organisational justice are represented in various industrial relations laws and codes of practice and, in many respects, articulate the minimum standards that need be achieved in order to protect worker's rights, minimise exploitation and harassment, and generally uphold fair standards of workplace practice. These laws are present in all industrialised countries and are critical for maintaining a fair and just society. However employment relations laws generally represent the minimum that is required in order to build fair working environments and organisations need to go well beyond these in order to meet employees' fairness perceptions.

A comprehensive stress prevention program is one that consists of an integrated set of strategies that address both the organisational origins of stress at work as well as the symptoms of distress exhibited by individual employees (Noblet & LaMontagne 2006). Although this approach emphasises pro-active strategies that can prevent or help minimise the incidence job stress, it is not always possible to prevent stressors and organisations need to have reactive strategies in place to effectively deal with the effects of excessive stress. Comprehensive stress management programs are much more likely to lead to favourable, long-term outcomes than programs that focus solely on the individual (e.g., Kompier, Cooper, & Guerts, 2000; Michie & Williams, 2003). One of the main reasons why comprehensive programs are thought to be more effective in the long-term is that the balance of organisational and individual-directed interventions helps to ensure that the "preventative benefits of the former can have a widespread impact across an organisation, whilst the curative strengths of the latter can target those (fewer) people who have already succumbed to occupational ill-health" (Bond, 2004, p.147).

When transferred to a justice-stress context, 'comprehensive' means taking steps to identify and, where possible, address the sources of injustice (including those emanating from 'non-justice' stressors such excessive job demands or low discretionary decision-making), while at the same time equipping the individual with the capacity to cope more effectively with the 'ups and downs' of modern worklife. Adopting a comprehensive approach to justice management also means having the capacity to react to employee perceptions of injustice and taking the action necessary to restore a sense of fairness, such as through justification, compensation or mitigation (see Vermunt & Steensma, 2005 for a detailed description of these 'restoring strategies').

The comprehensive approach to justice-stress management provides valuable opportunities for integrating justice-specific strategies with more mainstream stress prevention interventions. For example, justice-specific initiatives (such as training managers to undertake impartial and accurate performance reviews) would be couched within broader capacity and relationship-building strategies. (e.g., enhancing employee control, developing supportive leadership styles). Improving job control and supervisory support through strategies such as genuine two-way communication and timely, accurate feedback from supervisors can help employees address a range of potentially stressful conditions (not just those involving injustice). Integrating justice-specific strategies with a more general capacity-building approach oriented around control and support, would also serve to capitalise on the close conceptual and empirical relationships between these conditions and organisational justice, while reducing concerns about the lack of separation between stress and justice related variables (e.g., social support and interpersonal justice).

When developing comprehensive stress management programs, coordinators need to recognise that direct supervisors play a key role in perceptions of justice and stress and that they therefore represent a particularly important target group for justice-stress related interventions (Cropanzano, Goldman, & Benson III, 2005). The injustice experienced by employees can be decreased or even prevented by interpersonal justice from the direct supervisor and, according to some organisational justice scholars, this group represents the "best source for remedying against stress" (Vermunt & Steensma, 2005, p.396). However, it should also be recognised that supervisors generally have a dual role in the organisation (i.e., master and subordinate) that can create conflict between achieving efficiency goals on the one hand (and keeping superiors satisfied) and maintaining standards of justice (and satisfying followers' needs). In order to reduce this conflict, strategies need to also focus on the supervisor's superior (Vermunt & Steensma, 2005). Whilst training is considered to be an important strategy for helping managerial personnel develop the knowledge and skills required to promote high levels of fairness, the effectiveness of this training will be minimal if managers simply do not have the time to practice these newly developed techniques. Organisations therefore need to monitor the time demands of their managerial staff and ensure they have both the opportunity (time-wise) and the capacity (skill-wise) to provide adequate levels of justice-related support.

The potential lack of synergy between strategies designed to reduce injustice or stress and the overall culture/strategy of an organisation, raises the need for organisations to adopt an organisation-wide approach to stress management. High-investment human resource management (HRM) is an example of a macro-level strategy that can provide the broad foundation for developing a more systematic and consistent approach to managing stress and perceptions of injustice. High-investment HRM strategies are those that devote considerable resources to recognising and developing the skills, knowledge and general capacity of their employees and include empowerment programs designed to maximise employees' decision-making latitude, training and development opportunities, compensation and reward systems that promote equity and equality, learning-based performance management systems and, supportive leadership styles (Arthur, 1994; Guthrie, 2001).

While high-investment HRM can benefit the organisation, through improved performance-related outcomes, this approach to managing people has also been found to lead to increased job satisfaction, greater commitment to the organisation, and improved citizenship behaviours (Guthrie, 2001; Takeuchi, Marinova, Lepak, & Moon, 2004). Organisations adopting high-investment HRM not only look for opportunities for further boosting the expertise of its employees, but are also much more likely to be concerned about conditions, practices or policies that undermine employee capacities, particularly psychosocial stressors such as injustice. Although there is some research showing a positive relationship between high-investment HRM and procedural and distributive justice (Takeuchi, Marinova, Lepak, & Moon, 2004), further research in this area is required. Nevertheless, the strong connections between initiatives that can reduce stress and injustice on the one hand, and improve HRM capacities on the other, suggest that the high-investment HRM strategies may provide a valuable set of over-arching, organisation-wide strategies that can build fairer and more satisfying workplaces.

The final practical implication relating to the development of comprehensive justice-stress interventions relates to evaluation. Irrespective of how much planning and consultation was involved in developing strategies to reduce job stress, these initiatives may produce unexpected effects or fall short of expectations. Organisations therefore need to closely monitor the impact of their strategies and, where necessary, take early action to minimise the negative effects. Again, employees should be heavily involved in this process, especially in terms of assessing the value of existing strategies and developing more effective measures. Correctability is an important criterion for assessing procedural justice and hence a slow or non-response to a poorly performing strategy is likely to exacerbate perceptions of injustice and stress (Leventhal, 1976).

The role of occupational health psychologists and other organisational health personnel

At first glance, creating fairer organisations might appear to be the responsibility of management personnel, employee relations experts and other HR specialists. Although this may be the case when dealing with specific justice-related issues, such as compensation systems, performance appraisal programs, succession plans and organisational change initiatives, developing comprehensive justice-stress strategies requires a multi-disciplinary approach that spans a range of professions (management, HRM, employee relations, occupational health psychology [OHP], occupational health and safety [OHS] and workplace health promotion [WHP]). OHPs and other organisational health personnel (OHS, WHP) need to play a particularly prominent role in: exposing justice-related situations and conditions that contribute to stress and other adverse outcomes; advocating for justice-related issues to be high on the agenda of decision-makers, and; facilitating the development of comprehensive, needs-based stress prevention programs.

One of the key priorities of organisational health personnel is to create greater awareness of the importance of justice perceptions for individual and organisational functioning. Organisational justice dimensions have only just been recognised as a significant predictor of job stress and hence an important task of workplace health professionals at this stage is to generate a greater understanding of what these dimensions involve and how they can impact on employee health and performance. In particular, senior managers need to be are aware of the possible consequences of addressing (or not addressing) injustice and other sources of job stress. There is evidence that many organisations may be unaware, or even reluctant to acknowledge, the relationship between working conditions and employee health and performance (Mustard, 2004) and subsequently an early goal of OHPs and other health professionals may be to gather internal (e.g., employee surveys, exit interviews) and external data (e.g., published research, case studies) to underline the importance of this topic. Collecting data on outcomes that are important for organisational functioning (e.g., performance, absenteeism, turnover) would be especially useful in highlighting to senior personnel that stress and injustice represent a significant loss in human resources and, in an era when human capital is critical for competitive advantage, organisations can simply not afford to ignore the impact of psychosocial working conditions.

Once there is a general acceptance of the significance of fairness perceptions, personnel with responsibility for organisational health have a pivotal role to play in facilitating the development of comprehensive stress prevention initiatives. This role includes working with all levels of the organisation to identify and assess the specific conditions that are contributing to injustice or stress and using the results of these investigations to develop well informed needs-based strategies that can reduce their impact. OHPs are especially well equipped to develop data collection methods (e.g., questionnaires, interviews) that can accurately and reliably measure perceptions of justice and other psychosocial working conditions and thus they could adopt a more 'hands-on' role during this stage. They are also more likely to have expertise in data analysis and could provide organisations with valuable guidance when analysing and interpreting survey data. Further, these same skills would prove very valuable when evaluating the effectiveness of justice and stress management strategies and making decisions regarding initiatives that could have a more positive impact.

The aforementioned roles indicate that people with expertise in OHP, OHS and WHP should be actively involved in, first, creating an environment that understands and accepts the importance of justice perceptions in the workplace and, second, helping to develop processes that encourage the involvement of all sections of the organisation in identifying and addressing stressful and unjust working environments. Although issues involving justice may be outside the 'comfort zones' of many organisational health professionals (Fujishiro & Heaney, 2007), the close association between justice and employee wellbeing suggests that individuals and groups with a responsibility for health at work must be at the forefront of initiatives aimed at building fairer workplaces.

CONCLUSION

Literature focusing on the relationship between organisational justice perceptions and employee stress is rapidly expanding. While there is already a considerable body of evidence indicating that injustice can make significant contributions to employee stress, there are still doubts over the potential size of this contribution, especially when compared to traditional psychosocial stressors (e.g., support and control). There is also some uncertainty regarding the 'justice-as-moderator' hypothesis, although there are signs that the resource-oriented dimensions of justice (i.e., procedural, interpersonal and informational) could ameliorate the negative effects of non-justice sources of stress (e.g., job demands). Despite these limitations, there is sufficient evidence to suggest that justice should be high on the agenda of managers, supervisors, HRM, OHPs and other individuals or groups with people management responsibilities. In terms of developing appropriate strategies, justice management initiatives need to be integrated into comprehensive stress management programs. These programs should to be informed by, and address, the specific concerns and ideas expressed by employees and hence all levels of the organisation need be involved in (1) uncovering practices and policies that lead to injustice and job stress and (2) using the results of these investigations to develop strategies that can prevent and/or reduce the adverse effects of these conditions. Employees are particularly important stakeholders in this process – as they are the ones who appraise justice-related actions as just or unjust. Likewise, managers and supervisors need to be heavily involved, not just because their attitudes and actions will have a strong influence of employees' evaluations of fairness, but also because their support is required to prioritise and resource the recommended strategies. Finally, organisational health professionals such as OHPs have an important role to play in facilitating the development of comprehensive stress management programs that can help build fairer and less stressful workplaces. Issues involving fairness may appear to be more relevant to other disciplines (e.g., employee relations experts), however the effects generally include health-related outcomes and hence health professionals should be pro-active in identifying and addressing the conditions that contribute to these effects.

REFERENCES

Adams, J. S. (1965). Inequity in social exchange. In L. Berkowitz (Ed.), *Advances in Experimental Social Psychology* (pp. 267-299). New York: Academic Press.

Ambrose, M. L. (2002). Contemporary justice research: A new look at familiar questions. *Organizational Behavior and Human Decision Processes, 89*, 803 - 812.

Ambrose, M. L., Seabright, M. A., & Schminke, M. (2002). Sabotage in the Workplace: The role of organizational injustice. *Organizational Behavior and Human Decision Processes, 89*, 947 - 965.

Arthur, J. (1994). Effects of human resource systems on manufacturing performance and turnover. *Academy of Management Journal, 37*, 670-687.

Bakker, A. B., Schaufeli, W. B., Sixma, H., Bosveld, W., & Van Dierendonck, D. (2000). Patient demands, lack of reciprocity, and burnout: A five-year longitudinal study among general practitioners. *Journal of Organizational Behavior, 21*, 425-441.

Belkic, K., Landsbergis, P., Schnall, P., & Baker, D. (2004). Is job strain a major source of cardiovascular disease risk? *Scand J Work Environ Health, 30*(2), 85-128.

Bies, R. J., & Moag, J. (1986). Interactional justice: Communication criteria of fairness. In R. Lewicki, B. Sheppard & M. Bazerman (Eds.), *Research on Negotiation in Organizations*. Greenwich, Conn: JAI Press.

Bies, R. J., & Shapiro, D. L. (1988). Voice and justification: Their influence on procedural fairness judgements. *Academy of Management Journal, 31*(3), 676-685.

Bond, F. (2004). Getting the balance right: The need for a comprehensive approach to occupational health. *Work and Stress, 18*(2), 146-148.

Bond, F., & Bunce, D. (2003). The role of acceptance and job control in mental health, job satisfaction and work performance. *Journal of Applied Psychology, 88*, 1057-1067.

Brockner, J., & Wisenfeld, B. (1996). An integrative framework for explaining reactions to decisions: Interactive effects of outcomes and procedures. *Psychological Bulletin, 120*, 189-208.

Colquitt, J. A. (2001). On the dimensionality of organizational justice: A construct validation of a measure. *Journal of Applied Psychology, 86*(3), 386-400.

Colquitt, J. A., Conlon, D. E., Wesson, M. J., Porter, C. O. L. H., & Ng, K. Y. (2001). Justice at the Millennium: A meta-analytic review of 25 years of organizational justice research. *Journal of Applied Psychology, 86*(3), 425-445.

Colquitt, J. A., Greenberg, J., & Zapata-Phelan, C. P. (2005). What is

Organizational Justice? A Historical Overview. In J. Greenberg & J. A. Colquitt (Eds.), *Handbook of Organizational Justice* (pp. 3 - 56). Mahwa, New Jersey: Lawrence Erlbaum Associates.

CONLON, D. E., MEYER, C. J., & NOWAKOWSKI, J. M. (2005). How Does Organizational Justice Affect Performance, Withdrawal and Counterproductive behaviour? In J. Greenberg & J. A. Colquitt (Eds.), *Handbook of Organizational Justice*. Mahwah, New Jersey: Lawrence Erlbaum Associates.

CROPANZANO, R., BOWEN, D. E., & GILILAND, S. W. (2007). The Management of Organizational Justice. *Academy of Management Perspectives, November*, 34 - 45.

CROPANZANO, R., GOLDMAN, B. M., & BENSON III, L. (2005). Organizational Justice. In J. Barling, E. K. Kelloway & M. R. Frone (Eds.), *Handbook of Work Stress*. Thousand Oaks, California: Sage Publications.

CUTRONA, C. (1990). Stress and social support: In search of optimal matching. *Journal of Social and Clinical Psychology, 9*(1), 3-14.

DE BOER, E., BAKKER, A. B., SYROIT, J., & SCHAUFELI, W. B. (2002). Unfairness at work as a predictor of absenteeism. *Journal of Organizational Behavior, 23*, 181-197.

DE JONGE, J., REUVERS, M., HOUTMAN, I., BONGERS, P. M., & KOMPIER, M. (2000). Linear and nonlinear relations between psychosocial characteristics, subjective outcome and sickness absence: Baseline results from SMASH. *Journal of Occupational Health Psychology, 5*, 256-268.

ELOVAINIO, M., KIVIMÄKI, M., & HELKAMA, K. (2001). Organizational Justice Evaluations, Job Control, and Occupational Strain. *Journal of Applied Psychology, 86*(3), 418 - 424.

ELOVAINIO, M., KIVIMÄKI, M., STEEN, N., & VAHTERA, J. (2004). Job decision latitude, organizational justice and health: Multilevel covariance structure analysis. *Social Science and Medicine, 58*, 1659 - 1669.

ELOVAINIO, M., KIVIMAKI, M., & VAHTERA, J. (2002). Organizational Justice: Evidence of a New Psychosocial Predictor of Health. *American Journal of Public Health, 92*(1), 105-108.

ELOVAINIO, M., KIVIMÄKI, M., VAHTERA, J., & KELTIKANGAS-JARVINEN, L. (2003). Sleeping Problems and Health Behaviors as Mediators Between Organizational Justice and Health. *Health Psychology, 22*(3), 287 - 293.

FLETCHER, B. C., & JONES, F. (1993). A refutation of Karasek's demand-discretion model of occupational stress with a range of dependent measures. *Journal of Organizational Behavior, 14*, 319-330.

FOLGER, R., ROSENFIELD, D., GROVE, J., & CORKRAN, L. (1979). Effects of "voice" and peer opinions on responses to inequity. *Journal of Personality and Social Psychology, 37*, 2253 - 2261.

FOX, M. L., DWYER, D. J., & GANSTER, D. C. (1993). Effects of Stressful Job

Demands and Control on Physiological and Attitudinal Outcomes in a Hospital Setting. *Academy of Management Journal, 36*(2), 289-318.

Fox, S., Spector, P. E., & Miles, D. (2001). Counterproductive work behavior (CWB) in response to job stressors and organizational justice: Some mediator and moderator tests for autonomy and emotions. *Journal of Vocational Behavior, 59*, 291 - 309.

Francis, L., & Barling, J. (2005). Organizational Injustice and Psychological Strain. *Canadian Journal of Behavioural Science, 37*(4), 250 - 261.

French, J., Caplan, R., & Harrison, R. (1982). *The mechanisms of job stress and strain*. Chichester: Wiley.

Fujishiro, K., & Heaney, C. A. (2007). Justice at Work, Job Stress, and Employee Health. *Health, Education and Behavior* [Electronic Version], 1 - 18 DOI: 10.1177/1090198107306435.

Giga, S., Noblet, A., Faragher, B., & Cooper, C. (2003). Organisational Stress Management Interventions: A review of UK-based research. *The Australian Psychologist, 38*(2), 158-164.

Greenberg, J. (1988). Cultivating an Image of Justice: Looking Fair on the Job. *The Academy of Management Executive, 8*(2), 155 - 158.

Greenberg, J. (1990). Employee theft as a reaction to underpayment inequity: The hidden cost of pay cuts. *Journal of Applied Psychology, 75*, 561 - 568.

Greenberg, J., & Folger, R. (1983). Procedural justice, participation, and the fair process effect in groups and organizations. In P. Paulus (Ed.), *Basic Group Processes* (pp. 235-256). New York: Springer-Verlag.

Griffiths, A. (1999). Organizational Interventions: Facing the Limits of the Natural Science Paradigm. *Scandinavian Journal of Work, Environment and Health, 25*(6), 589-596.

Guthrie, J. (2001). High-involvement work practices, turnover, and productivity: Evidence from New Zealand. *Academy of Management Journal, 44*(1), 180-190.

Harden, A., Peersman, G., Oliver, S., Mauthner, M., & Oakley, A. (1999). A systematic review of the effectiveness of health promotion interventions in the workplace. *Occupational Medicine, 49*(8), 540-548.

Harlos, K., & Pinder, C. (1999). Patterns of organizational injustice: A taxonomy of what employees regard as unjust. *Advances in Qualitative Organizational Research, 2*, 97 - 125.

Hobfoll, S. (1989). Conservation of resources: a new attempt at conceptualising stress. *American Psychologist, 44*, 513-524.

House, J. S. (1981). *Work Stress and Social Support*: Addison-Wesley Publishing Company, London.

Janssen, O. (2000). Job demands, perceptions of effort-reward fairness and innovative work behaviour. *Journal of Occupational and Organizational Psychology, 73*(3), 287-302.

JANSSEN, O. (2001). Fairness Perceptions as a Moderator in the Curvilinear Relationships Between Job Demands, and Job Performance and Job Satisfaction. *Academy of Management Journal, 44*(5), 1039-1050.

JUDGE, T. A., & COLQUITT, J. A. (2004). Organizational Justice and Stress: The Mediating Role of Work - Family Conflict. *Journal of Applied Psychology, 89*(3), 395 - 404.

KARASEK, R., & THEORELL, T. (1990). *Healthy Work: Stress, Productivity, and the Reconstruction of Working Life*. New York: Basic Books.

KIVIMAKI, M., ELOVAINIO, M., VAHTERA, J., & FERRIE, J. E. (2003). Organisational justice and health of employees: prospective cohort study. *Occupational and Environmental Medicine, 60*(1), 27-34.

KIVIMAKI, M., ELOVAINIO, M., VAHTERA, J., VIRTANEN, M., & STANSFELD, S. A. (2003). Association between organizational inequity and incidence of psychiatric disorders in female employees. *Psychological Medicine, 33*(2), 319-326.

KIVIMÄKI, M., ELOVAINIO, M., VAHTERA, J., VIRTANEN, M., & STANSFIELD, S. A. (2003). Association between organizational inequity and incidence of psychiatric disorders in female employees. *Psychological Medicine, 33*, 319 - 326.

KIVIMÄKI, M., FERRIE, J. E., BRUNNER, E., HEAD, J., SHIPLEY, M. J., VAHTERA, J., et al. (2005). Justice at Work and Reduced Risk of Coronary Heart Disease Among Employees. The Whitehall II Study. *Archives of Internal Medicine, 165*, 2245 - 2251.

KIVIMAKI, M., FERRIE, J. E., HEAD, J., SHIPLEY, M. J., VAHTERA, J., & MARMOT, M. G. (2004). Organisational justice and change in justice as predictors of employee health: the Whitehall II study. *Journal of Epidemiology & Community Health, 58*(11), 931-937.

KIVIMAKI, M., HEAD, J., & FERRIE, J. E. (2003). Sickness absence as a global measure of health: Evidence from all-cause mortality in the Whitehall II study. *British Medical Journal, 327*, 364-369.

KOMPIER, M., COOPER, C., & GUERTS, S. (2000). A multiple case study approach to work stress prevention in Europe. *European Journal of Work and Organizational Psychology, 9*(3), 371-400.

KORSGAARD, M. A., SAPIENZA, H. J., & SCHWIEGER, D. M. (2002). beaten Before Begun: The Role of Procedural Justice in Planning Change. *Journal of Management, 28*(4), 497 - 516.

LAZARUS, R., & FOLKHAM, S. (1984). *Stress, Appraisal and Coping*. New York: Springer.

LEVENTHAL, G. (1980). What should be done with equity theory? New approaches to the study of fairness in social relationships. In K. Gergen, M. Greenberg & R. Willis (Eds.), *Social exchange: Advances in theory and research*. New York: Plenum Press.

LEVENTHAL, G. S. (1976). Justice in Social Relationships. In J. W. Thibaut,

J. T. Spence & R. C. Carson (Eds.), *Contemporary Topics in Social Psychology*. Morristown, NJ: General Learning Press.

LIND, E. A., & TYLER, T. R. (1988). *The social psychology of procedural justice*. New York: Plenum.

LIND, E. A., & VAN DEN BOS, K. (2002). When fairness works: Toward a general theory of uncertainty management. In B. M. Staw & R. M. Kramer (Eds.), *Research in Organizational Behavior* (Vol. 24, pp. 181 - 222). Boston: JAI Press.

MARMOT, M., BOSMA, H., HEMINGWAY, H., BRUNNER, E., & STANSFELD, S. (1997). Contribution of job control and other risk factors to social variations in coronary heart disease incidence. *The Lancet, 350*, 235-239.

MASTERSON, S. S., LEWIS, K., GOLDMAN, B. M., & TAYLOR, M. S. (2000). Integrating justice and social exchange: The differing effects of fair procedures and treatment on work relationships. *Academy of Management Journal, 43*(4), 738-749.

MICHIE, S., & WILLIAMS, S. (2003). Reducing work related psychological ill health and sickness absence: a systematic literature review. *Occupational and Environmental Medicine, 60*(1), 3-9.

MOLINER, C., MARTÍNEZ-TUR, V., PEIRÓ, J. M., RAMOS, J., & CROPANZANO, R. (2008). Organizational justice and extrarole customer service: The moderating role of wellbeing at work. *European Journal of Work and Organizational Psychology, 17*(3), 327-348

MURTA, S., SANDERSON, K., & OLDENBURG, B. (2007). Process Evaluation in Occupational Stress Management Programs. *American Journal of Health Promotion, 21*(4), 248-254.

MUSTARD, C. (2004). Work-related stress in the UK: A new, 'Management Standards' approach. *Work & Stress, 18*(2), 140-141.

NOBLET, A. J., & LAMONTAGNE, A. D. (2006). The role of workplace health promotion in addressing job stress. *Health Promotion International, 21*(4), 346-353.

NOBLET, A. J., & RODWELL, J. J. (in press). Integrating Job Stress and Social Exchange Theories to Predict Employee Strain in Reformed Public Sector Organisations. *Forthcoming in, Journal of Public Administration Research and Theory*.

POSTHUMA, R., & CAMPION, M. (2008). Twenty Best Practices for Just Employee Performance Reviews. *Compensation and Benefits Review, 40*, 47-55.

ROBERTSON, Q. M., MOYE, N. A., & LOCKE, E. A. (1999). Identifying a missing link between participation and satisfaction: The mediating role of procedural justice perceptions. *Journal of Applied Psychology, 84*, 585 - 593.

RODWELL, J. J., & NOBLET, A. J. (2007). *Organisational Behaviour in Victoria Police Project*. Paper presented at the Symposium on Organisational

Behaviour in Policing and the Public Sector (11-12 October 2007), Melbourne.

RODWELL, J. J., & NOBLET, A. J. (2008). *Assessing Job Strain Among Public Sector Personnel Using Job Stress and Organizational Justice Models*. Paper presented at the Academy of Management Conference, Anaheim.

ROSEN, A. D. (1993). *Kant's theory of justice*. Ithaca, NY: Cornell University Press.

RUPP, D., & CROPANZANO, R. (2002). The mediating effects of social exchange relationships in predicting workplace outcomes from multifoci organizational justice. *Organizational Behavior and Human Decision Processes, 89*, 925-946.

RYDSTEDT, L. W., FERRIE, J., & HEAD, J. (2006). Is there support for curvilinear relationships between psychosocial work characteristics and mental wellbeing? Cross-sectional and long-term data from the Whitehall II study. *Work and Stress, 20*(1), 6-20.

SAKSVIK, P., NYTRO, K., DAHL-JORGENSEN, C., & MIKKELSEN, A. (2002). A process evaluation of individual and organizational occupational stress and health interventions. *Work & Stress, 16*(1), 37-57.

SARASON, I. G., SARASON, B. R., & PIERCE, G. R. (1990). Social support: the search for theory. *Journal of Social and Clinical Psychology, 9*, 133-147.

SCHMITT, M., & DORFEL, M. (1999). Procedural injustice at work, justice sensitivity, job satisfaction and psycho-somatic well-being. *European Journal of Social Psychology, 29*, 443-453.

SHAPIRO, D., & BRETT, J. M. (1993). Comparing three processes underlying judgements of procedural justice: A field study of mediation and arbitration. *Journal of Personality and Social Psychology, 65*, 1167-1177.

SIDLE, S. D. (2003). Best Laid Plans: Establishing Fairness Early Can Help Smooth Organizational Change. *Academy of Management Executive, 17*, 127 - 128.

TAKEUCHI, R., MARINOVA, S., LEPAK, D., & MOON, H. (2004). Justice Climate as a Missing Link for the Relationship Between High Investment HRM Systems and OCBs. *Academy of Management Best Conference Paper*.

TEPPER, B. (2001). Health Consequences of Organizational Injustice: Tests of Main and Interactive Effects. *Organizational Behavior and Human Decision Processes, 86*(2), 197 - 215.

THIBAUT, J., & WALKER, L. (1975). *Procedural justice: A psychological analysis*. Hillsdale, NJ: Erlbaum.

VAN DER DOEF, M., & MAES, S. (1999). The Job Demand-Control (-Support) Model and psychological wellbeing: A review of 20 years of empirical research. *Work & Stress, 13*(2), 87-114.

VAN HORN, J., SCHAUFELI, W., & ENZMANN, D. (1999). Teacher burnout and a lack of reciprocity. *Journal of Applied Social Psychology, 29*, 91-108.

VERMUNT, R., & STEENSMA, H. (2005). How Can Justice Be Used to Manage Stress in Organizations? In J. Greenberg & J. A. Colquitt (Eds.), *Handbook of Organizational Justice* (pp. 383 - 410). Mahwah, New Jersey: Lawrence Erlbaum Associates.

WAGER, N., FIELDMAN, G., & HUSSEY, T. (2003). The effect on ambulatory blood pressure of working under favourably and unfavourably perceived supervisors. *Occupational and Environmental Medicine, 60*, 468 - 474.

WALSTER, E., WALSTER, G. W., & BERSCHEID, E. (1978). *Equity: Theory and Research*. Boston, MA: Allyn & Bacon.

WARR, P. (1987). *Work, Unemployment, and Mental Health*. Oxford: Oxford University Press.

WARR, P. (1990). The measurement of well-being and other aspects of mental health. *Journal of Occupational Psychology, 63*, 193-210.

XIE, J. L., & JOHNS, G. (1995). Job scope and stress: Can job scope be too high? *Academy of Management Journal, 38*(5), 1288-1309.

YLIPAAVALNIEMI, J., KIVIMÄKI, M., ELOVAINIO, M., VIRTANEN, M., KELTIKANGAS-JARVINEN, L., & VAHTERA, J. (2005). Psychosocial work characteristics and incidence of newly diagnosed depression: A prospective cohort study of three different models. *Social Science and Medicine, 61*, 111 - 122.

ZOHAR, D. (1995). The justice perspective on job stress. *Journal of Organizational Behavior, 16*, 487 - 495.

OCCUPATIONAL HEALTH PSYCHOLOGY: EUROPEAN PERSPECTIVES ON RESEARCH, EDUCATION AND PRACTICE

CONTENTS OF PREVIOUS VOLUMES

Back copies may be purchased at www.nup.com.
Also available at a discounted rate at EA-OHP events

Vol. 2 – 2007

1. Overtime work and well-being: Prevalence, conceptualization and effects of working overtime
   Taris, Beckers, Dahlgren, Geurts & Tucker

2. Occupational stress research: The "stress-as-offense-to-self" perspective
   Semmer, Jacobshagen, Meier & Elfering

3. Exploring the new psychological contract among temporary and permanent workers: Associations with attitudes, behavioural intentions and well-being
   De Cuyper and De Witte

4. Healthy Organisational Change
   Saksvik, Nytrø & Tvedt

5. Education in occupational health psychology in Europe: Where have we been, where are we now and where are we going?
   Houdmont, Leka & Cox

6. "Which mask do you prefer?": Changing occupational health behaviour
   Lunt, O' Hara & Cummings

7. Rehabilitation: Maintaining a healthy workforce
   Tehrani, MacIntyre, Maddock, Shaw & Illingworth

8. Necrocapitalism: Throwing away workers in the race for global capital
   Dollard

9. Work-family balance: Concepts, implications and interventions
   O'Driscoll, Brough & Biggs

10. Development, Implementation and Dissemination of Occupational Health Management (OHM): Putting Salutogenesis into Practice.
    Bauer and Jenny

Vol. 1 – 2006

1. Age as a factor in the relation between work and mental health: Results of the longitudinal TAS survey
   de Lange, Taris, Jansen, Smulders, Houtman & Kompier

2. Work stress and health: lessons for active ageing
   Siegrist & Dragano

3. Understanding task-related learning: When, who, why and how
   Wielenga-Meijer, Taris, Kompier & Wigboldus

4. Employee well-being and job performance: Where we stand and where we should go
   Demerouti & Bakker

5. Occupational Health Psychology: A US and UK perspective
   Tetrick

6. Education and training in OHP: The case for e-learning
   Houdmont, Leka & Cox

7. Occupational health psychology in practice: The rganization, its employees and their mental health
   Arthur

8. Developing occupational health psychology services in healthcare settings
   Wren, Schwartz, Allen, Boyd, Gething, Hill-Tout, Jennings, Morrison & Pullen

9. Building quality approaches to work-related violence training: Pillars of best practice
   Leather, Zarola & Santos

10. Combating psychosocial risks in work organisations: Some European practices
    Oeij, Wiezer, Elo, Nielsen, Vega, Wetzstein & Żołnierczyk